Ledbetters

from

Virginia

Roy C. Ledbetter,
William R. Ledbetter,
Justus R. Moll, and
James D. Tillman, Jr.

HERITAGE BOOKS
2019

HERITAGE BOOKS

AN IMPRINT OF HERITAGE BOOKS, INC.

Books, CDs, and more—Worldwide

For our listing of thousands of titles see our website
at
www.HeritageBooks.com

A Facsimile Reprint
Published 2019 by
HERITAGE BOOKS, INC.
Publishing Division
5810 Ruatan Street
Berwyn Heights, Md. 20740

Originally printed

Wilkinson Printing Company
Dallas, Texas

Library of Congress Catalog Card Number: 64-23709

International Standard Book Number
Paperbound: 978-0-7884-5877-4

LEDBETTER LOCALES IN EARLY VIRGINIA

WATERCOURSE SEGMENTS
ASSOCIATED WITH
EARLY LEDBETTERS

(1) Appomattox River

(2) Blackwater Swamp

(3) Brewers Branch

(4) Fontaine Creek

(5) Genito or Janeto Creek

(6) Great Creek

(7) Jones Hole Swamp

(8) Ledbetter Creek

(9) Meherrin River

(10) Rattlesnake Creek

(11) Rocky Run

(12) Warwick Swamp

(13) White Oak Swamp;
now Whiterock Creek

CHARLES CITY

PR. GEORGE

SURRY CO.

SURRY

DINWIDDIE

SUSSEX

SURRY CITY

CHARLES CITY

BRUNS-WICK

GREENS-VILLE

EARLY

Key Map Showing Prince George & Brunswick

VIRGINIA

NORTH CAROLINA

WRL 62

DEDICATED

TO

FUTURE GENERATIONS

"Our design in printing these genealogies is to gratify a natural desire, which most persons feel, to know something of their forefathers, and to show how family-trees in a few generations interlock their branches. It is more creditable to transmit an honorable name to one's children than it is to derive it from one's ancestors, and to be descended from good and true men than from a long line of unworthy forefathers, even though it be a line of kings and queens. But it seems to be unnatural and irrational to attach more value to the pedigrees of horses and herds than to pedigrees of men and women. One end of history is to reproduce the past for the gratification and instruction of the present; and it is surely (at least) an innocent curiosity to look back at those who in the past century cleared the land which we now till, and who laid the foundation of the institutions under which we live." Rev. Philip Slaughter, History of St. Mark's Parish, Culpeper County, Va. (1877)

CONTENTS

PREFACE

This volume traces the Ledbetters who settled in the Prince George County area of Virginia about 1635 and attempts to name all those who spread out from that area up to about 1800. In addition, the descendants of three of these are traced insofar as possible in a connected family line to the present time. The descendants of some five others have been traced in a connected line but are not published here except in general outline.

Many other families are mentioned. Mainly, these are families into which Ledbetter sons and daughters have married. Wherever known, the parents and sometimes grandparents are named. In a few instances the children of the former Ledbetter daughters are named. Additional names include those of neighbors, ministers, officials and even witnesses to documents. The general index lists families and given names under each. It is hoped that such names will serve as leads to those interested in tracing their families.

The first two chapters pertain to genealogy as distinct from specific family lines. Chapter One discusses the history and source of family names in general. It is surprising, but a settled fact, that as people grew from the tribal group the individual had only a given name. Family names began to arise less than a thousand years ago. Double given names did not come into use until about one hundred fifty years ago. Chapter Two discusses the racial origin and early migrations of the Ledbetters so far as known.

This volume also adds means of further research on the Ledbetter and other families. Under this part are included those named Ledbetter who engaged in the wars from the Revolution through the Civil War. Census and migration information is included. Search has been made of all appellate court cases in the United States to discover all parties named Ledbetter.

Included are very brief biographical sketches of the principal researchers for the past sixty years and of the writers who have produced this book. There are many more who furnished information. The culling and interpreting of material has been the responsibility of the authors. It is regretted that there is a limit on the amount of biography and history that can be published. The authors are engaged in additional writings based on the material gathered and other sources.

Yet, the facts given do add to biography and history. The reader may imagine the joy at the birth of each child, the merriment on marriage, and the grief at death. In this book those events are represented by "b," "m," and "d." Tradition and fiction are almost absent from this volume. Included are many leads for the historical novel, the fiction, as well as fact, of the frontier and hero or folk stories. Examples are the stories of the death of Colonel Daniel Ledbetter at the bloody battle of Manassas, the posthumous birth of Martin Van Buren Ledbetter after his father was killed by a bushwhacher in Arkansas, and the exploits of Bud Ledbetter in shooting robbers in the Indian Territory. Some of the marshall's exploits were the subject of a silent movie which used a wax figure of mustached old Bud to draw customers.

The authors trust that workers will follow us with as much pleasure as we have had in pooling to produce this volume. The record can be explored in the past or made as events occur. The mass of names was like a ball of twine. The more lines traced out, the easier it became as to the remaining mass. But we realize that we have charted only a small part of the many Ledbetters who have been born since the early migration to America. We are fully conscious that controversy exists. For example, since his grand-daughter named only nine of the twelve children of Colonel Drury Ledbetter and his wife Winifred Lanier, who are the remaining three?

As the authors pass on, we leave available our principal source material. The Genealogical Society of the Church of Jesus Christ of Latter Day Saints, Salt Lake City 16, Utah, has a microfilm. The Department of Archives and History of the State of Georgia in Atlanta is to receive a copy of the same microfilm and the original material.

May, 1964

ROY C. LEDBETTER
WILLIAM R. LEDBETTER

JAMES D. TILLMAN, JR.
1924 34th Ave.
Meridian, Miss.

James David Tillman was born February 6, 1882 in Carrollton, Mississippi. Graduated at Millsaps College in 1902, B. A. Degree, Kappa Sigma Fraternity. After graduating at Millsaps College, he attended Eastman Business College, Poughkeepsie, N. Y., graduating in Banking and Accounting in 1902. He is a Methodist, a member of all Masonic Bodies and Shrine, Fellow of the Institute of American Genealogy (an original member), member of Virginia Historical Society, Mississippi Historical Society, New England Historic Genealogical Society; Sons of the American Revolution (La. Society); member of National Exchange Clubs.

He has been collecting genealogical records on his families since 1898. His records on the Tillman Family were the foundation for the Tilghman-Tillman Family by S. F. Tillman. He has contributed data to many genealogical publications.

His ancestral lines are: Tillman, Ledbetter, Bennett, Randle, Johnson, Winfree, Goodrich, Dunn, Wynne, maternal; Bryan, Marshall, Turner, Eastman, Guice, Harman, Smith, Averett, Whitfield, etc. His wife's were Hamilton, Taylor, Foote, Bedinger, Swearingen, Morgan, Baird, Collins, Haynes. He has collected records on all of these families. Three volumes of records with indexes on these and other families have been printed.

MRS. FLORENCE LOUISE HEINEMANN
Albany, Georgia

Florence Louise Marshall, the daughter of Jennie Botterill Slaughter and Charles Henry Marshall, was born October 5, 1886 in Petersburg, Virginia. Her birth place was near "the place called Bristol" mentioned as the residence of Henry Ledbetter in 1668. Many Ledbetters remained in the area. She is a direct descendant of the elder Richard (d. 1767) and wife Hanna, through Drury (b. 1734) and wife Rebecca, Nathan (d. 1802) and wife Susanna Mayes, Gardner (1786-1866) and wife Nancy Jones, their daughter Martha (1820-1909) and husband John J. Slaughter and their daughter Jennie B. (1867-1944) and husband Charles H. Marshall, parents of the subject of this sketch. About 1912 she began research in the records of the original Virginia counties and in the archives at Richmond. Her research has contributed a great part of the information on the first Ledbetters in America.

Educated in the private and public schools of Virginia, Florence Louise Marshall was married December 18, 1906 to Charles H. Heinemann and they have one son, Charles H. Heinemann Jr. She is a member of the Episcopal Church, of National Society Daughters of American Revolution and Daughters of War of 1812.

The family lived in Petersburg, Virginia until 1939 when they located in Albany, Georgia, their present address.

CHRISTIAN ALBERT LEDBETTER

Christian Albert Ledbetter was born October 28, 1864 at Julian, North Carolina, in northeastern Randolph County. He was the son of Wesley A. and Margaret Kime Ledbetter and a grandson of William IV. He was the second of three boys and the fourth in a family of five. His parents were God-fearing people and had little of this world's goods but were very proud and strict.

He farmed with his parents until he was twenty-one, at which time he began following the carpenter's trade. Later he entered the shop where he became very proficient in the care and operation of the various woodworking machines.

In his youth he was a member of Shiloh Methodist (Protestant) Church in Randolph County, near Julian. He married Miss Martha Selina Craven on June 24, 1891 at Asheboro, N. C. She was the daughter of James Murphy and Elizabeth Woodell Craven and a grandniece of Professor Braxton Craven, founder of Trinity College, which later became Duke University. Here five of eight children were born. In 1903 he brought his family to Greensboro, where he stayed until late in 1905, when he moved to Julian, where the sixth child was born in early 1906. Sometime the next summer he returned to Greensboro where the last two children were born. He held residence in Greensboro until his death.

He began tracing the family tree in or about 1923 and was following some leads when an auto accident occurred that brought his death on July 18, 1938. He was laid to rest at Shiloh Methodist Church July 20, 1938. His family took new life in 1914 when the first of 16 grandchildren—10 granddaughters and 6 grandsons— was born. Then in 1935 the first of (at this writing) 26 great-grandchildren, 20 great-grandsons and six great-granddaughters, was born.

He examined many records in the counties and searched in archives in North Carolina. The research was particularly valuable in tracing the Ledbetters as they migrated from Virginia. But his interest included all Ledbetters. His correspondence was vast and he was ready to help everyone. He wrote an account of his ancestry from William, the youngest son of Richard the older, down to the date of his death.

From this family came four sons who serve in the printing trade. Two grandchildren are serving, one as a photo-engraver and another as a printer. Then in 1948 one of his granddaughters married a printer. It might be said that in addition to his genealogical research, his legacy to posterity was printers—yes, there are nine printers in the family.

His records unpublished are in the possession of his son, Charles A. Ledbetter, 1016 Portland St., Greensboro, N. C.

JUSTUS REINIGER MOLL
1329 Washington Ave.
Springfield 2, Mo.

Born April 16, 1893 at Mason City, Iowa, son of a railroad official, grandson of a railroad official, his first school was supervised by Mrs. Carrie Lane Chapman, whose name was later changed to Mrs. Carrie Chapman Catt. He was an ardent feminist during the remainder of his life. His mother, Mrs. Belle R. Moll (1866-1956) was a suffragist of The Woman's Party in Washington. His father, Alexander Henry Moll (1866-1921) was chief dispatcher on the CM&StP RR, later superintendent on CRI&P, B&O, Mo-Pac, CMStP&P, and Frisco Lines.

After schooling in Grafton, W. Va., Rock Island, Ill., Little Rock, Ark., Trenton, Mo., Kansas City, Osawatomie, Pueblo, Seattle and Fresno, Justus went into railroad clerical work. He organized the Brotherhood of Railway Clerks on the Frisco System, and for over twenty years was their General Secretary-Treasurer. In 1943, after ten years as Chief Clerk to the Secretary of State in Jefferson City, he took a temporary job with a law firm in Washington, D. C., and worked there until 1962. His wife and family remain in the Moll home, near Drury College Campus in Springfield, Mo. His wife, Cleadie Edith Atkinson Moll, is a Ledbetter of the Arthur Ledbetter line. His only child is William Alexander Moll, the father of Carol Sue and William Justus.

Moll became interested in genealogy in 1920, and spent much time on his own line, joining Sons of the Revolution and Society of Colonial Wars, and was a member of the Institute of American Genealogy and New England Historic Genealogical Society, and a member of the Missouri Historical Society. He was a Trustee of the State Historical Society and a member of the American Historical Association, American Association for State and Local History, and state historical societies of Kansas, North Carolina, Indiana, Mississippi, Alabama, and Florida. In 1930, he decided to tackle the Ledbetter line of his wife, and for many years conducted research by search of local courthouse records, and by correspondence. Many of the persons who contributed their own personal knowledge have since passed on, but Moll preserved the records carefully. Colonel Wm. R. Ledbetter has microfilmed these disintegrating papers, and their content will be preserved through Colonel Bill's efforts.

After going to Washington in 1943, the pressure of his work caused Moll to retire from active genealogical work, other than census research, and he prevailed upon Roy Ledbetter to assume the burden. Roy took the major part of Moll's files and worked them into shape. He encountered Colonel Bill, made a convert, and Roy and Bill have worked like two beavers ever since. Moll, who writes these words, is everlastingly grateful to these two beavers.

Moll is a lawyer, admitted to the Supreme Court of the United States, District of Columbia Appeals, District and Municipal Courts, U. S. Court of Claims, I. C. C., Treasury Department, F. C. C., Veterans Administration, General Accounting Office, Supreme Court of Missouri, Eighth Circuit Court of Appeals. He is a Baptist deacon, a Mason, and a Democrat. Although a member of The American Institute of Management, his life interest has been in union labor. His legal work in Washington is in the interest of labor unions. He has also had membership in the American Economic Association, The American Political Science Association, and The American Railway Historical Association.

Inasmuch as oldsters are prone to offer gratuitous advice, Moll suggests to readers of this book that they remember the words of Dr. David Starr Jordan, president of Leland Stanford University:

"Genealogy is the science of personal identification."
These seven words should be explored thoughtfully. Years ago, when Moll was researching the line of Gov. Forrest Smith of Missouri, he found his to be a descendant of one John Smith of Pittsylvania Co., Va., who lived during the era in which he could have been a soldier in the Revolution. There were 300 John Smiths in the county at that era. Many of hem were revolutionary soldiers or sailors. It would require a better genealogist than Moll to identify, scientifically, the John Smith we wanted.

His second short sentence was from his teacher of genealogy, his distant cousin, the late Idah Meacham Strowbridge, who said:

"Remember, young man, we trace by *place*, and prove by *date*."
It is unfortunate the old family Bibles recorded dates, but not places. But you must trace by place. Don't skim the index in county record books, especially deed, civil and criminal court records. Let the index lead you to the complete records, especially powers of attorney. Work the probate index, but let it lead you to the file of loose papers pertaining to settlement of the estate. In the non-Torrence portions of the South, look for old maps showing partitions of farm lands. If the court house records were burned, try the abstract offices and title companies.

I am indeed grateful that Roy C. Ledbetter and Colonel Bill Ledbetter have given so much time and money in the effort to publish and preserve this record for Ledbetter persons of coming generations. I am grateful; though I regret to state that I am not a Ledbetter descendant. My study of the family has resulted in my having a profound admiration for the Ledbetters of the South.

Roy Clifford Ledbetter
3516 University
Dallas, Texas 75205

Born 2 August 1893 in northern Alabama, Roy C. Ledbetter was removed at age two, with all the family, to Ferris, Ellis County, Texas, about twenty miles south of the city of Dallas. He lived four years in the Choctaw Nation of the Indian Territory, near Caddo, followed by the year 1908 near Gorman, Commanche County, Texas. The residence has remained in Dallas and Ellis Counties, except for the above five years and the time spent in the Army and at school. Schools attended include Ferris High School, Trinity University at Waxahachie in 1914, Sam Houston Teachers College, Huntsville, in 1916, and Texas University, where he received Bachelor of Arts and Bachelor of Laws degrees in 1921. Honorary societies included Phi Beta Kappa, Pi Sigma Alpha (Government), Phi Delta Phi and Chancellors (legal). Two years were spent teaching in the public schools and several terms as instructor on the subject of mortgages at Southern Methodist University Law School.

At the outbreak of World War I, Roy attended the First Officers Training Camp at Leon Springs, Texas; served until December 3, 1918, as Second and First Lieutenant and Captain of Infantry.

On receiving law degree, pursued general practice of law in Dallas, Texas until 1934, and thereafter in the legal department of Magnolia Petroleum Company assigned to litigation and industrial relations.

Mr. Ledbetter was President of the Dallas Bar Association in 1941; served as Member of House of Delegates, American Bar Association 1938-1942; served Dallas County Democratic Executive Committee 1946-1949.

Memberships include: Highland Park Methodist Church, Dallas, Texas; American Bar Associations; American Legion; Masons; Friends of the Land; The Dallas Agricultural Club; Dallas Estate Council; Local History and Genealogical Society of Dallas; The National Genealogical Society; The Society of Genealogists, England.

Writings included the following:

Preparation and Trial of a Land Suit, Southwestern Legal

Foundation, Institute on the Trial of a Land Suit, 1954, E. J. Storm Printing Company, Dallas.

Morgages on Land Affecting Subsequent Mineral Interests, 32 Tex. L. Rev. 740 (1954).

Frank Reaugh—Painter of Longhorn Cattle, The Southwestern Historical Quarterly, Vol. 54, July 1950.

Opinions (Legal) 1934-1955, in two volumes, unpublished. For three years edited "Dallas Bar Speaks."

As early as 1916 Roy C. Ledbetter began preserving notes on family history and since 1930 has followed the hobby rather intensively. Justus R. Moll furnished extensive files of correspondence, and largely through his inspiration research has been carried on since about 1930. Genealogical research has been made in Dallas Public Library, Virginia, North Carolina and Georgia archives as well as in many counties of those states and South Carolina and Texas. Inquiries have been made in the course of vacation travel. Travel only partially for genealogical research has been in all the states, Canada, Mexico, Central and South America, the western European countries, Russia and all the continents. Writing of family history began in 1946.

Despite a busy schedule, there has been time for hobbies— horses, farm, travel, teaching and genealogy.

WILLIAM R. LEDBETTER
3909 North 31st St.
Waco, Texas 76708

William R. Ledbetter is the grandson of a Chisholm Trail cowhand named Bill Ledbetter and of a South Carolina Rebel cavalryman named Duffy Gambrell, both of whom were attracted to Texas following the Civil war. After working the Trail for a number of years, the cowhand settled on a farm along the route near its Brazos River crossing in McLennan County, Texas thus starting another Ledbetter locale. Subject was born in the third generation there and named for his grandfather.

The namesake was graduated from Texas A. & M. College in 1940 with a degree in engineering. He is a registered professional engineer in the state of Texas and a career officer in the U. S. Army Corps of Engineers.

His major service in World War II was in the Asiatic-Pacific Theater. Subsequent assignments included supervision of design and contracted construction in Japan during the United States occupation and in support of the Korean War, and duties as advisor to the post-war Japanese Army Engineers.

After attending a one-year course in the Persian language and culture, the officer was assigned a tour as Technical Assistant Military Attache in the Middle East with station at Tehran, Iran.

Beginning in 1960 he served for more than two years as Deputy District Engineer of the five-state Army Engineer District headquartered at Mobile, Alabama, which was engaged in design, construction and real estate work for Army, Air Force, National Aeronautics and Space Administration, and Civil Works programs. His most recent assignment was to the Office of the Chief of Army Engineers in Washington, D.C., which followed a tour as engineer advisor with the Army of the Republic of Korea.

Other assignments included the usual troop duty and four years as Department Head for Reserve Officer Training at the University of Detroit in Detroit, Michigan.

Using the data collected by Justus R. Moll in the early 1930's, and with the expert guidance of Moll and Roy C. Ledbetter, subject pursued the *Arthur Ledbetter* line. The search for Ledbetter family information led Colonel Ledbetter to make personal searches in many records depositories. Among them were the National Archives, the Newberry Library in Chicago, and state archives and history files of eight southern states. In pursuit of the *Arthur Ledbetter* line, records of over 100 county courthouses were reviewed in varying degrees. Personal visits were also made with appropriately located elderly Ledbetters and to old burying grounds within the Georgia-Texas-Illinois triangle.

CHAPTER 1

ORIGIN OF FAMILY NAMES

Revised and adapted from a talk made by Roy C. Ledbetter to the Dallas Chapter of the Sons of the American Revolution, November 11, 1950

Originally individuals were known by a single name only, such as Peter, John, Paul. How early such individual names arose is not known. Perhaps the custom originated, along with a spoken language, before the dawn of history. The members of the royal family of England still have only individual names. On accession to the throne the ruler selects his own name, as does also the Pope at Rome. Even to this day the Church of England and the Roman Catholic Church recognize only the individual name by which the child is baptized. The baptismal name came to be known as the Christian name. The Christian name is also called the first, proper, or given name. Before the earth became crowded and communication common, one name was sufficient to distinguish each person among his family and neighbors. As family and tribe grew in size, individual names resulted in many duplications and confusions. The need of an additional name began to be felt. Among the first distinguishing words to be added were such as Peter the strong, John the hardy, and the peoples of Northern Europe began adding such as Oscar son of Carnuth.

The Roman Patricians in their later history evolved a system of family names. The first name described a quality, such as Gaius for joyful. The first name was called praenomen. This was followed by an adjective referring to the tribe, such as Caecilius. This middle name was called nomen. It was followed by a nickname, such as Pulcher, meaning handsome. This last was called cognomen and often became the family name somewhat in the sense that we know it today. With the influx of the barbarian tribes before the year 500, the Roman system of names ended and there was a return to the primitive custom of a single name.

Family names began to appear gradually about nine hundred years ago and have been in common use only about five hundred years. At first the family name might be used by the children or an entirely different name might be adopted. A custom developed

1

by which the child came to inherit the name of the father, called a patronym. Family names began to appear in England after the initial Norman conquest in 1066. By the time of the Doomsday Books in 1086, the rudiments of many family names had been established. As late as 1465 a statute was passed in England to compel certain Irish outlaws to adopt surnames: "They shall take unto them a Surname, either of some Town, or some Colour, as Blacke or Brown, or some Art or Science, as Smyth or Carpenter, or some Office, as Cooke or Butler." Teutonic names began to arise some nine hundred years ago, but as late as the year 1800 a decree in Germany and Austria compelled Jews to add a German surname to the single names which they had used up to that time. The Welsh names evolved about the time of the discovery of America. Family names for Indians in Alaska arose within the last seventy-five years. The schools established by the United States assigned family names usually from the animals, birds or fish of the area.

Generally the family or surnames may be divided into four sources of origin, arranged somewhat in the order of time in which they first came into use.

(1) To the given name of the father was added a prefix or suffix meaning son, such as son of John, which was shortened to Johnson. In Scandinavian the word is Johnsen. In Norman French Fitz means son; hence the family name Fitzpatrick. Among the Celts, including the Irish and Scots, the prefix Mc or Mac means son, such as McKay and MacFarlane. Among the Irish O' means grandson, such as O'Toole. In Welsh ap means son, such as in Bowen (ap Owain). In Welsh son of Gilbert has been shortened to such as Gibbs. Other names have the same origin, such as Jones and Edwards. Other suffixes meaning son include ing, kin.

(2) Personal qualities or nicknames added after the individual name became family names in many instances. John "the strong" became John Strong. Others are Jack Little, James Good, Peter Wise, Little John, John Campbell ("crooked lips").

(3) Place or locality of residence is perhaps the largest source of family names. The Norman French used their estates as names, such as found in the Roll of Battle Abbey (a Doomsday Book of the soldiers who came to England with William the Conqueror).

"Baldun de Brionne" in England was shortened to Bryans or Bryant. There is also the French Du (by) Pont (bridge), English Atwood and Atwell, German Von (of) Hindenburg, and Dutch Van. Other place names are obvious, such as Field, Marsh, Meadow. Johnston is made up from John and "tun" meaning an enclosure or stead as used in homestead. It is not true, as jokingly told by people named Johnson, that some of their relatives got into trouble and added a "t" in the name.

(4) The occupation became one of the last sources of names to arise. Examples are John the smith and William the tailor, becoming John Smith and William Taylor. The son usually followed the trade of the father and the occupation became the family name. In this class fall Miller, Barber, Wainwright—a wagon builder, and Latimer, an interpreter. In the Doomsday Book is listed "Busher" a person who cleared away brush for the hunter; hence the family name of Bush.

No doubt a great percentage of names fit into the four named sources of origin. But to classify all family names under the four sources of origin unduly simplifies the subject. All of us can readily call to mind family names from many other sources. Witness names from parts of the body, such as Hand, Head, Finger and Foot. Names from fowls include Bird and Swan. From animals there are Fox and Wolf. From shrubs there are Rose and Thorn. Examples could be multiplied.

At first, the name went by the sound only, and there was plenty of room for change. There has been a tendency to shorten the name as first used. A high percentage of literacy is of recent origin, hence the sound was often mistaken. Handwritings have changed even in the last hundred years and old ones cannot be deciphered. Even now handwritings may be illegible. Printing is relatively new. Many spellings for the sound appeared, such as the twenty-seven for William Shakespeare. The average number of spellings of each family name is said to be from four to a dozen.

There has been much research extending only for the past three hundred years. Many of the printed meanings are based on theory. Opinions differ as to the origin of a few names. Research will never be able to explain the origin and meaning of all family names.

There is no British law against taking any name desired. Such is usually the law in the several states except the alias cannot be taken in fraud to escape detection of crime. Usually an application for change of name is made to a district court but this is not necessary. In America is found the greatest variety of given and family names. They are principally names derived from English, Scots, Irish, Welsh, but the surnames of every race and nation are represented.

By custom in England and the United States the wife on marriage adopts the surname of her husband but in Scotland she retains her family name and adds that of her husband at the end. In Spain and in the Latin countries among the well-to-do, the child takes the surname of his father followed by the maiden surname of his mother joined by "y" meaning "and", but in the Spanish colonies the conjunction is often omitted.

In books on the origin of names, Ledbetter is explained as a trade name applied to those who made pewter vessels for household use. Mr.. Jesse E. Ames, who published *Leadbetter Records* in 1917, wrote me on October 21, 1953: "LEBETE seems to be the old surname—and in France where Dr. Hamilton studied the records for us—Le Lebete (The Beast) which tradition says was the emblem they bore on their shields—in those days of the clans." In letter of December 7, 1953, Mr. Ames wrote: "He (Dr. Hamilton) was satisfied that the earliest name—he called it the original name—was LEBETE and that the banner with the Beast prominent was at the period of the clans—responsible for the name." Dr. Hamilton was the President of Tufts University for many years.

On page 6 of his book Mr. Ames says:

"The old spelling 'Lebete' is still found in some provinces of France and several of the name 'Lebete' are or were very recently living in New Orleans, their ancestry being readily traceable direct to France. The established fact is that the English name 'Leadbetter' is a gradual evolution of the French name 'Lebete', and that from England one must go to France for the earliest generations of the family."

Again on page 9 he says:

"The spelling *Lebete* followed by De Lebete, or Le

Lebete is, however, the oldest known, followed during the next century by Le Ledbetter, and Le Ledbeter. The *Le* is dropped during the next hundred years, and the present Leadbetter and Leadbeater date back to about 1530, the change at that time being the introduction of the letter *a*.

"It is said that in the Western and Southern States about a hundred and thirty years ago the family dropped the *a* because the people of the South persisted in pronouncing the name *le-ad*-Better very broadly."

More intensive research shows that from 1668 to the present the almost exclusive spelling in the South has been Ledbetter. In the North, the accepted spelling is Leadbetter. Other spellings include Ledbitter, Ledbutter, Letbetter. The name has been found with twenty-six spellings. There can be added Ledbelly, the negro folk-singer discovered by John A. Lomax in a southern penitentiary. Leadbelly has lent luster and fame to the name by writing his song hit, "Goodnight Irene."

After family names became generally established, the custom of using only one Christian or given name continued. Signers of the Declaration of Independence had only a single given name. It is simply George Washington, Thomas Jefferson, John Adams. The son John Quincy Adams, became the first president of the United States with a middle name. Middle names did not become common until the year 1800. By 1917 if an enlistee did not have a middle name the Army gave him one. With the modern large cities and telephone directories, the middle name and even additional distinctions are necessary. John Henry Smith in the telephone directory means scarcely anything.

Perhaps two hundred years ago there came to be added after the family name additional distinctions such as Junior or Senior. At first, this simply meant that there was an older person and a younger person of the same name in the community. Gradually it came to mean that the Senior was the father and the Junior was the son of the identical Christian and family name. Even today the Junior and Senior do not form any part of the legal name. In most States the law also disregards the middle name.

The original meaning of the family name has ceased to have any significance as to present qualities. It matters not that the name originally was Jester, Porter, Wainwright, Nimitz or Eisenhower. The name of the particular family is made significant by the happenings to those who bear it. At first, it was merely a convenient label to distinguish one John from his neighbor. The family name developed as a part of the bearer's individuality. It passed to his children and grandchildren. Gradually it became the symbol not of one man, but of a family, and all that it stood for was handed down from generation to generation. It became associated with achievement, the tradition, and the prestige of the family. It is a truism that in each flock a black sheep may be found or there may be skeletons in the closet. But the name borne through every event of a man's life and through the lives of his ancestors, became a badge of honor and the symbol of a "good name" to be proud of and to fight for. The worthy deeds of generations have given it dignity and splendor and it has become a family rallying cry and the most treasured possession of those who bear it.

SOURCES

George F. Black, *The Surnames of Scotland*, New York Public Library (1946)

N. I. Bowditch, *Suffolk Surnames*, Trubner and Co., 60 Paternoster Row, London (1861)

C. L'Estrange Ewen, *History of Surnames of the British Isles*, The Macmillan Co., New York (1931)

S. Baring-Gould, *Family Names and Their Story*, Seeley & Company, Limited, 38 Great Russell Street, London, England (1910)

Elsdon C. Smith, *The Story of Our Names*, Harper & Brothers, New York (1950)

Ernest Weekley, *The Romance of Names*, E. P. Dutton & Company, New York City, (1914)

Encyclopaedia Britannica, 14th ed., "Names"

132 American State Reports 563-580 (1909)

The Media Research Bureau, Washington, D. C., *Why You Have a Family Name and What It Means To You*

Chapter 2

MIGRATIONS, RACIAL ORIGIN AND TRAITS

By Roy C. Ledbetter

From remains of human skeletons sometimes including skulls found in caves or unearthed during the last hundred years, it is estimated that man has been on the earth a million years. Until recorded history beginning about six thousand years ago, information is based on these skeletons, fossils, tools and other remains pertaining to man. How scanty is this information may be judged by the method of naming all the period prior to ten thousand years ago The Old Stone Age from the unpolished stones used principally as weapons. The New Stone Age (polished stones) covers the period between ten thousand and seven thousand years ago. The ages arrive later in some areas than in others. For instance, the age of Bronze has been applied to 4000 to 1800 B. C. in the Orient, and 2000 to 1000 B. C. in Europe. The Age of Iron has been in the Orient since 1800 B. C. and in Europe since 1000 B. C.

It is surmized that man was nomadic, living chiefly by hunting in his earliest periods. When he obtained domestic animals, man made a great advance. He became pastoral. Tilling the soil was another great advance.

No doubt the prehistory period was very important and fixed most of the physical features of man but these we can judge chiefly by the type of people found at the dawn of history. The Aryan race, also called Caucasian, in its Eastern section was occupying Armenia, Persia, Northern India and Afghanistan. The western Aryan included all of Europe except the Basques, Lapps, Magyars and Turks. There must have been many migrations and resulting mixture of peoples before the dawn of history but there is a difference of opinion as to the area where the Aryan was originally located. The usual conclusion is that they arose in Caucasia near the Caspian Sea. Celtic people as a division of Aryan were dominant in Central Europe from about 1000 B. C. to about 300 B. C. Celts were pushed to the western coastal areas by the Germanic tribes and the Romans. Today the Celtic stock is represented by Bretons of Western Brittany in France, the Cornish, Irish, Scots and Welsh. The Celtics were dominant in England when the Romans conquered the Islands about the time of Christ. As the Romans left about 400 A. D. the Germanic Angels, Saxons and Jutes began to invade England and were dominant until the Battle of Hastings 1066.

Most likely the particular division of Aryan from whom the Ledbetters arose was the Nordic from Scandinavia. The last mass migration into Continental Europe was from Norway, Sweden and Denmark. Beginning about 789 and lasting about two hundred years, the Scandinavians spread out along the coasts and rivers. This is a period as long as from the first settlement at Jamestown to the breaking out of the Civil War in the United States. These invaders were called Vikings, meaning sea-warrior. They were skilled seamen and sea fighters. They set out from the fjords in boats, some seventy-six feet long and small draft of about two and one-half feet and propelled by sixteen oarsmen on each side. A fairly accurate but dramatic description of these sea rovers, their equipment and fighting may be seen and heard in the recent movie The Vikings. They were regarded by their victims as fierce, cruel pirates. The invaders spread southeast and left settlements along the rivers of Russia. Norman structures are seen along the Amalfi Drive on the western coast of Italy and along the eastern coast of the Mediterranean in Palestine at Biblos. Vikings sailed up the St. Lawrence River and the east coast of North America. At first the parties merely raided and took away booty. Later groups settled Dublin, Ireland and Brittany in France. In 911 Charles III of France, called The Simple, made a treaty with Rollo ceding a part of Brittany to the Norsemen on condition that they became Christian. James Harvey Robinson, in his *History of Western Europe*, says:

> "For a considerable time the newcomers kept up their Scandinavian traditions and language. Gradually, however, they appropriated such culture as their neighbors possessed and by the twelfth century their capital, Rouen, was one of the most enlightened cities in Europe."

It was from Normandy that William the Conqueror invaded England. The Normans became the ruling group in England for three hundred years. The Anglo-Saxon at first did not cherish the ruling Normans. The hatred of the Saxon for the Norman is described in Sir Walter Scott's novel, *Ivanhoe*. In England the Celtic, Saxon and Norman Scandinavian, modified by their stay in France, now began to amalgamate. Speaking of the Danes who separately established themselves in Eastern England, as well as the Norsemen from Normandy, Sir Winston Churchill, in his *History of the English Speaking Peoples*, Vol. One, says:

> "When we reflect upon the brutal vices of these salt water bandits, pirates as shameful as any whom the sea has borne, or recoil from their villanous destruction and cruel deeds, we must remember the discipline, the fortitude, comradeship and martial virtues which made them at this period beyond all challenge the most daring race in the world."

Again he states:

> "The bloodstain of these vigorous individualists, proud and successful men of the sword, mingled henceforth in the Island race. A vivifying, potent, lasting and resurgent quality was added to the breed."

Hundred Rolls of Early English Families supposed to record those who came with or followed William the Conqueror into England lists Gounild De Lebete as in Buckinghamshire (Bucks) in 1248. Gonnilda le Lebetere was in the same shire in 1273.

Rog. LeLedbeter, Robs. LeLedbetter and Henr. LeLedebet appear on the subsidy rools of Lancashire in 1332. There was also a Henry Leadbetter of Knowsley, Lancashire, in 1582.

Richard Ledebatter and Robert Ledebeter resided in Yorkshire in 1379.

Burke's-Landed Gentry of 1939, says:

> "A member of this old border family, Walter de Ledbetere is mentioned in the Assize Roll of Northumberland 40 Henry III (1256) and is described 'of Heydon', which is in Warden Parish in N. W. division of Tyndale Ward. Seven of the name are found in the Muster Roll for Northumberland 1538."

The account and also Burke's Landed Gentry of 1914 set out a connected lineage from Matthew Leadbitter of Warden d. 1588 through his son Nicholas and succeeding generations to Thomas Francis Leadbitter b. 26 May, 1839 and Jasper Michael Leadbitter b. 25 September, 1912.

There was a John Leadbeater of London in 1561.

There were ten of the name Leadbetter or Leadbeater in the Diocesan Registry of Chester, 1572-1620. The Chester branch was represented in 1580 by William Leadbeater of Holmes Chapel. He had a son, Thomas who was the father of John, William, Samuel, Mary, Thomas, Anne, Elizabeth and Ellen. John, son of Thomas, had sons Thomas, John, Peter, Matthew.

Thomas Leadbetter was Vicar of Hinckley, Leicestershire, in the time of Charles II (1630-1685). It is established that Henry Leadbetter migrated from Hinckley to America and married Sarah Tolman of Dorchester (Boston), Massachusetts in 1658.

Dr. James McQueen Ledbetter of Rockingham, N. C. b. 19 August, 1869 said the Ledbetters migrated from Durham, England to Virginia. Dr. W. T. Whitsett in an address July 21, 1929, at the Ledbetter family reunion at Guilford Battle Ground, near Greensboro, N. C. said:

> "Durham County, England, is the ancestral home
> of the Ledbetter family and the first records that we find
> locate the family as living near Seaham Harbour."

William Leadbeater migrated from Northumberland into Ireland and there married Mary Shackleton who in 1744 published a short history of the family. She said the family was descended from French Huguenots who had fled France some years before the Massacre of St. Bartholomew in 1572. This specific statement is probably correct but there were Ledbetters in England at least three centuries earlier than that flight.

The extent of the mixture of the Nordic with the Celtic and Anglo-Saxon in England is a matter of surmise. In England the central area and eastern area where the Ledbetters are traced had a concentration of the invading Saxons and Danes.

In America our information is more accurate as to the Ledbetters who spread out from Virginia. A count of the racial origin of the names of the wives who married Ledbetters in the Southern States shows about 90 per cent of English origin, 4 per cent Irish, about 2 per cent German, 2 per cent French, and about 1 per cent of all others including Dutch, Scots and Swiss.

The records of soldiers in the armed forces of the United States as compiled by Lt. Col. Wm. R. Ledbetter, set out physical descriptions in a few instances. The heights of the Ledbetters ranged from five feet five inches to six feet one inch and the average is five feet nine inches. The eyes are described as blue, grey, or greyish blue. The complexion is described as light or fair and the hair is about equally divided between light and black.

The Norsemen had a mythological religion described in the Eddas, collected in writing about 1300 A. D. Their chief god was named Woden from which is derived the English word Wednesday. The oldest son of Woden was Thor, the Thunderer. He was the strongest of gods and men especially with the hammer. From the name Thor our word Thursday is derived. Freya was the goddess of love, music, spring, the flowers and fairies. From her we have Friday.

The Norsemen who settled in Normandy became Christian by the Treaty of 911 A. D. Those remaining in Scandinavia were converted about 1000 A. D. Immediately the Norman knights became avid crusaders to the Holy Land.

After conversion the Norsemen, no doubt in the main, followed the established church in France and England but there is evidence of some becoming Dissenters even before the Reformation. Scandinavia is Lutheran to the present day. In Virginia at first the Ledbetters were recorded in the established Episcopal Church. Before 1750 they became principally Baptist and Methodists and have remained so to the present.

The usual great variety of human conduct has been found in the study of the genealogy of the Ledbetters. Yet a general statement of the family traits has been attempted.

"The Le(a)dbetters have been described as generally vigorous, active and sociable, frequently studious and religious, and of somewhat quiet, unostentatious disposition."

CHAPTER 3

LEDBETTERS OF EARLY VIRGINIA AND THEIR PROBABLE FAMILY RELATION

By Roy C. Ledbetter

The first Ledbetter came to America in a sailboat two hundred years before steam came into use. Entering the wide James River in Virginia, he sailed about 35 miles up the James and the Appomattox Rivers before settling "at a place called Bristol." This first immigrant probably stopped at Jamestown, half the distance up the river, before settling on land near the south edge of the modern city of Petersburg.

This first Ledbetter, whose name is not known, came probably in 1635, and at least before 1655. He came not in literal search of gold and pearls and a waterway westward across North America as did the original Jamestown adventurers in 1607. He knew that the successive waves of settlers at Jamestown had struggled for existence against a warm, unaccustomed climate in a swampy tidewater area of southeastern Virginia, peopled with Indian tribes. In 1622 and 1631 the whites had been greatly reduced by Indian massacres. Long before the first Ledbetter came, it was known that cultivation of tobacco was the chief occupation in the Colony.

Strangely enough, the first record of a Ledbetter in America was a judgment of court for a debt. "At a cor't holden att mer'chts hope Jan'ry 2, 1659—Henry Leadbeater ordered to pay Mr. Jno. Cogan 816 lb. tobo." The court was held in Charles City County about four miles south of the James River, some fifteen miles northeast of the present city of Petersburg, near Merchants Hope Church, built about 1657, then in Martins Brandon Parish. We infer that Henry had been in the Colony long enough to raise some tobacco and purchase a few supplies from Mr. Cogan. The creditor's name is perpetuated in Coggin's Point on the south bank of the James River, the location from which, on January 10, 1781, Baron Von Steuben observed the British fleet as its leader, Benedict Arnold, fell back down the James River after he raided Richmond,

12

and D. H. Hill, of the Confederate Army, on July 31, 1862, bombarded McClellan's Camp on the north side of the River.

The second record is a patent dated April 29, 1668, issued by Sir William Berkeley to Henry Ledbetter for 224 acres of land on the south side of the Appomattox River in Charles City County at a place called Bristol, 125 acres of which was sold to Henry's father by Edward Tunstall and 99 acres for transporting to the Colony Margory Lurae and Mary House (spelling not legible). The father, whose given name is not known, we assume was the first immigrant to America. Just when Henry's father purchased the land from Edward Tunstall we do not know. On August 16, 1637, land in Henrico County, Virginia, had been granted to Edward Tunstall. In Bristol Parish, on the north side of the Appomattox River there was the mouth of a neck called Tunstalls.

The third record of a Ledbetter in Virginia was about October 1673. "Jugt. to Mary Ledbetter agt. Tho: Walton for 1000 lb. tobo. for accomodacon cloathing and levyes expended X-deft." Mary most likely was the widow of the first Ledbetter and mother of Henry, Senior.

For nearly one hundred years, up to about 1729, the Ledbetters remained in the area within about twenty miles south and southwest of what became the town of Petersburg in 1737. The places of residence were all east of the present U. S. Highway Number 1, running southwest from Petersburg and west of or very near the present Highway Number 301, running south from Petersburg. The area became a part of Charles City County on its establishment as one of the eight original shires in 1634, with Charles City, just north of the James, continuing the county seat to the present day. In 1702 Prince George County was created, covering the land south of the Appomattox River. Prince George town is the county seat. The southern part of Prince George County became Brunswick County in 1720, with Lawrenceville established as the county seat in 1732. The western part of Prince George County became Dinwiddie County in 1752, with Dinwiddie town as the County seat.

Bristol Parish was created in 1642 covering the area south of the Appomattox. In January 1741 Bath Parish was established, covering substantially the area which was to become Dinwiddie

County in 1752. John Ledbetter, whose wife's name is always left blank in the record, Richard, whose wife was Hanna, and perhaps other Ledbetters were in the area included in Bath Parish and Dinwiddie County. Other Ledbetters resided on the western border of Prince George County, near the eastern boundary of Dinwiddie County.

It may be noted that, although records were made of many events, these have decayed or been lost by time, fire, war, or other casualty. In general, the period of about one hundred years from 1650 to 1750 was marked by great growth but is largely a silent colonial period. There are fairly good records and writings on political history; economic and family history largely was not recorded. The established Episcopal Church had a vestry book of minutes and register of births. The minutes and registers of some of the parishes have ben preserved in part. Very few of the land records are available but these are the best source. There are scraps of court records available.

The Prince George-Hopewell Story by Francis Earl Lutz published in 1957 by the William Byrd Press, Inc., Richmond, Virginia, is a narrative of the particular area where the Ledbetters settled. The chronological events are told in a connected story with emphasis on the development of the area since World War II. No Ledbetter is mentioned in the volume except there are set out among the seven hundred sponsors, Mr. and Mrs. Paris I. Leadbetter, teachers, who have not traced their ancestry.

The lands patented or conveyed to the Ledbetters had descriptions not capable of exact location but named creeks which drained the land. As already stated, the lands of Henry were near Petersburg, and those owned by others extended farther south with each grant. Second Swamp Creek, with Alder Branch and Ashen Creek as tributaries, appears to be the stream nearest the Appomattox River. Then come the two forks of the Warwick Swamp Creek which join to form the Blackwater Creek, flowing eastward and southward. Procock Swamp Creek appears to flow into Warwick Swamp Creek on its south side. Brewers Creek, at the mouth of Hog Pen Branch, is mentioned. Jones Hole Creek with Roberts Branch appear to be farther south of Warwick Swamp Creek.

Stoney Creek and Rocky Run are in a southern location and drain into the Nottaway as it flows east before reaching Surry County.

Sappony Branch arises about a mile east of the present town of McKenney on Highway Number 1, south of the town of Dinwiddie. Near this point was built in 1727 Old Sappony Church, where Protestant Episcopal services still are held. About a mile south of the old church, on a slight elevation on the east side of the road, stands a two-story residence formerly occupied by Gardner Ledbetter (1786-1866), a great grandson of the original Richard and wife Hanna.

Included in this volume is a sketch of the areas where early Ledbetters were found in Virginia. The sketch was drawn by Lt. Col. Wm. R. Ledbetter from several of the best sources of information.

About 1729 several Ledbetter families moved about twenty miles southwest from their former residences into the western part of the frontier area of Brunswick County, near the boundary of North Carolina. The first land grant was in 1724 to Richard, whose wife was Hanna, recited as residing in Surry County. There followed grants in Brunswick County to Henry, Jr., whose wife was Edith Williamson, to William whose wife was Francis; and to John, Jr., whose wife was also Francis. All these, with other Ledbetters, including William whose wife was Sarah, had actually moved to Brunswick County by about 1729. They represented perhaps the fourth generation in Virginia. They or some of their descendants remained in Brunswick County more than half a century.

Most of the Ledbetters in Brunswick County owned land adjoining each other. The land was on both sides of Meherrin River. Rattlesnake Swamp or Creek was on the south with Fountain Creek a north tributary and White Oak Swamp a tributary on the south side of Rattlesnake Creek. Another apparent tributary of Rattlesnake Creek is Janeto Creek on which was located Long's meadow. Swiss Creek with two branches is mentioned. Little Creek is also mentioned. Up the Meherrin River, Hoands Creek is another tributary. Ledbetter Creek, with nearby Ledbetter Church house, is farther up the Meherrin. Bell in his *The Old Free State* says land south of Meherrin and Rattlesnake was granted to Henry and Richard Ledbetter in 1726. He adds "It was from this family, an early name in Prince George County, that Ledbetter Creek in Lunenburg undoubtedly took its name." Perhaps all the Ledbetters moved on because none is named in the well preserved Lunenburg County deed records or in the Cumberland Parish Vestry Book (1746-1816).

There were many Ledbetters of whom we have no record. This is shown by the voters' list of 1748 in Brunswick County, naming two Henrys and two Williams, of whom we can account for only one of each given name. We know very few of the children of known Ledbetters. Also, we find several Ledbetters whose parents we are unable to trace.

In the arrangement below by generations a relation is assigned on the basis of probability. Where relation and other facts can be established by record, references are often made herein. That the families were closely related is shown by their living in the same communities and removing together to a new home. Often the repetition of unusual given names is a clue to kinship. Henry, Richard, Thomas, as well as the very common John and William, appear as given names in practically every generation of the early Ledbetters. Francis as a given name was common at first but almost disappeared after one hundred years. In Prince George County other families owned land adjoining the Ledbetters, and no doubt their daughters married Ledbetter sons, thereby bringing into the Ledbetter family such unusual names as Buckner, Coleman, Drury, Jones and Osborne. Ledbetter as a given name similarly was brought into at least the Jones and Lanthrope families, who owned land in Prince George County adjoining the land of the original Henry, John, and Francis Ledbetters. Unusual Bible names bestowed on Ledbetter sons continued to appear in later generations. These include Ephraim, Daniel, Isaac and Joel.

This discussion names all the Ledbetters who have been found in the early records, so that further work may be done in tracing ancestry back to those named. In a few instances the family chain to the present has been traced. For the most part, these family lines are set out in discussion by particular authors in later chapters. In each of some eight instances where connected lines of ancestors have been traced, they go back to a Ledbetter in Prince George or

Brunswick County, Virginia. Accordingly, we conclude all Ledbetters coming through the southern states originated from Virginia. A few have been traced back to Georgia or Tennessee without as yet being able to connect with a Ledbetter in Virginia.

The account here covers substantially the period 1635 to 1800. It is thought that, by search of the U. S. Census and other records, many in the several states may trace a connected Ledbetter family line to some of those in this discussion.

In order to prevent confusion of those of the same given name and to make the account as clear as possible, a number and generation is assigned to each individual. When the next generation is discussed the parent's name, with the assigned number in parenthesis, is repeated followed by marriage and children constituting such succeeding generation.

I. *First Generation in Virginia*

1. Thomas Ledbetter, b about 1600, perhaps near Durham in the northeast part of England near the coast, d about 1655 in Charles City County, Virginia, in that part south of the James and Appomattox Rivers, which became the northern part of Prince George County in 1702 and was included in Bristol Parish in 1642.

In chapter two of this volume we have referred to the tradition that Ledbetters migrated from Durham to Virginia. A search of all the published lists of emigrants to America has not disclosed the name of any Ledbetter.

Burke's Landed Gentry is credited with stating that a Thomas Ledbetter was in Virginia in 1635. No Ledbetter is shown in the original Jamestown list of colonists, nor in the census of Jamestown in 1623.

II. *Second Generation in Virginia*

Thomas is not named in any record. We assume that he or the first immigrant had at least one son:

2. Henry, Senior, b probably 1623 in England, d probably before 1700 in Charles City County, Virginia. "Henry Ledbetter ordered to pay Mr. Jno. Cogan 816 lbs. tobo," as shown in Vol. 11, page 217, Order Book Charles City County, Virginia. Virginia Colonial Abstracts by Beverly Fleet, 1941.

On 29 Apr 1668, as shown in Patent Book Vol 6, page 134

in the Land Office (now Archives), Richmond, Virginia, patent issued by Sir William Berkeley to Henry 224 acres of land in Charles City County (Prince George County after 1702) at place called Bristol, of which the present Petersburg is the approximate location. The patent recited that 125 acres had been sold to Henry's father, unnamed, and the date not stated. On 29 Oct 1668 a patent was issued to Robert Coleman for 283 acres recited as adjoining Henry Ledbetter, Patent Book Charles City County, Vol 6, p 189, and William and Mary Quarterly number 13.

Under date of Oct 1673, "Judgment to Mary Ledbetter against Tho. Walton for 1000 lb tab for accomodation cloathing and levys expended plus debt," Vol 12 Court Orders, Charles City County page 549 original. Mary was likely the widowed mother of Henry.

Under date of 15 Aug 1678 Fragments of Court Order Book, Charles City County, p 318 by Ann B. Peebles (unpublished), "Wm. Range, dec'd, left to the use of Henry Ledbeater one mare filly which by Roger Rice delivered to said Henry, and prays the same be recorded. Mr. John Sturdevant desired to see the same branded for use of said Henry."

Under date of 12 Feb 1716, Court Order Book Prince George County, p 105 by Ann B. Peebles (unpublished), "Hugh Lee, Sr, exhibited a judgment of 12 Feb 1716, and desired it recorded and execution issued thereon against Henry Ledbetter and John his son, and they ordered to pay said Lee—and 5 S, costs of execution." This probably meant that Henry was dead and that was the reason for issuing execution against his son John. It will be noted that in Charles City Patent Book 7,—387, the patent of 548.32 acres to Francis Ledbetter recited "adjoining Hugh Lee's land."

III. *Third Generation in Virginia*

We do not have any record as to any brothers and sisters of Henry. Francis, Senior, could be a brother of Henry but is more likely his oldest son. A sister or daughter of Henry had likely married Wm Jones and had Ledbetter Jones, who married a Martha and they on Jan 1721 became the parents of Elizabeth Jones and 19 July 1725 became the parents of Francis Jones. We do not have the name of Henry's wife or date of marriage. Henry and wife likely had the following sons:

3. Francis, b about 1653 in Charles City County, Virginia, d before 1743 at the same place, then in Bristol Parish, Prince George County. Francis is first mentioned 3 Dec 1677 in Order Book of Charles City County, p 257, Ann Peebles, unpublished record, in suit by Eusebius King against Francis for debt. In the same court during 1678 and 1679, as shown by fragments of the records, Francis was sued for debt at least by Thomas Hermison, Thomas Clarke, Francis Epps and Major General Abraham Wood. In the same court during the same period Francis brought suits for debt at least against Wm Dodson, Thomas Parke and John Sturdivant. Also at Westover in 1678 Francis took out administration on the estate of Henry Foster, deceased, because Francis had boarded him and kept him in time of sickness. On 16 Aug 1678 Francis bought a white faced sorrel horse and black mare from Indians. On 3 June 1679 Francis was on the jury in Charles City. 20 April 1694 a patent was issued by Lieutenant Governor Edward Andrews to Francis and John Ledbetter, whom we conclude were brothers, and to William Jones, whom we conclude married their sister. The grant was for 300 acres of land in the forks of Warrock Main Swamp, then in Charles City County, in consideration of their having transported six unnamed persons to the colony. The patent is found in Book 8, p 367, of Charles City County Grant Book in the Archives of Land Office at Richmond. 26 April 1694, as shown in Charles City County Patent Book 7, p 387, and also in Nimmo's Manuscript Notes, there was granted to Francis Ledbetter 548.32 acres of land adjoining Hugh Lee's land on the south side of the Appomattox River in Charles City County in the part which became Prince George County after 1702. The land was in the same vicinity and perhaps a little south of the 300 acres. In 1704 Francis is listed as owning 100 acres of land and John 400, as disclosed by the Quit Rent Rolls of Prince George County, 28 Virginia Magazine of History and Biography, p 334.

13 June 1743 a patent issued to Henry Ledbetter for 200 acres of land in Prince George County between Procock and Warwick Swamp "on the line of Francis Ledbetter, deceased, and below the house of said Henry," Prince George County Grant Book 20 p 552. How long Francis had been dead we do not know but judging from the usual slowness in the issuing of patents it might have

been a few years before 1743. We are also of the opinion the Henry was the one called Junior who moved to Brunswich County about 1729. The recital of "house of said Henry" also represented a historical fact inasmuch as such recitals often occur long afterwards. We also conclude that the above patent is some evidence that Henry, Jr, was a son of Francis, and the patent issued to Henry after the death of his father. This conclusion is also aided by the recital in the St Andrews Parish minutes in Brunswick County in 1745 to the effect that Henry was paid 1200 lbs. of tobacco "for keeping his mother," who probably came to live with him after the death of Francis in 1743 or earlier.

4. John, Senior, b 1664 or earlier in Charles City County and d 1730 or later at the same place, then in Bristol Parish, Prince George County, Virginia.

John is first mentioned in the patent of 20 Apr 1694 issued to the three as mentioned above under Francis. Under date of 3 Oct 1696 John Ledbetter sued Jacob Colson, and neither party appearing, the case was dismissed, Charles City County Court Order Book, p 592, by Ann B. Peebles.

10 Oct 1702 Robert Bolling surveyed for John Ledbiter 400 acres of land in Charles City County on the south side of Blackwater, "English Duplicates of Lost Virginia Records," by Louis des Cognets, Jr. (1958). 17 March 1711/12 there was surveyed for Samuel Lee, 172 acres on the north side of Warwick Swamp on the east side of the Great Branch thereof, "beginning on John Leadbiter's corner," Plat Book Prince George County from a photostatic copy p 79 in the Archives, Richmond.

John was rather active in Prince George County from about 1711 to 1727. His activities included: 10 Jan 1714/15 witnessed deed from John Hamlin to Cuthbert Williams; 12 March 1715/16 on jury to divide land in suit Stitch Bolling v. Robert and Thomas Bolling; 10 May 1715 on grand jury of Prince George County; and on the jury on dates 14 May 1717 at Merchants Hope, 11 Nov 1718, 14 Feb 1720/21. On 14 Feb 1720/21 overseer of road from south side of Warwick to Nottaway Road.

John was appraiser on estates of deceased: Elizabeth Spell, widow of George, on 2 Jan 1716, George Spell 15 July 1716, Richard Tidmarsh 11 July 1726.

18 June 1726 John and Mary had slave b named Tab; 30 Dec 1726 John's slave Robin died.

24 July 1727 John and Samuel Lee, under order of Bristol Parish Vestry held at Ferry Chapple Church, were to procession land on the south side of Bristol Parish in Worocock Swamp, and about the same date the land of John Ledbetter and Samuel Lee, "the parties being present," was processioned. This meant to mark the boundaries anew, perhaps by hacking or glazing trees. This is the last record on John and wife Mary.

30 May 1712 Robert Bolling surveyed for John "100 acres on the north side of Warwick, adjoining his old land," Prince George Plat Book, p 751. On 18 June 1712 Robert Bolling surveyed for Richard 116 acres south side Jones Hole. On 1 March 1721-22 an indenture and release from John, Sr, and wife Mary to Richard "200 acres now in possession of said Richard, situated on both sides Worocock Branch adjoining Hugh Lee" was witnessed by James Thweat and John Edwards as shown Deed Records Prince George County, p 520-21, Richmond Archives. Before the same witnesses on 8 March 1721-22, as shown in the same record, pages 523-24, Richard made an indenture and release to William (whose wife was Francis), "50 acres now in possession of said William, on the Main Worocock Branch on the north side thereof, at the mouth of the Alder Branch, thence up the 2 branches."

The items in the last paragraph above are evidence that Richard was a son of John, Senior, and wife Mary. But we have no direct record that John and Mary had any children. Richard might have been a nephew, and as a part of the same transaction conveyed to his brother William. In any event, we shall see later in this account that William (whose wife was Francis) was certainly the son of Francis, Senior.

5. Drury, b probably 1666 in Charles City County d perhaps 1740 in Brunswick County. This original Drury is mentioned in a suit for trespass in Brunswick County in 1732. There is no other record of this Drury. There is a Drury b 24 Nov 1734, son of Richard and Hanna, and the famous Colonel Drury b 1743, son of Henry d 1751.

6. William, b about 1668 or earlier in Charles City County

d 1743 in Brunswick County. This probably was the William first mentioned 3 Feb 1691 where Captain John Taylor commenced suit against William who did not appear, as shown in Court Order Book Charles City County, p 388, Ann B. Peebles' unpublished Fragments; and 3 March 1791 William confessed judgment "for 2837 lbs. tobacco with cash and costs of execution, due by bill," as shown at p 391. In the same court 9 Nov 1694 Richard Bland, assignee of Thomas Swan, sued William (p 537) and 3 Dec 1794 William appeared in replevy of attachment, p 540.

9 Oct 1716 Randle Platt sued William but suit was dismissed for failure to prosecute, Prince George County Court Order Book, p 85. On 10 Nov 1719 in same court, p 294, Richard Bland sued William for debt and case was dismissed for failure to prosecute.

We cannot be positive whether the suits were against the same William. We place him here because he fits by date and place as a younger son of Henry, Senior, and because in the Bristol Register we find William and Rebecca had a daughter Mary b 28 Dec 1720. She, with her brother, can be traced later in the St. Andrews Parish Vestry, Brunswick County, as taking care of William and Sarah. There could be a William who married Rebecca and a different William who married Sarah but I conclude Rebecca was the mother of the children and after her death William m (2) Sarah.

We also list here other William Ledbetters whom we have been unable to trace and hence have not assigned an identification number to them:

8 Dec 1708 William Ledbeter will probated Somerset County, Maryland, beneficiaries Dorothy Earington, Mary wife of Francis Hepth, "late master." This William is probably an entirely separate family from the Ledbetters in Prince George County, Virginia.

March 1721—William Ledbetter deed to John Bowen, 610 acres south side Marattuck River, Chowan County, North Carolina, Chowan County, Register of Deeds, Book C No. 1. 2 July 1721 Wm Ledbetter witnessed sale at Edenton, North Carolina. Chowan County being very large and adjoining Brunswick County, this could be William b about 1696 in Charles City County, m Francis Vandiver about 1718 and was son of the original Francis Ledbetter.

LEDBETTERS OF EARLY VIRGINIA 23

IV. *Fourth Generation in Virginia*

(3) Francis m about 1677 or later to wife whose name is not known but she died 1745 according to our conclusion from the fact that Henry, Jr. was paid 1200 lbs. of tobacco in that year by St. Andrews Parish Vestry "for keeping his mother," who probably came to live with Henry after death of Francis as above mentioned under Francis. We conclude Francis, Senior, had at least:

7. Henry, Junior, b about 1690 or earlier in Charles City County d 1751 Brunswick County, Virginia. Under Francis above we gave our conclusion that Henry, Junior, was a son of Francis.

Henry is first mentioned on 10 March 1718-19 as one of three witnesss who had witnessed will of John Lanthrope dated 9 Jan 1718-19 and probated at Merchants Hope on testimony of the three witnesses. Henry witnessed by mark H. L. as he did his own will probated 1751 in Brunswick County. We conclude Henry, Senior, had died earlier or at least by 1716.

On 13 Nov 1721 a patent issued by King George to Henry Ledbitter, Junior, "for good reason and money paid" covering 98 acres on south side Ashen Creek, Prince Gorge County Land Grant Book 11, p 79. At first it was thought Henry, Junior, was a son of Henry, Senior. Ways and Means of Identifying Ancestors, by Evan L. Reed (1947), p 37, says that Senior and Junior did not as a rule imply father and son until after 1800.

Henry, Junior, d 1751, is traced in a separate chapter by James David Tillman, Jr.

8. William, b about 1696 in Charles City County in what became Bristol Parish, Prince George County, and d as a fact in 1775 in Brunswick County, Virginia. This is William whose wife was Francis, and he is not to be confused with the older William (number 6 above) whose wife was Rebecca or Sarah. The present younger William is proved to be a son of Francis, Senior, by recitals in patent dated 5 Aug 1751 issued to William, Prince George County Grant Book 29, p 505. The grant was for 561 acres in Prince George County on both sides of Procock adjoining Francis Ledbetter's land being a part of the grant of 548 acres to Francis and prior grant of 250 acres to William 31 Oct 1726, Prince George Grant Book 13, p 41, and another grant to William

9 Feb 1737 for 142 acres Prince George Grant Book 17, p 504, and 199 acres never before granted. Under the same date of 31 Oct 1726 as shown in Brunswick County Deed Book 13, p 61, a grant of 320 acres to Richard, at p 63 grant of 240 acres to Henry, and at p 64 a grant of 340 acres to William all in the same vicinity, is strong proof that the three were brothers according to the tradition to that effect.

(4) John, Senior, m perhaps 1687 to Mary who d after 1727 in Prince George County. Under John above is discussion that he and Mary probably had one son:

9. Richard, b about 1690 in Charles City County d as a fact in 1767 in Brunswick County.

As early as 1712 there was a survey for Richard followed by patents to Richard in the same location in Prince George County as the original grants to Francis and John.

Richard, on 2 Feb 1724, was the first Ledbetter who acquired land in the then pioneer County of Brunswick. Richard owned the most land, followed in order by William and Henry. Richard was appointed Constable in Brunswick County in 1738 and overseer in 1739. In 1748 Richard and his son Richard were on the roll of voters in Brunswick County.

(6) William (the eldest) m (1) Rebecca by whom he had his children, and m (2) Sarah and the latter died 1747 in St. Andrews Parish, Brunswick County. William and Rebecca had at least:

10. John, Junior (whose wife was Francis) b about 1699 in Prince George County. 13 Oct 1727 a patent issued to John for 318 acres on the south side of Meherrin River, adjoining land of Richard, Brunswick Land Grants Book 13, p 205. On 5 Nov 1743 grant to John of 196 acres "beginning at Ralph Jackson's Corner a little below the Islands" on the north side of Meherrin, Brunswick County. On 5 June 1744 John and wife Francis sold the above 196 acres of land to Joseph Fisher, who married his sister, Brunswick Deed Book 2, p 461. John perhaps moved and there is no further record where he can be distinguished from others named John.

11. Josephina, a daughter, who m before 1744 to Joseph Fisher.

12. Mary, b 28 Dec 1720, recited as dau of William and Rebecca, and baptized 26 Feb 1721 as shown in Vestry Book of Bristol Parish, p 329, by Gibson Chamberlayne, m Simmons before 1743.

The above three are proved to be children of William whose second wife Sarah by the Vestry Book of St. Andrews Parish, Brunswick County, where in 1743 John Ledbetter was paid 250 lbs. of tobacco for keeping Sarah Ledbetter three months, and in the same year Mary Simmons was paid for keeping William and Sarah Ledbetter; in 1746 Josephina was paid for keeping widow Ledbetter and in 1747 for burying Sarah Ledbetter, a poor parishioner.

In this period in Prince George County, in the Bristol Parish, which met at the brick church on Well's Hill near the eastern line of what became Bath Parish in 1741 and Dinwiddie County in 1752, there was a John whose father likely was Francis, Senior, and a Francis, Junior, whose parents are even more uncertain.

13. John, b about 1698 or earlier in Bristol Parish, Prince George County, and lived there at least until 1744, after which we are uncertain. The Vestry held at the brick church paid John for keeping Thomas Tedstall (Tedstill) for each of the years 1740 through 1743, as shown at pp 99, 105, 108, 115 of the Vestry Book of Bristol Parish by Chamberlayne. Tedstall might have been the father of John's wife whose name is left blank in all records.

We think that this John, with his sons John, Henry (Calvinist preacher), and Ephraim moved to Granville County, North Carolina in 1745. See discussion when his children are named below under (13) John.

14. Francis, Junior, b about 1715 or earlier in Bristol Parish, Prince George County and might have d about 1775 or removed to Henrico, an adjoining county in Virginia, in 1764. It is concluded that the father of Francis died in 1752 or earlier and that his mother died in 1756. This is based on the minutes of the Vestry meetings at brick church each November 1752 to 1756 when Francis was paid allowance for keeping his mother, the period being five months in 1756. See pp 150, 155, 160 and 163 of the Vestry Book, Bristol Parish, by Chamberlayne.

15. George, b about 1720, place unknown, was a soldier in

French and Indian Wars and married in 1746 in the Province of Pennsylvania. Nothing more is known and he is likely a different family of Ledbetters. In 1740 a grandson of Richard, the elder, was named George. It is likely that several Ledbetters moved to the Northwest Territory claimed by Virginia. This included the later states of Ohio, Indiana, and Illinois.

V. *Fifth Generation in Virginia*

(7) Henry's descendents have been traced by James David Tillman in another chapter.

(8) William, m about 1718 in Prince George County to Francis Vandiver, dau of John Vandiver, who in his will in 1719 in Prince George County mentions his dau Francis Ledbetter. She could be the wife of John whose wife was also Francis, and the last named had a son William b 19 Feb 1720 in Prince George County. William and Francis certainly had at least two sons:

16. John, b about 1719 in Prince George County, Virginia. Wm and wife Francis 12 Feb 1774 gave their son John 200 acres of land patented to Wm 15 July 1760 and recorded at Williamsburg, Brunswick County Deed Book 11, p 237. His brother James and Isaac witnessed the deed. There is no further record of this John.

17. James, b about 1730 in Brunswick County, Virginia, and d there in 1821. Deed 15 Feb 1774, William and wife Francis to their son James, 200 acres on Rattlesnake Creek, "land whereon I now live and my watergrist mill," Brunswick County Deed Book 11, p 268.

(9) Richard, Sr, m in Prince George County about 1715 to Hanna, who d about 1775 in Brunswick County. All their sons are known:

18. Richard, b about 1716 in Bristol and d 1749 in Brunswick County. Richard was surveyor of Brunswick County and on his death was succeeded by his brother John.

19. John, b about 1720 in Bristol Parish, Prince George County, Virginia, d 1785 in Chatham County, N. C. 29 Dec 1763 John and wife Amy gave a deed to Owen Myrick, who married Sarah, dau of his deceased brother Richard, conveying 120 acres on the north side of Rattlesnake Creek, "said land granted by patent

to Richard Ledbetter (Senior) Sept 28, 1732," Brunswick County Deed Book 7, p 411. Similar recitals are in deed dated 2 Dec 1769 between the same parties, Book 9, p 582. By 1765 John had moved to Orange County, N. C., probably in that part which became a part of Chatham County upon its creation in 1770. See deed, 5 Dec 1765 executed by John in Orange County, Brunswick County Deed Book 8, p 474. 31 March 1780 was granted 800 acres on Cub Creek, Chatham County, N. C. as shown Land Grant, Raleigh, N. C. On 3 Nov 1785 John, Sr, conveyed to his son John 100 acres of this land.

20. Drury, b 24 Nov 1734, as shown in Vestry Book and Register of Bristol Parish, p 332, by Chamberlayne, and d in Dinwiddie County, Virginia, in 1789. See Revolutionary War where this Drury served as a private.

21. Charles, b about 1738 in Brunswick County. Deed 20 Dec 1757 was executed by Richard to his son Charles, Brunswick County Deed Book 6, p 232. On 5 July 1763 Charles, then in Bath Parish, Dinwiddie County, Virginia, apparently unmarried at the time, sold the land given to him by his father to Charles Collins, Brunswick County Deed Book 5, p 332. On 2 Nov 1774, Charles and wife Francis sold to John Dun of Brunswick County (had also sold him land in 1764) a part of 512 acres patented to Charles in 1763, Brunswick County Deed Book 12, p 74. Charles is not to be confused with Charles of about the same age who was son of Henry and who married Mary Randall and moved to Montgomery County, N. C. in 1772. There is no further record of Charles and his wife Francis.

22. William, the youngest son of Richard and Hanna, was born 22 March 1740 and d 1812 in Chatham County, N. C., where he had moved in 1771. Although the parents had moved to Brunswick County, the son's birth was recorded in Bristol Parish, Prince George County, p 332 Chamberlayne. He is probably the William who in 1767 sold beds, furniture, cows, hogs, guns, etc to Marmaduke Daniel, Brunswick County Deed Book 9, p 21. He may be the William who on 7 May 1771 petitioned for four hundred acres in Saint Phillips Parish, Georgia, and recited "that he had been sometime resident in the province with his family consisting of a

wife, two children and three negroes," as shown Colonial Records
of Georgia, Vol XV, p 335, which petition was granted but no
further record unless he is a William in Revolution.

(10) John m Francis and had at least one son:

23. William b 19 Feb 1720. The Vestry Book and Register
of Bristol Parish, p 329 by Chamberlayne, shows John and wife
Francis had son William b 19 Feb 1720 and baptized 22 July 1721.
This may be the William whose estate was inventoried in Brunswick County, Will Book 5, p 213, Henry Walton, administrator
in 1787. Also in 22 Virginia Magazine of History p 377. No
further positive identification.

(13) John, whose wife's name is always blank in the record,
had the following sons:

24. John, b and baptized perhaps two months later on 23
July 1720, as recorded in Slaughter's Bristol Parish, p 129; perhaps
d about 1784 in Washington County, Georgia.

25. Henry, b 19 Nov 1721 in Prince George County, Virginia,
d 1785 in Caswell County, N. C. It is not known for certain who
the parents were but John and wife (blank) fit by date and place
and the possible migrations referred to often naming other children.
A separate chapter has been written on Rev. Henry and his descendents by Roy C. Ledbetter.

26. "Ephrain son of John and——Ledbetter born" 30 Dec
1742, as recorded p 333 Vestry Book, Bristol Parish, Prince George
County, by Chamberlayne.

27. William, b 1745 Prince George County, according to
James David Tillman who thought he was son of John, Sr. and
wife———. John, Senior, had died perhaps fifteen years before
this birth and besides Mary was always stated in the record as wife
of John, Sr. It is entirely possible that John and Mary were the
grandparents.

It is known that Rev. Henry (Calvinist) migrated about 1745
to Granville County, N. C. On 30 Jan 1748 Henry gave a deed to
John for 120 acres in Granville County, Book A Deed Records,
Granville County. On 17 Oct 1752 John of Granville County sold
the 120 acres. In March 1752 Henry sold 80 acres on Gunter
Creek in Granville County. On 7 Oct 1766 John Ledbetter of

Granville County sold 240 acres in that county. The John in these deeds likely was the father supposed to have been born about 1698 or could be his son, certainly born in 1720.

On 6 Feb 1778 Henry Downs gave a deed to John and Ephraim Ledbetter for four acres on the Savannah River, as shown in Richmond County, Georgia, Deed Book B-2, p 3. This was likely the above brothers John and Ephraim.

In 1828 in the northern part of Madison County, Alabama, an Ephraim Ledbetter died without a will and Moses Ledbetter was made administrator with surities Thomas Ledbetter and James Hozzle who in 1821 married Patsy Ledbetter in Madison County, Alabama. This was likely the Ephraim born 1742 in Prince George County. The occurrrence of the peculiar bible name is quite significant.

(14) Francis m about 1736 to Ann and had the following children:

28. Ann b about 1738. On 9 Sept 1760 Francis paid to the church wardens of Bristol Parish "for his daughter Ann's fine for having a bastard child," p 180 Parish Register of Bristol Parish by Chamberlayne.

29. Osburn, b 14 Feb 1740, son of Frances and Ann Ledbetter, p 332 Chamberlayne. In 1764 Osburn was included in a list of insolvents (p 225 Chamberlayne) and apparently thereby excused from paying tithes to the church. In the same year an Osburn was said to be in Henrico County, Virginia, and there is no further record.

30. Mary b 5 Dec 1741 and baptized 20 Feb 1742, p 333 Chamberlayne.

31. "Woodie b 5 Apr 1745 son of Francis and Anne Ledbetter" and baptized 9 June 1745, p 333 Chamberlayne. No further record of this Woodie.

VI. *Sixth Generation in Virginia*

(17) James m about 1765 Mary, as shown in his will in 1821, Brunswick County Wills, Vol 9, p 165, and in 22 Virginia Magazine of History, p 377, James and Mary had:

32. Osburn (Osborne) b about 1778 in Brunswick County, Va. See War 1812. An Osborne is shown on the tax list in 1812 for

Prince George County as owning 50 acres of land north of War-
rick Swamp near the town of Blandford, now City of Petersburg.
This may be the same Osborne because a James, who was probably
same James who was the father, was on the personal property tax
list in Prince George County for 1800 to 1802 as shown in State
Library at Richmond. In 1826 he and his brother Hubbard partitioned land, Brunswick County Deed Book 26, p 458. In 1827
Ozburn executed a deed of trust to Cook in Greenville County, Va.

33. Hubbard b about 1780 in Brunswick Co, Va, d 1860 in
Brunswick Co, as shown by inventory in estate of Hubbard filed
in Vol 19, p 73, Brunswick Co. See War 1812. 16 Dec 1808
Marriage Bonds Brunswick Co, Hubbard Ledbetter to Thirza Mosely.
In 1824 Herbert Ledbetter and wife Thursey Moseley gave deed
to Harris Moseley in Brunswick Co. He was in 1810, 20, 30 Census
Brunswick Co. There is no further information on Hubbard.

34. Hamlin b about 1785. See War 1812. Oct 22, 1804
Marriage Bonds Brunswick Co, Hamlin m Dicey Wright. No
further information. Deed 7 Oct 1779 from James and wife Mary
to William Whiteley covering 100 acres was shown to have been
witnessed by Hamlin Ledbetter, James Mason and Balaam Essell,
Brunswick County Deed Book 17, p 460. This would be an earlier
Hamlin of whom we have no record.

35. Winnifred (Winney).

36. Mary.

(18) Richard, Jr, m about 1737 in Brunswick Co, Va, to
Mary Walton who d Brunswick Co 17 July 1779, dau of George
Walton. By deed dated 4 Nov 1741 George Walton gave his
daughter Mary Ledbetter 369 acres of land, Brunswick County
Deed Book 1, p 496. Isaac Rowe Walton, son of George Walton
in his will dated 19 June 1770 mentioned his sister Mary Ledbetter,
Will Book Brunswick Co 4, p 29. As shown in will of Mary
Ledbetter dated 28 March 1778, probated 26 July 1779, Brunswick
County Will Book 5, p 57, also 22 Virginia Magazine of History
377, Richard, Jr and Mary had three sons and three daughters:

37. Richard b 1738 in Brunswick Co, Va, d 22 Jan 1841 on
Hightower River, Lumpkin County, Ga, Historical Collections
Joseph Habersham DAR, Vol 2, pp 610-613, biography of Richard.

On 28 Nov 1752 the original Richard deeded to his grandson Richard 100 acres of land on the south side of Rattlesnake Creek patented to the elder Richard 13 Oct 1727, Brunswick County Deed Book 5, p 289. On 23 Oct 1769 Richard and his brother Isaac sold this land, Brunswick County Deed Book 10, p 253. By about 1770 Richard, likely with his sister Mary and her husband George Bradley migrated to the western part of North Carolina on the French Broad River. See Revolutionary War. Richard lived in Brunswick County, Va, from 1781-90 and apparently his brother George was there with him for a short time. He is likely the Richard shown in the U.S. Census 1790 in Morgan District, Lincoln County, N. C. with his family of three males under 16, four females and 16 slaves His brother George is shown in the same census with family of three males over 16, five females and 14 slaves. The U. S. Census 1810 for Rutherford County, N. C. shows a Richard over 45 years of age with family two males under 10 and one 16 to 26 and two females under 10 and one 10 to 16, one 26 to 45 and wife over 45 and twelve slaves. Probably Johnston Ledbetter on the same Census was his son. There was another Richard on the same Census and each was over 45. Some date after 1830 Richard moved to Lumpkin County, Ga.

38. George b about 1740 in Brunswick County, Va, d about 1792 in Rutherford County, N. C. George continued to live in Brunswick County at least through 1774 when he was one of the tithers in the Episcopal Church Meherren Parish Book 13. On 30 Jan 1774 George and wife Elizabeth sold to John Taylor 400 acres, Brunswick Deed Book 11, p 285. Clarence W. Griffin in his History of Old Tyron and Rutherford Counties, North Carolina 1730-1936, Miller Printing Co., Asheville, N. C. (1937) p 117, says "George Ledbetter, a member of the Conventions (to ratify the Constitution of U.S.) of 1788 and 89, was a man of unusual ability, well educated for his day, and one of the county's (Rutherford, N. C.) leading men. He was an officer in the Revolution and Commanded a company under Col. Andrew Hampton at the Battle of Kings Mountain. He served as Justice of the Peace in Rutherford County from 1784 to 1791. He shortened his days by too free use of spiritous liquors." See Revolutionary War. A George is also shown as a member of the Georgia Conventions of 1788 and of 1789.

39. Mary b about 1742 in Brunswick County, m about 1760 to John Bradley who d about 1778. They lived on French Broad River in Rutherford Co, N. C. and her mother's will of 1778 recited that Richard might trade land in Brunswick County to Mary Bradley, widow, for the land on Broad River. They had a daughter Mary Bradley of Brunswick Co.

40. Elizabeth b about 1743, Brunswick Co, m before 1760 John Williams. See deed 27 Nov 1760, Richard and Hanna to John Williams, Brunswick County Deed Book 6, p 529. Also, 8 April 1778 her brother Richard and wife Nancy deed to George Williams, Brunswick Deed Book 13, p 100.

41. Sarah b about 1747 Brunswick Co, Va, m about 1763 Owen Myrick. See deed 29 Dec 1763 John (her uncle) and wife Amy to Owen Myrick witnessed by her brother Isaac, Brunswick Co, Deed Book 7, p 411.

42. Isaac b about 1741 Brunswick Co, d same place July 1785. See Revolution. Isaac owned extensive lands in Brunswick Co, and in 1783 and 84 he was on the personal property tax list for 10 slaves.

(19) John, son of Richard and Hanna, m about 1745 in Brunswick Co Amy, who d after 1784 in Chatham Co, N. C. They had three children:

43. John b about 1747 in Brunswick Co, Va, d 1794 in Chatham Co, N. C. He is probably the John with wife Elizabeth of Wake County, N. C., who in 1779 sold 175 acres on the north side of Rattlesnake Creek in Brunswick Co, Va. John, son of John and Amy, 30 Oct 1783 with wife Elizabeth gave a deed to John Ferrington for 317 acres on Cub Creek, Chatham Co, N. C. He is not shown in the Census 1790.

44. Sarah

45. Cleo

(20) Drury (Private) m about 1754 in Brunswick Co to Rebekah who d 1801 in Dinwiddie Co, Va, as inferred from the personal property tax list of Dinwiddie Co, in State Library, Richmond, showing Drury from 1782 to 1790 and Rebekah from 1791 to 1801. They had only one child.

46. Nathan b about 1755 in Brunswick, d after 1802 in Din-widdie Co, Va. In 1789 he was administrator of his father's estate in Brunswick Co. From 1782 to 1799 Nathan is on the personal property tax list of Dinwiddie Co.

(22) William, youngest son of Richard and Hanna, m about 1761 in Brunswick Co, but his wife's name is not known. William, in his will probated 2 April 1812 in Chatham Co, N. C. mentions by name only Coleman and William, then gives to his grandchildren, unnamed (probably children of his deceased son John) and the remainder of his property to be divided equally between his other children, unnamed. The U. S. Census 1790 shows William in Hillsborough District, Chatham Co, N. C. with a family of two other males over 16 (probably William and Alsey) and two males under 16, whose names have never been accounted for, and four females. In the same district, living alone and apparently unmarried, were Coleman and John. From the above we name the following children of William:

47. Coleman b about 1762 in Brunswick Co, Va, d after 1826 in Guilford Co, N. C. to which county he moved that year with his three sons.

48. John b about 1765 in Brunswick Co, Va, probably d about 1810 in Chatham Co. No further record.

49. William b about 1775 in Chatham Co, N. C. No further record.

50. Alsey b about 1776 in Chatham Co. 8 Aug 1808 Alsey was deeded land in Chatham Co by his grandfather William. Perhaps he is the same Alsey who, with Patsy Bright his wife, while residents of Harden Co, Tenn, in 1839 gave power of attorney to Ambrose Forshee recorded in Chatham Co, N.C. No further record.

51. J. Luther b about 1778 in Chowan Co, N. C. No further record.

VII. *Seventh Generation in Virginia*

(32) Osborne, son of James and Mary, m 7 Dec 1809, as shown by Brunswick Co Marriage Bond to Polly Delbridge. They had at least seven children:

52. David Egbert b 1813 in Brunswick Co, m 1837 Polly H. Smith. Removed in 1830 to Lowndes County, Ala, where he died 1870.

53. William Osborne m 1838 Sarah E. Delbridge.

54. John James m Eliza Ann Bates.

55. Thomas Jefferson m Elizabeth Phillips.

56. Roanna m William Cassady.

57. Mary E. no descendants.

58. Alexander Hamilton m Nancy Elliot .

(37) Richard (the Revolutionary soldier who lived to be 103 years old) m about 1765 in Brunswick Co Nancy Johnson who d 1785, dau John Johnson; m (2) in Rutherford Co, N. C. 24 April 1822 Elizabeth Berry b 1773 d after 1854 in McDowell Co, N. C.

Richard and Nancy had several children, including two daughters, not named in the record, who were murdered by the Indians. Their children included:

59. Johnson b about 1770 m about 1804 in Rutherford Co, N. C. to Nancy Whiteside, dau of John Whiteside, Jr, and his wife Eleanor Kelly. Johnson and Nancy had a son Richard O. Ledbetter.

60. Elizabeth m William Whiteside, brother of Nancy Whiteside.

61. Polly m a man named Harris.

62. Richard m Mary Whiteside, sister of Nancy. U. S. Census for Rutherford Co, N. C. for 1800, 1810, 1840 and 1850 likely show this Richard and his son Richard. Elizabeth Whiteside, another sister, m John Ledbetter, whose family relation we have been unable to trace.

63. Jonathan b 14 June 1773 in Brunswick Co, Va, d 19 April 1845 in McDowell Co, N. C., m Jan 1822 to Nancy Wells and had fourteen children. The scope of the present chapter does not extend to the period of the fourteen children. One of the fourteen was Dr. Jonathan.

The soldier Richard, having named his first child Johnson from his wife's maiden name and having named another son Jonathan, these names have confused the family as they appear in succeeding generations.

(38) George m 27 June 1772 in Brunswick Co to Elizabeth Walton, dau of Isaac Rowe Walton and of Elizabeth Ledbetter. U. S. Census 1790 shows George in Rutherford Co, N. C. with family of three males and five females. Of the several children only one can be easily identified:

64. Isaac b perhaps 1780 in Mumford's Cove, Rutherford Co, N. C. The U. S. Census of 1810 for Rutherford County, N. C. shows Isaac and his wife between 26 and 45 years of age and no children at the time. His wife's name is unknown. They had a son James b 4 July 1812, d 5 May 1871. James m his first cousin, Rebecca Bradley b 3 April 1822 d 23 March 1917. James and Rebecca had eight children, including J. Caloway and William Miller Ledbetter. In U. S. Census 1850 James and Rebecca were in McDowell Co, N. C.

(42) Isaac m before 1763 to Jane Johnson, sister of Nancy (wife of his brother Richard). They had two daughters and a son:

65. Virginia (Betsy) m 22 Dec 1789 in Brunswick Co to Thomas Howard, overseer of her mother's plantation.

66. Isaac b about 1775 in Brunswick Co, Va, d 1819 in Rutherford Co, Tennessee, m 2 Dec 1797 in Brunswick to Nancy King.

(43) John, son of John and Amey, m before 1779 to Elizabeth. In his will probated in Chatham Co, N. C. (Will Book 1789-1794, p 46) John mentions his wife Elizabeth and children James, Viney and Tas. James and Tas must have died young because Viney and her mother on 1 July 1799 sold 70 acres of the estate to Tom Cole and on 22 Feb 1804 Viney sold 100 acres of the estate in Chatham Co to Tom Cole. No further record.

(46) Nathan m Susanna Mayes who d 1815 in Dinwiddie Co, Va, dau of Robert Mayes and Judith Morris. They had eight sons and three daughters.

67. Richard b 1784 d 1837, m about 1804 to Martha Roper and had a son Joseph and a daughter Mary, who m William Dodd. Joseph and Mary in 1847, while residing in Hinds Co, Miss, gave a deed to land in Brunswick Co, Va. The land had been acquired through their ancestors Richard and Drury (Private in Revolution).

68. Gardner b 1786 in Dinwiddie Co, Va, d there in 1866. See War 1812.

69. Martha b 1788 in Dinwiddie Co, Va, d 1857 in Brunswick Co, m 1809 to David Pilkington.

70. William b 1791 in Dinwiddie Co, d there in 1856. Was in War 1812 with his brother Gardner. William m Anne Bland, dau of Wm Bland of Prince George Co and they had son John who moved to Baltimore, Md.

71. Peter M. b about 1791, unmarried, killed horseback riding. Served in War 1812 with his two brothers.

72. Judith P. m 1821 to William Womack of Chesterfield Co, Va.

73. Benjamin P. b about 1798 m 26 March 1840 in Petersburg to Luvany Scoggins. They had a son who was a minister in Brunswick Co.

74. Henry W. b about 1800 in Dinwiddie Co. No further information.

75. Nathan b 19 Jan 1802 Dinwiddie Co, d 30 May 1852 same county, m 6 Nov 1828 Martha Gum.

76. Joel b 1804 d 1857, m Martha Chambers. Their children included Robert Fulton Ledbetter whose descendents lived in Richmond, Va.

(47) Coleman m about 1777 to Elizabeth, perhaps in Chatham Co, Hillsborough District, N. C. and their children included at least three sons:

77. William b about 1777 in Chatham Co, N. C. About 1826 he with father and two brothers removed to Guilford Co, N. C. William m about 1803 to Sarah Mitchell and their children include:

Isaiah (1804-1875) m Delilah Wright.

Henry Clay (1808-1880).

William (1806-1855) m Eunice Siler.

Chesley (1802—) m Martha Siler.

78. Hiram b about 1780 in Chatham Co, N. C. m about 1802 and his children included:

Anderson Charles (1804-1884) m in Missouri to Elizabeth Gordon.

James m Jennie Millikan.

79. John b about 1785 d perhaps Rockingham Co, N. C. m perhaps 1810 in Chatham Co, N. C. His children included James m Susie Reid, Leonard, a Baptist minister who moved to Tennessee about 1856. Leonard of Clarksdale, Miss, about 1930 could be a descendant of the preacher.

In addition to the Ledbetters listed under numbers 1 to 79 above and arranged in seven generations, there were others in Virginia born before 1800 whom we list as follows:

80. Henry b about 1740, perhaps in Charles City Co, d there 1797. William Irby in Charles City Co was appointed guardian of Jacob, Isaac, and Henry, whom we conclude were minor sons of Henry. In 1785 Hardyman Dancy conveyed land to Henry Ledbetter. Later the same land was conveyed to Turner Christian by Henry Ledbetter (we suppose the son) and wife Elizabeth, and Isaac Ledbetter of Richmond and by Jacob Ledbetter. Most likely Henry and Isaac are the same who enlisted from Richmond in War 1812.

81. Joseph, Senior, b 1725 or earlier in Prince George Co, d there 1782 or later. Joseph on 19 Dec 1758 witnessed a deed from Thomas Pillion of Bristol Parish, Prince George Co, to Edward Woodlief (brother of Joseph's wife Ann) conveying 150 acres on "the Great Branch." On 10 May 1759 will of Edward Woodlief gave 200 acres of land to Joseph Ledbetter and also appointed him as one of his executors and provided "Joseph Ledbetter to have his share of crop as overseer," William and Mary Quarterly June 1901. Will also mentions his sister Ann Ledbetter, presumed to be wife of Joseph.

The father of Joseph is not known. His father could have been John, whose wife was Francis, or John whose wife's name is always left blank, listed in items 10 and 13 of this account.

Joseph, Senior, m before 1745 Anne Woodlief, d perhaps 1788, dau of Thomas Woodlief of Prince George Co and their children include:

82. Joseph, Junior, b about 1745 in Prince George Co and d there 1796. On 3 Feb 1787 Joseph, Junior, sold a slave to Daniel Davenport "now in possession of said Daniel and his wife,

Elizabeth, daughter of said Ledbetter," Prince George Deed Book 1, p 164. Deed was witnessd by William, brother of Joseph, Junior. On 10 Feb 1789 Joseph "for natural for his brother," Wood deeds to him 104 acres on Procock Swamp adjoining David Davenport, Prince George Deed Book 1, p 216. Joseph and wife Mary in 1789 sold land to Allen Hadden as shown by Deed Records of Dinwiddie County. In 1790 Joseph and wife Mary were on the tax list of Dinwiddie County. Joseph was on tax list of Prince George Co from 1782 to 1796. Joseph m about 1765 Mary, d 1808, dau of John Lanthrop and wife Rebecca. They had Elizabeth, m before 1787 Daniel Davenport. Perhaps Joseph and Mary also had Joseph b about 1770 who became the father of Task Wilkinson Ledbetter b about 1810.

83. Wood b 1750 or earlier and d 1804 or later in Prince George Co. 17 Feb 1778 he was appraiser in the estate of Edward Edwards, Prince George Co. From 1782 to 1804 Wood was on personal property tax list of Prince George Co. Presently no information on marriage or descendants.

84. William b 1760 or earlier d 1810 or later in Prince George Co. 8 June 1790 Henry Bonner and his wife Ann gave a deed to William Ledbetter for "100 acres on north side of Jones Hole Road beginning at said Ledbetter's line on said road to line of David Davenport," Prince George Deed Book 1, p 365. This land and land conveyed by Joseph, Jr, to his brother Wood above on 10 Feb 1789, was in same location as land surveyed for Richard in 1712 and same location as land granted to William, whose wife was Francis, on 31 Oct 1726 on western branch of Procock adjoining John Lanthrop, Prince George County Grant Book 13, p 41. William was on the tax list of Prince George Co for the years 1783 to 1810. He also likely is the William who appeared on the U. S. Census of Prince George Co 1810.

85. Herbert b 1762 or earlier d 1795 or later. On 13 April 1790 Herbert witnessed a deed for Joseph Kirkland to Hartwell Kirkland in Prince George Co. Herbert is on the tax list of that county in 1794 and 1795. Herbert could possibly be the one of that name appearing on U. S. Census 1830 for Botetourt Co, Va. He is placed as a brother largely on the tax list and his being in the same location in Prince George Co.

86. Arthur, who has been traced in a separate chapter by Lt. Col. William R. Ledbetter, we feel sure was born in Virginia. His son John C. was born 16 Jan 1785 and another son Washington was born 1789 somewhere in Virginia, at a time when the family had returned from North Carolina and before moving to Georgia and Tennessee.

87. Rowland b 1764 in Brunswick Co, Va, d 1842 in Marshall Co, Tenn. The date and place of his birth were set out in his pension application as a Revolutionary soldier made 2 Sept 1839. This date and place of birth fits as the second son of Col. Drury and wife Winifred. That Rowland was such a son is confirmed (a) by the statement of Rowland's son, Rev. James Johnson Ledbetter, made about 1860 in the presence of John Wade, then about 12 years old, and related in Nov 1937 to Christian Albert Ledbetter. The preacher had married the oldest sister of John Wade's father, whom she and the preacher were then visiting; (b) Isaac Johnson Ledbetter b 9 Aug 1844 and living at Morrillton, Ark, told Justus R. Moll in 1931 that Col. Drury was the father of Rowland who was Isaac's great grandfather. Also, the places of Revolutionary service by Rowland fit the places of residence of Drury in North Carolina. U.S. Census of 1790 shows Rowland in Nash Co, N. C. and Census of 1810, Anson Co, N. C. shows Roland b before 1765. According to family tradition, Rowland migrated about 1811 from Anson Co, N. C. to Lincoln County, part of which later became Marshall County, Tennessee.

Rowland m about 1787 to Sarah Vaughan of Chesterfield Co, S. C. (adjoining Nash Co, N. C.) who d 2 June 1833 in Lincoln Co, Tenn. They had the following eleven children:

88. Nancy b 1787, perhaps in Nash Co, N. C. d in McNairy Co, Tenn. She married William Wilkins.

89. Rev. Henry (Methodist) b 28 Oct 1789 in Robeson Co, N.C., d 1859 in Perry Co, Tenn. About 1812 he, with parents, removed to Linden, Tenn, and in 1830 removed to Richland Creek, Perry Co, Tenn. This Rev. Henry married in 1812 in North Carolina to Ann Phillips. They had seven daughters and five sons who for most part lived in Tennessee, but his grandchildren and great grandchildren removed to Farmington and Columbia, Missouri, to Cicero and Cartersville, Illinois.

90. Jesse b June 1791, perhaps in Nash Co, N.C., d Lauderdale Co, Tenn, in 1855. Had grandson Isaac Jonathan, b in 1844 in Ripley, Tenn, and living in 1931 at Morrillton, Ark.

91. Wesson b March 1793 in Anson Co, N.C. d Perry Co, Tenn, about 1872. He may be the Weston Ledbetter of Fayetteville, Lincoln Co, Tenn, who served in War 1812. He had a grandson, C. H. Ledbetter, living at Pope, Tenn, in 1931.

92. Betsy b 1797, m James Haslip and d in Marshall Co, Tenn.

93. Rebecca, b 1798, m in North Carolina to James Powell.

94. Henrietta b in North Carolina 1799, m Laban Haislip and d before 1861 near Humboldt, Tenn.

95. Isaac b 1801, perhaps Anson Co, N.C. d in Perry Co, Tenn.

96. Katherine b 1803, m James McMullen and d 1835 in Wayne Co, Tenn.

97. Rev. James Johnson (Methodist) b Nov 28, 1807, perhaps Anson Co, N. C., d Lewis Co, Tenn, about 1865. He m about 1824 Jane Wade of Montgomery Co, N. C. They had a son, Rev. Taylor (Methodist) who married a daughter of Rev. Pinkey Ledbetter and they in turn had a son, S. A., residing at Fresno, Calif., in 1931.

98. William Riley b 1810, d 1833, just after m Eliza Meesy of Giles Co, Tenn.

99. William Leadbeater from Leicester, England, settled in Occoquan, Virginia, in 1830, according to account by his great grandson Clarence Chandlee Leadbeater of Alexandria, Va, as published 1909 in Men of Mark In Virginia, Vol V, by Lyon G. Tyler. The article says the Leadbeater Drug Store at Alexandria was founded in 1792 by Edward Stable, another ancestor of Clarence Chandlee Leadbeater.

A folder of four pages advertises The Stabler-Leadbeater Apothecary Shop, 107 South Fairfax Street, Alexandria, Va, as having been founded in 1792. In the Archives at Mt. Vernon in 1933 there was a document showing Martha Washington ordered from the Leadbetter Drug Store.

The Leadbeaters of Alexandria likely did not have an immediate family connection with the Ledbetters of Prince George Co, Va.

CHAPTER 4

THE LEDBETTER FAMILY OF VIRGINIA

By JAMES DAVID TILLMAN, JR.

Introduction

The data from which these records are compiled is found in the Land Office at Richmond, Virginia, a few records from Prince George County, the Bristol Parish Register at Petersburg, the Brunswick Co., Va. records, Thomas Benson Ledbetter of Rockingham, N.C., L. S. Ledbetter of Cedartown, Ga., Mrs. Florence M. Heinemann of Petersburg, Va. and others, also from old Bible records.

Mr. J. E. Ames of Boston, Mass. has written a very interesting history of the Leadbetter Family of Maine and Massachusetts. The family was traced from the original name of Le Betre and was very old, and I am of the opinion that all of the names were probably related. The Maine family was descended from a Henry Leadbetter who came to this country from England about 1650. He was possibly a near relative of Henry Ledbetter who settled near Petersburg, Virginia about the same date.

The traditions of our family claim that there were three brothers who came from Ireland to this country and settled at Jamesown. I find the name variously spelled: Leadbeater, Ledbetter, Leadbitter, Leadbiter and Ledbeater. The Coat of Arms as given in Burke's Peerage is for Leadbiter, Deptford near Sunderland, County Durham, England, and is described thus: Gules on a Chev. order three crosses patee sa. between as many plates. Crest: Out of a mural coronet gu. a demi unicorn erminois, erased of the first, armed and crind or. Many of the names are still to be found in England, and especially in Liverpool, the spelling is usually Ledbetter.

In the Land Office at Richmond, Va. we find that April 29, 1668, Henry Ledbeater was granted 224 acres of land on the south side of the Appomattox River in Charles City County, for the transportation of two persons to the colony. Part of this land had formerly been sold to his father, so the record states, and that proves that Henry Ledbeater's father must have emigrated at an earlier date than 1668.

April 26, 1694, Francis Ledbetter was granted 548 acres in same county on the south side of the Appomattox River at a place known as Warrockhock near Bristol, for the transportation of eleven persons to the Colony.

April 30, 1694, Edmond Andros, Lieut. Governor, granted Francis Ledbetter, John Ledbetter and William Jones 300 acres of land in Bristol Parish, Charles City Co., in the forks of Warick (or Warroch) Main Swamp, for the transportation of six persons to the Colony.

Now these seem to be the ancestors of all the Ledbetters in Virginia and of the Southern States, the records, however, are very incomplete and we are unable to establish the exact relationship between the early settlers. They were all closely related and lived in the same neighborhood, which was originally Charles City County, but later became Prince George County. Subsequently Brunswick and Dinwiddie Counties were formed in part from Prince George County. Virginia in 1634 was divided into eight shires, James City, Henrico, Charles City, Elizabeth City, Warwick River, Warrosquijooke, Charles River and Accomac. These later were divided into many counties, and as a result we often find a family to have lived in several counties without having moved.

We have only the Brunswick records complete from 1726, but the Bristol Parish records give many dates of births. We find that the Ledbetters were neighbors and friends of the Tillmans, and connected with many prominent families of the state. They were active and energetic in the development of their country, and were of that pioneer stock that means so much to the settlement of a new country.

There were so many Ledbetters of the same name living at the same time that they are very easily confused. So without trying to establish the relationship between the early settlers, we will commence this record with Henry Ledbetter who died in Brunswick Co., Va. in 1751, leaving a will. He was first mentioned in Prince George County in 1720 as Henry Ledbetter, Jr., and was probably a son of the first named Henry or of Francis. He was living at the time of his death on White Oak Swamp, and his place adjoined

George Walton and Richard Ledbetter. Richard Ledbetter had a
wife named Hanna and sons Drury (born Nov. 4, 1734), Charles,
Richard and William (born 1740). The descendants of Henry
Ledbetter will now be given in detail.

DESCENDANTS OF HENRY LEDBETTER
OF BRUNSWICK COUNTY, VIRGINIA

1. *Henry Ledbettter.*

Among the many grants of land in Brunswick County the
following will show that Henry, William and Richard Ledbetter together with George Walton (first Justice in the
County, 1732) all lived on adjoining places. They were
brothers or closely related:

Oct. 31, 1726. Henry Ledbetter was granted 240 acres on
south side of Meherrin River.

Oct. 31, 1726. William Ledbetter (whose wife was
Frances) was granted 340 acres on south side of Meherrin River at the Rattlesnake Swamp. (They sold this
land May 28, 1754.)

Oct. 31, 1726. Richard Ledbetter was granted 320 acres
on south side of Meherrin River at the corner of William Ledbetter's line on both sides of Rattlesnake Creek.
This Richard, whose wife was named Hanna, had a
land grant Sept. 16, 1740 on White Oak Swamp adjoining George Walton and Henry Ledbetter.

Will Book No. 3 records Henry Ledbetter's will dated
Sept. 23, 1749 as follows:

WILL OF HENRY LEDBETTER
OF BRUNSWICK COUNTY

In the name of God, Amen.

I, Henry Ledbetter of Brunswick Co., Virginia, knowing the
following uncertainty of human life and being now in perfect
mind and memory do make and ordain this my last will and
testament in manner and form following:— Item, I give
and bequeath to my daughter Elizabeth Walton one mulatto
girl, Lucy. One negro boy, Hercules. I give and bequeath

to my son, Charles Ledbetter, one negro named Moile, one negro boy James and one ship-saw. I give and bequeath to my son, Henry Ledbetter, two negro boys, Abraham and Cato. I give and bequeath to my son, Drury Ledbetter, one negro named Daniel and one negro named Amaca. I also give him 240 acres of land by Patern whereon I now live and a survey of 400 acres adjoining to him and his heirs forever only leaving my loving wife Edith Ledbetter the use of it. I give to my loving wife Edith Ledbetter the residue of my Estate not heretofore mentioned but of what or quality so ever. Lastly I do hereby nominate and appoint my loving wife, Edith and Isaac Rowe Walton Executors of this my last will and testament.

Hereby revoking and disannuling any wills by me heretofore made. As witness to my hand this 23 day September in the year of our Lord Christ 1749.

Henry Ledbetter
(his mark) /—

In presence of

Nathan Harris
William Johnson
William Gwathmey

Probated March 26, 1751

(Copied at Brunswick County Court House by F. M. H. P.S. died at White Oak Swamp, on land adjoining his relatives Richard Ledbetter and George Walton)

His wife was Edith Williamson. (After Henry Ledbetter's death she married Henry Britt who died in Brunswick Co. —will dated 1765) Children given in Henry Ledbetter's will were:

1. Elizabeth Ledbetter, married Isaac Rowe Walton
   (see No. 2)

2. Charles Ledbetter, married Frances Randle
   (see No. 3)

3. Henry Ledbetter, married Winnefred Wall
   (see No. 105)

4. Drury Ledbetter, married Winnefred Lanier
   (see No. 117)

2. *Elizabeth Ledbetter* (see No. 1)

She was born about 1730. She married Isaac Rowe Walton, son of George Walton and wife Elizabeth Scott (See *Harris Family* by Gid C. Harris). Some say George Walton married Elizabeth Rowe. George Walton left a will probated in Brunswick County Jan. 26, 1767 in which he mentioned his wife Elizabeth and children, John Walton, Mary Ledbetter, Catherine Harris, Isaac Rowe Walton. His wife, Elizabeth Walton in will dated Feb. 12, 1771 mentions same children and grandchildren, George Simms, Sarah Simms and Isaac Rowe Simms.

Nathan Harris who married Catherine Walton was born 1716, was son of Edward Harris who left will dated April 27, 1733. Nathan had a sister Martha Harris who married ───────── Williamson. Richard Ledbetter who married Mary Walton (her will probated July 26, 1779) had these children: Isaac Ledbetter, George Ledbetter, Richard Ledbetter, Elizabeth Williams, Mary Bradley wife of John Bradley, and Sarah Mirick.

Isaac Rowe Walton left will dated June 19, 1770. He died in 1771, left wife Elizabeth and these children:

1. Mary Walton married ─── Mabry.
2. Henry Walton
3. Daniel Walton
4. David Walton
5. Isaac Rowe Walton, born 1765; d. 1833; Mar. 1st 1787, Elizabeth Allen (1773-1805); mar. 2nd. 1808, Polly Lanier
6. Drury Walton
7. Elizabeth Walton, mar. June 27, 1772 George Ledbetter, son of Richard Ledbetter and Mary Walton (1715-1779)
8. Fanny Walton
9. Nancy Walton

3. *Charles Ledbetter* (see No. 1)

He lived in Brunswick Co., Va. on Rattlesnake Creek near Roanoke River. (This would be in the southwest corner of the County. In 1904 I visited Col. Stephen Tillman who lived in this section near Rattlesnake Creek. J.D.T.) He was probably born about 1732 and married before 1758 Frances Randle dau of Peter Randle who married February 15, 1742 Frances Barrett. Her brother Peter Randle, Jr., born about 1744, married in Brunswick Co. Mary Sims and Peter, Sr. died in Montgomery Co., N.C., Aug. 9, 1786; and her brother William Randle (1747-1790) mar. Lucy Simmons. Her father Peter Randle was born in King William Co., Virginia 1714, son of John Randle and Mary Johns, daughter of Richard Johns (will in King William Co. Va.) John Randle's will was probated in Brunswick Co. Aug. 28, 1753; wife Frances and children Josias, Susanna, John, William, Peter and Frances Randle.

Charles Ledbetter and wife Frances on Jan. 25, 1764 deeded land to Jeckonias Randle (He was her uncle, born in King William Co., May 1, 1710, son of John Randle and Mary Johns.) On Nov. 2, 1774 Charles Ledbetter and Frances sold their land in Brunswick Co. and "refugeed" from Tories to what was then Anson Co., N.C., later Montgomery County. At about the same time his brother Drury Ledbetter and many related families left Brunswick and settled in the same section. Among these were Randles, Ledbetters, Davidsons, Prichards, Quinceys, Johnsons, Laniers and Tillmans. Frances Randle (sometimes called in error Mary Frances) wife of Charles Ledbetter died and Charles then married the widow of Dr. Thomas Johnson of Brunswick County, Va. and three of the Ledbetter children married Johnson children. Charles Ledbetter and both wives are buried in Stanley Co., N.C. on west bank of Pee Dee River. The following letter of Quincey Davidson is of interest. He was the son of George W. Davidson and Mary Randle, whose parents were Peter Randle, Jr. and Mary Simms. Peter Randle, Jr. was a brother of Frances Randle, the wife of Charles Ledbetter.

Mission Valley, Texas
January 12, 1903

Mr. James D. Tillman
Carrollton, Mississippi

Dear Sir:

Yours of Dec. 24, 1902 is to hand, and contents noted. My answer to Question 1 is that I knew John Tillman and his mother (She was Ann Randle, wife of Richard Tillman, who died in Montgomery Co., N.C. about 1800. J.D.T.) when I was a small school boy. They lived about two or three miles from Lawrenceville (Montgomery Co., N.C. J.D.T.) where I was at school. John's brother David was living with an old Aunt east of the County of Montgomery (She died in Granville Co., N.C. J.D.T.). At her death he came back and settled in Montgomery County on the west side of PeeDee River in about three miles of my father's place. His wife was Henry Ledbetter's daughter. I have heard him, L. preach frequently. Ledbetter's mother was a Randle (you misspell the name). She was sister to William, "Dumb Johnny" and Peter Randle. Richard Tillman's wife must have been sister to said men. (She was cousin. J.D.T.) My mother was the daughter of the said Peter Randle. Ledbetter's first wife was the sister of William Johnson of old Sneedsboro (Anson Co., N.C. J.D.T.). I cannot go any farther back on the Johnson side, but I do know there was one John Randolph a celebrated statesman of Virginia and there was some relationship of the Johnson and Randolphs. I know not what. You will excuse my poor writing. My first excuse is that I am in my ninety first year, the next sometime ago I was attacked by a vicious dog, and in the fight my thumb was bitten off. I was a citizen of Mississippi at one time, and visited Carrollton in 1893. I stopped to see some friends, and will probably pay them another visit before I die.

Yours with highest regards,

Quincey Davidson Sr.

Another letter written by Walter Steele Little, son of
Sarah Elizabeth Ledbetter born 1820 and half sister of Rev.
Henry Willis Ledbetter both grandchildren of Charles Led-
better and Frances Randle. The letter was written to his
first cousin Virginia Ledbetter, daughter of Rev. Henry
Willis Ledbetter. This letter runs as follows:

Ansonville, N.C.
December 3, 1890

Dear Cousin Jennie:

Your note enclose in Cousin Addie's letter came safely.
The best information I can give you is such as I get from
mother and does not amount to much.

Henry Ledbetter as you know was our grandfather. His
father was Charles Ledbetter who came from Brunswick Co.
Va. about 1773 when Henry Ledbetter was 5 years old and
was a farmer. Had several sons and daughters:—Charles,
Henry and Gray and John, Edith Harris, Sallie Harris, Betsey
Bell. Charles and Henry were Methodist preachers. Charles,
Henry and Gray married the three daughters of Dr. Johnston
who had married their mother after the death of Charles
Ledbetter Sr. Charles (I think) married Elizabeth Johnston.
Gray married Celia Johnston. Henry Ledbetter married Mary
Johnston. Henry Ledbetter joined the Conference when
quite young before was ever married and preached four years
(or I should say) rode the circuit four years. Mother does not
know what year he joined the conference. After riding four
years he married Mary Johnston and had 5 children. His
wife died and he traveled and preached four years more then
married the widow Dunn. Had 5 children:— Mary, Nancy,
Charles 1st (who died in infancy), Charles 2nd and Tabitha.
Charles 2nd is still living in Polkton, N.C. though in quite
feeble health. Henry Ledbetter's second wife died and he
married Polly Steele and had four children. The wife of
Charles Sr. was Frances Randall. This is all the history I
can learn from mother. I might learn something further from
Uncle Bob Ledbetter and I may write to him if I do and
learn anything will let you know. Uncle Charles is the only

òne of the older children living. All of the younger set are alive. Cousin Fannie Cooley is living with her daughter Bettie Harlee or rather Bettie lives with her in Morven, Anson Co. where they have a very pretty little home and are very comforably situated. Cousin Dave and family and Cousin John are at the old homestead. Cousin Bill spends most of his time in Wadesboro. I have not been to the old homestead since Aunt Patsy died. Cousin Jim L. Smith and wife of Texas were to see us last summer and I had a letter from his wife last week. I think she is a splendid woman. Cousin Jim has made a big lot of money and is doubtless rich. He is a strong Methodist and seems to be very liberal. He and his wife have been to see us twice and have made themselves very pleasant. Col. Wm. C. Smith died several years since in Texas. Cousin Mary Ann lives with Ida. Cousin Pat married Will Cox and I think they are now living in Mt. Airy, N.C. Cox has busted two or three times and from some cause seems never to have done much. Cousin Fanny married John McGregor who is now sheriff of this county. McGregor also failed in business but has been twice elected sheriff. Cousin Jim Tillman Smith is somewhere in Texas successfully (I suppose) practicing law. His first wife did not live a great while after he went to Texas and he has married a second time. I think he has several children, don't know how many. Probably all of this I have written will be of little interest to you but it is writ and I suppose I may as well send it on as it won't cost anything and you are not compelled to waste your time on it. My fire has died down and the chilly night air comes creeping around and warns me that it is high time for me to bid you good night, drop the curtain and retire.

With much love as ever,
Your affectionate cousin,
W. S. L.

Montgomery Co. N.C. tax lists 1782
Charles Ledbetter   560 acres 15 slaves
Drury Ledbetter   720 acres 10 slaves
Zedekiah Ledbetter   50 acres   2 slaves

The children of Charles Ledbetter and wife Frances Randle were:

1. Rev. Henry Ledbetter b. 1769; mar. 1st Mary Johnson (see No. 4)

2. Rev. Charles Ledbetter b. 1771; mar. Elizabeth Johnson (see No. 94)

3. Gray Ledbetter b. 1776; mar. 1799 Celia Johnson (see No. 95)

4. John Ledbetter died in infancy.

5. Edith Ledbetter b. 1763; mar. 1778 Col. West Harris, Jr. of Rowan Co., N.C. He is buried in Harris grave-yard on bank of Yadkin River, Stanley Co. He was member of State Senate 1797-1801. He had daughter, Edith Ledbetter Harris, who married ——— Bruner. (Edith Ledbetter Harris was great grandmother of Mrs. James K. Moore of Salisbury, N.C.)

6. Zedekiah Ledbetter born in Va. 1758; lived in N.C.; buried on Little River, Montgomery Co.; had daughter Ony, who married James Raiford, afterwards married ——— Shankle and moved to Alabama.

7. Elizabeth Ledbetter, b. 1767; mar. Benjamin Bell and had son Jonathan Bell who died in Stanley Co., N.C., leaving sons Frank and Littleton Bell living near Albermarle, Stantley Co., 1916.

8. Sarah Ledbetter b. 1761; mar. Dr. ——— Cato. No records.

9. Frances Ledbetter b. 1765; mar. Arthur Harris of Montgomery Co., N.C., who was a member of the legislature in 1798. They had four children who moved to Tennessee. He afterwards married a Miss Clark.

4. *Rev. Henry Ledbetter* (See No. 3)

Rev. Henry Ledbetter was born in Brunswick Co., Va. Jan. 29, 1769 and died in Anson Co., N.C. April 1, 1852, aged 83, leaving a will. He was baptized at Rattlesnake Church, Brunswick Co. He was a pioneer circuit rider of N.C. and S.C., licensed to preach in 1788 and admitted to Methodist

Conference 1789, located 1794. He is buried in Wadesboro, N.C. cemetery. He was a very wealthy man.

He was married three times: 1st about 1792 to Mary Johnson, by whom he had 5 children; 2nd about 1810 to Mrs. Dunn, nee Anne Pritchard by whom he had four children. (She was a relative of Senator Pritchard of N.C. She had a son Thomas Dunn and a daughter Elizabeth Dunn, who married George Mendenhall.); 3rd to Mary Steele on Oct. 19, 1819, by whom he had four children. Mary Steele died Jan. 24, 1828.

His children in order by each marriage, but not in order by birth:

1st Marriage:
1. James Ledbetter mar. Elizabeth Forrest (See No. 74)
2. William Johnson Ledbetter (See No. 5)
3. Martha Ledbetter, b. Dec. 24, 1794 (See No. 9)
4. Henry Willis Ledbetter b. June 1800 (See No. 79)
5. Frances Ledbetter, mar. Col. Duncan McRae, had son James Ledbetter McRae b. 1831 and living Albermarle, Stanley Co., N.C. in 1916, daughter Minerva McRae and son Duncan McRae

2nd Marriage:
6. Tabitha Randle Ledbetter b. July 24, 1811 (See No. 75)
7. Mary Washington Ledbetter b. Oct. 28, 1808 (See No. 87)
8. Nancy Ledbetter, mar. Charles Robinson and (1) Ann Eliza Robinson mar. Thomas Colson, (2) James Robinson, (3) Keziah Robinson, (4) Cora Robinson mar. John Eason.
9. Charles W. Ledbetter b. Jan. 1, 1814 (See No. 88)

3rd Marriage:
10. Sarah Elizabeth Ledbetter b. 1820 (See No. 89)
11. Robert Steele Ledbetter (See No. 91)
12. John Fletcher Ledbetter (See No. 92)
13. Thomas Benson Ledbetter (See No. 93)

5. *William Johnson Ledbetter* (See No. 4)

William Johnson Ledbetter mar. Dec. 16, 1830 Martha Wall Leake who died Sept. 6, 1850. He died Dec. 17, 1857 in Anson Co., N.C. Their children were:
1. Col. Henry Wall Ledbetter (See No. 6)
2. William Pickett Leake Ledbetter (See No. 7) mar. Emma Porter.
3. Mary Ann Ledbetter b. 1836; mar. F. M. Kennedy.
4. Eliza John Ledbetter (See No. 8)
5. Tabitha Cole Ledbetter b. 1846; d. 1851

6. *Col. Henry Wall Ledbetter* (See No. 5)

Henry Wall Ledbetter was born Nov. 8, 1833 in Wadesboro, N.C.; died June 15, 1897; married 1st, 1860, Elizabeth Stanback, 2nd, Dec. 1876, her sister Mary Stanback (1841-1919). Children by his first wife were:
1. William P. Ledbetter, mar. Texanna M. Gray (See No. 65); lived in Wadesboro, N.C. and had daughter Bessie Ledbetter.
2. George Stanback Ledbetter (1873-1924), mar. Mollie Lockhart who was born Dec. 8, 1870, died May 9, 1944.
3. Lillie May Ledbetter, mar. John William Masemore (See No. 66)
4. Mary A. Ledbetter, m Cyrus Cole Bryan (See No. 65)
5. Martha Elizabeth Ledbetter, b. Jan. 12, 1865; died May 30, 1933; mar. William A. Sloan. (See No. 63)

7. *William Pickett Leake Ledbetter* (See No. 5)

Born 1831; married Emma Jane Porter of Tennessee. They had a daughter, Emmie Ledbetter, who married Dr. Thomas May Hunter in 1885, and had children: (1) Thomas M. Hunter, Jr, mar Josephine Phillips, and (2) William Lewis Hunter mar. Myrtie Humble.

8. *Eliza John Ledbetter* (See No. 5)

Born 1839; died 1912; married William Bennett Little; lived in Wadesboro, N.C. Their children were:
1. William Ledbetter Little mar. Netta Hardison. (See No. 68)

2. Frank Milton Little (See No. 69)
3. George Kennedy Little, died young.
4. Edward Robert Little, died young.
5. Henry Wall Little (See No. 70)
6. Mary Ledbetter Little (See No. 71)
7. Julia Little (See No. 72)
8. John Leake Little (See No. 73)

9. *Martha Ledbetter* (See No. 4)

She was born December 24, 1794 and died in Anson County, North Carolina on January 3, 1882. On October 22, 1818 she married her cousin, David Tillman, who was managing the plantation of her father Rev. Henry Ledbetter. David Tillman was born in Montgomery County, North Carolina, December 21, 1784. He was the son of Richard Tillman, who came from Brunswick County, Virginia to Anson County, North Carolina in 1783 and wife Ann Randle, daughter of William Randle, who died in Brunswick County April 1771. David Tillman was a member of 10th Co. 7th Regiment of the Montgomery County Militia in the War of 1812. He died in Anson County North Carolina on April 21, 1859. Their children were:

1. Richard Henry Tillman (See No. 10)
2. Mary Ann Tillman (See No. 30)
3. Dr. James Alexander Tillman, born October 27, 1824. He was educated at the University of Virginia. He married Cornelia Pettigrew and he died in Wadesboro, N.C. on January 7, 1882. No children.
4. Frances Eliza Tillman (See No. 38)
5. Martha Ledbetter Tillman, born May 31, 1829 died June 15, 1855. Not married.
6. William Ledbetter Tillman, born July 17, 1831 in Stanley Co., North Carolina. He was a Major of Militia during the Civil War. He died 1907 in Montgomery County. (I visited him in 1902, J.D.T. Jr.) He never married.
7. David Chiles Tillman (See No. 46)

8. John Randolph Tillman was born April 14, 1837 and
    died in Anson County, North Carolina, February 2,
    1897. Never married.

10. *Dr. Richard Henry Tillman* (See No. 9)

He was born in Granville County July 3, 1819 while his
father was looking after the affairs of an old grandaunt,
Sarah Lumpkins who was the daughter of George Tillman
and wife Mary Goodrich of Brunswick County, Va. He
studied medicine at the University of Pa. Philadelphia 1841.
November 11, 1841 he married Narcissa Bennett, daughter
of James Charles Bennett and Mary Ella Winifree of Anson
Co. N.C. He died December 23, 1864, and is buried in
Wadesboro, N.C. His widow moved with part of her family
to Carroll Co. Mississippi in 1867 and died February 24,
1899 and is buried in Carrollton, Mississippi. Their children
were:

1. James David Tillman (See No. 11)
2. Mary Ella Tillman (See No. 14)
3. Ann Elizabeth Tillman (See No. 17)
4. Martha Frances Tillman (See No. 18)
5. Charles Henry Tillman (See No. 24)
6. William Edwin Tillman (See No. 25)
7. Helen Bennett Tillman (See No. 26)
8. Adela Cleveland Tillman born in Anson Co. N.C.,
    February 28, 1855; married October 21, 1885 her
    first cousin William S. Bennett at Black Hawk in
    Carroll Co. Mississippi on October 13, 1889. No child.
9. Minnie Ethline Tillman (See No. 29)
10. Leila Hortense Tillman died in infancy.

11. *James David Tillman* (See No. 10)

He was born in Anson County North Carolina on November 8, 1842 and died January 1, 1932 in Meridian, Mississippi. He served throughout the Civil War with Co. C 14th
N. C. Regiment was on honor roll. He came to Carroll
County, Mississippi in 1867. He married in Carrollton, Miss.
on Decmber 21, 1880 Rachel Caroline Bryan who was born
December 13, 1850 and died Dec 26, 1946 in Meridian,

Miss. She was the daughter of Samuel Washington Bryan, a native of Johnson Co. N.C. and wife Martha Ann Marshall of Carroll County, Miss. Children were:

1. James David Tillman, Jr. (See No. 12)
2. Carrie Bryan Tillman (See No. 13)
3. Anne Boleyn Tillman, born March 14, 1886, married Albert McLemore who died June 1, 1952 in Greenwood, Miss.
4. Mary Lena Tillman, born April 3, 1888, died November 19, 1897.
5. Addie Tillman, born August 8, 1889, living in Meridian, Miss. in 1954. D.A.R. No. 243144.
6. Samuel Henry Tillman, born Feb. 1, 1891 died April 3, 1894.

12. *James David Tillman, Jr.* (See No. 11)

He was born February 6, 1882 in Carrollton, Miss. Graduated at Millsaps College in 1902, B.A. Degree, Kappa Sigma Fraternity, member of all Masonic Bodies and Shrine, Methodist. Married January 3, 1911, Anne Sigisimunda Hamilton, daughter of John Moore Taylor Hamilton and Sarah Elizabeth Collins and descended from many old Virginia families. She was born in Meridian, Miss. and killed in Tornado, April 20, 1920 at Meridian, Miss. Children are:

1. James David Tillman III, born April 3, 1912 in Carrollton, Miss. Enginering graduate at Georgia School of Technology, married 1st June 6, 1933 to Sara Gaither of Atlanta, Georgia, one child Floyd Gaither Tillman born July 12, 1934. Married 2nd on January 12, 1947 to Mildred Boucher who was born in Murphysboro, Ill. No children. In 1954 living in New Orleans, La. wholesale Electric Supply Business, Masonic order and Shriner, Kappa Sigma, Methodist. Served through 2nd World War now Lieut. Col. in Reserve.
2. Sara Hamilton Tillman born March 6, 1914 in Meridian, Miss. Graduate of Mississippi State College for Women. Married August 27, 1939 to Dwight F.

Blissard, Okolona, Miss. one child Dwight F. Blissard born February 25, 1943. Her D.A.R. membership was No. 283352 (Richard Tillman)

3. Rachel Anne Tillman born July 24, 1919 in Meridian, Miss. Graduated at M.S.C.W. also M.A. degree from University of Miss. Member of Delta Gamma. Married December 19, 1947 to Dr. Frank Miller Laney, Jr. of Tupelo, Miss. He was born November 2, 1918 graduated from the University of Miss. and PHD from the University of Virginia. In 1954 Assistant Professor of History at Millsaps College, Jackson, Miss. He belongs to Phi Delta Theta. He served through 2nd World War and is now Major Reserves. She was a Lieutenant Jr. Grade in the WAVES during war. Children are:

1. David McLemore Laney, born in Atlanta, Ga. on June 20, 1950.
2. Frank Tillman Laney, born in Atlanta, Ga. on July 23, 1953.

13. *Carrie Bryan Tillman* (See No. 11)

Was born October 10, 1883 in Carrollton, Miss. She married November 11, 1908 John Taylor Hamilton, son of John Moore Taylor Hamilton and wife Sarah E. Collins of Meridian, Miss. In 1954 living in Meridian, Miss. Children are:

1. John Taylor Hamilton, born Jan. 30, 1912, graduated from Mississippi State College and served World War II Captain, now with U. S. Engineers at Galveston, Texas, married October 18, 1941 Frances Jane Hines of Texas. Children are:
1. Rebecca Jane Hamilton
2. Sarah Ann Hamilton
2. James David Tillman Hamilton, born March 27, 1914. Graduated from University of Mississippi, member of Phi Delta Theta, graduated from Duke University with Master's degree. Served in World War II now a Lieut. Col. U. S. Engineers in Washington, D. C. and lives in Falls Church, Va. He married Nancy Laprade

of Durham, N. C. daughter of Dr. W. H. Laprade, Dean of History Department at Duke University. Children are:

1. James David Tillman Hamilton
2. Susan Elizabeth Hamilton
3. William Thomas Hamilton
4. John Lloyd Hamilton

3. William Morgan Hamilton, born January 31, 1916, attended University of Mississippi, member of Phi Delta Theta. Engineering Consultant at Meridian, Mississippi. Married Ann Tobias, daughter of Col. R. B. Tobias, U. S. Army retired, and wife Mary Dunlay. She served in WAVES during World War II, Lieut. Jr. Grade. Children are:

1. Mary Ann Hamilton
2. William Morgan Hamilton
3. Bobby Jack Hamilton

4. Caroline Hamilton, died in infancy.

5. Rachel Elizabeth Hamilton, born Jan. 17, 1920. Graduated from University of Mississippi, member of Delta Delta Delta. She married William Hailey Willis of Meridian, Miss. PHD from Yale University, now Professor of Latin and Greek at the University of Mississippi. Served during World War II, now a Major in the Reserves. Children are:

1. Caroline Claire Willis
2. Lissa Catherine Willis
3. Millicent Helen (Robin) Willis

14. *Mary Ella Tillman* (See No. 10)

She was born in Wadesboro, N.C. on May 23, 1844, married W. Brantley Pettigrew, July 11, 1865 and moved to Florence, S.C. where he died June 26, 1884. She died in Marion, S. C. Jan. 1932. Children were:

1. Louis Mowry Pettigrew, born Sept. 20, 1866 (See No. 15)
2. Henry Tillman Pettigrew, born Dec. 14, 1867, died July 6, 1885.

3. Mary Ella Pettigrew, born August 14, 1869, died Sept. 12, 1870.

4. Mattie Lane Pettigrew, born Aug. 12, 1871, married Aug. 12, 1919, to Prof. T. N. Rhodes of Marion, S. C. He died June 1940. They had no children.

5. William Brantley Pettigrew, born October 28, 1870 (See No. 16)

6. James Bennett Pettigrew born July 23, 1880, died 1880.

15. *Lewis Mowry Pettigrew* (See No. 14)

Married June 19, 1895 to Anne Blackwell. He died Jan. 16, 1931. Lived in Marion, S. C. Children are:

1. Robert Sanders Pettigrew, born 1898, married in Marion, S.C. to Gladys Galloway and lived in Atlanta, Ga. One child, Robert Sanders Pettigrew, Jr. born 1929.

2. Sarah Pettigrew, born 1907, married Hagood Martin and lives in Marion, S. C.

16. *William Brantley Pettigrew* (See No. 14)

Married Mary Wade of Farmville, Va. and died in Florence, S. C. March 22, 1940. Children are:

1. Virginia Pettigrew, married Stuart Claire lived in Atlanta, Ga. later moved to S. C.

2. William Brantley Pettigrew, born 1918 living in Houston, Texas in 1940.

17. *Ann Elizabeth Tillman* (See No. 10)

Born in Anson Co., N. C. on December 23, 1845, died at the home of her brother James David Tillman, Carrollton, Mississippi on Jan. 25, 1880. She married her first cousin Robert Burns McCaskill on October 31, 1873. He was an attorney and died in Meridian, Mississippi in 1874. Left one child:

1. William Burns McCaskill born July 1874, reared by his uncle, James David Tillman in Carrollton, Miss. Studied medicine and settled in Idabel, Okla. Major in

Medical Dept. World War I. Married 1906 to Catherine Adams of Texas. Children were:

1. Robert Burns McCaskill, born 1906, Capt. in Signal Corps. World War II, married Helen Rotramel, living in Tulsa, Okla. Children: 1. William Burns McCaskill. 2. James Robert McCaskill.
2. Samuel James McCaskill, born 1909, Lt. in World War II, married Lucille Davidson, living in Oklahoma City.
3. Tillman McCaskill, born 1913, Captain in Armored Division in World War II.

18. *Martha Frances Tillman* (See No. 10)

Born in Anson Co. N. C., April 20, 1847, and married Dec. 7, 1865, J. E. Pettigrew, onetime member of South Carolina legislature, lived in Florence, S. C. She died, Sept. 25, 1903. Children were:

1. Elizabeth Pettigrew (See No. 19)
2. Leila Pettigrew (See No. 20)
3. James Alexander Pettigrew (See No. 21)
4. Joseph Edward Pettigrew (See No. 22)
5. Mary Pettigrew (See No. 23)
6. Rev. George Robert Pettigrew, married Pauline Fore. He is a Baptist Preacher in Chappell, S.C. No children.
7. Addie Pettigrew, died young 1903.

19. *Elizabeth Pettigrew* (See No. 18)

She died in 1919, lived near Florence, S. C., married Edward S. Burch, onetime Sheriff of County (I visited them in 1903, J.D.T.) Children were:

1. J. Furman Burch, married Eva Howell. Lived in Charlotte, N. C. No children.
2. Nora Burch, married Oswald Carpenter, lived in Fayetteville, N. C. One child, Elizabeth Carpenter.
3. Eugenia Burch, married Claude Spears, living in Fayetteville, N. C. Children: 1. Caroline. 2. Eugenia.
4. Kate Burch married Leon Perkins, lives in Virginia or Bennettsville, S. C. No children.

20. *Leila Pettigrew* (See No. 18)

    Married J. Sanders McKenzie and lived in Bannockburn, S. C. Both died about 1939. Children were:

    1. Leila Mae McKenzie married November 3, 1915 to William Marshall Bridges, attorney at Florence, S.C. Children are: 1. Mae Bridges born 1917. 2. Wm. Marshall Bridges. 3. Sanders Bridges.

    2. William J. McKenzie married Margaret Calais, live in Dillon, S.C.

    3. J. Sanders McKenzie married Jira Lee Hartzog, St. George, S.C. No children.

    4. Edward McKenzie died young.

21. *James Alexander Pettigrew* (See No. 18)

    Married in Florence, S. C. to Irene Papot and died in 1939. Children are:

    1. Richard Pettigrew, professor of English, Howard College. PHD at Duke University, June 1930.

    2. Edna Pettigrew, Florence, S.C.

    3. Elizabeth Pettigrew, married Joe Durante, child Irene Durante.

    4. James Alexander Pettigrew.

22. *Joseph Edward Pettigrew* (See No. 18)

    Married Edith Wannamaker, lived in Florence, S. C. Children are:

    1. Frances Pettigrew married Henry T. Owen, Prof. at New York Univ. One child, Mary Frances Owen. 3524-78th St., Jackson Hts., N.Y.

    2. J. Edward Pettigrew lives in Florence, S.C.

    3. George Wannamaker Pettigrew born 1912 md. Ruth Critchett.

    4. James Alexander Pettigrew born 1912 lives in Florence, S. C.

    5. Edith Pettigrew born 1914 lived in Washington, D.C.

    6. Lilly Elizabeth Pettigrew born 1919, Florence, S.C.

23. *Mary Pattigrew* (See No. 18)

    Born in Florence, S. C., married Thomas Oswald Lee and was living in Arlington, Va. 1952. Children were:

1. Thomas Oswald Lee, died young
2. George Lee, died young
3. Addie Lee
4. Mary Lee, married ———— Register, Arlington, Va.
5. Elizabeth Lee, married Rev. Kyle Hazleton and live in Yonkers, New York. One child, Kyle Hazleton, Jr. (or Haselden)

24. *Charles Henry Tillman* (See No. 10)

Born in Anson County, N. C. on November 14, 1850, died in Vaiden, Miss. on February 13, 1927. Married on December 1877 to Mollie Fullilove. Children were:

1. Charles Henry Tillman, never married
2. Susie Mae Tillman, married Layton Bankston and died July 1937, in Tallulah, La. one child, Layton Tillman Bankston.
3. Thomas Rivers Tillman, lived in New Hampshire, no children.
4. Addie Boleyn Tillman, married Oct. 3, 1928 to John R. Jenkins of Durant, Miss. No children.
5. Willie Bennett Tillman, died young
6. Rosa Elliot Tillman, died young

25. *Dr. William Edwin Tillman* (See No. 10)

Born August 26, 1851, Anson Co., N.C., studied medicine in Louisville, Ky. married Lizzie B. Willis of Orange County, Va. Lived at Graysport, Grenada County, Miss. where he died Jan. 2, 1925. One child:

1. Lucetta Bouton Tillman, who married James G. Coman and settled in Mexia, Texas. Children:
   1. James G. Coman, living in Houston, Texas 1954.
   2. Jack Coman, Professor of music at Judson College, Ala.

26. *Helen Bennett Tillman* (See No. 10)

Born on April 16, 1853 in Anson Co., N. C. and married Charles A. Redditt in Carroll County, Miss. April 30, 1880. She died 1920 and he died 1918 at McCarley, Miss. Children were:

1. Helen Boleyn Redditt (See No. 27)

2. Stella Amanda Redditt born Dec. 8, 1884 married Dec. 6, 1905 her cousin James B. Turner lived in Glendorn, Miss. No child.
3. Charles Harison Redditt (See No. 28)

27. *Helen Boleyn Redditt* (See No. 26)
Born March 18, 1882 and on Dec. 17, 1902 was married to her cousin Hall W. Turner. Lived in McCarley, Miss. Children were:
1. Mary Stella Turner, born Oct. 25, 1903
2. Helen Boleyn Turner, born April 28, 1910

28. *Charles Haridson Redditt* (See No. 26)
Born August 16, 1889 in McCarley, Mississippi, he married on April 12, 1925 to Appie Stoker and lived in Scott, Miss. Children were:
1. Helen Elizabeth Redditt, married 1949 to Charles Eckford Reid, Jr. of Greenville, Miss. He graduated at the U.S. Naval Academy, June 3, 1949.
2. Ada Virginia Redditt, married June 28, 1954 to Lt. Ambrose Roy Morrell of Kennewich, Washington.

29. *Minnie Ethline Tillman* (See No. 10)
Born in Anson Co. N.C. September 4, 1857, married on December 21, 1880 to Richard Cross Price in Carrollton, Miss. the same date her brother James David Tillman married Rachel C. Bryan. Richard C. Price was educated at Davidson College, N.C. Died April 20, 1901. Children were:
1. Richard Cross Price, born July 8, 1882. Not married.
2. Hattie Irby Price, born Aug. 3, 1884. Not married.
3. Annie Bennett Price born Aug. 17, 1886, died Sept. 28, 1928.
4. Minnie Price born Dec. 31, 1888 and died 1889.
5. Charles Tillman Price born November 28, 1892 lives in Carrollton, Mississippi.

30. *Mary Ann Tillman* (See No. 9)
Born in Anson Co. N. C. on October 5, 1882 married there to Col. William Calvin Smith, born April 25, 1824 died March 12, 1886. She died Dec. 14, 1899 in Cleburne, Texas. Children were:

1. James Tillman Smith (See No. 31)
2. Mary Frances Smith (See No. 32)
3. Martha Cornelia Smith (See No. 37)
4. Fannie Eliza Smith (See No. 36)

31. *James Tillman Smith* (See No. 30)

Born in Anson Co. N. C., September 8, 1843 died in Fort Worth, Texas on Jan. 30, 1908. During the Civil War was a member of Co. C. 14th N. C. Anson Guards. Was a prominent man in Texas. Member of State Senate 1876. He married 1st November 27, 1867 to Ellen Pegues who was born March 1845 and died March 3, 1870. One child.——
Married 2nd, June 17, 1874 to Emma Adele Demaret who was born November 28, 1846. Children were:

1. Ellen Tillman Smith, by first marriage who married on July 27, 1910 to Pickens Butler Bookman, born June 18, 1857 and died April 29, 1927. She was living in Navasota, Texas in 1937, one child Ellen Pegues Bookman, born October 5, 1911 who married Marshall Curtis Peters.
2. William Calvin Smith, born July 7, 1879 lived in Fort Worth, Texas.
3. Demaret Smith, born July 2, 1881, in Fort Worth, Texas.
4. Selwyn Smith, born February 20, 1883, lived in Fort Worth, Texas.
5. Felix Carson Smith, born July 1887 lived in Fort Worth, Texas.

32. *Mary Frances Smith* (See No. 30)

Born in Anson Co. N. C., March 9, 1846. She married Dec. 15, 1868 to John William McGregor, born Aug. 9, 1840. He was one time Sheriff of Anson County and lived near Wadesboro. Children were:

1. William Smith McGregor, born Sept. 18, 1869 died June 8, 1914 married Anne Estelle Tolson and lived in Rocky Mt., N. C.
2. John Duncan McGregor (See No. 33)
3. James Tillman McGregor (See No. 34)
4. Phillip Archibald McGregor (See No. 35)

33. *John Duncan McGregor* (See No. 32)

Born August 28, 1872, married August 24, 1904 to Georgie Steele McMurray who was born June 30, 1876. Lived near Lilesville, N. C. Children were:
1. Julia Little McMurray, born May 21, 1905
2. Frances Smith McMurray, born August 22, 1909

34. *James Tillman McGregor* (See No. 32)

Born October 2, 1874, married February 1, 1906 to Tommie Ethel Culp and lived near Wadesboro, N.C. and had children:
1. James Tillman McGregor, born Nov. 1906
2. Mary A. McGregor, born October 1913

35. *Phillip Archibald McGregor* (See No. 32)

Born in 1876 and married April 20, 1910 to Verna May McSwain. Children were:
1. John William McGregor, born April 4, 1911
2. Teresa McGregor, born June 2, 1915

36. *Fannie Eliza Smith* (See No. 30)

Born January 21, 1850 married ——————— Willingham, lived in Cleburne, Texas. Children were:
1. Smith Willingham
2. Mary Willingham
3. Pattie Willingham
4. Helen Willingham

37. *Martha (Patty) Cornelia Smith* (See No. 30)

Born March 9, 1848 and died 1897, married W. E. Cox and lived in Mt. Airy, N. C. Children were:
1. Berta Cox
2. Essie Cox

38. *Frances Elizabeth Tillman* (See No. 9)

Born June 1827 in Montgomery County, N. C. and died March 1899. She married in Wadesboro, N.C. Earle Cooley, son of Earle and Rhoda (Graves) Cooley of Middletown, Conn. Children were:
1. Elizabeth Cooley (See No. 39)
2. Edgar Earle Cooley (See No. 42)

39. *Elizabeth Cooley* (See No. 38)

Born October 12, 1856 in Wadesboro, N. C. Married David Stuart Harllee who died April 16, 1891, moved to Greensboro, N. C. Children were:
1. Frederick Earle Harlee (See No. 40)
2. Edgar Cooley Harlee, born 1884
3. David Stuart Eugene Harlee (See No. 41)

40. *Frederick Earle Harllee* (See No. 39)

Born October 21, 1879 in Anson County, N.C. He married Marjorie Fisher, daughter of George Fisher and wife Mary Marquis. Children were:
1. Eleanor Marquis Harllee born November 22, 1910
2. Frederick Earle Harllee born January 17, 1911
3. Marjorie Ferne Harllee born February 19, 1914
4. Victoria Fisher Harllee born March 23, 1918

41. *David Stuart Eugene Harllee* (See No. 39)

Born Jan. 1, 1886 in Anson County, N.C. He married Mattie Mae McIntyre, daughter of Dr. Archie McIntyre, and had children:
1. Mary Elizabeth Harllee, born December 25, 1913

42. *Edgar Earle Cooley* (See No. 38)

Born December 25, 1861 in Anson County, N.C. and died Sept. 20, 1942. He married 1900 to Cornelia Caroline Webb, daughter of Rev. Wesley of Rockingham, N. C. Children were:
1. Francis Earle Cooley, born Dec. 30, 1901 who married Lois Speed 1943 and lives in Raleigh, N. C.
2. Edgar Eugene Cooley, born 1903 married 1942 to Carmille Swindell, living in Newport News, Va.
3. Elizabeth Caroline Cooley (See No. 43)
4. Tillman Webb Cooley (See No. 44)
5. Margaret Frances Cooley (See No. 45)
6. David Harllee Cooley, born Nov. 2, 1921 serving in U.S. Navy 1945

43. *Elizabeth Caroline Cooley* (See No. 42)

Born 1906 married in 1932, William L. Parker, address: 222 Priser Street, Suffolk, Va. Children were:
1. Caroline Webb Parker, born 1940

44. *Tillman Webb Cooley* (See No. 42)

Born December 9, 1913 in Suffolk, Va. He married June 6, 1942 Margaret Elizabeth Burgym, daughter of Judge W. H. S. Burgym of N. C. Superior Court. They live in Suffolk, Va. Children are:

1. Caroline Webb Cooley, born 1940

45. *Margaret Frances Cooley* (See No. 42)

Born August, 1919. She married 1941 William Baskerville of Blackston, Va. Children:

1. William Baskerville, born Sept. 22, 1942

46. *David Chiles Tillman* (See No. 9)

Born in Montgomery County June 14, 1835 and died April 21, 1904 in Anson County, N. C. at Deep Creek (His father's home place.) In the Civil War he was a member of Co. C. 14th N.C. Anson Guards as was his nephew James David Tillman. He married June 19, 1863, Martha Elizabeth Arnold who was born Sept. 9, 1845 and died November 11, 1911. Children were:

1. Fredereick Shailor Tillman, born Dec. 30, 1865. Died in Wadesboro, N.C. 1937. Never married.
2. Everard Ebert Tillman, born Aug. 30, 1867, died Aug. 1930. No descendants.
3. John Chiles Tillman born Jan. 21, 1869. No descendants.
4. Frances Ella Tillman (See No. 47)
5. Elizabeth Gertrude Tillman (See No. 53)
6. David Arnold Tillman (See No. 56)
7. William Ledbetter Tillman (See No. 57)
8. James Eugene Tillman (See No. 58)
9. Richard Henry Tillman (See No. 60)
10. Rosa Cooley Tillman, born April 27, 1893, married Jan. 29, 1923 to James William Wilkes, lived in Kennedale, Texas.

47. *Frances Ella Tillman* (See No. 46)

Born December 23, 1871 in Perry, Kansas. She married April 10, 1888 to James Argyle McLaughlin and settled in Weatherford, Okla. Children were:

1. Elizabeth Anna McLaughlin (See No. 48)

2. Katherine McLaughlin (See No. 49)
3. John Calvin McLaughlin born July 14, 1898, died Sept. 1916
4. Rosamond McLaughlin born Jan. 7, 1900 (See No. 51)
5. Martha Mac McLaughlin born Dec. 1, 1903, died 1904.
6. Frances McLaughlin (See No. 52)
7. James Argyle McLaughlin, born Dec. 22, 1910

48. *Elizabeth Anna McLaughlin* (See No. 47)

Born August 3, 1889 in Meridian, Kansas. She married Aug. 5, 1914 to Herbert Meeting, living in Anadarko, Okla. Children were:

1. Herbert McLaughlin Meeting born June 18, 1917
2. Betty Ann Meeting born March 9, 1920

49. *Katherine McLaughlin* (See No. 47)

Born March 7, 1895 in Wadesboro, N. C. She married June 22, 1916 Wayne F. Clegern, lives in Oklahoma City, Okla. Children are:

1. William Argyle Clegern, born July 3, 1917 (See No. 50)
2. Harriet Clegern, born Sept. 24, 1920
3. Frances Eleanor Clegern, born March 31, 1925
4. Wayne McLaughlin Clegern, born November 25, 1929

50. *William Argyle Clegern* (See No. 49)

Born July 3, 1917, married Roberta Hughes. Children are:

1. William Henry Clegern, born June 23, 1941
2. Robert Wayne Clegern, born February 28, 1943

51. *Rosamond McLaughlin* (See No. 47)

Born Jan. 7, 1900 in Anson Co. N.C. She married Sept. 16, 1927, Troy O. Morgan. Children are:

1. Troy O. Morgan, born Aug. 4, 1928

52. *Frances McLaughlin* (See No. 47)

Born November 17, 1906 in Mangum, Okla. She married July 25, 1926 Paul Francis Pearson, lived in Stillwater, Okla. Children are:

1. Paul Francis Pearson, born July 31, 1928

     2. Carolyn Pearson, born Aug. 18, 1929

     3. Jeanne Pearson, born March 25, 1930

     4. Andrea Pearson, born April 9, 1932

     5. James McLaughlin, born November 28, 1933

53. *Elizabeth Gertrude Tillman* (See No. 46)

     Born January 5, 1876 in Anson Co. N.C. She married June 19, 1907 John W. Stitt, attorney of Fort Worth, Texas. Children:

     1. Arnold Haymie Stitt, born April 14, 1908 died 1909

     2. William Tillman Stitt (See No. 54)

     3. David Leander Stitt (See No. 55)

54. *William Tillman Stitt* (See No. 53)

     Born May 27, 1910 and married June 21, 1934 Christine Sawyer of Brownfield, Texas. Children:

     1. Ticia Elizabeth Stitt, born Aug. 4, 1935

     2. John Monroe Stitt, born Aug. 11, 1938

55. *David Leander Stitt* (See No. 53)

     Born October 5, 1912. He married Sept. 10, 1940 to Jane Dupuy of Greensboro, N. C. He is President of Austin College, Sherman, Texas. Children:

     1. David Tillman Stitt, born April 9, 1943

     2. John Dupuy Stitt, born Jan. 16, 1945

56. *David Arnold Tillman* (See No. 46)

     Born Sept. 9, 1873 in Anson County, N.C. and died in Bennettsville, S.C. October 14, 1931. He married October 6, 1909, Catherine Cornelis Lilly who is living in Bennettsville, S.C. Children:

     1. Catherine Lilly Tillman, born Sept. 22, 1911 and married June 24, 1933, Herbert Stanley Brown, child:

         1. Catherine Stanley Brown, born Dec. 25, 1935

     2. Elizabeth Arnold Tillman, born March 26, 1913

     3. Anna Marshall Tillman, born Aug. 18, 1914, married Nov. 22, 1941 Lanier Mayo Williams. Child:

         1. Mattie Lou Williams, born Sept. 19, 1943

     4. David Arnold Tillman, born April 12, 1921. He married Nov. 1943 Dicksie Bradley Bandy.

57. *William Ledbetter Tillman* (See No. 46)

     Born March 7, 1878 in Wadesboro, N.C. He married Jan.

24, 1906 Grace Allen who was born Aug. 4, 1882. They settled in Bennettsville, S.C. Children:

    1. Martha Elizabeth Tillman, born November 23, 1906
    2. Margaret Tillman, born September 19, 1908

58. *James Eugene Tillman* (See No. 46)

    Born July 29, 1880, Anson Co. N.C. He married August 5, 1902 Sallie V. Robinson and settled in Wadesboro, N.C. Children:

    1. Mary Hardison Tillman, born July 29, 1905
    2. Frederick Shailor Tillman (See No. 59)
    3. Martha Arnold Tillman, born February 2, 1911
    4. Thomas Robinson Tillman, born June 15, 1913
    5. Sarah Elizabeth Tillman, born June 15, 1913
    6. James Eugene Tillman, born June 28, 1918, Capt. in World War II
    7. William Henry Tillman, born June 9, 1920

59. *Frederick Shailor Tillman* (See No. 58)

    Born May 29, 1908 married Dec. 30, 1941 to Effie Lambeth Allen daughter of Dr. Charles Allen (grandson of Dora Bennett, of Wadesboro, N.C.) He served in World War as a staff sergeant in the Air Force. Children:

    1. Frederick Shailor Tillman, born Dec. 14, 1942
    2. Mary Lambeth Tillman, born July 6, 1945

60. *Sarah Elizabeth Tillman.* (See No. 58)

    Born Sept. 11, 1916. She married 1st ———— and had Sally Ann, born Sept. 20, 1937, married 2nd Major Walker Ralph Wheatley of the Air Force.

60-b. *Richard Henry Tillman* (See No. 46)

    Born September 12, 1884 in Anson Co., N.C. He married December 21, 1910 to Frances Taisey Nelson, and lives in Riderwood, Baltimore, Md. He was associated many years with the Baltimore Power & Light Co. Children were:

    1. Richard Nelson Tillman (See No. 61)
    2. Arnold Lee Tillman, born Aug. 4, 1913 married June 27, 1938 Ida Mae Turnbull.
    3. James Rogers Tillman, born Jan. 18, 1915
    4. David Franklin Tillman (See No. 62)

61. *Richard Nelson Tillman* (See No. 60-b)

Born April 4, 1912. He is a doctor and lives in Kerne-
wood, Baltimore, Md. He married February 19, 1938. Child:

1. Hole Nelson Tillman, born Sept. 9, 1941

62. *David Franklin Tillman* (See No. 60)

Born March 5, 1916. Married July 1, 1938, Elizabeth
Watkins lives in Baltimore, Md. Children:

1. Richard Henry Tillman, born Nov. 19, 1939
2. Joseph Edmund Tillman, born Jan. 14, 1941
3. James Lee Tillman, born March 17, 1943

63. *Martha Elizabeth Ledbetter* (See No. 6)

Died May 30, 1933. Married William A. Sloan. Children
were:

1. William Ledbetter Sloan, born Oct. 17, 1885, md.
   Eunice Pareicnick
2. Mary Stanback Sloan, born Feb. 21, 1888, md. A. W.
   Huntley, one son, Wilson Sloan Huntley, died World
   War II
3. Henry Sloan, born Feb. 9, 1890 died Feb. 1910
4. Frank Alexander Sloan (See No. 64)

64. *Frank Alexander Sloan* (See No. 63)

Born March 31, 1892 died June 13, 1942, married 1st
1915 to Julia Lockhart who was born Sept. 1893 and died
Oct. 1927, daughter of Henry and Louisa Lockhart. Children
were:

1. Louisa Sloan, married June 13, 1942, James Ledbetter,
   son of Dr. James M. and Bessie Steele Ledbetter of
   Rockingham, N.C. (See No. 93-b)

Frank Alexander Sloan, married 2nd Sadie O'Connell

65. *William Presley Ledbetter* (See No. 6)

Born October 17, 1867, died Sept. 12, 1924. Married
January 6, 1892 to Texanna M. Gray, born October 15, 1867,
daughter of James Mattison and Laura Ann Lee Gray. Child:
Laura Elizabeth Ledbetter, born Jan. 18, 1894 died Jan.
8, 1919. She was called Bessie. (I had a letter from
her in Wadesboro, N.C. dated July 7, 1916. J.D.T.)

66. *Lillie May Ledbetter* (See No. 6)

Born December 8, 1870 and died May 9, 1944. She mar-

ried John William Masemore who was born May 10, 1852 and died Jan. 9, 1940. Children:
1. John Ernest Masemore, born Oct. 6, 1893, died 1894.
2. Elizabeth Virginia Masemore, born July 22, 1897 and married John Spencer
3. Ann Little Masemore, born June 20, 1900.

67. *Mary A. Ledbetter* (See No. 6)
Married Cyrus Cole Bryan, born March 24, 1871, he died 1942. Children were:
1. Mary Ledbetter Bryan, born April 13, 1906
2. Emma Pamelia Bryan, born Sept. 1908

68. *William Ledbetter Little* (See No. 8)
Married Netta Hardison. Children were:
1. William Bennett Little married Cornelia Harris, of Wadesboro, N.C. Children:
   1. William Bennett Little
   2. Edmund Strudwick Ashe Little
2. George Kennedy Little married Iva Ratliff, Wadesboro, N.C. one child: Genet Little
3. Netta Little, Wadesboro, N.C.
4. Sarah Little married Boyce Riley, Wadesboro, N.C.
5. Edward Robert Little, married Mattie Ratliff. Child: Jane Little.
6. Mary Little married Marcus Ham, has Ledbetter Ham, Wadesboro, N.C.

69. *Frank Milton Little* (See No. 8)
Married Elizabeth Lilla Ingram, Wadesboro, N.C. Had child:
1. Mary Kennedy Little married James Matheson Davis, and lives in Wadesboro, N.C. 1954. Children:
   1. James Matheson Davis, Jr. married Harriet Elizabeth Jones. One child: Amy Lynn Davis
2. Mary Elizabeth Davis, married James William Reid, Raleigh, N.C.
3. Frances Lee Davis
4. Frank Little Davis
5. Robert Lee Davis

70. *Henry Wall Little* (See No. 8)
    Married Effie Allen and had:
    1. Henry Wall Little, died young
    2. Allen Little, Columbia, S. C.
    3. Hal W. Little, married Mary Louise Robbins. Children:
        1. Henry W. Little, Wadesboro, N.C.
        2. Dora Ann Little, Wadesboro, N.C.
    4. Thomas Marshall Little, married Katherine Smith. Children:
        1. Frances Little, Wadesboro, N.C.
        2. Thomas Marshall Little, Jr.
        3. Effie Jean Little
        4. "Chris" Little
    5. Dora Bennett Little, married A. Paul Kitchen, children:
        1. A. Paul Kitchen, Jr., Wadesboro, N.C.
        2. Henry Little Kitchen, Wadesboro, N.C.
    6. William Bennett Little, married Wildren Williamson
    7. Charles Lemuel Little, married Lucy Pate, Wadesboro, N.C. Has: 1. Corinne Pate Little
    8. H. Frank Coleman Little, married Hilda Hardison. Children: 1. Hilda Hardison Little; 2. Betsey Little

71. *Mary Ledbetter Little*
    Married Nelson Thomas Fletcher, Gibson, N.C. Children:
    1. Nelson Thomas Fletcher, Jr. Married and has Nelson Thos. Fletcher III
    2. Mary Little Fletcher, married George Hamrick, has:
        1. George Hamrick, Jr.

72. *Julia Little* (See No. 8)
    Married Richard A. Kellam, Atlanta, Ga. have children:
    1. Elsie Kellam married Nelson Rector, have:
        1. Richard Kellam Rector
        2. Mary Chisholm Rector
    2. Mary Ledbetter Kellam, married Gordon Buckey. Live in Charlotte, North Carolina. Children:
        1. Gordon Buckey, Jr. (dead)
        2. Richard Buckey

73. *John Leake Little* (See No. 8)
    Married Lila Brent, Charlotte, N.C. Children:

1. Julia Marshall Little, married Kermit Chapman.
   1. Lila Chapman
2. Frank Milton Little, married Sarah Thomas. Child: Mary Elizabeth Little
3. John Leake Little, Jr., Statesville, N.C.

74. *James Ledbetter* (See No. 4)

Married Elizabeth Forrest, born 1812 and had children:
1. John A. Ledbetter
2. Henry W. Ledbetter
3. William P. Ledbetter
4. Eliza D. Ledbetter, married Thomas H. Tomlinson
5. Mary J. Ledbetter, married David Pemberton
6. Martha Ledbetter, married Lemuel DeBerry

75. *Tabitha Randle Ledbetter* (See No. 4)

Born July 4, 1811 and married Stephen William Cole (1813-1889) and died Sept. 17, 1858. Children were:
1. William Cole
2. Judith Cole
3. Ann Cole married Luke Blackmer
4. Mary Cole married John Boyden
5. Sarah Steele Leake Cole (See No. 76)

76. *Sarah Steele Leake Cole* (See No. 75)

Was born June 12, 1838 and died Jan. 12, 1915. She married Presley Nelme Smith, born July 26, 1835, Anson Co. N.C. and died July 11, 1900. Children:
1. Annie Cole Smith (See No. 77)
2. Mary Ledbetter Smith, born June 15, 1871, teacher in Savannah, Ga.
3. Sallie Shelton Smith, born Sept. 30, 1875, married Oct. 11, 1903 to Peter Frank Down. Child:
   1. Raiford Franklin Down

77. *Annie Cole Smith* (See No. 76)

Born Dec. 12, 1869 and married July 11, 1888 to William Alfred Winburn born 1863, lived in Savannah, Ga. Children:
1. William Alfred Winburn, born May 17, 1889. Served in World War promoted to Captain. He is soliciting Freight Agent, Central of Georgia in Savannah, Ga.

    2. Susan Cole Winburn (See No. 78)

    3. James Randle Winburn, born No. 29, 1898, married Virginia Van Giesen on May 5, 1918 and lives in Savannah, Georgia.

78. *Susan Cole Winburn* (See No. 77)

Born April 11, 1891. Educated in Washington, D. C. a very gifted violinist. She married Dec. 9, 1914 Dr. Antonio Johnston Waring, Jr. of Savannah, Ga. He is a medical graduate of Yale University. He lives in Savannah, Ga. and is a baby specialist. Was Captain in World War I. Children:

    1. Antonio Johnston Waring, Jr., born Aug. 17, 1915

    2. Annie Waring, born March 16, 1918

79. *Henry Willis Ledbetter* (See No. 4)

Born June 1800 in Montgomery Co. N.C. married April 12, 1836 to Belinda Herndon and lived in Cokesbury, S.C. but moved to Russell Co., Ala. His wife was widow of Mr. Mitchell. Henry Willis Ledbetter was a noted Methodist Preacher. He died 1876. Children were:

    1. Sarah Herndon Ledbetter, born Feb. 12, 1839, died Jan. 18, 1840 buried Cokesbury, S.C.

    2. William Henry Ledbetter, born Oct. 16, 1840, died Feb. 10, 1910 buried Emory Chapel Church, eight miles from Newman, Ga. (See No. 80)

    3. Mary Virginia Ledbetter, born May 10, 1842, died Dec. 18, 1899, unmarried buried at Emory Chapel

    4. Rev. Benjamin Edwin Ledbetter, born April 4, 1844, died Jan. 18, 1910, buried So. Boston, Va. (See No. 82)

    5. Rev. Joseph Herndon Ledbetter, born May 13, 1846, died Feb. 21, 1902, buried Denver, Colo. (See No. 83)

    6. James Osgood Andrew Ledbetter, born Sept. 23, 1848, died Sept. 18, 1853, buried Cokesbury, S.C.

    7. Charles Cole Ledbetter, born June 15, 1850, died Aug. 9, 1909, unmarried, buried Hillibee Camp Ground in Tallapoosa Co., Ala.

    8. Frances Tillman Ledbetter, born Sept. 17, 1852, living in 1931 (See No. 84)

9. Rev. Robert Newton Ledbetter, born Nov. 25, 1854, died April 2, 1913, buried near Paris, Texas. (See No. 85)
10. Barbara Ada Ledbetter, born Sept. 16, 1856, died Oct. 23, 1917, buried Meridianville, Ala. (See No. 86)
11. Julia Ledbetter, born in Ala. July 4, 1861, died Sept. 11, 1861, buried Glennville, Ala. All born in Cokesbury S.C. except the last. These are all the children recorded in the family Bible of Rev. Henry Willis Ledbetter.

80. *William Henry Ledbetter* (See No. 79)

Born October 16, 1840 died Feb. 10, 1910, married May 14, 1874 to Belle Lester of Georgia. She died Sept. 11, 1880. Children:

1. Virginia Belle Ledbetter, born Mar 18, 1875, living, married Jan. 31, 1897 to John G. Davis. Res: Newnan, Ga. (See No. 81)
2. William Herndon Ledbetter, born Nov. 27, 1876, died 1878
3. Robert Henry Ledbetter, born June 1, 1878, living, unmarried.
4. Belle Lester Ledbetter, born May 20, 1880, died Oct. 1880

81. *Virginia Belle Ledbetter* (See No. 80)

Married John G. Davis. Children:
1. Edna Davis, born Nov. 14, 1897; married Dec. 6, 1916, Sam P. Cook, res: Fairmont, Ga. Children:
   1. Juanita Cook, born July 28, 1920
   2. Sam P. Cook, Jr., born April 23, 1925
   3. La Rue Cook, born Oct. 26, 1926
   4. John Cook, born March 7, 1930
2. Dorothy Davis, born March 14, 1900; married July 9, 1922, Embry Van Houton, Res: Newnan. Children:
   1. Embry Van Houten, Jr., born March 17, 1924
   2. Donald Van Houten, born Dec. 5, 1926
   3. Robert Van Houten, born Nov. 5, 1929

3. Leo L. Davis, born Sept. 22, 1902; married Jan. 5, 1924 to Mary LeSuer. Res: Chicago, Ill. Child: Jere Davis, b. Aug. 1925
4. John G. Davis, Jr. born Oct. 11, 1904, married May 16, 1930 Theora Chamber, res: Newnan. Child: Sue Davis, born May 28, 1931
5. Virginia Davis, born Feb. 20, 1907, married June 30, 1929 to W. L. Holland. Res: Texas
6. Edith Davis, born June 20, 1910, married July 2, 1931 Ralph Bess. Res: Geneva, Ala.
7. Albert & Alleyne Davis, twins, born July 20, 1913
8. Joel Davis, born March 7, 1919

82. *Rev. Benjamin Edwin Ledbetter* (See No. 79)

Born April 4, 1844, died Jan. 19, 1910 and married May 7, 1873 to Emily L. Donalson of Ga. She died 1924.
Children:

1. Benjamin Herndon Ledbetter, born Sept. 1876, married in 1919 to Willie Baskerville. Res: South Hill, Va. No children.
2. Frances Maude Ledbetter, born Feb. 1, 1881, married John Lacy who died Nov. 3, 1931. His widow lives at So. Boston, Va.
3. Mae Wightman Ledbetter, born May 1, 1884, married John Collie. Res: So. Boston, Va. Children:
    1. Edwin Collie, born 1908
    2. John Collie, Jr., born 1910
    3. Frances E. Collie, born 1918
4. Ethel Harman Ledbetter, born Dec. 1886, married Arthur Barkesdale, Res: Princeton, W. Va. Children:
    1. Arthur Sydnor Barkesdale, born 1911
    2. Frances Mae Barkesdale, born 1918
    3. Donaldson Barkesdale, born 1921

83. *Rev. Joseph Herndon Ledbetter* (See No. 79)

Born March 13, 1846, died Denver, Colo. Feb. 21, 1902, married Nov. 25, 1869 to Susan M. Meredith, she died Feb. 21, 1902. Children:

1. Josephea ("Jodie") Herndon Ledbetter, born Aug.

25, 1870 married Thomas S. Bishop. Res: Phoenix, Ariz. Children:
1. ————— Bishop, married Victor Davis, living in Calif.
2. Meredith Bishop.
2. William Meredith Ledbetter, born Oct. 5, 1872, married —————. Res: St. Louis, Mo.
   1. Helen M. Ledbetter
   2. Alleen (Deceased)
3. Henry Willis Ledbetter, born Sept. 28, 1876, died Feb. 1879
4. Lillian Alice Ledbetter, born June 15, 1880, married Paul E. Grantham. Res: Tyler, Texas

84. *Frances Tillman Ledbetter* (See No. 79)

Born Sept. 17, 1852, living 1932, married July 7, 1886, George Moody Bentley. He was born April 6, 1848 and died Nov. 20, 1911. Children:
1. Lillian Herndon Bentley, born Sept. 4, 1891, died Sept. 14, 1892
2. Willis Gay Bentley, born Jan. 12, 1893, married May 5, 1918 to Leila Louise Gayle. She was born July 26, 1894. (Compiler of this genealogical sketch on Rev. Henry Willis Ledbetter.) Children:
   1. John Gayle Bentley, born March 10, 1919
   2. Leila Norfleet Bentley, born July 2, 1922

85. *Rev. Robert Newton Ledbetter* (See No. 79)

Born Nov. 25, 1854 and died April 2, 1913. Married 1st on Dec. 9, 1879 Luella V. Dunn of Ala. She was born Nov. 26, 1854 and died Feb. 14, 1886. Married 2nd, June 22, 1887 Sarah Ella Barnes of Ala. She was born April 11, 1864 and died Oct. 13, 1913.

Children by 1st:
1. Rev. Robert Edgar Ledbetter, born June 17, 1881 and married June 17, 1913 Mary Simpson of Texas. She was born Sept. 14, 1891. He is preaching at Hughes Springs, Texas, 1932. Children:
   1. Robert Edgar Ledbetter, Jr., born Nov. 10, 1915

      2. Llewellyn Harper Ledbetter, born July 8, 1917
      3. Mary Katherine Ledbetter, born Dec. 30, 1921

2. Llewellyn Herndon Ledbetter, born Aug. 6, 1883, married 1916 Neva Fulton. Children:
      1. Llewellyn Herndon Ledbetter. Is an M.D. living in Beaumont, Texas
      2. Marion Ledbetter, born 1917
      3. William Robert Ledbetter, born 1920

3. Nellie Ledbetter, born Feb. 3, 1886, married June 22, 1910 Charles H. Russell. He was born Aug. 23, 1887. Living in Birmingham, Ala. Children:
      1. Irma Belle Russell, born May 3, 1911, married Dec. 22, 1931 to J. Clyde Cruse.
      2. Ellaree Herndon Russell, born Oct. 31, 1912

Children by second wife:
    4. Eugene Hendrix Ledbetter, born Jan. 10, 1889, died Jan. 19, 1889

    5. Francis Bernard Ledbetter, born April 17, 1891, married Jan. 2, 1917 Virginia Caldwell. Res: Berkley, Calif. Children:
      1. Frances Virginia Ledbetter, born Jan. 4, 1922

    6. Carl Eldridge Ledbetter, born July 19, 1894, married June 15, 1921 Helen Burke, res: Pasadena, Calif.
      1. Margaret Ella Ledbetter, born Oct. 29, 1923

    7. Willis Earl Ledbetter, born June 14, 1896, married July 15, 1918 Julia C. Armstrong. Res: Paonia, Colo. Children:
      1. Robert Kenneth Ledbetter, born Mar. 13, 1920
      2. Betty Jane Ledbetter, born June 29, 1921
      3. James Earl Ledbetter, born Jan. 31, 1923
      4. Barbara Helen Ledbetter, born Feb. 2, 1924
      5. Jules Bradley Ledbetter, born May 24, 1925
      6. Bertha Glynn Ledbetter, born July 3, 1931

    8. Bertha Glynn Ledbetter, born Oct. 27, 1898, married Aug. 29, 1919 Shirley Dare Vogler. Res: Kimball, Nebr. Children by adoption:
      1. James Berton Vogler, born April 13, 1928
      2. Shirley Dare Vogler, born Aug. 7, 1930

9. Joseph Morgan Ledbetter, born Nov. 1, 1900, died Nov. 21, 1907
10. Julia Evelyn Ledbetter, born Aug. 7, 1903, married May 30, 1925 George P. Steiner. Res: Oakland, Calif. Children:
    1. George Paul Steiner, born May 30, 1926
11. Kate Lee Ledbetter, born Mar. 20, 1906, married Apr. 15, 1925 Lewis E. Gard, Res: Los Angeles, Calif. Children:
    1. Kathleen Joy Gard, born June 2, 1926

86. *Barbara Ada Ledbetter* (See No. 79)

Born Sept. 16, 1856, died Oct. 23, 1917, married 1st, Dec. 28, 1898 John M. Chambliss of Ark. He b ca 1842 d July 20, 1899. She married 2nd on Nov. 1903 Howard Anderson of Ga. He died Apr. 11, 1914. No children by either marriage.

87. *Mary Washington Ledbetter* (See No. 4)

Born Oct. 28, 1808, married Dec. 21, 1832 Thomas Jefferson Smith, who was born July 13, 1810. (He was a brother of William Calvin Smith who married Mary Tillman). She died July 14, 1882, he died Jan. 18, 1887 and both are buried in Mexia, Texas.
Children:
    1. Mary A. Smith (See No. 106)
    2. James Ledbetter Smith (See No. 107)
    3. Sally Eliza Smith (See No. 109)
    4. Lewis Phillip Smith (See No. 116)
    5. William Charles Smith, born Dec. 19, 1848 in Anson County, N. C. d. 1849.
    6. Thomas J. Smith, born Nov. 20, 1849, died in Texas 1860.
    7. Henry Ledbetter Smith, born Oct. 2, 1842, died 1844.

88. *Charles W. Ledbetter* (See No. 4)

Born Jan 1, 1814, died at Polkton, N.C. 1892, married Roxie Bennett, daughter of Nevill Bennett and Katherine Harris had one child:
    1. Charles Bennet Ledbetter, married 1st . . . . Crump, 2nd Martha DeBerry, lived in Polkton, N.C.

He died prior to 1950.

Children: (Had 9)

    1.   Charles Ledbetter, married and has son Charles Ledbetter.

89. *Sarah Elizabeth Ledbetter* (See No. 4)

    Born 1820, died 1895, married William Little lived in Ansonville, N.C. Children:

    1. Walter Steele Little, no descendants

    2. Robert Eugene Little (See No. 90)

    3. John Richard Little

    4. Leonides L. Little, born July 29, ... married Lula Smith.

90. *Robert Eugene Little* (See No. 89)

    Prominent attorney of Wadesboro. One time State Senator, married Mary Austin Bennett, daughter of Col. Risdon Tyler Bennett and Kate Shepherd whom he married Aug 26, 1863. Col. Bennett commanded the 14th N. C. Regiment during the Civil War and was afterwards a member of Congress and Judge. (In 1903 I spent a week in his home J.D.T.) Mary Austin Bennett was born Jan. 1866. Children of Robert E. Little and Mary A. Bennett were:

    1. Robert Eugene Little, Jr.

    2. Risdon Tyler Bennett Little

    3. Augusta Shepherd Little

    4. Mary Bennett Little, born 1902

91. *Robert Steele Ledbetter* (See No. 4)

    Born Mar. 2, 1822, died 1896, married Oct. 27, 1854 Martha J. Steele. Lived in Rockingham, N. C. died Feb. 22, 1896. She was youngest daughter of Robert J. Steele, Jr. They had five children:

    1. Henry Ledbetter, who married . . . . . . Scales, lived in Rockingham N. C. Had children.

92. *John Fletcher Ledbetter* (See No. 4)

    Born February 5, 1824 died Aug. 31, 1902. He married May 24, 1844 Judith Harriet Little who died Sept. 26, 1900. Children were:

    1. Anna Jane Ledbetter, born Mar. 22, 1845, died 1846

2.   Preston Adolphus Ledbetter, born Sept. 3, 1846
3.   John Steele Ledbetter, born Oct. 11, 1848
4.   William Henry Steele Ledbetter, born Oct. 18, 1852, died July 16, 1905
5.   Mary Elizabeth Steele Ledbetter, born March 3, 1856

93. *Thomas Benson Ledbetter* (See No. 4)

Born Dec. 28, 1825 and died Jan. 16, 1913 in Rockingham, N.C. He was a fine Christian gentleman, a Methodist, and owned a cotton yarn mill near Rockingham. (In 1902 I spent a very enjoyable Christmas with him and other relatives. He gave me much valuable information about the family, being the youngest grandson of Charles Ledbetter and Frances Randle. J.D.T.) He married 1866 Ella McQueen, daughter of Major John McQueen, and had:

1.   Mary Benson Ledbetter, born May 27, 1871, married Rawlins D. Best, Cincinnati, Ohio.
2.   Henry David Ledbetter (See No. 93A)
3.   Dr. James McQueen Ledbetter (See No. 93B)

93A. *Henry David Ledbetter*

Born July 21, 1867 in Rockingham, N.C. married May 1912 Johnsie Poythress Wall, and children were:

1.   Florence Dockery Ledbetter, born June 14, 1913.
2.   Henry David Ledbetter, born May 1, 1915.
3.   Thomas Benson Ledbetter, born April 27, 1919.

93B. *Dr. James McQueen Ledbetter* (See No. 93)

Born in Richmond Co. N.C. Sept. 19, 1869, married in Rockingham, N.C. April 26, 1911 Martha Elizabeth Steele, daughter of Robert Leake Steele and wife Martha E. Little. He died in Rockingham before 1951. Children were:

1.   James McQueen Ledbetter, born May 16, 1912, married June 13, 1942 Louise Sloan (See No. 64).
2.   Martha Elizabeth Ledbetter born June 18, 1916.

94. *Rev. Charles Ledbetter* (See No. 3)

Born 1771 in Va. married Elizabeth Johnson, daughter of Dr. Thos., and moved to Middle Tenn. about 1792 (See History Hickman Co. Tenn. page 206). He was a Methodist preacher and had:

1.   Rev. William Ledbetter, born July 31, 1803, who

married Martha Knott, daughter of William Knott of N.C. She was born Aug. 22, 1802 and had child:

1. Rev. Henry Ledbetter born Aug. 18, 1831.

2. Pinkney Ledbetter, preacher and attorney, came from N.C. to Middle Tenn. and had:

 1. Charles Ledbetter

 2. . . . . . . Ledbetter, who married Rev. Taylor Ledbetter, a Methodist preacher. He was son of Johnson Ledbetter also a Methodist preacher. In 1924 they had a son, S. A. Ledbetter, living in Clovis, California. (I met him in Meridian, Miss. He was on his way to Conference of Methodist Church in Baltimore, Maryland. Rev. Johnson Ledbetter was son of Rowland Ledbetter who married . . . . . . Vaughn (Had son Rev. Henry Ledbetter who had son Rev. Mack Ledbetter, born Dec. 18, 1830 living near Pope, Tenn. in 1916)

95. *Gray Ledbetter* (See No. 3)

Born in Anson Co. N.C. 1776, married in 1799 Cecilia Johnson, daughter of Dr. Thomas Johnson. She was born in Brunswick Co. Va. Jan. 8, 1775 and died Oct. 25, 1856. They moved from Alabama to Lowndes Co. Miss. about 1834. Children:

1. Rufus Ledbetter, lived near Crawford, Miss. No children.

2. William J. Ledbetter born 1813 in Montgomery Co. N.C. No child.

3. Thomas R. Ledbetter, Dec. 9, 1800 in Montgomery Co. N.C. died Crawford, Miss. Aug 3, 1841. No children.

4. John M. Ledbetter (See No. 96)

5. Willie Ledbetter, born June 13, 1806, died Sept. 10, 1836. (There is also buried in the Crawford, Miss. Cemetery, Alonzo, son of J. V. and M. A. Ledbetter, born Aug. 21, 1800 and died Aug. 13, 1840).

96. *John M. Ledbetter* (See No. 95)

Born June 21, 1802 in Anson Co. N.C. died in Crawford, Miss. Nov. 14 1887, married 1834 Eliza H. White, born 1817, d. 1876, came to Miss. 1834 and settled near Crawford, Miss. Children:

1. Leon S. Ledbetter (See No. 98)
2. Alexander Hamilton Ledbetter (See No. 99)
3. John McGee Ledbetter (See No. 100)
4. Mat Ledbetter, md. 1st . . . . . . Terrell, 2nd H. H. Smith, lived in Crawford, Miss.
5. Letitia Ledbetter, md. . . . . . . Hinkle
6. Sallie Ledbetter, never married
7. Clara Ledbetter (See No. 102)
8. Emma C. Ledbetter (See No. 103)
9. Laura Ledbetter (See No. 104)
10. Mary E. Ledbetter, born Jan 6, 1837, died Sept. 10, 1844

98. *Leon S. Ledbetter* (See No. 95)

Born 1858, died April 13, 1938 in Crawford, Miss. Married Ida Crymes, and had children:

1. Warren Ledbetter
2. Mattie Bell Ledbetter, md. . . . . . . Masters lived in Denver, Colorado
3. Claire Ledbetter, md. . . . . . . Gibson, Detroit, Mich.
4. Lucille Ledbetter, Crawford, Miss.

99. *Alexander Hamilton Ledbetter* (See No. 96)

Born Sept. 28, 1838, died in Miss. April 18, 1871 married Lucy Ann Osborne. Children were:

1. Alexander O. Ledbetter, died 1895, md. Annice B. Puller. No child.
2. Bee Hamilton Ledbetter, md. Mattie Reeves 1916 was storekeeper of Southern Railway in Meridian, Miss. No children.

100. *John M. Ledbetter* (See No. 96)

Born May 22, 1846 died about 1942 married his cousin Maggie Randle (granddaughter of Wiatt Randle who came to Miss. 1834 from N.C.) She died 1926. She had a brother James Randle. They lived in Crawford, Miss. He was a member of Board of Supervisors of Lowdnes County for many years. Children were:

1. Walter D. Ledbetter (See No. 101)
2. Shep Randle Ledbetter md. Bernice Cunningham, grandson of James Richard Randle and Eleanor Brooks. He is with Southern Bell T. & T. Co. in Jackson, Miss. Have one child. Lenore Ledbetter.
3. Lewis Ledbetter md. . . . . . . Lawrence
4. Gray W. Ledbetter, lives in Seminole, Okla. md. . . . . . . Children: 1. Gay Ledbetter 2. . . . . . . girl
5. Maggie Lou Ledbetter
6. John M. Ledbetter, md. . . . . . . Norwood, child: Jack Ledbetter
7. Albert Ledbetter

101. *Walter D. Ledbetter* (See No. 100)

Married Mamie Hinkle. Children:
1. Mamie Ledbetter
2. Christine Ledbetter
3. Margaret Ledbetter
4. Bessie Ledbetter

102. *Clara Ledbetter* (See No. 96)

Married Alonzo Hartman. 1938 lived in Crawford, Miss. Children:
1. Jack Hartman
2. William Hartman
3. Henry Hartman
4. Mary Hartman
5. Lonnie Hartman
6. Laura Hartman
7. Doc Hartman

103. *Emma C. Ledbetter* (See No. 96)

Born 1846 married in 1869 Walter W. Scales, born 1846 lived in Starkville, Miss. Children were:
1. Walter W. Scales, died May 19, 1935, prominent merchant of Starkville, had son: Walter W. Scales.
2. Dr. Webb Scales
3. Dr. Hunter Scales

4. Lillie Scales, md. D. E. Slaughter and lived in Starkville, Miss. She was born 1876 and died Oct. 16, 1952.
Children were.
1. Dr. Daniel Walter Slaughter. Has children.
2. . . . . . . Slaughter, md. C. B. Stephenson of
Portland, Oregon. Children:

104. *Laura Ledbetter* (See No. 96)
Married 1st Nealy Nance. 2nd . . . . . . Thorpe lived in
Crawford, Miss. Had three children.

105. *Henry Ledbetter* (See No. 1)
Lived in Brunswick Co. Va. and died there 1794, he married Winnefred Wall who was born Jan 20, 1728, daughter
of Joshua Wall and wife Martha, and niece of Agnes Wall
of same county. Children:
1. Mary Ledbetter, who married William Gray, Oct. 13,
1786 in Brunswick Co.
2. Winnefred Ledbetter, md. Aug. 24, 1783 Edward
King in Brunswick Co.

106. *Mary A. Smith* (See No. 87)
Born Oct. 2, 1833 in Anson Co. N.C. died Feb. 8, 1912.
Married General Thomas Walter Blake, born in Fayetteville, N.C. about 1822. He died Jan. 14, 1905 both buried
Plantersville, Texas. Children:
1. Mary C. Blake born Feb. 18 . . . . died Nov. 6, 1915.
Never married.
2. Thomas Smith Blake born Dec. 25, 1874, md. Annie
M. Harper, born July 14, 1888. Child: Thomas Smith
Blake, Jr. b. Feb. 17, 1918, Galveston, Texas
3. Sallie Eugenia Blake, born Nov. 3, 1876. Not married.
4. James Phillip Blake, born Aug. 31, 1873, died 1917,
not married.

107. *James Ledbetter Smith* (See No. 87)
Born Oct. 15, 1840 in Anson Co. N.C. died May 13, 1906
in Mexia, Texas, married 1868 Eugenia Womack born July
2, 1851. Children were:
1. James Sanford Smith (See No. 108)
2. Mary Eugenia Smith, born Nov. 10, 1873, married
James H. Steedman, born 1867 Norwood, Ga.

    3.   Jesse Phillip Smith (See No. 114)

    4.   Sally Fanny Smith, born Feb. 4, 1876, married Dr. J. L. Metcalf, of Mexia, Texas.

    5.   Benjamin Shaw Smith (See No. 115)

    6.   William Blake Smith, born Feb. 22, 1882, married Lanere Camp. He discovered the Mexia Oil Field and became a millionaire, President City National Bank and a big oil operator. Had one child: William Blake Smith, Jr., born Feb. 18, 1912.

108. *James Sanford Smith* (See No. 107)

    Born Jan. 31, 1870 in Mexia, Texas, married Ruby Fay Kelly, born April 22, 1871. Children were:

    1.   James Fort Smith, born May 20, 1895 in Mexia, Texas, married Lucy Garby, born June 19, 1889.

    2.   Virginia Smith, born Dec. 19, 1899, Mexia, Texas. Married Peter W. Cawthon of Oak Cliff, Dallas, Texas, one son Peter Cawthon, Jr. born Aug. 2, 1921.

    3.   Emma Jean Smith born July 22, 1909, Mexia, Texas.

109. *Sally Elizabeth Smith* (See No. 87)

    Born Oct. 18, 1844 Anson Co. N.C. died May 27, 1913, married Jan. 31, 1866 Sanford Gibbs born July 7, 1819, Union District, S.C. He died Sept. 30, 1886, buried Huntsville, Texas. Children:

    1.   Wilbourn Smith Gibbs (See No. 110)

    2.   Mary Alla Gibbs, born Aug. 11, 1868 Huntsville, Texas, married Henderson Yoakum Robinson, two sons:

        1.   Herndon Yoakum Robinson, born Oct. 28, 1904.

        2.   Wilbourn Thomas Robinson, born Dec. 26, 1898.

    3.   Thomas Clifton Gibbs (See No. 111)

    4.   Sarah Sanford Gibbs, born Sept. 6, 1873 married Dr. Oscar Laertins Norsworthy, they live in Houston, Tex. one child: O. L. Norsworthy, died an infant.

    5.   Dr. James Phillips Gibbs (See No. 112)

    6.   Luteola Gibbs (See No. 113)

    7.   Annie Ledbetter Gibbs, born July 10, 1883 died an infant.

110. *Wilbourn Smith Gibbs*

Born Nov. 12, 1866, died Sept. 17, 1921. He married June 26, 1900 Annie Nugent of Jackson, Miss. They moved to New Orleans, La. Children:

1. Wilbourn Sanford Gibbs, born Feb. 28, 1909.
2. 2 children who died infants.

111. *Thomas Clifton Gibbs* (See No. 109)

Born Feb. 7, 1870 in Huntsville, Texas. Sept. 20, 1893, he married Jamesetta Hunt of Caldwell, Texas. Children:

1. Thomas Clifton Gibbs, born June 7, 1894, died infant.
2. Pauline Gibbs, born Oct. 14, 1896, married on Nov. 19, 1919, Jesse Vernon Butler, one child: Pauline Butler.
3. Cecile Gibbs, born Nov. 20, 1898.
4. Edith Gibbs, born Aug. 7, 1902.
5. Anne Kathleen Gibbs, born Jan 18, 1908.

112. *Dr. James Phillips Gibbs* (See No. 109)

Born April 3, 1875, married Oct. 18, 1905 Mary Brent McAshan, born Dec. 1, 1883. Children were:

1. Virginia Sandford Gibbs, born Nov. 23, 1906.
2. Sarah Elizabeth Gibbs, born Oct. 1, 1910.
3. James Phillips Gibbs, born Oct. 9, 1916.

113. *Luteola Gibbs* (See No. 109)

Was born June 10, 1878, Huntsville, Texas, Nov 18, 1903 married Henry Houston Hawley, born Jan. 6, 1868, Walla Walla, Wash. He is a wholsesale jeweler in Dallas, Texas, and they reside at 5701 Gaston Avenue, Munger Place, Dallas, Texas. Children:

1. Henry Houston Hawley, Jr. born July 14, 1906.
2. Sarah Alla Hawley, born March 30, 1918.

114. *Jesse Philip Smith* (See No. 107)

Born Feb. 4, 1878 on Dec. 31, 1902 married George Duffield live in Dallas, Texas. Children:

1. Philip Duffield Smith, born Mar. 20, 1905 died infant.
2. Jack Womack Smith, born July 2, 1910.
3. George Duffield Smith born Dec. 6, 1908.
4. Helen Frances Smith born Jan. 29, 1914.

115. *Benjamin Shaw Smith* (See No. 107)

Born March 29, 1880, married Natalie Machan, children:
1. James Ledbetter Smith, born Aug. 19, 1905.
2. Margaret Machan Smith, born . . . . . . 28, 1910.
3. Benjamin Shaw Smith, born Jan. 23, 1917.

116. *Lewis Philip Smith* (See No. 87)

Born in Anson Co. N.C. Jan. 3, 1847, died Oct. 24, 1886, md. 1st Aurelia Walton, born July 18, 1851, died Aug. 31, 1873. He then married 2nd Mattie Beeson, born Jan. 24, 1855, lived in Mexia, Texas. Children:

1. Mary Walton Smith, born Sept. 12, 1870, married 1st Dr. Robert Long had one son, Robert Lee Long, Jr. married 2nd: Thomas A. White, Mexia, Texas, one son: Leonard Philip White, born Oct. 16, 1900.
2. Thomas Frank Smith, born Feb. 12, 1873, married Jasper Kate Gibbs, born April 8, 1878. Children: Maxwell Chandler Smith, born Jan. 24, 1904. 2. Mary Ann Smith, Dec. 17, 1906.
3. Emma Aurelia Smith, born Feb. 24, 1878, md. Dr. Perry C. Baird. They live at 4603 Munger Ave., Dallas, Texas. Children:
   1. Perry C. Baird, born July 8, 1903.
   2. James Garrity Baird, born Oct. 31, 1905.
   3. Martha Catherine Baird, born Jan. 13, 1908.
   4. Lewis Philip Baird, born Feb. 28, 1920.
4. Sallie Eugenia Smith, born Feb. 15, 1880, married Fred S. Torley Karner, one child Fredericka Stanley Karner, born Sept. 28, 1901.
5. Luella Ross Smith, born June 7, 1885, died July 21, 1904.
6. Philip Smith, buried in Mexia, Texas.

117. *Drury Ledbetter* (See No. 1)

Born in Brunswick Co. Va. about 1734. He married when 20 years old, before 1770 Winnefred Lanier, as on Jan. 7, 1771 The Brunswick Co. Records show he and wife Winnefred sold 240 acres a patent to his father Henry Ledbetter, Oct. 31, 1726. She was daughter of Sampson Lanier and Elizabeth Chamberlain whom he married before 1740.

Sampson Lanier was a vestryman for Saint Andrew's Parish, Brunswick Co. one of the Justices and High Sheriff and was son of Thomas Lanier and Elizabeth Washington, daughter of Richard Washington of Surry Co. Va. and wife Elizabeth Jorden. Richard Washington was son of John Washington and wife Mary, widow of Charles Flood all of Surry Co. Va. Marriage contract signed Sept. 15, 1658. John Washington was son of Sir John Washington who md. 1st: Mary Curtis. After selling his land Drury Ledbetter moved to what was then Anson Co. N.C. where a deed was signed by him 1774 land on Grassy Creek. He was very prominent in Anson Co. Colonel of Militia, Sheriff, etc. Took seat in Senate from Montgomery Co. N.C. (formed from Anson Co. 1779) Jan. 1781. He took up land (military Bounty) in Wilkes Co. Ga. a few years later about 1884 with his wife Winnefred settled there where he died about 1799. She afterwards married James McClesky and moved to Hall Co. Ga. Smith's History of Georgia shows that Walton Harris moved from Brunswick Co. Va. via N.C. to Wilkes Co. Ga. He was born about 1739 married 1760 Rebecca Lanier, daughter of Sampson Lanier. She was sister of Drury's wife Winnefred and had: Buckner, Sampson, Augustin, Walton, Elizabeth, Littleton and Gen. Jeptha Vining Harris (Joel, Edwin, Nathan, and Simeon all died infants)   of Athens, Ga. Drury bought 200 acres in Anson Co. N.C. Oct. 2, 1772. Montgomery Co. N.C. tax lists show him with 720 acres, 10 slaves. Children of Col. Drury Ledbetter and wife Winnefred were:

1. Lewis Ledbetter born before 1763 as he was a land-owner in Washington Co. Ga. Dec. 14, 1784.

2. Buckner Ledbetter was in Overton Co., Tenn. Census of 1820 1 male 45 years up, 1 female 45 up, 6 children males 6 females

3. Williamson Ledbetter

4. Nancy Ledbetter b. 1769 md. James Gardiner.

5. Caroline Ledbetter, born 1771, md. Col. A. Y. Nichol, a son was Judge John C. Nichol of Savannah, Ga. Had only two children.

6. Susan Washington Ledbetter (See No. 118)
7. Washington Ledbetter (See No. 122)
8. Agathy Ledbetter
9. Lewis Ledbetter
10. Lucy Ledbetter
11. . . . . . . Ledbetter
12. Mary Ledbetter, born 1781, youngest child (See No. 124)

118. *Susan Washington Ledbetter* (See No. 117)

Born about 1773, married Major Thomas Martin of U. S. Army. Their children were:

1. Ann K. Martin (She lived to be 90) md. Capt. . . . . Bryson of U. S. Army.
2. Elizabeth Washington Martin (See No. 119)
3. Susan L. Martin, md. Maj. . . . . . . Sanford, of U. S. Army.
4. Mary F. Martin, md. Mr. Winston, a lawyer, and had: Sabella Winston who md. Governor Stevenson of Kentucky.
5. Harriet Martin, who md. Judge Joyes.
6. Louisa Martin, who md. . . . . . . Prather.
7. Thomas Martin
8. James Martin

119. *Elizabeth Washington Martin* (See No. 118)

Married Major Richard Oldham (son of Col. William Oldham and Penelope Pope) and had:

1. Jane Oldham (See No. 120)
2. William Henry Oldham
3. Thomas Martin Oldham
4. Catherine Martin, md. John W. Edgerton.
5. John Pope Oldham
6. Penelope Abigail Oldham, md. William A. Violett.
7. Mary Oldham, md. John B. Robertson.
8. George Washington Oldham, who md. Miss Miller of Louisville, Ky.

120. *Jane Oldham* (See No. 119)

Married Willard Wetmore, and lived in New Orleans, La. had children:

1. Florence Wetmore, md. . . . . . . Russwurm.
2. Mary Wetmore, md. . . . . . . Porter.
3. Oldham Wetmore, md. . . . . . . Oglesby of New Orleans.
4. John Wetmore
5. Leona Wetmore (See No. 121)

121. *Leona Wetmore* (See No. 120)

Married Paul Jumonville Coulon de Villiers, lived in New Orleans, and had:

1. Viola Aimee Jumonville Coulon de Villiers, married . . . . . . Schlegel, had daughter Viola Schlegel in 1935 living 8011 Hickory Street, New Orleans.

122. *Washington Ledbetter* (See No. 117)

Married Lucy Bostwick of Jefferson Co. Ga. and died a few years after 1867. Children were:

1. Eliza Ledbetter
2. Agathy Ledbetter
3. Drury Ledbetter
4. Winnefred Ledbetter
5. Susan M. Ledbetter
6. Littlebury Ledbetter
7. Hull Ledbetter
8. Malden Scott Ledbetter
9. Caroline E. Ledbetter
10. William R. Ledbetter
11. Lewis L. Ledbetter (See No. 123)

123. *Rev. Lewis L. Ledbetter* (See No. 122)

Born in Greene Co. Ga. 1816 and died June 9, 1867 was member of the North Ga. Methodist Conference, married 1842 Cornelia J. Byrd, daughter of Rev. Elijah and Anne E. Byrd of DeKalb Co., Ga. Children:

1. Alice A. Ledbetter, md. W. T. Revill of Greenville, Ga.
2. Cornelia M. Ledbetter, md. R. N. Ellis of Greenville, Ga.
3. Dennis Hawkins Ledbetter, md. Susan Cooper of La Grange, Ga.
4. Lewis Summerfield Ledbetter, md. Lula Dodds. He

was in 1903 Vice-President Bank of Cedartown, Cedartown, Ga.

5. William P. Ledbetter, md. Mrs. Lerzer of Floyd Co., Ga.
6. Francis M. Ledbetter, md. Cornelia H. Gresham, daughter of Judge D. C. Gresham of Greenville, Ga.
7. Melville Scott Ledbetter
8. Mary Hadessa Ledbetter married W. J. Woddey of Washington, Ga.
9. Rev. Samuel Byrd Ledbetter, md. Susie A. Ellis of Greenville, Ga.
10. Rev. Charles M. Ledbetter, md. Lula Maddox.
11. Emma Eufaula Ledbetter, born 1862, md. Rev. James W. Lee of North Ga. Conference, later was pastor of the largest Methodist Church in St. Louis, Mo. She was living there in 1932.
12. Carrie H. Ledbetter, md. J. W. Hughes of Atlanta.
13. Ernest L. Ledbetter, md. Addie Tomlinson of Cedartown, Ga.
14. Amelia J. Ledbetter, md. Rev. J. Tillman Eakes of the North Ga. Conference.

124. *Mary Ledbetter* (See No. 117)

Youngest daughter of Col. Drury Ledbetter was born 1783 and married at their home in Greensboro, Ga. June 6, 1802, as 2nd wife of Francis Philip Fatio. He died Mar. 9, 1831. She died April 9, 1828 in Florida, at New Switzerland, Duval County, their plantation, left 8 children, including Susan Fatio, md. John Claudius L'Engle (See No. 125)

125. *Susan Fatio* (See No. 124)

Was born 1806 and died 1897, married 1830 John Claudius L'Engle (1801-1864) Lieut. in the 3rd U. S. Artillery, a graduate of West Point Military Academy, class 1819. Child:

1. William Johnson L'Engle (1835-1861) md. Madeleine Saunders, and had daughter:
    1. Caroline L'Engle who married Bion Hall Barnett and in 1932 living 536 Riverside Ave., Jacksonville, Fla.

CHAPTER 5

REV. HENRY LEDBETTER B 1721 BRISTOL PARISH, PRINCE GEORGE COUNTY, VA., AND HIS SONS JOEL, SR. AND DANIEL OF ANDERSON, S. C.

By ROY C. LEDBETTER

This narrative attempts to show the descendants of Reverend Henry Ledbetter up to the year of 1957. For convenience the account is divided into generations. Eight generations are included and work begun on the ninth. Each individual is given a number. The number is necessary because the same Christian name has been given to different individuals. The number in parentheses indicates that the person has been named previously; the number is repeated in parentheses along with the name when tracing the children. Thus the direct ancestry and descendants can be traced by following the numbers.

In the general index, references are made to given names. The number assigned to each individual helps to distinguish from others of the same given name.

I. *First Known Ancestor of Continuous Line*

1. Rev. Henry Ledbetter, b 19 Nov 1721 in Bristol Parish, Prince George Co, Va, d 1785 Caswell Co, N.C.

Christian Albert Ledbetter, Greensboro, N.C., who died in 1938, says in his unpublished book No. 2 arranged in loose-leaf form:

> "Henry Ledbetter was born in Brunswick County, Virginia November 19, 1721. Was a son of John or Frances Ledbetter (undetermined)."

Francis and John, who were granted 300 acres of land in Charles City Co, Bristol Parish, Va 20 Apr 1674, each would be too old to be the father of Rev. Henry Ledbetter. Francis probably died in 1730. His wife, whose given name is unknown, died in 1756 in Bristol Parish, Prince George County, while living with her known son William, who was born about 1696 and died in

93

1775 in Brunswick Co, Va. John, Sr. and wife Mary had a son Richard born about 1690, died 1767. It is possible that Rev. Henry was a son of John, Jr. and wife Francis Ledbetter, who had a son William born 19 Feb 1720. It is possible, and even probable, that Rev. Henry was the son of another John whose wife's given name is nowhere mentioned, but who had a son John baptized 23 July 1720 in Bristol Parish, Prince George County, Va.

Henry removed before 1748 from Prince George (could be Brunswick at this time because in 1720 Brunswick was created from Prince George but did not operate until 1732) to Granville County, N. C. which was organized on the northern boundary of that state in 1746. Orange County was organized from Granville in 1752. From the northern part of Orange County there was created Caswell County in 1777. In 1748 he joined the Upper Fishing Creek (Baptist) Church on Reedy's Creek in the east central portion of present Warren County, in which he was ordained to preach in 1750. "Becoming in a few months a Calvinist he went to South Carolina and became a preacher at Lynch's Creek" in Craven County. (As per Christian Albert Ledbetter of Greensboro, N. C. in a letter in 1935 to J. R. Moll.) "He returned to North Carolina in 1761 for the remainder of his life."

Before 1748 Henry acquired 120 acres on the north side of Fishing Creek in Granville County, N. C. On 30 Jan 1748 Henry gave a deed to John for this 120 acres (Book A Deed Records, Granville Co, N. C.) On 17 Oct 1752 John of Granville County sold this land. In March 1752 Henry Ledbetter sold 80 acres of land on Gunters Creek in Granville County, N. C. On 7 Oct 1766 a John Ledbetter of Granville County, N. C. sold 240 acres in that county. "This is the same Henry that turned preacher, went to S. C. and returned to N. C. later for the remainder of his life." (Christian Albert Ledbetter in letter dated 31 Mar 1935 to J. R. Moll.)

The distinguished genealogist and author Clayton Torrence, 3318 Hanover Ave., Richmond, Va, wrote William Logan Martin that the land was in the present Persons County formed in 1791 from the east half of Caswell. He advised that up to 1935 he had not been able to determine the relationship between Henry (the

Calvinist Baptist preacher) and the other Ledbetters mentioned in the records.

There was a Kehukee Association of Primitive Baptists organized in 1765. Certain churches divided into "Regulars" and "Separates" in 1775. In August 1777 at Elder James Bell's Meetinghouse Sapponey, in Sussex County, Virginia the ten churches settled their trouble and became known as "United Baptist." One of the six "Regulars" thus united was "The Church in Granville County, North Carolina, under the care of Elder Henry Ledbetter—70 members." (P. 698 History of the Church of God from creation to 1885 by Edgar Cushings Hassell, published by Gilbert Beebe's Sons, Publishers, Middleton, Orange County, N.Y. 1886.)

In History of North Carolina Baptists by George Washington Paschal, Vol. 1, covering the years 1663 to 1803, printed 1930 by Edwards & Broughton Company, Raleigh, N. C. and found in the Kirby Library, Southern Methodist University, Dallas, Texas, it is stated, at page 178, note 82:

"Morgan Edwards account (date 1772) of Rev. Henry Ledbetter is as follows: 'Mr. Ledbetter was born, 17—, in Prince George County in Virginia. Reared a churchman. Embraced the principles of the Baptist Feb. 1748/9 and had the ordinance administered to him by Rev. Josiah Hart of Scotland Neck, N. C. Ordained Aug. 1750 along with Mr. Smart by Rev. Mess. Wm. Walker and William Washington. He was then a general Baptist, but in about 6 months after embraced the Calvinistic doctrines. He came to Linches Creek in 1754 from Welsh tract. In 1757 he went to Flat River in North Carolina. He married Edy Clark by whom he has children Joel, Jaene, William.' "

It is further stated:

"In 1772-3, Morgan Edwards at Philadelphia set out on a visit to get material for a history of the Baptist of America, traveling through provinces from New Hampshire to Georgia. Such information as he could gather he assembled into notebooks, one for each province visited. These notebooks are now to be found in the library of the American Baptist Historical Society, at Chester, Pennsylvania. Later Mr. Edwards expanded each notebook into what he called a volume which included some matter not found in the original. These were left in manuscript but were freely used by Benedict in his History of the Baptist. That for North Carolina, entitled materials towards the History of the Baptist of North Carolina, has been published with annotations in the North Carolina Historical Review for July, 1930. The notebooks have never been published. A manuscript copy of that for North Carolina was made about a half century ago by Mr. J. C. Birdsong for the North Carolina State Library."

II. *Second Generation—Children of Reverend Henry*

(1) Rev. Henry m to Eady (Edy, Ede, Eddie, Ed) Clark. To them were born either in N. C. or S. C. at least five children:

2. Joel, b about 1751, d 1815 in the New Hope Community, near Huntsville, then Mississippi Territory but Alabama after 1819.

3. Daniel, b about 1753, d 1827 near Townville, Anderson County, S. C.

4. Prudence. No further record.

5. Elizabeth. No further record.

6. A daughter m before 1785 to Shadrach Forest of Orange County, N.C.

Before 1777 when Caswell County was organized Rev. Henry acquired 365 acres of land just south of Rocky Run Branch, an east tributary of Hickory Fork of Deep Creek. On 10 Nov 1784 the State of North Carolina patented to Joel 350 acres just east of his father's land and to Daniel 100 acres just west of his father's land. The father and the two sons appear on the tax list of St. James District of Caswell County in the years 1777, 1778, 1780, 1783, and 1784. Each owned as many as four horses and eleven head of cattle and Henry owned one slave which his widow Ede owned after his death in 1785. Ede and her two sons appear on the tax list for 1785 and 1786.

A bond dated 15 Apr 1785 on file in the office of the clerk of the Superior Court of Caswell County, N. C. was executed by Joel Ledbetter, Daniel Ledbetter, Prudence Ledbetter, and Elizabeth Ledbetter of Caswell County and Shadrach Forest of Orange County, N. C. "being heirs to the estate of Henry Ledbetter, deceased" left "the whole of the estate (except the land interlined before signed) of the said deceased Ledbetter in possession of Eddie Ledbetter, late wife of the said Henry Ledbetter, and there to remain during her natural life of widowhood and then to be divided equally amongst us."

Joel of Caswell County 14 July 1786, for fifty pounds, sold to Daniel 136 acres of land on both sides of Duck Creek of Flat River in Caswell County, N. C.

The First U. S. Census of 1790 shows Joel Ledbetter, Daniel and Ed (evidently Eddie their mother) Ledbetter of Hillsborough District, Caswell Co, N. C. All information as to them is left blank in Heads of Families North Carolina printed in 1908.

On 12 May 1794 Daniel McCollum as grantor deeded 300 acres of land in Pendleton District to Daniel Ledbetter (Book B p 258 Deed Records Anderson Co, S. C.). On 23 June 1795 Abraham Odam conveyed 122 acres on Generostee Creek in Pendleton District, S.C. to Joel Ledbetter "of the State of Ga." and the instrument was witnessed by Daniel (Book C p 14 Deed Records Anderson Co, S.C.) From this it is concluded that soon after 1790 Joel and perhaps his brother Daniel, and others removed from Caswell Co, N.C. to an unknown county in Ga. Then by about 1794 they removed from Georgia to a place northwest of the present Anderson near Townville, S.C. The above were the first of several deeds of land by Joel and Daniel either as grantee or grantor.

On 12 Oct 1801 Joseph Waldron conveyed land in Anderson Co, S.C. to Matthew Ledbetter (Vol G p 68 Deed Records Anderson Co, S.C.) Rebeccah was perhaps his wife. The relation of Matthew is not known.

On 11 Oct 1803 H. (Henry) Ledbetter as Justice of Peace in Pendleton District, S.C. took acknowledgment on a deed to John Ledbetter (Vol G 22 355-6). A store was operated by Henry Ledbetter under the name "Ledbetter and Hartgraves."

In 1804 Henry died, leaving a will mentioning only his wife Patience.

On 15 July 1802 Henry gave a note for $16. to Eady Ledbetter (supposed to be daughter of Daniel but could be mother). The relation of this Henry is not known. He could be a son of Rev. Henry's brother. W. Ledbetter witnessed the early deeds.

On 1 June 1812 Stephen Strange conveyed 100 acres of land in Anderson County to William Ledbetter (Book L p 363 Deed

Records Anderson Co, S.C,). Perhaps one of these was the older son of Daniel.

In a deed Daniel Ledbetter is called "Planter." He remained in Anderson County where he died and his will was probated in 1827. For the most part, his descendants today live in or near Anderson, S. C.

Quite in contrast, the descendants of Joel, Sr. are widely scattered over Alabama, Georgia, Arkansas, Louisiana, Texas and other states.

III. *Third Generation—Grandchildren of Reverend Henry*

(2) Joel m Kitty (Catherine) d 1814 Madison County, Ala. On 7 Apr 1810 Joel conveyed to his son John 650 acres of land on Richland Creek, Pendleton District, S. C. It was recited to be his home place. (Deed was recorded in Anderson County Deed Records Vol K—128 and also at Walhalla, Oconee County, being just north of Anderson County and being the extreme northwestern county of South Carolina.)

Apparently Joel, Sr. with his younger sons immediately thereafter departed for Egbert County, Ga and soon continued his journey, settling in the New Hope Community about ten miles southeast of Huntsville in Madison County, Ala. This territory had been given up by the Creek Indians to the United States only in 1809. It was called Mississippi Territory until about 1819. Old Joel bought land. On 8 Apr 1814 by deed recorded in Book H p 418 Deed Records Madison County, Ala, Joel, Sr. divided 160 acres of land and made settlement with his sons, Joel, Jr, Ephraim, Daniel and his youngest son, Henry Burford, then a minor.

A supplemental account has been written covering additional information about Joel, Sr. in Madison County, Ala. The supplemental account traces his daughters, Lydia, Edy, Abby and his sons, Joel, Jr. Ephrame, Samuel, Daniel and Buford. In the present account we trace the descendants of Daniel, son of Reverend Henry (Calvinist) and of John, son of Joel, Sr. But for convenience we name all of the known six sons and six daughters of Joel, Sr. and wife Kitty:

7. John b 25 Dec 1774 Orange County (Caswell after 1777),

N.C. d 25 Jan 1831 near Providence Church, Townville, near Anderson, Anderson County, S. C.

8. Joel, Jr b about 1777 Caswell County, N. C. d 1820 Madison County, Ala.

9. Lydia b about 1778 Caswell County, N. C. d Madison County, Ala.

10. Edy b about 1880 in Caswell County, N.C. d Madison County, Ala.

11. Ephrame b 1784 Caswell County, N.C. d 4 July 1841 Pope County, Ark. Soldier, War 1812.

12. Samuel b about 1790 in Caswell County, N.C. d about 1853 Madison County, Ala.

13. Daniel b 1792 in Georgia d 15 Mar 1856, Madison County, Ala.

14. Abby b about 1796 d in Madison County, Ala.

15. Buford b 1798 in Pendleton District, S.C. d after 1850 in Madison County, Ala.

(3) Daniel, son of Rev. Henry m Nancy who died 7 Dec 1833 near Anderson, S.C. They had two sons and four daughters:

16. William b about 1785 in Granville County, N.C. d about 1841 in Bedford County, Tenn. He lived in Pendleton District until it was created Anderson County, S.C. in 1826. He and his family appear in the U.S. Census for that District in 1810 and 1820. Soon thereafter he with his family removed to Bedford County, Tenn.

17. Jenny b about 1787 in Caswell Co, N. C. m Robert Gilmer.

18. Abner b 23 Dec 1788 in Granville, N. C. d 11 Aug 1830 in Anderson County, S.C. Both he and his wife were buried at Old Stone Churchyard near the present Pendleton in northern Anderson Co, S.C. On 12 June 1812 Daniel conveyed land to his son Abner (Vol L p 363 Deed Records Anderson County, S.C.). The U. S. Census of 1800, 1810 and 1820 for Pendleton District, S.C. show Daniel with a son of the age of Abner. Abner appears in the 1830 Census of Anderson Co, S. C.

19. Nancy b about 1790 m John Calhoun, son of Alexander Calhoun, said to be a kinsman of the famous U. S. Senator John C. Calhoun.

20. Rhoda b about 1792 m about 1827 to Jacob Gordon and they migrated to Polk County, Ga about 1828 and settled at Cedartown about 1831.

21. Ede b about 1796 in Pendleton District, S.C. m John Russell.

22. Lavina m Reuben Townes.

The U. S. Census shows Daniel had only four daughters but the family name five as above listed.

IV. *Fourth Generation*

(7) John, son of Joel, Sr, m 14 Apr 1803 to Mary Verner b 11 Nov 1782 at Abeville, S.C. d 29 Sept 1860 and buried at Providence Church, Hart County, Ga. Mary was a daughter of David Verner, Revolutionary soldier, b 20 Feb 1760 d 10 June 1852, and his wife Estra. David Verner was the son of John Verner, Sr, also a Revolutionary soldier, b 1725 d 1800 and his wife Mary Pettigrew b 1736 in Ireland d 1796. Mary Pettigrew was a daughter of James Pettigrew, a Revolutionary soldier b April 1713 in Ireland, landed 15 Nov 1740 at New Castle, Del, d 24 Dec 1784 in Pendleton District, S.C. and his wife Mary Cochran b 1732 in North Ireland. (See D.A.R. No. 191432, Mrs. Edward McMurry.)

John and Mary had seven sons and three daughters, all born in Pendleton District, S. C.:

23. Henry b 10 May 1805. On 29 Sept 1829 Charles Verner conveyed 74 acres of land to Henry (Vol S p 476 Deed Records, Anderson Co, S.C.). On 10 Jan 1849 the heirs of John, presumably including Henry, conveyed land to Joel. (Vol A-2 p 448 Deed Records, Anderson Co, S. C.) On 3 Oct 1849 the same heirs conveyed lands to George (Vol C-2 p 1 Deed Records, Anderson Co, S. C.) Henry m 11 July 1825 Charity Shockley. They removed to Mississippi and there is no further record.

24. Rev. James Verner b 21 Feb 1807 d 23 Apr 1863 in Franklin Co, Ga. On 27 Oct 1851 Zephenia Herndon conveyed land to James (Vol A-2 p 445 Deed Records Anderson Co, S. C.). James m 14 July 1829 Martha B. Sisk. The 1840 Census of Anderson Co. S. C. shows they had two sons and two daughters. They moved to Franklin Co, Ga. and in 1860 Census are in Calhoun Co, Ala. Rev. James and Martha Sisk had at least three daughters and

five sons: dau b 1830, son b 1832, James b 1836 m 1860 Lorena b Ala 1842, dau b 1838, David b 1843, Joseph b 1845, son b 1848, all in S. C., Martha b 1852 in Ga.

25. Rev. John b 7 Feb 1809 d 2 July 1856 in Franklin Co, Ga. to which he removed in 1836 at which time he purchased a farm two miles west of Red Hill and about one mile north of Old Allen Camp Ground.

26. Rev. Joel b 27 July 1811 d 25 Oct 1873 at Lavonia, Franklin Co, Ga to which place he had moved in 1852.

It will be noted that three sons of John Ledbetter and Mary Verner were preachers. Their grandfather Henry had been a preacher in the Primitive Baptist Church. His grandson John was brought to the Methodist Church by his wife, Mary Verner. From about 1795 to 1859 members of this family lived near Providence Methodist Church in what is now northwestern Anderson County, S. C. Obituaries of Mary and her sons, John and Joel, have been preserved by a descendant, Mrs. Edward R. McMurry, deceased of Lavonia, Georgia. In 1802 when she was twenty years old, being the year before she married, Mary Verner joined the Methodist Church. "At the request of her husband she prayed in the family before he embraced religion, and even afterwards assisted when called on. She often led in prayer at church. She was well versed in Biblical knowledge and well understood the doctrines of the M.E. Church. She instructed her children correctly in the great principles of Christianity. Her house was always a home for the preachers."

All of her children joined the church. All of her sons were officials in the church except Daniel, who died young. Of John, it is said he came up in the class meetings. At about 17 years of age "he went to camp meeting a mourner but returned without the blessing. One Sabbath evening after meeting, he took his Bible and went to the woods. About sunset he returned rejoicing in the Lord from a sense of love of God shed abroad in his soul. It was his conversion." In 1831 he was licensed to exhort. In 1836 he was licensed to preach.

Joel was licensed to exhort in Pendleton Circuit, S.C. 21 Nov 1839 and was licensed to preach in the same circuit 9 Dec 1842. He was ordained a Deacon by Bishop W. M. Capers at

Spartanburg, S.C. 24 Dec 1848. He was ordained as Elder in Georgia by Bishop J. T. Pierce 18 Dec 1854. Rev Joel preached among other places at Poplar Springs Camp Ground in eastern Franklin County, Ga. Henry Walter Ledbetter, a grandson of Rev. Joel, was a retired Methodist preacher residing at Shreveport until his death about 1954.

27. Catherine b 24 Dec 1813 d 15 Mar 1875 unmarried and is buried at Providence Church, northern Hart County, Ga.

28. Esther b 3 June 1816 d 23 Nov 1885 m John Martin son of Matthew Martin, Sr, a Revolutionary soldier. Both Esther and John Martin were living in Franklin Co, Ga, when they died.

29. David Turner b 4 Feb 1819 d 1877 at his farm north of Jacksonville, Calhoun County, Ala. Injury received from a team of oxen caused his death. He is buried in Green Cemetery near his farm, which is owned by a great grandson. On 7 Feb 1843 Thomas A. Patrick conveyed 150 acres of land to David. (Vol Z p 311 Deed Records, Anderson Co, S.C.) About 1853 his family moved to Benton Co, which in 1858 became Calhoun Co, Ala.

30. Mary Caroline b 2 Feb 1821 d 19 June 1881 unmarried.

31. Daniel Lewis b 1 Apr 1823 d 28 Aug 1844 unmarried.

32. George Montgomery, the youngest child of John and Mary, b 26 Mar 1825 d 17 Apr 1904 on Shoal Creek, Hart Co, Ga. and is buried at Providence Church in that county. He had given eight acres of land on which the old Providence Church in Anderson Co, S.C. was still standing in 1933. (J. W. Baker, History of Hart County.) He served in the Confederate Army as private, Co. B, 2nd Georgia Regiment, State Troops, under Captain John H. Patrick and Samuel H. Mosely until the surrender.

(16) William, son of Daniel, m Anna and their children included at least two sons:

33. Bettie m Javors.

34. Winnie.

35. Jones m William Forest of Chapel Hill, Tenn.

36. Madison b 1 Sept 1811 Pendleton Dist, S. C. d 1 Jan 1895 Holly Springs, Marshall Co, Miss.

37. Jesse Mercer b 1814 Pendleton Dist, S. C. d May 1881 in Bedford Co, Tenn.

(18) Abner, son of Daniel m Sarah Ann Calhoun, b 12 Mar 1797 d 13 Sept 1852 dau of Alexander Calhoun and had one son:

38. Daniel Alexander b 1825 Townville, Anderson Co, S.C. killed 29 Aug 1862 at Second Battle of Manassas. Lieut. Col. Daniel Alexander Ledbetter was six feet six inches tall. He commanded a regiment of Orr's First South Carolina Rifles. At the Second Battle of Manassas his regiment was defending the railroad cut which was Stonewall Jackson's key to the fight. While with his staff in front of his tent, he was picked off by a sharpshooter. On a lonely hillside in the Virginia Mountains, in the center of the battleground, his son Daniel erected to his memory a marble shaft fenced with an iron railing.

Col. Daniel Alexander Ledbetter who died at Manassas is not to be confused with Gen. Danville Ledbetter b 24 Aug 1811 at Leeds, Maine, d 26 Sept 1866 in Canada. Danville was a graduate of West Point and served in the U. S. Regular Army 1836 to 1857 when he resigned as Captain. He owned a plantation in the south. He served in the Confederate Army 1861 to 1865 with distinction and rose to a General. Danville was a remote descendant of Henry Ledbetter who in 1659 was married to Sarah Tolman at Dorchester, Massachusetts. The descendant of this Henry formed the subject of the well-written volume Leadbetter Records, published in 1917 by Jesse E. Ames, now of Boston, Mass.

V. *Great Great Grandchildren of Rev. Henry—Fifth Generation*

(25) Rev. John, son of John, m 30 Dec 1830 Anderson Co, S. C. Susan Williams. They had two sons and five daughters, including:

39. John Turpin, b 1831 in Anderson Co, S.C. He enlisted pvt G 3rd Ga. Inf and no more was heard of him. He married Elizabeth Parks and they had a son John who died about 50 years of age unmarried, and a daughter Parmelia who married Willie Ward. After the Civil War all the family moved to Texas.

40. Mat and her twin sister, b about 1833 m (1) . . . . . . Scott, and (2) Jonathan Sam Morgan and moved to Ala.

41. Mollie, the other twin, m Joel Mabry, son of James Mabry and wife Sallie of Franklin Co, Ga. Mollie and Joel Mabry had four sons and two daughters.

42. Caroline, m Green Morgan and moved to Texas about 1882.

43. Joel Parks, b Feb 1848 in Franklin Co, Ga, d 1923 just north of Carnesville, Ga.

44. Julia, m Albert Vandiver and moved to Baldwin Co, Miss. They had a daughter Hallie.

(26) Rev. Joel, m 27 Feb 1834 Mary (Polly) Parker, b 3 July 1811, d 10 May 1889, dau of Joseph A. Parker and Barbara Redwine of Hart Co, Ga. (John William Baker, History of Hart Co, p 130). To them were born seven sons and three daughters:

45. William Henry, b 25 Dec 1834, Anderson Co, S. C. d 28 Oct 1924 at Alexandria, La, and buried at Simsboro, La. He served in the Infantry in the Civil War and was a prisoner two years at Chicago. He was a lay Methodist preacher from young manhood until his second marriage. From about 1884 to 1887 he owned a sawmill, where he lost all his savings.

46. Elizabeth C., b 10 Dec 1836, d 3 Sept 1885 at Lavonia, Ga, unmarried.

47. John P., b 30 Dec 1838 Anderson Co, S.C. d Dec 1887 of Pneumonia on the road between Lisbon and Homer, La.

48. Matilda Frances, b 11 Apr 1841, d 14 Mar 1900, buried in Lavonia Cemetery. Never married.

49. Joel Lewis, b 16 June 1843, d 6 May 1874 at Lavonia, Ga. (No further record)

50. Robert Newton, b 18 Aug 1845 Anderson, S.C. d 19 Dec 1923 at Prescott, Ark. In 1866 William Henry, Robert Newton and James Stacy removed by ox and mule wagon from Lavonia, Ga to ten miles west of Farmersville, Union Parish, La. Late in 1870 all removed about 35 miles northward to new homes about 16 miles west of El Dorado, Union Co, Ark. About 1872 Robert Newton moved to Pine Bluff, Ark and later settled at Prescott, Navado Co, Ark. About 1877 William Henry and James Stacy moved from Union Co, Ark to the town of Arizona, Claiborne Parish, La. In 1881 James Stacy returned to Union Co, Ark.

51. James Stacy, b 12 Oct 1847, Anderson Co, S. C. d 22 July 1904 at Cornie, Union Co, Ark.

52. David Benson, b 29 May 1851, Anderson Co, S.C. d Feb 1918 at Jeffersonville, Ga.

53. Mary Eliza Jane, b 11 Mar 1853 in Ga, m Russell Crump and d one year later.

54. Oliver Parker, b 16 Oct 1856 in Ga, d 2 Feb 1899 and buried Lavonia, Ga. Oliver, David Benson, Elizabeth and Matilda were charter members of the Lavonia Methodist Church organized in 1880.

(29) David Turner, m 5 Nov 1840 Nancy Tilly b 1821 Anderson Co, S.C. d May 1885 at the home north of Jacksonville, Calhoun Co, Ala. To them were born six sons and three daughters:

55. Louise E., b 1842, m Tom Green. A daughter m Newman and her descendants live at Sherman, Grayson Co, Tex.

56. George Whitfield, b 21 Sept 1843 Anderson Co, S.C. d 1859 Jacksonville, Ala.

57. Augustus (Gus) Benson, b 24 Oct 1845 in Anderson Co, S.C. d 13 Dec 1912 Anniston, Calhoun Co, Ala. Never married. He served as pvt G 3 Ala Cav and near the end of the Civil War lost his right arm by accidental discharge of a gun. He served as tax assessor of Calhoun Co, Ala. He also taught school when a young man.

58. Eliza Jane, b 21 Oct 1848, d 29 Mar 1879, buried Pine Cemetery west of Anniston, m J. Harve Davidson.

59. Cephas Andrew, b 2 Nov 1850 Anderson Co, S.C. d 1891, buried Green's Cemetery north of Jacksonville, Ala.

60. David Carlisle, b 17 Feb 1855 Calhoun Co, Ala, d 1919, buried Green's Cemetery.

61. Julius Lafayette, b 30 May 1857 south of Jacksonville, Ala, d 29 July 1898 four miles southeast of Ferris, Ellis Co, Texas, to which place all of his family had removed by train from Keener, Etawah Co, Ala in the fall of 1895. He is buried at the new cemetery at Ferris, Texas, where his grave is marked by a monument.

62. Cornelia Adeline, b 1 Nov 1859, m John Davidson, brother of J. Harve Davidson.

63. Franklin Perry, b 4 Apr 1863 north of Jacksonville, Ala, d 10 June 1933 Bowden, Ga.

(32) George Montgomery, youngest son of John, m 27 Apr 1848 Sarah Jane Martin b 23 Sept 1829 d 4 Feb 1903, dau of Matthew Martin, Jr of Anderson Co, S.C. The children of George and Sarah Jane are:

64. Caleb Martin, b 4 Mar 1849 Anderson Co, S.C. d 31 Mar 1924 Hart Co, Ga, m 16 Nov 1871 Mary Elizabeth Parker but no present record of their children.

65. Susanna Nancy Jane, b 24 May 1853 Anderson Co, S.C. d Lavonia, Ga.

66. William Franks, b 4 Oct 1857, d Atlanta, Ga, m 24 Nov 1892 at Lavonia, Ga Lizzie Black, b 19 Apr 1855 in La, d 17 April 1904 Hart Co, Ga dau John Black and Mary Latimer Black of Loudsville. William Franks had two daus. Jennie Eulalia, b 12 Feb 1893 m 2 July 1922 Charles W. Thomas, Atlanta, Ga; and Emma Morena, b 21 May 1895, address 264 Rawson St, Atlanta, Ga.

66. John Martin, b 11 July 1861, d 31 Aug 1861.

67. George Richardson, b 16 Oct 1864 Shoal Creek, Hart Co, Ga d 6 Mar 1908 in Hart Co, Ga, buried Allen's Church Cemetery, Franklin Co, Ga.

68. James, b 22 June 1868, d 27 Sept 1868.

(36) Madison, son of (16) William and grandson of (3) Daniel, m 22 Sept 1835 Margaret D. Nolen, b 8 Feb 1818 Marshall Co, Tenn, d 12 July 1891 Holly Springs, Miss. She and Madison had only one child:

69. Millard Johnson Camiel, b 11 Mar 1859 Holly Springs, Marshall Co, Miss, d 31 July 1930, Blue Mountain, Miss.

(37) Jesse Mercer, m (1st) Mary Shearin and had:

70. Maggie, m Garrett of Lewisburg, Tenn.

71. Sarah, m Ray and lived at Ladonia, Texas.

72. James Madison, b 1849 d Lewisburg, Tenn, 18 Apr 1918.

Jesse Mercer m (2nd) Bircheen and they had five children:

73. John H. lived at Columbia, Tenn. (No further information).

74. Ellen, m Beaty.

75. Merideth Gentry.

76. Isaac Newton.

77. Mary m Long.

The last four lived at Lewisburg, Tenn and there is no further information.

(38) Col. Daniel Alexander, son of Abner, m Elizabeth Earl Vandiver and they had:

78. John Peter, b 1856 Townville, S.C. and d there 11 Oct 1927.

79. Maria, b 2 Oct 1854 Townville, S.C. m Dr. Winfield Kennedy Sharp.

80. Daniel Alexander, b 6 Nov 1862 at Townville, d 29 Feb 1920 Anderson, S.C. He was six feet and four inches tall and weighed 300 pounds. In this respect he was like his father, Col. Daniel Alexander Ledbetter, who fell at the Second Battle of Manassas just before his birth. His mother took him as a baby in arms from their home in South Carolina to Virginia to see his father. At Richmond she was turned back with the news that her husband was dead. No record of the grave was kept except that he was buried "on the battlefield." For more than 20 years the family did not know the spot of his burial. A boy then ten years old watched the burial of two soldiers on his father's farm on the battlefield. Later he wrote a poem "Two Soldiers in Gray." It appeared in the Charleston News and Courier. The son read the poem which named his father, Col D. A. Ledbetter. The son left at once for Virginia and the author of the poem pointed out the spot "on a lonely hillside in the Virginia Mountains" where the father was buried. The son, then twenty-one years of age, was working in a store at Townville, his home place, and saving his money until he would have enough to move to Anderson and go into business for himself. He spent the savings to erect the marble shaft which now commemorates Col. Daniel Alexander Ledbetter on the Manassas Battle Ground.

VI. *Sixth Generation—Great Great Great Grandchildren of Reverend Henry*

(43) Joel Parks, son (25) Rev. John, m 1870 Mary Miller, b Nov 1845, d 24 Dec 1924 Lavonia, Ga, dau of Samuel Miller of Tacoa, Banks Co, Ga. They had two sons and five daughters, all born at the old home place of Rev. John.

81. Emma b 1871, m 8 June 1889 at Atlanta, Ga, Asa M. Cox and lived at Atlanta, Ga. They had Jesse Lee d young, Blanch, Lou Ella, Irene, and Boyd.

82. John Samuel, b 5 Sept 1872, m Alice Thompson Sewell, dau J. N. Thompson and wife Jane Alice. In 1948 they were living

at Royston, Ga. They had four daughters born Lavonia, Ga:
Wynona Boyce m Francis Rees Edwards, live Athens, Ga; Charles
Nelle m Howard Meffert Woddle, live West Point, Ga; Marian
Montine m Moody Goss Thomas, live Alta, Ga; Janie Bob m John
O. Hill, live 1601 Jackson St, Amarillo, Texas.

83. Sue, b 9 Nov 1875, d 1918 m Jan 1909 Walter Davis,
Tocoa, Ga.

84. Parmelia, b 4 Feb 1877, m 3 Jan 1900 Tom Aderhold,
lived Clarkston, Ga.

85. Gaines, b 1879, d Jan 1903, m Dec 1901 Effie Toney
and had one child Floyd, Lavonia, Ga.

86. Myrl, b 2 Sept 1880, m Jan 1901 Tom Bailey, lived
Mauldin, S.C.

87. Sallie, b 1882, m 2 Nov 1905 Hubert A. Kelley, lived
Decatur, Ga.

(45) William Henry, son of (26) Rev. Joel, m 1st 14 Aug
1860 Mary Elizabeth Powledge, b about 1839, d July 1881 at
Minden, La, dau of Powledge of Merriweather, Ga. Of this marriage there were two daughters and four sons:

88. Lula, b 1861 at Merriweather, Ga, d 1880 at Arizona, La,
m Tom J. Whitehead. Some of their descendants named Whitehead
live in Dallas, Texas.

89. William Raymond, b 16 Mar 1866 at Merriweather, Ga.
Lived Bunkie, La, Route 1.

90. Mollie, b 1868 near Cornie, Union Co, Ark, d 1905
Jonesboro, La, m W. Austin Harris, son of Rev. Austin Harris.
They had five sons and three daughters.

91. Rev. Henry Walter, Methodist minister, b 4 July 1870
Cornie, Ark, d Shreveport, La. about 1954. From 1896 to 1946
he preached in many churches in northern La. Twelve church
houses were erected under his ministry. He wrote numerous poems.

92. Edgar, b 1874 Union Co, Ark, d 18 Apr 1948, Ruston, La.

93. Joel Martin, b 1876 Cornie, Ark, d 23 Apr 1948, Simsboro, La.

(45) William Henry, m 2nd 12 Dec 1881 Emma Goodwin
b 1858, d about 1910 at Homer, La, dau of James Goodwin of
Lincoln Parish, La. By the second marriage there were three
daughters and two sons:

94. Annie Mae, b 1883 Arizona, La, m about 1904 Rev. Glasspool, Methodist, at Homer, La. Resided San Antonio, Texas.

95. Laura, b about 1885. Never married. Nurse, San Antonio, Texas.

96. Parker Redwine, b about 1887 at Arizona, La. Lived Ponca City, Oklahoma.

97. Mildred, b about 1888 Homer, La, m James Ferguson and was a nurse at San Antonio, Texas.

98. Roy, d six months of age.

(47) John P., son of (26) Rev. Joel, had five sons and four daughters but we have a record of only six children:

99. Joe, b about 1868, d about 1899 at Arizona, La, m about 1891 Betty Willis, d about 1897, dau Tom Willis of Arizona, La. They had only one child, a girl.

100. John.

101. Willie.

102. Lee, All three died before grown, unmarried.

103. Dora, m

104. Fred, b about 1883 in Ga and removed about 1885 with family and lived Heflin, Bossier Parish, La, with his wife and children.

(50) Robert Newton, son of (26) Rev. Joel, m Feb 1881, Missouri Beaver, who d 7 July 1928 Prescott, Ark, dau of Hugh Beaver of Homer, La. Robert Newton and wife had three sons and two daughters:

105. Joseph Columbus, b 2 Sept 1883 at Bluff City, Ark. Resided Prescott, Ark.

106. Robert Franklin, b Apr 1885, d 12 Aug 1888, Bluff City, Ark.

107. Willie Walter, b about 1887 and in 1947 resided at Gladewater, Texas, m 1st Alley Brown, m 2nd Lola Benton.

108. Ida Mae Ela, b about 1889, m Neil White and resided Prescott, Ark.

109. Della Penella, b about 1895, m Tatum and resided Prescott, Ark.

(51) James Stacy, son of (26) Reverend Joel, m 1883

Cornie, Ark, Sarah Louvenia Peace, d 1 Apr 1927 Wesson, Ark. They had:

110. Lela Pearl, m Davis, resided Emerson, Ark.

111. Mary Etta, m Owens, resided Wesson, Ark.

112. Florence Edna, b 25 Dec 1888 at Cornie, Ark, m 28 Feb 1905, Cornie, Ark, Henry Kirk Beaver, b 13 Nov 1884, son of Henry Stevan Beaver of Lancaster, S.C. They resided Bluff City, Ark.

113. David Parks, resided Wesson, Ark, m Catherine Fielder.

114. Myrtel, m Waller and resided Wesson, Ark.

115. James Oliver, Midland, Texas.

116. Myra Catherine, d before 1932, m Fielder.

117. Earnest Layville, d before 1932.

(52) David Benson, son of (26) Rev. Joel, m 1st Burnett Morris of Pickens, S.C., 2nd Sallie Cunningham, but there is no record of their children.

(54) Oliver Parker, youngest son of (26) Rev. Joel, m about 1884 Nettie Ragsdale and had:

118. Edith, m and lived Jeffersonville, Ga.

119. Olien, Jeffersonville, Ga.

120. Hubert.

121. Ruth, m and d about 1920.

122. Carl, Macon, Ga.

(59) Cephas Andrew, son of (29) David Turner, m Narcissus Reaves, dau of Carter Reaves, Jacksonville, Ala. All their children were born at Jacksonville.

123. Albert Monroe, b 15 Oct 1875, d 2 June 1929 at Columbia, La. He was a jeweler at Columbia in the same building where his son, Milton, now runs the business.

124. Andrew Harrison, b 1876, d 1936, Miami, Fla.

125. Lee Ronie Rosetta, b 7 Apr 1881, m in 1905 Simpson Ferrill, son of Rev. Jim Ferrill. Separated and retained name Ledbetter and had one child, Willis Albert Ledbetter, b 17 Aug 1906, m 1 Jan 1932 Minnie Francis Holder, dau of Jess Holder and Adline Hardy.

126. James Wesley, b 10 Nov 1883, d about 1954 Anniston, Ala.

127. Collie Peyton, b 9 Mar 1885, d about 1956 at Piedmont, Ala.

128. Luther Gaston, b 1 Aug 1887, d 19 Nov 1945, Atlanta, Ga, buried Central Cemetery, near Douglasville, Ga.

128. Louisa Jane, b 13 Aug 1889, d 1947 Piedmont, Ala, m 23 July 1908 Charlie Green, son of James Thomas Green and Josie Griskie.

130. Turner Hill, b 11 June 1891, d 15 Feb 1937, Birmingham, Ala.

(60) David Carlisle, son of (29) David Turner, m 21 Dec 1882, Millie Elizabeth Dempsey, dau John Dempsey and Lucy Wilson, Calhoun Co, Ala. Children of Carlisle all born in Calhoun Co, Ala.:

131. Lily Euphema, b 3 Nov 1883, d 3 May 1932, Calhoun Co, Ala, m Joe Reeves, son of John Reeves and Laura Dempsey; Lily had no children.

132. Lena May, b 13 Dec 1884, d 22 Sept 1885.

133. Laura Ada, b 2 Feb 1886, m Carl Benton Farmer, d 25 Mar 1931, son of Shade Farmer and Maggie Wilkerson, Calhoun Co, Ala. Lived Piedmont, Ala.

134. David Levi, b 26 Mar 1888, d 4 Aug 1910, unmarried.

135. Mary Frances, b 9 Feb 1890, d about 1949, m 12 Sept 1910 William Arthur Dempsey, son of Levi Dempsey and Louisa Reeves. Lived Jacksonville, Ala.

136. Jocey Alma, b 13 May 1895, d Dec 1899.

137. Malcolm Young, b 15 Apr 1895, m 1916 Cuba Harmon, dau John William Harmon and Lela Smith. Lived Jacksonville, Ala.

138. Lester, d as baby.

139. Floyd Turner, b 11 Jan 1901. Never married, Lived Piedmont, Ala.

(61) Julius Lafayette, son of (29) David Turner, m 28 Sept 1879, Calhoun Co, Ala, Emily Elizabeth Littlejohn, b 22 Oct 1861 Calhoun Co, Ala, on the farm of her grandfather, Charles Littlejohn, d 24 Dec 1924 at Stephenville, Erath Co, Texas, buried as Lizzie, then wife of J. F. Briley in Allard Cemetery about seven miles east of Stephenville. She was the only child of Daniel Littlejohn, who died Sept 1862 in Civil War and Sarah Cochran, d 1896 Ferris, Texas. Sarah Littlejohn m 2nd Jim Brown. Children of Julius Lafayette:

140. Theodocia Inez, b 13 May 1880 about seven miles north of Jacksonville, Calhoun Co, Ala, d Ferris, Texas 7 Oct 1958.

141. Elector Esterham, b 12 Aug 1882, Millerville, Union Co, Miss, d 4 Apr 1941, Carrollton, Dallas Co, Texas, to which place he had moved from Ferris, Texas, Jan 1916.

142. Marvin Phelps, b 2 June 1884 north of Jacksonville, Ala, d 1 Oct 1885.

143. Essie Leola, b 13 Nov 1886, d May 1889.

144. Van Buren, b 25 Dec 1887, d Jan 1888.

145. Mary Euphema, b 14 Dec 1889 near Keener, Etawah Co., Ala.

146. Jodie, b 15 Jan and d Feb 1892.

147. Roy Clifford, b 2 Aug 1893, resides 3516 University Blvd. Dallas 5, Texas.

148. Easter May b 7 Apr 1895, resides 2712 Gibbs Williams Road, Dallas, Texas.

149. Joe Wesley, b 28 Mar 1897 four miles southeast of Ferris, Ellis Co, Texas to which place the family migrated from Keener, Ala in the fall of 1895. Resides 1010 N. Neblett St, Stephenville, Texas.

(63) Franklin Perry, youngest son of (29) David Turner, m Lottie Giles, dau Samuel Giles and Margaret Thatcher. Franklin had five sons and five daughters.

150. Charles Absalom, b 8 June 1888, Cleveland, Tenn, d June 1954. All remaining children of Franklin were born near Bowden, Ga, on the western border near the Alabama line and still live near that address.

151. Emma Gertrude, b 25 June 1890, m 10 Sept 1936, Lynn Buchanan, son of Manse Buchanan and Cindy Williams. No children born to Emma.

152. Florence Lavada, b 25 Apr 1893, d Oct 1898.

153. Pinkney Monroe, b 25 Jan 1896, d 9 Sept 1911.

154. Julia Bell, b 29 Aug 1898, m Marcelous Robinson, son of John Robinson and Nancy Crider, Waco, Ga, Route 2.

155. Walter Benson, b 10 June 1901, lives Bowden, Ga, Route 3.

156. Virgil Franklin, b 1 July 1905. He is six feet six inches tall. Lives Bowden, Ga, Route 3.

George Montgomery Ledbetter (1825-1904) and Wife

Emily Littlejohn Ledbetter (1861-1924) and her children: Front left, Ma
Conn (1880-1958); Standing Left to Right, Joe Wesley Ledbetter, Roy
882-1941), E. M. Ledbetter.

157. Jesse Carl, b 12 Feb 1908, lives Heflin, Ala, Route 2.

158. Carry Lee (twin) b 12 Feb 1908, m Ike Abercrombie, son of Leonard Abercrombie and Zodie Lambert. Lives Waco, Ga, Route 2.

159. Mamie Lou, b 18 Oct 1910, d 16 Dec 1943 unmarried.

(65) Susanna Nancy Jane, dau of (32) George Montgomery, m 17 Nov 1874 Thomas Higginbotham of Hart Co, Ga, and had only one child: Arnetta, b at Shoal Creek, northern Hart Co, Ga, and d about 1942, Lavonia, Franklin Co, Ga. She married Edward Russell McMurray, merchant of Lavonia, Ga. They had a son Winfred McMurray, d Oct 1956. The only other child was Edna McMurray who married B. Frank Shadburn and resides at Lavonia, Ga.

Mrs. Edward R. McMurray was a genealogist and did much work on Ledbetter family of Pendleton, S.C. and connected families. She left her records to the Georgia State Archives, Peachtree St, Atlanta, Ga. In her application National Number 191432 to the John Benson Chapter of the National Society of the Daughters of the American Revolution in the records of that chapter at the court house, Hartwell, Ga, she sets out her direct ancestry including the ancestors of Mary Verner. The Bible records of John, b 1774, who married Mary Verner, and of their youngest son George Montgomery are in the possession of her family.

(67) George Richardson, son of (32) George Montgomery, m 8 Dec 1892 Addie Lucinda Clodfelter, b 24 Mar 1866, d 5 June 1941. They had one daughter and four sons:

160. Alice Cleo, b 18 Sept 1893, m 16 Nov 1930 at Anderson, S.C., William Parrot Knight, b 2 Mar 1891 at Ware Shoals, Laurens Co, S.C., where the family still lives with one surviving child, Mary Louise, b 12 Sept 1931, m 20 Dec 1953, James Jackson Haygood, b 16 Sept 1930 Anderson, S.C., and also lives Ware Shoals, S.C., Route 1.

161. George Franklin, b 25 Mar 1895, d 21 Nov 1949, buried Cemetery Hollywood, Habersham Co, Ga.

162. David Turner, b 22 May 1896, resides Clarksville, Ga.

163. Henry Baxter, b 22 Feb 1900, resides Tallulah Lodge, Ga.

164. Wallace Smith, b 10 Oct 1905, Carnesville, Ga. All of

his brothers and sisters were born at Lavonia, Ga. Resides St. Simons Island, Ga.

(69) Millard Johnson Camiel, son of (36) Madison, m 28 Mar 1899, Holly Springs, Miss, Mabel Buliah Mullihan, b 11 Mar 1858, living 1932, Blue Mountain, Miss, dau Charlie Mullihan, York, Neb. Millard and wife Mabel had three daughters and two sons, all born Holly Springs, Miss:

165. Juliet Lettie Carrie, b 9 Feb 1900, m 2 June 1925, Samuel L. Hill of New Albany, Miss.

166. Charlie Madison, b 16 Sept 1901, d 9 Oct 1918 in World War I.

167. Hazel Ellen, b 19 Sept 1904, m James A. Sage, New Albany, Miss.

168. William Jennings Bryan, b 19 Sept 1907. No further record.

169. Eva Margaret, b 20 Apr 1911, m 17 July 1931, Jimmie McSkelly of Ripley, Miss.

(72) James Madison, son of (37) Jesse Mercer, m Jan 1876 Lewisburg, Tenn, Hattie M. Long, d 17 Dec 1920. They had a daughter and three sons:

170. Mittie, m 1st J. G. Stinson, m 2nd O. C. Miller, lived Lewisburg, Tenn.

171. James Ozro, b 3 Oct 1878, Farmington, Tenn, lived Winchester, Tenn.

172. Walter Mercer, b 23 Aug 1881 Lewisburg, Tenn, living Tracy City, Tenn.

173. Myrt Coleman, b 23 Feb 1883, Lewisburg, Tenn, lived Pulaski, Tenn.

(78) John Peter, son (38) Col. Daniel Alexander, m Clara Cox, d 17 June 1908 Townville, S.C. they had:

174. Mattie, m J. Walter Dickson, Townville, S.C.

175. John Hill, unmarried.

176. Elizabeth Helena, unmarried.

177. Emma Lee, m J. Samuel McClellan, Anderson, S.C.

178. Daniel Ralston, m Grace Martin. No further record. Resided Townville.

179. Rev. James Edward (Missionary Baptist). Served in World War I. Unmarried.

180. Clara Aline, unmarried.

181. Rev. Virgil Kennedy, b 28 Nov 1897, Townville; Resided 1938 at Anaheim, Calif.

182. Annie Mae, m Eugene Smith and resided Wellford, S.C.

183. Harold Cox, resided Townville, m Louise Wells. No further record.

(80) Daniel Alexander, son of (38) Col. Daniel Alexander, m 28 Oct 1891 Annie Pinckney Brown. They had two daughters and three sons, all born and living at Anderson, S.C.

184. Louis Randolph, b 19 July 1892. Served as Lieutenant in Infantry World War I. He is in wholesale mercantile business, Anderson, S.C.

185. Julia Reed, b 11 Dec 1896, m John Aull Russell, Orlando, Fla.

186. Fred Brown, an architect at Anderson, S.C.

187. Elizabeth Vandiver.

188. Joseph Brown.

VII. SEVENTH GENERATION—*Great Great Great Grandchildren of Reverend Henry*

(89) William Raymond, son of (45) William Henry, m 10 Oct 1889 Arizona, La, Annie Maud Harris, b 14 Sept 1871, d 24 Jan 1944, Bunkie, La, dau Rev. William Austin Harris, a Missionary Baptist preacher at Lisbon, La. Children:

189. Glynn Harris, b 11 July 1890 Arizona, La. He graduated L.S.U., Baton Rouge, and served as sugar chemist, spending part of each year in the Dominican Republic, m 1924 Clistie Meek, dau J. M. Meek, Eugene Oregon. To them were born two daughters, Patricia and Millicent.

190. Thomas Reed, b 13 Apr 1892, Arizona, La, m Dec 1918 Maud Hickenberg, dau Henry Hickenberg, Cheneyville, La, and had William Henry, b 1919, resides Pineapple, Ala; Thomas Reed, b 1925; Charles Harris, b 1927, d 1931; Wilhelmina Cordelia.

191. Walter Raymond, b 14 Aug 1893, Arizona, La. Resides 3217 Stanford, Dallas, Texas, m 20 June 1923 Eleanor Bonnycastle, Shreveport, La and have two children, both born Shreveport,

La: Dorothy Eleanor, b 6 June 1924; Walter Raymond, b 3 Sept 1929.

192. Ralph Claude, b 13 Apr 1896 Weston, La, d Oct 1922, Pineville, La, unmarried.

193. Gladys Milner, b July 1898 Alexandria, La, m 1926 Burton Broussard, resides Alexandria, La.

194. William Wallace, b Sept 1900 Poland, La, lives Lake Charles, La, m 1st Ruby Brown (divorced), m 2nd Elizabeth James. No children.

195. Annie Flora, b 23 Nov 1903, m 1938 Erskine Donald, Snow Ball, Ala, resides Pineapple, Ala.

196. Mary Elizabeth, b 1906 Poland, La, m 1927 Sterling Bain, who was accidentally killed Nov 1930. Two children, Beverly Glyn and Sterling C, m 2nd 1942 Clyde H. Smith, resides Bunkie, La.

197. Billy Louise, b Mar 1910, m 1931 Lt. Col. F. L. Miller, resides Washington, D.C.

(92) Edgar, son of (45) William Henry, m Clara and had:

198. Blanchard, resides Ruston, La.

199. Ruth, d about 1936, unmarried.

200. Max, m John Davis, Cotton Valley, La.

201. Frankie, m Ernest Hill, resides Ruston, La.

(93) Joel Martin, son of (45) William Henry, m Ella Madden, Simsboro, La, and had:

202. Bryan, resides in Missouri.

203. Roy, resides Arcadia, La.

204. Walter, resides Simsboro, La.

205. Mildred, resides in Calif.

(105) Joseph Columbus, son of (50) Robert Newton, m 15 Dec 1910, Prescott, Ark, May Collingham, b 12 June 1887, dau of J. L. and Francis Collingham. They have six children all born and reside in Prescott, Ark.

206. Dennis Ferris, b 11 Oct. 1911.

207. Dale Newton, b 19 Nov 1913. He and his four younger brothers served in World War II.

208. Dorius Goodone, b 15 Dec 1915.

209. James Ottis, b 1 June 1921.

210. Wallace Raymond, b 22 Dec 1923.

211. Ellis Eugene, b 2 Feb 1926.

(123) Albert Monroe, son (59) Cephas Andrew, m 1894 Austin, Texas, Betty Elizabeth Daniel, b 1876, dau George Washington Daniel and Harriet Orpha Singleton, Gainesville, Ga. Betty lives at Columbia, La. Their children:

212. Cecil Elmore, b 14 June 1896 Ruston, La, d 15 Dec 1943, Lake Charles, La, m Mamie and had one son who resides at Lake Charles, La.

213. George Henry, b 14 Mar 1898, Lincoln, Orleans Parish, La, m 2 Jan 1926 Alice Elizabeth Jarrell, Greenville, Ga, and have one dau Joanne, b 4 Apr 1927, New Orleans, La, m Briley; one son George Ronald, b 18 Dec 1932, Charlotte, N.C.

214. Wade Thomas, b 14 Feb 1900, Ruston, La, m Jewel Manley, dau of Steve Manley and wife Isabell. Wade has a son Jack, b 16 Mar 1929 and dau Shelba Jean, b 11 Nov 1942.

215. Milton Andrew, b 13 July 1902, Columbia, La, where he is a jeweler, m 12 Mar 1922 Annie Adelia Brown, dau Stephen Emanuel Brown and Molly Hubb, Waco, Texas. Milton has two daughters and one son; Marien Jennette, b 25 Apr 1924, resides San Francisco, Calif; Peggy Martell, b Sept 1926 and m Clyde I. Smith; Klien Beve, b 5 May 1929, m Bonnie Merrill Waldrop, Columbia, La.

216. Flossie May, b 7 Aug 1904, m 1st Pete Lehr, d 29 June 1946 had two sons, George Edward, b 23 Jan 1927; and Albert Landen, b 19 Jan 1931, m 2nd Henry R. Tanner.

217. Richard, b May 1905, d two weeks of age.

218. Fonzer Lewis, b 1 Aug 1907, live Columbia, La, m 11 Feb 1948 Maude Nellie Agnes Etier.

219. Arthur Herbert, b 9 July 1909, resides Charlotte, N.C.

220. Bonnie Pearl, b 13 Aug 1911, m 3 Oct 1938 Earl Foreman, son Frank Foreman and Lilla Greenberg. Resides 6015 Burgundy, Dallas, Texas. Bonnie has two dau, Dwanna Rae, b 9 Jan 1940 and Jackie, b 31 July 1942.

221. Grace Dimple, b 15 Aug 1915, m Dallas Calk, reside 3137 Lillian St, Shreveport, La. Grace has two dau: Barbara Ann, b 9 July 1936, m Roland Nichols, son of Jake Nichols: Janie Gayle, b 28 July 1940.

222. Hazel Marie, b 16 Apr 1917, m 17 Apr 1946, Ollie Lee

Biedenhorn, Jr, son of Ollie Lee Biedenhorn and Adelle Zehntner. Reside 1106 Richmond Circle, Shreveport, La.

(124) Andrew Harrison, son (59) Cephas Andrew, m Oct 1893 Ella Moody. They had five sons and three daughters:

223. Tim Wheeler, b 10 Jan 1895.

224. Clifford Wakefield, b 10 July 1903, d 5 June 1946, Miami, Fla, m Aug 1919 Rosie Collins, Piedmont, Ala. Had a daughter Lois Mae, b 30 Apr 1927, and son Fred Eugene, b Mar 1925.

225. John Clarence, b 5 June 1905, unmarried.

226. Myrtle Odell, b 22 Oct 1909, m 1927 Marshall Crouse, Miami, Fla, and had Betty Jean, b 11 Apr 1928; Carroll Francis, b 1 Mar 1931; Marshall, b 1 June 1935.

227. Eula Mae, b 30 May 1911, m 1929 Henry Rollins, Miami, Fla, and had Dolores, b 5 May 1931, and Elain, b 30 June 1930.

228. Hubert Thomas, b 6 Dec 1914, m 1935 Pearl Colby, Miami Fla, and had Janice, b 16 Jan 1936; Jean b 3 Oct 1938 and Tommie, b 2 Apr 1941.

229. Maudy Esta, b 15 Jan 1918, m 1935 H. B. Robertson, Miami, Fla, and had Terry, b 1937 and John Franklin, b 1946.

230. William Franklin, b 12 May 1922.

(126) James Wesley, son (59) Cephas Andrew, m 7 July 1901 Margaret Ellen Doss, dau Samuel Alexander Doss and Louisa Missouri Holder. They had three sons and two daughters:

231. Oscar Lee, b 13 Dec 1903, lives Anniston, Ala, as do all his living brothers and sisters. Married. No children.

232. William Claudie, b 15 Nov 1906, d 6 Apr 1910, near Jacksonville, Ala.

233. Buena Mae, b 8 May 1909, m 6 Feb 1937 James Herbert Walker and adopted James Richard, b 13 Jan 1940.

234. Cecil Samuel, b 7 May 1911, unmarried.

235. Burnett Francis, b 28 Mar 1915, m 24 Jan 1935 Elbert Lewis Shears, son James Franklin Shears and Lula Margaret Hutson and has two children: Robert Lewis, b 28 May 1939; Margaret Ellen, b 10 Apr 1943.

(127) Collie Peyton, son (59) Cephas Andrew, m 24 Dec 1906 Lucy Dempsey, dau Levi Breckenridge and Louisa Reaves.

They had five sons and five daughters born at Piedmont, Ala.:

236. Talbot Jessie, b 6 Oct 1907. He and his father owned and resided on the tract of land which David Turner Ledbetter acquired about 1853. Talbot m 19 Dec 1931 Cora Bell Bonds, dau William Canada Bonds and Willie Head and they have a son Kerry Knox b 8 Oct 1937.

237. Julius Oneal, b 1 Feb 1909, d 29 Nov 1924.

238. Lola Lee, b 22 Jan 1911, m 13 Apr 1933 George Leo McGathey, son of Worth McGathey and Violet Houston. Lola Lee has five children: Beatrice Jeanette, b 18 May 1934; Eva Jocelyn, b 18 July 1936; Judith Ann, b 31 May 1940; Kirby Jean, b 20 June 1942; and Larry O'Neal, b 19 June 1946.

239. Thomas Alvin, b 28 Apr 1913, m 26 May 1937 Leola Mangum, dau of Richard Mangum and wife, Mattie Alvin, has Kenneth Allen, b 8 Aug 1938; Joyce Gail, b 29 June 1942; Carroll Jean, b 6 June 1946.

240. Dovie Luvenia, b 13 Jan 1915, m

241. Eva Pauline, b 5 Apr 1917, m 26 Sept 1941 Thomas Walden, son Cicero Carson Walden and Mary Helms. Eva has Bobby Dennis, b 30 Aug 1942 and Janice Sue, b 9 Nov 1944.

242. Leamon Earl, b 30 Dec 1919, m 1946 and has a child born in Dallas, Texas. Served World War II in Iceland 1942-1944; in Philippines and Japan in 1945.

243. Ivy Lydell, b 11 Apr 1921, m 25 Aug 1945 Edna Mildred Livingston, dau Pat Livingston and Maud Fry.

244. Edda Margaret, b 1 July 1923, m 1 May 1945 Ollie Rogers, Jr., son of Ollie Rogers and Tacolla Moore.

245. Kirby Columbus, b 10 Mar 1925; was in World War II and died unmarried soon after returning from the Pacific area.

(128) Luther Gaston, son (59) Cephas Andrew, m 11 Nov 1922 Winiford Savanah Anderson, dau John Logan Anderson and Francis Almitie Watkins. Luther had one child, Francis Almitie, b 25 Feb 1924, m 21 Apr 1942 James Robert Brown, son of John Alexander Brown and Allie Launna Head. Francis Brown had Mary Ellen, b 2 Apr 1944 and James Robert, Jr, b 14 June 1945.

(130) Turner Hill, youngest son of (59) Cephas Andrew, m Annie Holder, dau of Dock Holder and Mollie Owens. Turner had two sons and three daughters, all living in Birmingham, Ala:

246. Emmett Edward, b 18 Aug 1906.

247. Velma Louise, b 19 Sept 1909, m 19 Apr 1932, James Austin Funderburg.

248. Nellie Mae, b 15 Oct 1910, m 13 Jan 1927 William Clyde Dorr, son of L. L. Dorr and Beula Adair. Nellie Dorr had Betty Louise b 18 Oct 1929 and Clyde Franklin, b 30 June 1935.

249. Ray Lee, b 10 Dec 1913. Ray is a contractor of heavy machinery at Birmingham, Ala.

250. Violet Kathleen, b 10 Sept 1917, m 15 July 1935 Robert Walter Cockrell and has three sons and a daughter: Robert Turner, b 16 July 1937; Nancy Grace, b 27 Aug 1939; Walter Ray, b 12 Feb 1941; and James Edward, b 22 Oct 1942.

(137) Malcolm Young, son of (60) David Carlisle, m 1916 Eula Harmon, dau John William Harmon and Lela Smith. Their children are:

251. Otis William, b 14 Oct 1917. Resides Anniston, Ala.

252. David Jessie, b 13 Oct 1919. Served in Army July 1941 to 16 Sept 1945 and was in Europe.

253. Dorothy Cordia, b 16 Feb 1922, m Jan 1939 D. R. Cook. Resides Piedmont, Ala.

254. John Pelhorn, b 11 Feb 1925. Resides Piedmont, Ala.

255. Jewel Matilda Elizabeth, b 20 Sept 1927, m 15 Dec 1945 William Lipscomb. Resides Piedmont, Ala.

256. James Ruben, b 29 June 1933.

(140) Theodocia Inez, dau (61) Julius Lafayette, m 8 June 1899 Ferris, Texas, John Robert Conn, b 24 Dec 1864 in Tenn just north of Corinth, Miss, d 6 Oct 1952, Ferris, Texas, son of Samuel Conn (Coln) and Emily Brookshire Berry b 1816 d 31 Dec 1915. All children born near Ferris, Texas.

257. Bessie Emeline, b 14 May 1900, unmarried.

258. Sammie, b 3 May 1901.

259. John Robert Conn, b 27 Jan 1905, m Adele Thompson. No children. John died 1959 at Dallas, Texas.

260. Mary Hazel (Dollie), b 19 Nov 1906.

261. Ana Belle, b 11 Dec 1909.

262. Davis Duff, b 10 Oct 1911, d 19 Mar 1912.

263. Ford Babb, b 4 Jan 1913. Served in U. S. Engineers as Mess Sgt. 1940 to 1946 and was in N. Africa, France and Germany.

264. Mattie Docia, b 2 June 1914.

265. Edna Doan, b 26 Dec 1916, d 25 Jan 1927.

266. Cal Joe Conn, b 20 Oct 1920, d Sept 1962, Ferris, Texas.

267. George Amond, b 7 June 1922. Served in Merchant Marine and later became a Baptist preacher.

(141) Elector Esterham, son (61) Julius Lafayette, m 2 Jan 1908, Ferris, Texas, Eugenia, b 10 Dec 1879 Blue Springs, Union County, Miss, within a few miles of the place where her husband was born, dau Aaron David Bryant and Callie Kennedy. They had nine children:

268. Leeman Buren, b 14 Nov 1908 one mile east of Ferris, Texas. Resides Carrollton, Texas.

269. Letha Bernice (twin), b 14 Nov 1908.

270. Arnold David, b 18 Feb 1911 three miles east of Ferris, Resides Lewisville, Texas.

271. Leola Gladys, b 1 July 1913, Ferris.

272. Morris Lee, b 12 Jan 1916 four miles west of Carrollton, Dallas Co, Texas. All remaining children born at same place. Resides Lewisville, Denton Co, Texas.

273. Marjotie (twin), b 12 Jan 1916.

274. Mazie Kathryn, b 17 May 1920.

275. Julia Mae, b 24 Feb 1922.

276. Henry Alton, b 25 May 1924. He served as Sgt in Infantry and military police while in Honolulu and is Capt. in Dallas Fire Department.

(145) Mary Euphema, dau (61) Julius Lafayette, m Roy Washington Norwood, b 29 May 1888 d about 1950, son of George Norwood and Addie Reeves. Mary Norwood had two sons both born about two miles east of Wilmer, Dallas Co, Texas. Mary Norwood resides at Wilmer, Texas.

277. Roy David Norwood, b 13 July 1912, d 8 May 1963, Longview, Texas.

278. Troy Luther Norwood, b 18 Oct 1915. Resides Seagoville, Texas.

(147) Roy Clifford, son (61) Julius Lafayette, m 5 June 1918 Houston, Texas, Marguerite Tomlinson, b 30 June 1899 Willis, Montgomery Co, Texas, died 7 Nov 1959, dau John Wesley

Tomlinson and Ellen Georgette Collard. Roy and Marguerite had three daughters:

279. Georgia Elizabeth, b 15 June 1919 at Seton Infirmary, Austin, Texas, m 21 Mar 1948, Dallas, Preston Roy Phillips. Reside Dallas, Texas. No children.

280. Anice Myrl, b 24 Nov 1920 at Seton Infirmary, Austin, Texas.

281. Nancy Ellen, b 16 Feb 1937 Methodist Hospital, Dallas, Texas, m 27 June 1959 to John Madison Kindle, Jr, son of John Madison Kindle Sr. Resides 6515 Desco Drive, Dallas, Texas.

(148) Easter May, son (61) Julius Lafayette, m 12 Sept 1926 Rucker, Texas, Christelle Allgood, b 1 Mar 1902, dau William Sanford Allgood and Mary Ida Stevenson. They had a son and a daughter:

282. Sanford Truett, b 28 May 1929, El Paso, Texas, killed by overturning his roadster, 30 Oct 1953.

283. Emily Marlene, b 3 June 1939, Methodist Hospital, Dallas, Texas, m 3 June 1960 to Regis Farris Rhea, son of Farris W. Rhea.

(149) Joe Wesley, youngest son (61) Julius Lafayette, m 21 Oct 1917, Stephenville, Erath Co, Texas, Ida McDowell, b 1 Aug 1900 dau J. Wiley McDowell and Rosie Keeney. They have a son and a daughter, each born near Stephenville:

284. Robert Lee, b 17 Nov 1921. He served as cook in the Army during World War II. Resides Stephenville, Texas, Route 4.

285. Joyce Erline, b 3 July 1940.

(150) Charles Absolom, son (63) Franklin Perry, m 1st Josie Stevens, dau of John L. and Mary. Children by first marriage:

286. Cecil, b 12 Apr 1910 resides Gadsden, Ala.

287. Ethel, b 1912.

288. Clara May, b 1914.

Charles Asolom m 2nd Georgia Daugherty by whom he had:

289. Guy, b 1919.

290. Carlos, b 1920.

291. Jesse Lee, b 1921.

292. Dal, b 1923.

293. Cal (twin), b 1923.

294. Pauline, b 1926.

(154) Julia Bell Robinson, dau of (63) Franklin Perry had:
295. Hazel, b Mar 1926.
296. Grace, b 2 July 1927.
297. Ruby, b 29 July 1929.
298. Curtis, b about 1931.
299. Roy Hugh, b 28 Jan 1936.
300. Betty Sue.

(155) Walter Benson, son (63) Franklin Perry, m Estelle
Smith, dau Jess Smith and Theodora Knowles. All their children
were born near Bowden, Ga:
301. Howard, b Dec 1924. Served in World War II.
302. Buren, b 6 May 1926. Served in World War II.
303. James Roy, b 28 Jan 1937.

(156) Franklin, son (63) Franklin Perry, m 21 July 1935
Carrie Elizabeth Robison, dau Rufus Robison and Roxy Elizabeth
Key. They have one child:
304. Franklin Rufus, b 1936.

(157) Jesse Carl, youngest son of (63) Franklin Perry, m
Jewel Beck 6 Dec 1914, dau Lewis Beck and Lydia White. Their
children were all born near Bowden, Ga;
305. Vernell, b 11 Apr 1933.
306. J. L., b 24 Oct 1934.
307. Johnny Lewis, b 14 Aug 1936.
308. Hoyt, b 28 Sept 1938.
309. Henry Thomas, b 19 June 1941.
310. Mary Grace, b 25 June 1943.
311. F. Videra, b 7 May 1945.

(158) Carry Lee Abercrombie, dau (63) Franklin Perry had
two sons:
313. Roy Frank, b about 1936.
314. Jerry Glen.

(161) George Franklin, son of (67) George Richardson, m
22 Feb 1923, Ga, Dixie Taylor b 14 Aug 1904 Habersham Co, Ga.
George and Dixie had two sons:
315. George Franklin, Jr, b 14 Mar 1924, m 23 Jan 1953
Mary Elizabeth Smith, b 9 Nov 1920 Carrollton, Carroll Co, Ga,
and they had one son Gregory Franklin, b 15 Mar 1955 at Carrollton, Ga.

316. Aubrey Charles, b 11 Nov 1926 Hollywood, Ga, m Nov 1950 Barbara Jean Bowden, b 27 Oct 1931, Vienna, Ga. They reside Rome, Ga. and have two children: Charles March, b 7 Oct 1952 Albany, Ga, and Sally Ann, b 25 May 1957, Rome, Ga.

(162) David Turner, son (67) George Richardson, m 28 Oct 1920 Lillian Ossie Brown, Carnesville Ga. and had two sons:

317. Dr. Richard Brown Ledbetter, b 11 July 1925. He is at Veterans Hospital, Thomasville, Ga. He m 27 June 1948 at Gainesville, Ga, Mary Ann Moore, b 15 Aug 1927 and they have two children: Richard Brown, Jr, b 19 Aug 1951 and Deborah Ann, b 13 Mar 1953.

318. Dr. Allison Ledbetter, b 11 Nov 1926 Tallulah Falls, Ga. and practices at Dahlonega, Ga. He m 13 Aug 1950 Habersham City, Ga, Dorris Oneil Hill, b 4 July 1933 and they have two sons: Robert Allison, Jr., b 14 July 1952 and David Jay, b 15 June 1954.

(163) Henry Baxter, son (67) George Richardson, m Cora Iola Brady b 18 Feb 1902 and had two daughters:

319. Lucy Ruth, b 19 July 1928, m 22 Dec 1947 Guy Howell Simmons and they live at Smyrna, Ga.

320. Betty Jean, b 12 Jan 1931, m 31 Aug 1950 Rev. David Herbert Long and they reside at East Tallassee, Ala.

(164) Wallace Smith, youngest son of (67) George Richardson, m 23 July 1929 Fraser Livingston, b 23 June 1905 Bookman Brunswick, Glynn Co, Ga. and they had one son:

321. Wallace Smith Ledbetter, Jr b 30 Aug 1930 at Way-Cross, Ga and resides Orange Grove Plantation, St. Simons Island, Ga. He m 20 Sept 1952 June Hemenway Fendig, b 17 Mar 1930, Brunswick, Ga and they have two children: Wallace Smith Ledbetter III, b 11 Nov 1953 and Susan Jane, b 17 Aug 1956.

(171) James Ozro, son (72) James Madison, m 17 Nov 1900 Ida Virginia Pickens, b 29 Nov 1877, dau W. D. Pickens and wife Mary Ann of Lewisburg, Tenn. They had two children:

322. Margaret Kareen, b 16 May 1903.

323. James Ozro, Jr, b 15 June 1906.

(172) Walter Mercer, son (72) James Madison, m 9 Oct 1901 at Forney, Texas, Mildred F. Gaither and had the following children:

324. Harry M., b 23 Oct 1919.

325. J. David, b 6 June 1921.
326. James W, b 5 Jan 1925.
327. Lloyd S, b 22 Mar 1927.
328. Mary N, b 3 Apr 1929.

(173) Myrt Coleman, son (72) James Madison, m 15 Oct 1903 Victor Partin and had four children:
329. Marion Coleman, b 31 Aug 1904.
330. Margarette Victoria, b 8 Dec 1913.
331. Catherine Lucy, b 26 Oct 1916.
332. James Fred, b 17 June 1920.

(181) Rev. Virgil Kennedy, m 31 Mar 1925 at Fullerton, Calif, Merle Simon, b 23 Dec 1905, dau Michael and Jessie B. Simon. Rev. Virgil has:
333. Virgil Dean, b 2 Apr 1927.
334. John Edward, b 19 Sept 1928.
335. James Robert, b 14 July 1931.

(184) Louis Randolph, son of (80) Daniel Alexander, m 1 June 1917 Laura Horton, dau of E. R. Horton and Laura McDavid. Louis has one daughter.
336. Julia Elizabeth, b 20 Dec 1922.

VIII. EIGHTH GENERATION—*Great Great Great Great Great Grandchildren of Reverend Henry*

(223) Tim Wheeler, son (124) Andrew Harrison, m Aug 1919 Fanny Collins of Piedmont, Ala, and they had seven children:
337. Harris Lee, b 8 Aug 1923, d 1 Aug 1945.
338. Ruth, b Sept. 1925.
339. ———, b 7 Mar 1927.
340. Ola, b Jan 1929.
341. Milton, b Apr 1931.
342. Leon, b Mar 1933.
343. Merl, b June 1936.

(246) Emmett Edward, son (130) Turner Hill, m Arline Favors, dau of Will Henry Favors and Allie Bradshaw and had three children:
344. Allie Ann, b 20 Sept 1929.
345. Dorothy Joyce, b 16 Mar 1932.
346. Emmett Edward, Jr, b 1 Mar 1945.

(249) Ray Lee, son (130) Turner Hill, m 13 Oct 1934 Claudine Walker, dau of Menter Gordon Walker and Sallie Johnson. Ray and Claudine had four children:

347. Gail Elaine, b 2 July 1937.
348. Ray Lee, Jr, b 2 Oct 1939.
349. Roy Wayne, b 6 Nov 1941.
350. Carry Allen, b 15 Dec 1946.

(258) Sammie, dau (140) Docia Ledbetter Conn, m Clarence David Dickerson, son of Will Alexander Dickerson and Ruth Connor. Sammie and Clarence Dickerson had:

351. Jewel, b 25 Jan 1925.
352. Billy Bob, b 11 June 1923, d 22 Sept 1961.
353. Betty Joe, b 16 Nov 1927.
354. David Cenell, b 13 Apr 1930.
355. Docia Ruth, b 8 Aug 1933.
356. Roy Clifford, b 4 Sept 1936.

(260) Mary Hazel, dau (140) Docia Ledbetter Conn, m Milburn Lusk, son of John William Lusk and Addie Massie. Hazel Lusk had:

357. John Samuel.
358. Mary Louise.
359. Evelyn Jane, b 20 Dec 1938.

(261) Ana Belle, dau (140) Docia Ledbetter Conn, m 19 Nov 1929 James Boone Hardin, son of Tilden Hendrix Hardin and Lillian McQueen. Ana Belle Hardin has five living daughters.

360. Clara Ann, b 16 June 1931.
361. Lillian Inez, b 2 Dec 1932.
362. Dorothy Sue, b 21 Feb 1943.
363. Elizabeth Sharon, b 4 Sept 1945.
364. Jimmie Nell, b 13 May 1949.

(263) Ford Babb, son (140) Docia Ledbetter Conn, m 12 July 1947 Frieda Joyce Green, dau William Ellis Green and Ella Bell Dodson of Rockwell, Co, Texas and has three daughters:

375. Guylyne, b 18 Aug 1949.
376. Johanna Adell, b 13 Dec 1951.
377. Bobbie Joyce, b 4 Apr 1957.

(264) Mattie Docia, dau Docia Ledbetter Conn, m 14 Nov

1942 Morris Shepard Hawkins, son of Henry Mark Hawkins and Beulah Jones of Fannin Co, Texas. Mattie and Morris have one daughter:

378. Morris Anne, b 15 Sept 1945.

(266) Cal Joe, son (140) Docia Ledbetter Conn, m 7 Aug 1940 Maxine Whitley, dau Cecil Martin Whitley and Maggie Lou Holbert, and had seven children: (Cal Joe Conn died Sept 1962.)

379. Bobby Joe, b 2 Mar 1941.
380. Billy Mack, b 24 Oct 1942.
381. Barbara Adell, b 29 May 1944.
382. Betty Lou, b 30 June 1947.
383. Benny Jack, b 27 Aug 1950.
384. Brenda Beth, b 25 Sept 1952.
385. Boyd Michael, b 17 July 1954.

(267) Rev. George Amond, youngest child of (140) Docia Ledbetter Conn, m 3 June 1941 Beatrice Hooper, dau Addie Lee Hooper, and has two sons:

386. George Olin, b 9 Apr 1942.
387. John Lloyd, b 13 Feb 1951.

(268) Leeman Buren, son of (141) Elector Esterham, m 22 Sept 1934, Willie Pearl Alton, dau Marion Hampton Alton and Ola Gertrude Swindle and have a son and a daughter:

365. Marian Joyce, b 6 July 1937, (Twin Mary Janice died three days after birth).
366. John Wesley, b 5 Dec 1940.

(269) Letha Bernice, dau (141) Elector Esterham, m 30 Nov 1933 Henry Graham, son of James Albert Graham and Cora Ella Atteberry and has:

388. Helen Anita, b 28 Dec 1941.
389. Stephen Henry, b 11 Nov 1946.
390. Doris Joan, b 13 Mar 1949.

(270) Arnold David, son (141) Elector Esterham, m 24 Dec 1929 Ruby Lenora Alton (sister of Pearl Alton who married Buren Ledbetter). Resides Lewisville, Texas, and has two daughters:

391. Betty Jean, b 5 Nov 1934.
392. Letha Jane, b 11 Aug 1943.

(271) Leola Gladys, dau (141) Elector Esterham, m Russell

Lyle Wrigley 21 Sept 1934. Reside Cameron, La, and has one daughter:

    393. Lora Louise, b 8 Jan 1937.

(272) Morris Lee, son (141) Elector Esterham, m 12 Oct 1935 Gertrude Johanna Duwe, dau of Otto Paul Duwe and Martha Anna Elizabeth Dollenger, both b near Berlin, Germany and she migrated to Texas at four years of age with her parents. Morris Lee lives at Lewisville, Texas, and has five children:

    367. Martha Jean, b 6 Dec 1936.
    368. David Paul, b 9 Feb 1941.
    369. Linda Jo, b 28 Mar 1943.
    370. James Howard, b 24 Jan 1948.
    371. William Henry, b 2 Oct 1951.

(273) Marjorie, dau (141) Elector Esterham, m 1st George Lowry. Divorced in 1941 and married 2nd 2 May 1951 Harold Monroe Yelton, son of Edwin Forest Yelton and Mayme Gosney of Ft. Thomas, Ky. One daughter by first marriage:

    394. Barbara Anne Lowry, b 25 Nov 1936.

(274) Mazie Kathryn, dau (141) Elector Esterham, m 3 Sept 1938 Edgar Elbert Albright, son John Willie Albright and Clara Belle Powell and has three daughters:

    395. Margaret Arlene, b 21 Aug 1939.
    396. Virginia Kathryn, b 5 Dec 1940.
    397. Alice Annette, b 3 June 1944.

(275) Julia Mae, youngest dau (141) Elector Esterham, m 29 July1944 Herbert Dightman Coburn, Jr, son of Herbert Dightman Coburn and Miriam Ware of New York. Reside Dallas, Texas and have two sons:

    398. Herbert Bryant, b 14 Nov 1950, Jacksonville, Texas.
    399. Randall Nye, b 30 Jan 1957, Dallas.

(276) Henry Alton, youngest son of (141) Elector Esterham, m 13 Dec 1947 Virginia Katherine Smith, dau William Nathan Smith and Myrtle Carlton. Henry has three daughters and one son:

    400. Carolyn Diane, b 28 Oct 1948.
    401. Jan Alane, b 21 July 1952.
    402. Amy Laura, b 29 Mar 1957.
    403. Mark Nathan, b 11 Sept 1958.

(277) Roy David Norwood, son (145) Mary Ledbetter, m 9 Nov 1935 Elinor Mae Nokes, dau Robert Franklin Nokes and Lenna Mae Farmer and has:
404. Robert David, b 10 Dec 1936.
405. Charles Edward, b 1 May 1939.
406. Kenneth Roy, b 31 May 1947.

(278) Troy Luther Norwood, son (145) Mary Ledbetter, m 12 Jan 1938 Eula Mae Ranton, dau Grover Ranton and Lonnie Jones and has three children:
407. Garey Luther, b 27 Nov 1941.
408. Marilyn, b 30 Mar 1944.
409. Linda Kay, b 20 Oct 1947.

(280) Anice Myrl, dau (147) Roy Clifford Ledbetter, m 25 Dec 1941 Edwin Hartzel Styron, b 10 Mar 1914, son of Charles Styron and Mary Pedelta Hale. Resides Stamford, Conn, and has four daughters:
410. Lucina Kay, b 22 Sept 1942 Alexandria, Va.
411. Hazel Ann, b 8 July 1946 at Florence Nightingale Hospital, Dallas, Texas.
412. Mary Anice, b 18 June 1949.
413. Jane Francis, b 19 May 1951.

(284) Robert Lee, son (149) Joe Wesley Ledbetter, m 15 May 1942 Agnes Lucille Pack, dau Thomas James Pack and Mary Elizabeth Watson of Erath Co, Texas, and has three sons:
372. Don Wesley, b 10 Sept 1945, San Francisco, Calif.
373. Charles Edward, b 17 Oct 1947.
374. Larry Wayne, b 13 Jan 1951.

(285) Joyce Erline, dau (149) Joe Wesley Ledbetter, m Jan 1958 George Austin Cooke b 1 Jan 1939, son of James Randolphe Cooke and Mildred Marie Mason of Erath Co, Texas. Reside Stephenville, Texas, Route 4, and have son:
458. Rickey Wayne, b 23 Aug 1959.

IX NINTH GENERATION — *Great Great Great Great Great Great Grandchildren of Reverend Henry.*

(351) Jewel, dau (258) Sammie Conn Dickerson m 1st 16 Sept 1941 Billy Lavage Lanford, son of William James Lanford

and Mattie Pearl Featherstone. Married 2nd Kenneth Reynolds. Following children by first marriage:

414. Billy Leon Lanford, b 26 Apr 1946.

415. Lance Darrell, b 13 Oct 1950.

416. Cecil Dennis b 23 June 1954.

(352) Billy Bob, son (258) Sammie Conn Dickerson, m 15 Oct 1946 Margie Frances Whitley, dau Cecil Martin Whitley and Maggie Lou Holbert. Billy Bob had four sons: (Billy Bob died 22 Sept 1961.)

417. James David, b 25 May 1947.

418. Bruce, b 10 Dec 1949.

419. Donald Ray, b 11 Dec 1952.

420. Steven Dane, b 24 Sept 1954.

(353) Betty Joe, dau (258) Sammie Conn Dickerson, m Sept 1946 Billy Jean Pyle and has:

421. Larry.

422. Terry.

423. Sheralyn.

424. Belinda Grace.

(354) David Cenell, son (258) Sammie Conn Dickerson, m Oct 1959.

(355) Docia Ruth, dau (258) Sammie Conn Dickerson, m Herbert Moore and has:

425. Lonnie.

426. Rhonda (twin Ronnie died at birth)

(356) Roy Clifford, son (258) Sammie Conn Dickerson, m 20 May 1955 to Helen Toy McCothan and has:

427. Debbie Faye.

428. Peggy Ellen.

429. Jewell Jeanette.

(357) John Samuel, son of (260) Mary Hazel Conn Lusk, m Connie Marie Pledger, dau James H. Pledger and has:

430. John Samuel Lusk, Jr, b 13 Jan 1950.

431. David Wayne Lusk, b 2 Feb 1953.

(358) Mary Louise, dau (260) Mary Hazel Conn Lusk, m Francis Lavoy Oats and has:

432. Ellen Bess, b 11 Mar 1946.

433. Debbie Elaine, b 20 Nov 1952.

(359) Evelyn Jane, dau (260) Mary Hazel Conn Lusk, m 1st Williams and has son: Evelyn Jane m 2nd Jerry Byrum.

434. Rickey Conn Williams, b 23 Jan 1958.

(360) Clara Ann, dau (261) Ana Belle Conn Hardin, m 24 Oct 1947 Herman L. Day, son Lester D. Day and Ora Ann Hutcherson, and has:

435. Linda Gail, b 15 Aug 1948.
436. Larry Thomas, b 12 June 1952.
437. Robert Hendrix, b 13 July 1954.
438. Peter John, b 14 Nov 1955.
439. Elizabeth Ellen, b 26 Nov 1959.

(361) Lillian Inez, dau (261) Ana Belle Conn Hardin, m Mar 1949 Bill Lawson. Reside Houston, Texas, and has:

440. Mary Jane Lawson, b 4 Nov 1949.
441. James Barton, b 26 Dec.
442. William David, b 23 Nov.
443. Lawrence Daniel, b 28 June 1957.

(362) Dorothy Sue, dau (261) Ana Belle Conn Hardin, m 8 June 1962 David Emmett Edwards, son of Emmett Edwards of Waco, Texas.

(380) Billy Mack Conn, son (266) Cal Joe, m 14 Aug 1961 Jean Wright, dau A. V. Wright and Balfa, and lives at Ben Wheeler, Texas.

(365) Marian Joyce, dau (268) Leeman Buren Ledbetter, m 6 June 1961 Lloyd Ashley Webb, son James Ashley Webb and Edith Brananhan, of Carrollton, Texas, and has:

459. Cynthia Ann, b 1 Dec 1962.

(366) John Wesley, son (268) Leeman Buren Ledbetter, m 2 Sept 1961 Marguerite Mary Dusak, dau of Joe Dusak, Carrollton, Texas, and has:

444. Kamie Denise, b 10 Mar 1962.

(388) Helen Anita, dau (269) Letha Bernice Ledbetter Graham, m 31 Jan 1960 James Dale Crader, son of Harold Wayne Crader and Artie Inez Wright, and has:

445. James Wayne, b 22 Feb 1961.
446. Lisa Cavell, b 13 Oct 1962.

(391) Betty Jean, dau (270) Arnold David Ledbetter, m 9 June 1959 Floyd Ray Robertson, son of Floyd Ray Robertson and Bertha Mae Taylor and has:

447. Kimberley Jean, b 28 Jan 1962.

(392) Letha Jane, dau (270) Arnold David Ledbetter, m 30 May 1959 David George Groves, son of J. S. Groves and Eva May Gunner, and has:

448. John Charles, b 24 Dec 1960.

(393) Lora Louise, dau (271) Leola Gladys Ledbetter Wrigley, m 30 Mar 1956 Edwin Garey Abrahams, son Henry A. Abrahams of Lake Charles, La, and has:

449. David Glenn, b 20 Oct 1957, in Lake Charles, La.

450. Steven Garey, b 8 Feb 1960, in Fairbanks, Alaska while his father was a Capt. in the U. S. Army.

(367) Martha Jean, dau of (272) Morris Lee Ledbetter, m 28 June 1955 Carl Ray Dungan, son of Byron L. Dungan and Daisy Guolden of Denton Co, Texas and has:

451. Dennis Dawyne, b 28 Feb 1956.

452. Carl Ray, Jr, b 7 June 1959.

453. Byron Lee, b 5 Nov 1960.

(369) Linda Jo, dau (272) Morris Lee Ledbetter, m 9 June 1962 William Foster Walker, with Denton, Texas, Police Department.

(394) Barbara Anne Lowry, dau (273) Marjorie Ledbetter Yelton, m 31 Aug 1957 Carl Edward Hand, son Clarence Crell Hand and Mary Katherine White, and has:

454. Celia Elaine Hand, b 28 Sept 1958.

455. Lisa Caroline, b 26 Aug 1961.

(395) Margaret Arlene, dau (274) Mazie Kathryn Ledbetter Albright, m 30 Aug 1958 Tommy Wayne Stockard, son of Frank Stockard, and has:

456. Philip Wayne, b 1 Sept 1959.

457. James Lynn, b 30 May 1962.

(396) Virginia Kathryn, dau (274) Mazie Kathryn Ledbetter Albright, m 28 July 1962 James Sherwood Polser, son Aubrey H. Polser, Lewisville, Texas.

ADDITIONAL DESCENDENTS OF JOEL LEDBETTER,SR. IN MADISON COUNTY, ALABAMA

By Roy C. Ledbetter, 3516 University, Dallas, Texas, and Kathleen Paul Jones, New Market, Alabama

The account of the descendents of Reverend Henry Ledbetter (Calvinist) when first written in 1947 traced his descendents so far as known at the time. The original account as revised traces Daniel and Joel, Senior, sons of Reverend Henry. Of the children of Joel Senior, only John, the oldest son who remained in Anderson County, South Carolina, was traced. Additional information since discovered calls for the writing of this supplement on the sons of Joel, Senior who migrated with him to Madison County, Alabama.

The local records have been searched by Kathleen Paul Jones. In the meantime her daughter has married Dr. John Riley Ledbetter, Junior, one of the descendents. The records from Madison County include deeds, marriages, probate, gravestones, and newspapers. In addition, the U. S. Census for Jackson, Madison and Marshall Counties, Alabama, has been revealing.

Before discussing the various descendents, we should like to set out here the probate sale in Madison County, Mississippi Territory, in 1815 in the estate of Joel, Sr. The purchasers give clues as to the relatives of Joel, Sr., particularly those who likely married his daughters. The items in the estate also are very revealing as to the life, customs, and occupation of the time. We also fancy that several of the items had belonged to Joel's father Henry, who came down from Virginia and preached in North Carolina and South Carolina. The saddle that sold for the then enormous sum of fifty dollars must have been very durable and decorative. We can almost see the old preacher father riding a horse on his curcuit. Horses were among the items shown on the tax lists in Caswell County, North Carolina, as owned by Reverend Henry and his sons Joel and Daniel. The best description that can be deciphered, the items and purchasers at the probate sale are as follows:

"LIST OF SALES OF THE PROPERTY OF JOEL LEDBETTER, DEC'D.,
DATED 1815:

Samuel Clark	1 cow and calf	$13.37½
	1 cow	13.12½
Benjamin Wilson	1 speckled heifer	5.00
	1 brindle steer	5.00
	2 spotted sows	12.00
	8 shoats	16.00
William Baugher	2 1st choice hogs	20.25
John Killingsworth	2 2nd choice hogs	20.25
	2 6th choice hogs	15.00
Ezekiel Craft	2 3rd choice hogs	19.50
John Stringfield	2 4th choice hogs	17.25
Benjamin Hynds	2 5th choice hogs	15.25
John Connelly	3 7th choice hogs	19.12½
	3 plains	2.37½
John Stringfield	1 shot gun pouch and horn	6.25
Sampson Skelton	1 shovel plow	1.31½
	1 hoe	1.00
James Edge	1 Gopher plow	.75
John Henry	1 broad axe	3.87½
Jackson Patrick	1 chopping axe	2.37½
William Simpson	1 chopping axe	2.25
Isom Hopkins	1 chopping axe	2.50
	1 shot gun	6.12½
Littleberry Vaughn	1 chopping axe	2.62½
	1 iron wedge	1.68¾
James Edge	1 Chopping axe	1.06¾
Ephraim Ledbetter	1 hand axe	.50
	1 cane hoe	.62½
William Simpson	1 mattock	2.12½
Littleberry Vaughn	1 mattock	2.25
	1 fro	1.20
	1 pr shot moles	1.06¼
Jasper Moon	1 handsaw	1.00
John Roark	1 tenon saw	3.25
Daniel Ledbetter	4 Augers & 5 chisels	6.08¼
	1 shoe box and tools	1.37½
	1 bed sted cord & furniture	24.25
	1 Gimblet	.12½
	1 deer skin	1.56¼
John Clock Sr.	1 drawing knife	3.00
Robt. Givens	1 Foot Adz	1.75
Ephraim Ledbetter	1 iron Square	.75
	1 large hammer	.37½
	1 pr stretchers	3.81¼
	1 sett waggon boxes	28.

Joseph Walters	1 p compasses	.25
George Anyan	1 log chain	5.00
Joel Ledbetter	1 hammer	.25
	1 bay mare	25.25
	1 bridle	1.06½
	1 pot & hooks	3.00
	1 pot rack	2.06¼
	1 ladle	.31¼
	1 pr spoon moles	2.56¼
	100 lb seed cotton	4.00
	A parcel of unbroken flax	1.31¼
Jackson Patrick	1 black horse	10.00
Henry Brazleton	1 currying knife	2.12½
	1 hackle	2.00
	1 flax wheel	.87½
Stephen DeBow	1 pr Hilyards	1.50
	1 single tree ironed	.62½
	1 keg	.50
	1 looking glass	2.25
	25 # tobacco	2.06¼
Thomas Riddles	2 pr Bitts & Bridle	.25
Sampson Skelton	2 Clevises	.50
	1 tub	1.12½
	5 barrels corn	10.56¼
	1 Piggin	.31¼
James Hannah Junr	1 saddle	50.00
	1 fire steel	.18¾
	1 bed stead corn & furniture	19.81¾
	100 lb cotton	4.18¾
George Anyan	1 oven lid & hooks	1.81¼
	1 iron hammer & bolt	1.25
William Kent	1 skillet	.62½
	1 hoe	1.50
Ephraim Ledbetter	2 smoothing irons	.50
	1 churn	.81¾
	1 bulk hand tobacco	3.12½
	5 pewter plates	2.56¼
	1 do dish	2.00
	1 calf skin	.62½
	1 pr trucks (?)	.06¼
Francis L. Adams	1 pr tongs	1.50
	4 pewter spoons	.50
	1 Indian basket & 2 combs	.31¼
Joseph Barclay	1 basket old iron	2.68¾
	1 grindstone	1.56¼
	1 pr cards	.31¼
	100 lb cotton	4.00
	1 guttering plain	.31¼

William Vann	1 Jug	2.00
John Hannah	1 bottle and jug	.25
	1 barrel	.75
	1 do	1.50
James Gordon	1 Slay & Harniss	.75
James Edge	1 pr hames	.25
Henry Brazelton	1 pr hame hangings	.43¾
	1 pail	.37½
	1 small trunk	.50
Joel Rice	1 half bushel	1.00
	1 collar	.50
	25 lb Tobacco	2.00
	1 cotton wheel	1.25
Bolen Lacy	2 powdering tubs	1.18¾
	1 churn	.50
Thomas Woodall	1 empty barrel	.50
	1 loom	9.12½
	1 pr cards	.12½
Joseph Loyd	1 piggin	.25
	1 large bason	1.81¼
Jordan Lacy	25 # tobacco	2.18¼
	400 # seed cotton	16.50
	3 sides of leather	8.93¾
Daniel Givens	20 # tobacco	1.81¼
	1 large trunk	1.81¾
	5 barrels corn	10.56¼
Peggy Pickens	1 bread tray & sifter	.37½
	3 tin cups & teapot	.12½
William Baugher	1 pr cards	.25
William Green	1 chair	.56¼
	1 deer skin	.93¾
	1 do do	1.31¼
William Calvert	5 plates	2.18¾
	1 dish	1.87¼
William Kent	1 large bason	3.31¼
	6 iron spoons	.81¼
Bolen Lacy	2 earthen plates	.12½
James Hannah	2 bells	.25
	3 rows peach trees	2.12½
William Wilson	10 barrels corn	20.06¼
Robert Givens	10 barrels corn	20.06½
Ezekiel Craft	10 barrels corn	11.25
Henry Stires Senr.	200 # cotton	10.12½
	1 side leather	3.00
John Childers	100 # cotton	4.06¼
Bolen Lacy	3 small skins	.62½
	266 cabbages	2.25

James G. Holmes	2 deer skins	.56¼
	2 saddle trees	.25
James Gordon	1 deer skin	.81¼
Thomas Riddles	450 bundles fodder	4.12½
Robert Givens	1 row peach trees	.93¾"

The 1800 census of Pendleton District (later Anderson County), S. C., showed Joel, Sr., over 45 years of age, and wife (known as Kitty or Catherine), also over 45 years of age. The census showed in the family six free white males, presumed to be sons, and six free white females, presumed to be daughters, and four slaves. Two sons were listed 16 to 26 years of age, two 10 to 16, and two under 10. As listed below, the sons are positively identified, except there remains a doubt as to Samuel.

John, the oldest son, remained in Anderson County, S. C., and his rescendents have been traced in the original account. So far as possible, the descendants of the remaining sons will be traced in this supplemental account. Possibly some of the older married daughters remained in Anderson County. Only four daughters can be tentatively identified in Madison County.

FIRST GENERATION IN MADISON COUNTY, ALABAMA

1. John b 25 Dec 1774 Orange County (Caswell after 1777), N. C., d 25 Jan 1831 near Providence Church, Townville, near Anderson, Anderson County, S. C., where his family remained when Joel, Sr. and his other sons and daughters migrated to Madison County.

3. Edy b about 1778 in Caswell County, N. C., m 14 Dec 1812 in Madison County, then Mississippi Territory, to John H. Childress, one of the purchasers at probate sale in the estate of Joel, Sr.

4. Lydia b 1780 in Caswell County, N. C., d 22 June 1847 "in 67th year of her age" in Madison County, Ala, m about 1801 in Pendleton District, S. C., Henry Brazelton b 5 April 1777 Frederick Co, Md, d 10 Dec 1851 Madison Co, Ala. Son Jacob Brazelton b 27 June 1749, d after 1826, and wife Hannah (Green) b 8 April 1757 d 11 Oct. 1832. Jacob Brazelton was a revolutionary soldier. Henry Brazelton, about 1810, also "other relatives by the name of Woodal, Skelton, Grayson, Pickens, and Scales, all located

in Madison County, Ala,", according to letter written by Allison Ledbetter to Col. William Logan Martin 17 Oct 1914.

Henry Brazelton and Lydia had two sons, Silas M. and Jason Madison, and five daughters, who have many descendants living in the area of Madison County, Ala. The oldest daughter Selina Brown Brazelton b 30 May 1804 in S. C., d Nov 1892, perhaps in Ladonia, Fannin Co, Texas, where her son Joseph W. Pickens had moved. Selina Brazelton m 31 Dec 1818 in Madison Co, Mississippi Territory Joseph Pickens b 31 Aug 1794 in Pendleton District, S. C., d 1870 Madison Co, Ala. He was the only son of Andrew Pickens and wife Margaret (Dowdle) Middleton. Andrew was a son of Captain Pickens and his wife Elenor Pickens, a cousin. The Captain, who was killed at Fort Ninety-Six, was a brother of General Andrew Pickens.

5. Joel, Jr. b about 1777 Caswell Co, N. C. d 1820 Madison Co, Ala. In 1816 Joel is on tax list Madison Co, Mississippi. See War 1812.

6. Ephrame b 1784 Caswell Co, N. C. d 4 July 1841 Pope Co, Ark. See War 1812.

7. Samuel B. b about 1790 in Caswell Co, N.C., d after 1861 probably in Jackson Co, Ala. He was listed in the censuses of Madison Co, Ala. for 1830 and 1840 but not in any other census for Jackson, Marshall, or Madison Counties. On 31 March 1823 he witnessed a deed from Daniel and Ephraim Ledbetter to Sampson Skelton who married Nancy, the widow of Joel, Jr. From this deed, from his being in the same locality, and from his sons Samuel B. and Silas M. having shown in the census of 1880 of Madison Co, Ala, that their father was born in North Carolina, we conclude Samuel, Sr, was an older son of Joel, Sr, so shown by age group in the census of 1800 for Pendleton District, S. C.

8. Daniel b 1792 in Georgia, d 15 March 1856 Madison Co, Ala. See War 1812. The deed of 1814 from Joel Sr. to his four sons definitely proves Daniel was a son. Daniel appeared in the 1840 and 1850 censuses of Madison Co, Ala, where he and all of his children are well identified. Most of his descendants are now traced.

9. Mary b about 1794, m Joseph Barclay (Barkley).

10. Abby b about 1796, m 5 April 1823 John Lyons of Madison Co, Ala.

11. Buford (Burfet) b 1798 Pendleton District S. C., d after 1850 in Madison Co, Ala, m 7 Dec 1819 Ann Pickens in Madison Co, Ala. On 12 Dec 1825 in Madison Co, Ala, he and his wife Ann executed a deed to Absolom Cornelius. They must have left Madison County because he does not appear in a census until 1850. He then appears as part of the family of Pascal E, son of his brother Daniel. We conclude his wife Ann had died and that they had no children.

SECOND GENERATION IN MADISON COUNTY, ALABAMA

(5) Joel, Jr, m about 1801 to Nancy b about 1785, d after 1840, perhaps while living with her son Absalom (Abarham). After death of Joel, Jr in 1820 his widow Nancy m 5 April 1824 in Madison Co, Ala, to Sampson Skelton, who d 1826 in Madison Co, Ala, and his estate was administered and different guardians were appointed for their minor children. From this file and the Censuses we conclude Joel, Jr and Nancy had at least two and possibly four sons, as follows:

12. Asa b about 1805, d after 1840, and more probably removed from Madison Co, m about 1827 but no record of the marriage. The 1830 census of Madison Co, Ala, shows the family consisting of two males 10 to 15 years of age (probably younger brothers), one male 20 to 30 being himself, two females under 5, and a female 20 to 30, being his wife and daughters, and a female 40 to 50, probably his mother Nancy. The 1840 census of Madison County shows Asa with wife and two sons and four daughters all under 10 years of age. There is no further record of the family.

13. Absalom (Abarham) b about 1808 in Georgia, d after 1850, perhaps in Hopkins County, Texas. The 1830 census of Madison Co, Ala, showed two sons under 5. In 1839 the family moved to Arkansas, County unknown, and perhaps in 1848 to Hopkins Co, Texas, where he and wife and six children, which did not include the two older sons who probably remained in Arkansas.

14. David b perhaps 1816, d after 1840. The 1840 census of Madison Co, Ala, shows David with Asa and Shelman living

near each other and near Samuel, Daniel, and Ephrame, whom we have listed as sons of Joel, Sr. David had a wife who, with himself, was in the 20 to 30 age group, and two sons under 5. We have no further record of David.

15. Shelman b April 1818, d after 1855, perhaps in Franklin Co, Ala, m Margaret Hughes in Madison Co, Ala, in 1839. He was in the Cherokee Removal of 1838. Shelman is in the 1840 census of Madison Co, Ala. There were shown two males 20 to 30 years of age, which included himself and possibly a half brother named Skelton, being perhaps the two boys 15 to 20 years of age with Asa in the census of 1830. There was a female 50 to 60 years of age who could be his mother Nancy, who was with Asa in 1830 census. There is no further record.

(6) Ephrame m 24 Jan 1808 in Elbert Co, Georgia Hester Smith b 1790 in South Carolina, d after 1850 in Marshall Co, Ala, had nine sons and three daughters:

16. Gardner Caswell b 25 Oct 1808 in Pendleton District, S. C., d 15 Dec 1892 at Rome, Georgia, (See Cherokee Removal) and was also with Andrew Jackson and in Confederate Army, and was made a prisoner at Ft. Donaldson. He taught school, was a merchant, and farmed. In 1840 and 1850 census of Madison Co, Ala, and 1860 and 1870 census of Marshall Co, Ala. All the remaining children of Ephrame were born in Madison Co, Ala.

17. John Westley b 28 Aug 1810 d 14 Feb 1895 at Anniston, Calhoun Co, Ala.

18. Daniel T. b 1812 d after 1860 in Ark.

19. Archie, killed in young manhood in Limestone Co, Ala, by a man named McKinney, whom his older brother Gardner traced into Arkansas but was unable to apprehend.

20. Joel P. b about 1818 d near Huntsville, Ala, 19 Nov 1870. He and his wife's brother J. J. Dillard were contractors and graded the first railroad built in Northern, Alabama.

21. Soloman Smith b 1825 d about 1899 near Guntersville, Marshall Co, Ala. He was constable in Marshall Co in 1858. In 1870-1 he was tax collector of Marshall Co. He was an officer in Forrest's Cavalry. He and a good portion of Forrest's Command cut their way out rather than surrender at Ft. Donaldson, and later fought at the Battle of Shiloh.

22. James b in Arkansas d in Infancy.

23. Kittie b in Arkansas died young.

24. Nancy Jane b 4 Jan 1827 d 28 July 1853 in Madison Co, Ala, m 23 Jan 1845 David S. Nowlin and had sons Beverly Angelo Nowlin b 27 Jan 1847, living in 1914 near Collinsville, Ala, and Archie Wade Nowlin b 16 July 1858 d June 1909.

25. Kate b about 1829 d about 1912 at Talladega, Ala, m (1st) Dr. W. B. Harrison, Guntersville, Ala, who practiced at Talladega, and had an only son Dr. W. W. Harrison, who also practiced at Talladega. Kate also had two daughters: Nancy Moore Harrison m Charles Riddle of Birmingham, and Minnie m one Hendricks of Talladega and moved to Texas. Kate m (2nd) William R. Stone, merchant of Talladega.

26. Henry Burfett, the youngest son of Ephrame and Hester, b about 1831 in Madison Co, Ala, removed before 1860 to Naples, Texas. He married Miss Roundtree in Jackson Co, Ala, and had an oldest son Gardner, who lives at Naples.

(7) Samuel B. m (1st) about 1819 to Nancy who died before 1836. In the 1830 census of Madison County he and his first wife are shown to have two daughters 5 to 10 years and two under 5, and a son under 5. We do not know the names of any of the children by the first wife. Samuel m (2) 5 Dec 1837 to Mildred M. Buford Bondurant, dau of Henry Buford, and she died 31 Jan 1851 in Madison Co, Ala. The census of 1840 of Madison Co accounts by age for children of the first marriage of Samuel and Mildred, with probably his oldest daughter having already married and ceased to be a part of the family. By 1850 Samuel is not shown in the Madison Co census. But in the meantime Pascal E, son of Daniel, had married Harriet Bondurant, dau of Mildred M. by her first marriage. Harriet's sister Julia A. C. Bondurant and her brother John M. Bondurant, as well as her half brothers Samuel B. and Silas M. Ledbetter, were a part of the family of Pascal. If we are correct about Samuel, Sr being a son of Joel, Sr, then the last two were first cousins of Pascal. Being unable to name the children of Samuel, Sr by his first marriage, we name below his two sons by his second marriage to Mildred:

27. Samuel B. b 1839, d after 1880 in Madison Co, Ala.

28. Silas M. b 1843, d before 1887 in Madison Co, Ala.

(8) Daniel m 18 May 1818 in Madison Co (then Mississippi Territory) to Harriet Buford b 1803 in Virginia d 31 Jan 1851 Madison Co, Ala, dau of Henry Buford. Children of Daniel and Harriet:

29. Pascal E. b 1820, Madison Co, Ala, d before 1870. He served as a private, Co H, 49th, Alabama Inf, C.S.A. and was a carpenter.

30. John (Jack) H. b 1827 Madison Co, Ala, d about 1908 in Marshall Co, to which he moved in 1852.

31. Elizabeth C. b 1829 in Madison Co, Ala, m 28 Dec 1858 in Madison Co to John Selvidge.

32. Albert D. b 1830 in Madison Co, Ala, m 27 Sept 1857 in Madison Co, Ala, to Nancy G. Grayson, dau of William Grayson. No further record.

33. William M. b 1832 in Madison Co, Ala, d after 1880 in Marshall Co, Ala.

34. Rueben Bondurant b 11 Nov 1833, Madison Co, Ala, d 1917 in Marshall Co, Ala. Enlisted at Huntsville, Ala April 1861 in 49th Alabama Inf. Co B, discharged Oct 1861 for illness. On 8 Jan 1862 reenlisted in Co H, 31st Alabama Inf, captured at Port Hudson and paroled.

35. Susan Mildred b 1837 Madison Co, Ala, d 1888 Coahoma Co, Miss, m 12 July 1857 in Madison Co, Ala, William W. Bondurant and had children Laura, Harriet, W. H. Bondurant, who were living in Coahoma Co, Miss in 1891.

36. Daniel L. W. b 1841 in Madison Co, Ala, d after 1880 probably in Marshall Co, Ala. Pvt. Co H, 49th Alabama Infantry.

THIRD GENERATION IN MADISON COUNTY, ALABAMA

(13) Absalom (Abarham) son of Joel, Jr, m 5 June 1827 in Madison Co, Ala, to Mary Ann Lacy, b 1808, dau of Jordan Lacy. In the 1850 census of Hopkins County, Texas, there are listed Absalom and wife Mariann, who are thus shown to be the same as the Madison Co, Ala, people. The census reflects four daughters and three sons of Abaslom and Mary Ann:

37. Jane b 1831 in Alabama.
38. Mariann b 1837 in Alabama.
39. Andrew b 1839 in Alabama.

40. Margaret b 1843 in Arkansas.

41. Shelman P. (evidently named after his father's brother) b 1845 in Ark.

42. Franklin M. b 1849 in Texas.

(16) Gardner Caswell, son of Ephrame, m 1 Jan 1834 in Madison Co, Ala, to Elizabeth Chappell Glover, b 1815 in Ala, d 26 Jan 1889, had four daughters and three sons:

43. Martha Catherine b 6 April 1835, m D. S. Nowlin in 1854, d 1856.

44. Oliver Green d in infancy.

45. Arkansas Ann d in infancy.

46. Allison Woodville b 15 April 1843 in Madison Co, Ala, d 8 March 1929 at Rome, Floyd Co, Georgia. Allison Woodville served as Capt. Co K 9 Alabama Inf. from Marshall Co, Ala. On 17 Oct 1914 while residing at Rome, Ga, he compiled and wrote in a letter to Col W. L. Martin, his cousin who had been elected Attorney General of Alabama, a sketch of eleven pages relative to the migrations and descendants of Ephrame and wife Hester. This sketch aided in tracing the ancestry of Ephrame, his father Joel, Sr and connecting back to North Carolina and Virginia.

47. John R. b 1846 d 1856.

48. Mary Jane b 9 Dec 1849, d 12 May 1899, m 2 Jan 1868 W. M. Elgin, whose descendants were residing in and near Birmingham, Ala, in 1914.

49. Nancy Belle b 1852 made a school teacher and d 1870.

(17) James Westley m (1st) 1830 Martha Ann Glover, b 4 Jan 1813 in Ga, d 15 May 1861, had:

50. Gardner Caswell, Jr, b 14 July 1832, d 5 Jan 1863. He was a Capt. in Co H 49 Alabama Inf from Madison Co, was in siege of Ft. Hudson, where his health was broken and he died.

51. James Logan b 29 March 1834, d 20 June 1906 at Weaver, Ala.

52. R. A. b 6 Aug 1836, d 30 June 1841.

53. G. W. b 30 June 1839, d 13 Dec 1841.

54. Kitty Ann b 19 July 1842, d 3 Aug 1893, m Dr. Robert E. Cochran.

55. John Malone b 29 June 1846, d 22 July 1912. He was

a 1st Lt. in C 26 Alabama Calvary from Calhoun Co, said to be a guerrilla band under command of Rev. Milus B. Johnson known as "Bushwhacker Johnson" operating in northern Ala.

56. William Gordon b 27 Dec 1849 Madison Co, Ala, removed 1877 to Anniston, Calhoun Co, Ala, where he d 27 Dec 1910. He was a banker.

57. Martha Elizabeth (Lizzie) b 12 March 1853, d 4 April 1892, m ——Haden.

(18) Daniel T., son of Ephrame, m (1st) 1835 to Mary B. Glover, making the third brother who married Glover sisters. To this marriage were born three sons and two daughters:

58. John, d in Arkansas before marrying.

59. Dr. Joel C b 9 July 1838, d 5 April 1872 at Bluntsville, Ala. Pvt. K 4 Alabama Cavalry enlisting from Jackson Co, m Miss Newson at Bluntsville and had one daughter.

60. Senia S, youngest son, b Pulaski, Ark. Served as Pvt. 3 Ark Cavalry and d in prison.

61. Elizabeth d in infancy.

62. Nancy Glover b 7 May 1851, m Isaac Henry of Summitt, Ala, and moved to Birmingham, Ala, where he died leaving a large family.

(18) Daniel T. m (2nd) Lizzie Lowe and by her had two sons and a daughter whose names are not in the record.

(20) Joel P., son of Ephrame m in Jackson Co, Ala, Jane C. Dillard and their children were:

63. Frank W. (W.F.) b 1849 Marshall Co, Ala d 1922 Anniston, Calhoun Co, Ala, m Sallie Jones. He left a son Joel F. who resided at Gadsden, Ala, and son Roy and daughters Ethel, Kate, and Helen.

64. James Henry b 1851 in Marshall Co, Ala, living with parents at Paint Rock, Jackson Co, Ala at the 1860 census, m Ida Draper of Anniston, Ala, and d before 1914 leaving four daughters.

65. Fanny b 1860 Jackson Co, Ala, m Mr. Hurt of Jackson Co, Ala, who died before 1914 and the widow and children moved to Talladega, Ala.

66. Tom P., youngest son, m Lou Elgin and lived in Meridian, Miss, and later moved to Birmingham, Ala, where he died.

67. Margaret C. (Maggie), youngest daughter of Joel P. and Jane, m Col. William Logan Martin, Sr. who was elected Attorney General of Alabama and moved to Montgomery. Their oldest son William Logan Martin, Jr. was also elected Attorney General of Alabama in 1914. He was a distinguished lawyer who practiced at Birmingham. He was active in the American Bar Association and was a member of its Board of Governors. He corresponded and collected information on the Ledbetter family until his death in 1958.

(21) Solomon Smith m 1849 Elizabeth Douglas and had a daughter and two sons:

68. Laura J. (Jimmie) b 1850 Marshall Co, Ala, m William C. Grason before 1870 and had at least one son, John.

69. Ephrame A. d 46 years of age unmarried.

70. Edward B. (Ned) b 1854 Marshall Co, Ala, m Miss Walker and they had three sons and four daughters who are not named in the report. In 1914 the family was living at Route No. 1, Grant, Marshall Co, Ala.

(27) Samuel B. m 19 Sept 1874 in Madison Co, Ala, to Rosa Vann.

The 1880 census of Madison Co, Ala, shows two sons:

71. Wm. C. b 1877. No further information.

72. John W. b 1879. No further information.

(28) Silas M. m 7 Jan 1873 Madison Co, Ala, to Sarah C. Maples, d before 1880, dau of Peter Maples, in whose estate in Madison Co, Ala, in 1885 his daughter Sarah was dead, leaving two children with an aunt, while the father was in Pilot Point, Texas. The two children also shown in 1880 census of Madison Co, Ala, are:

73. Sarah Catherine b 1875 in Mississippi.

74. Silas M. b 1877 in Ala.

(29) Paschal E., son of Daniel, m about 1843 in Madison Co, Ala, to his cousin Harriet B. Bondurant b 1825 in Madison Co, d before 1870 in Madison Co, dau of Mildred (Buford) Bondurant, and they had at least seven children, all born in Madison Co, as shown by U. S. Census 1860:

75. Reubin H. b 1844. Likely is the R. H. in Co. H, 49 Ala Inf. Unless he is the R. H. who m 9 Jan 1890 in Madison Co to Mrs. A. J. Worchard, there is no further record.

76. Mildred C. J. b 1846.

77. Julia A. C. b 1849. The first of the name of Julia A. C. Bondurant b 1821 and still single in the 1850 Census.. Evidently Paschal's Julia A. C. was named after father's mother's sister. A Julia A. Vann is shown as heir to estate of Wm. Henry Buford in 1850. He was the grandfather of Julia A. C. Bondurant.

78. Mary b 1851.

79. Martha b 1859. It is suggested that this family probably moved somewhere in Texas with the movement following the reconstruction era about 1880.

(30) John H. m 3 March 1852 in Madison Co, Jane Hannah and moved immediately to Marshall Co where they had:

80. Hannah J. b about 1854 and no further record.

81. William Albert b 8 Jan 1856, d 25 Aug 1936, buried in Kennamer Cemetery, Madison Co, although he had lived across the line in Marshall Co.

82. Nancy Addie b 1859.

83. John Daniel b about 1861, d in Arkansas. Had six daughters, of whom three were living in Maxine, Texas in 1952.

(33) William M., son of Daniel, m (1st) 13 Jan 1857 in Madison Co, to Harriet E. Dilworth, d before 1876, leaving daughters Lucy, m Aug 1880 to James B. Click and Nancy, a minor; m (2nd) to Sarah in Marshall Co before 1880 but no record of children by second marriage.

(34) Reuben Bondurant, son of Daniel, m (1st) 5 Nov 1852 his first cousin Caroline Vann, dau of Dempsey Vann and Julia Ann Buford, separated 1856 and divorced 1859. They had two daughters, one perhaps died. The other was Julia b 1854 m 23 May 1871 to George E. Vann. The mother Caroline and daughter Julia are shown in 1860 and 1870 census of Madison Co with the Dempsey Vann family.

Reuben B. m (2nd) 17 Nov 1867 in Madison Co to Martha P. Freeman b 1844 in Madison Co, and d before 1917 in Madison

Co, Ala. Dau of Meridith and Elizabeth Freeman. Reuben and Martha had seven children, all born in Madison Co.

84. John Wesley Taylor Daniel b 25 March 1869. In 1917 lived in Anderson Co, Texas and in 1952 living in Tyler, Texas.

86. Rosa Belle b 1871, d 1947 in Dallas Co, Texas, m 1889 Woodward Sharp and was living in Throckmorton Co, Texas in 1917. She had 14 children, including Bob Sharp, living in Dallas, Texas in 1952.

87. Hattie b 1873, m 1893 Fonza Towry and in 1917 and 1952 was living in Huntsville, Ala.

88. Mary R. b 1875, m 1895 G. J. Fisk, who died before 1917. In 1917 and 1952 she was living in Huntsville, Ala.

89. William R. b 1879, m Rosie and in 1917 was living in Clarke Co, Ark.

90. Eula b 1881, m Richard Bradford and in 1917 they were living in Madison Co, Ala.

91. A. Tate b 14 March 1881, m 1904 A. M. Branum. In 1917 they were living in Clarke Co, Ark. In 1952 Mrs. Tate Branum was living in Gurley, Ala, the home of her father and mother before their death in 1917.

(36) Daniel L. W. m (1st) 3 Jan 1861 in Madison Co to Mahala Moon, who probably died soon. m (2nd) Oct 1870 Martha b 1852 as shown in 1870 census of Madison Co. In 1880 census of Marshall Co Daniel is listed with wife Mary E., 26 years of age, likely same as Martha, with children:

92. James R. b 1872.

93. Daniel H. b 3 Sept 1873, d 11 Jan 1917 Marshall Co.

94. John W. b 1874.

95. Nancy E. b 1877.

96. William H. b July 1880.

FOURTH GENERATION IN MADISON COUNTY, ALABAMA

(46) Allison Woodville m 22 Oct 1867 to Elizabeth Josephine Green b 14 Aug 1849, d 28 June 1914, dau of Jacob Ross Green and Elizabeth Journey Boyd. Children of Allison Woodville and Elizabeth were:

97. John Whatley b 26 Aug 1869 d 23 May 1926 at Rome, Floyd Co, Georgia.

98. Elizabeth b 10 Dec 1871, m Leonard G. Todd and resided East Third St, Rome, Ga.

99. Mary Lee b 17 Sept 1873 at Alexandria, Ala, m 1897 to Albert Beta Arrington b 22 June 1869 at La Grange, Ga, d 29 April 1918 at Rome, Ga.

100. Oliver Green b 26 June 1876, d 8 Oct 1919, m Mrs. Bohn Mathias Smith and had one child, Elizabeth, b 8 Oct 1903, m 1933 to George Kelley.

101. William Taylor b 17 May 1880.

(51) James Logan m 1866 Elizabeth Cochran, d 14 June 1890 at Rome, Ga. Their children were:

102. Minnie Lou m W. C. Legrand and both d before 1933.

103. John Wade never married.

104. Mattie Swan. Never married. Both she and her brother John Wade Ledbetter were missionaries to China.

105. Robert Ernest b 21 July 1875 at New Hope, Ala, and resided Montgomery, Ala.

106. Thomas Gordon d before 1933.

107. Lonnie Lee. resides Anniston, Ala.

(55) John Malone m Mary L. McDonald and had one son:

108. Emmet W. b at New Hope, Ala, resided at Anniston, Ala.

(56) William Gordon m 1877 Sarah Draper, dau of Daniel D. Draper and Caroline (Woods) Draper of South Carolina. Their children are:

109. Ruth m Charles E. Burgoon and resided at 2208 East Beach, Gulfport, Miss.

110. Ralph Waldo b 13 Aug 1886 at Winston-Salem, N. C. Resides 205 East 4th St, Anniston, Ala, where he is employed with the Alabama Power Company.

111. Grace who also lived in Gulfport, Miss.

112. Willie G.

There were also three other children who died young.

(81) William Albert m 15 Sept 1875 in Marshall Co, Ala, to Sarah Kirkland b 18 Dec 1854, d 18 Jan 1937, dau of Riley and Rebecca (Birdwell) Kirkland:

113. John Riley b 1876, school teacher Guntersville, Ala.

114. Rebeca b 1878 as shown in 1880 census Marshall Co.

115. Cora m (1st) R. H. Jones, d 1937, m (2nd) J. H. Wood, Decatur, Ala.

116. Belle d New Hope 14 Feb 1937, m Seaborn Keel, Jr.

117. Mary m D. R. Click.

118. Eliza d July 1945, m Robert L. Walls.

119. Rosa m 17 Sept 1920 Otho M. Butler and lives Ardmore, Tenn.

120. Oma m Emmett Anderson.

In addition, four children of William Albert and Sarah Kirkland died in infancy.

(84) John Wesley Taylor Daniel Ledbetter, m 23 Oct 1889 at Larkinsville, Ala, Lula Purkerson, d 25 Oct 1949 at Tyler Smith Co, Texas. Their children are:

121. James Luther b 15 Aug 1890 in Jackson Co, Ala. In 1952 he lived at 102 N.E. 12th St, Big Spring, Texas, and had a son and a daughter.

122. Alvin Rubin b 24 July 1892 in Jackson Co, Ala. Lives at Athens, Henderson Co, Texas, Route 2 and has two sons and two daughters.

123. William Martin b 16 March 1894 in Texas, d 8 Jan 1933, leaving three sons.

124. Roy Malcolm b 11 March 1897. Engages in construction of highways and his address was unknown to his father in 1952. Has a son and a daughter.

125. Charlie Daniel, a carpenter, b 1 Aug 1900. Lives at 533 Dogwood Ave, Houston, Texas. He has a daughter and three sons.

126. Sam Lewis b 24 Feb 1903. Lives at Route 2, Box 35, Bivens, Texas. Has a daughter.

127. Kate Mahaney b 24 Feb 1903 (twin of Sam), m (1st) Powell from Louisiana; m (2nd) Tim Bivis of 624 E. Line St, Tyler, Texas. Has a daughter and a son.

128. Annie Pearl b 1 April 1906, m Meroworth. Lives 404 Virginia Ave, Big Spring, Texas, and has four daughters.

129. John Leonard b 3 Aug 1908, a carpenter. Lives Route 3, Box 236, Tyler, Texas. Had two sons (one deceased), and a daughter.

130. Carl b 11 March 1912. He is a painter and carpenter and lives at Tyler, Texas, with his father. No children.

FIFTH GENERATION IN MADISON COUNTY, ALABAMA

(97) John Whatley m 3 Oct 1900 Olive Cecilo Williamson b 4 April 1874, dau of Thomas Jefferson Williamson, b 25 Dec. 1844 and Martha Cleo Dykes, b 2 April 1848, d 12 July 1925. Father and mother of Thomas Jefferson Williamson were George Williamson b 4 Oct 1811, d 4 Oct 1859, and Jane Daniel b 22 June 1819, d 12 Feb 1902. The father and mother of Martha Cleo Dykes were Allen Hill Dykes b 4 Mar 1791, d 11 June 1864, and Polly Bleadsen b Oct 1794, d 2 Aug 1862. The children of John Whatley and Olive C. Ledbetter were:

131. Allison Woodville II b 24 Oct 1901, m 26 Feb 1930, Rosa Kingsberry Harvin and had one child Allison Woodville III b 16 April 1932.

132. Dorothy b 21 March 1910, m Dr. Boni J. De Laureal, 2905 Chestnut St, New Orleans, La. Dorothy continues to be interested in all lines of her family.

(101) William Taylor, son of Allison Woodville, m Cleo Williamson (sister to his brother John Whatley's wife). They had four children:

133. Martha Cleo b 22 Nov 1908.

134. Francis Lipscomb b 9 March 1911.

135. William Taylor b 4 Feb 1914.

136. Jackson Dykes b 16 Sept 1918, d 18 March 1943.

(110) Ralph Waldo m 24 Dec 1910 at Helena, Ga, Laura Esther Davenport b 3 April 1888, dau of James Terry Davenport and Laura Clementine (Wilson) Davenport. Ralph and Laura had five children:

137. Grace Evelyn b 24 Dec 1911 at Helena, Ga, m 17 July 1930 at Heflin, Ala, to Nick Ware III.

138. James Gordon b 15 July 1914 at Birmingham, Ala, m 20 July 1935 Elaine Theott b 6 Feb 1916. James Gordon Ledbetter lives in Anniston, Ala.

139. Sarah Draper Ledbetter b 8 Oct 1916 at Birmingham, Ala, m before 1947 and lived in N. J.

140. Ralph Wilson b 28 Feb 1921 at Anniston, Ala, m before 1947 and lives at Memphis, Tenn.

141. John Wayne b 28 Dec 1927 at Anniston, Ala.

(113) John Riley m Sarah Elizabeth Walls, a descendant of Daniel Walls of War 1812, d 1814 in Madison Co, Ala, and his wife Sarah Harless, dau of Henry Harless, Revolutionary soldier b Montgomery Co, Va, d 1815 Madison Co, Ala. John Riley Ledbetter and Elizabeth had:

142. John Riley, Jr. b 11 April 1922, A.B. University Alabama 1941, M.D. Alabama Medical College 1950, m 22 June 1949 Edith Gay Jones b 16 Oct 1922 at Huntsville, Ala, dau of Howard Criner Jones and Kathleen Paul Jones. Edith has BA 1944 U. of Ala; M.D. 1950 Medical College of Ala. Both she and her husband practice medicine at Rogerville, Ala. John Riley and Edith have Susan Lyne b 28 Oct 1952 and John Kennon b 15 June 1961.

143. Elizabeth m Robert Haden, M.D. Medical College Alabama and have Robert Haden, Jr. They live at Guntersville, Ala.

144. Rayford m Mary Jean Townson and lives at Guntersville, Ala.

CHAPTER 6

ARTHUR LEDBETTER LINE,
OVERTON COUNTY, TENNESSEE[1]

By LT. COL. WM. R. LEDBETTER

Arthur Ledbetter was born of English ancestry about 1740, possibly in Brunswick County, Virginia, and died "in the West" in 1814. His first marriage was to Frances Brooks, a native of Ireland. Such information has been passed down by word of mouth. The name of his second wife is not recorded. She may have been Franky, who died between 1828 and 1830, probably in Overton County, or Nancy, who is mentioned below.

Arthur's descendants, over 100 years after his death, say he was a true Whig and took an active part in the Revolutionary War. No record of such service has been found. Tradition tells us the Tories took him out of his house one day and hit him on the head with the flat of a sword so hard that the blade was heard to ring. Official recordings that indicate an Arthur Ledbetter existed are (a) a bill of sale dated 12 Aug 1777 recorded in Chatham County, North Carolina, which is signed by an Arthur, (b) an Arthur listed as owning 1,000 acres of taxable land in Wilkes County, Georgia, in 1792-94, (c) an Arthur and Nancy recorded in the Court Minutes of Blount County, Tennessee, from February 1800 to May 1801, (d) an Arthur listed as being taxable in White County, Tennessee, on 1 Jan 1812, and (e) an Arthur recorded as witness to a deed in the latter county on 25 Feb 1813.

It is most reasonable to assume that there had been three or four generations of Arthur's ancestors in Virginia. There is a tradition that he came from England with brothers varying in number from three to seven. This probably arose because there was no family record handed down naming the generations in America. The tradition that he landed from England in North Carolina has the element of fact that he did migrate to that state before 1777.

It is further tradition that Arthur and some of his sons visited Tennessee to determine its suitability as a new home, then returned to Georgia to bring back their families. Available records sub-

152

stantiate this. Such records indicate the location of Arthur and/or his early descendants to have been:

1777 to 1783 North Carolina, Probably Chatham County.

1785 to 1789 Virginia, at places unknown.

1792 to 1795 Georgia, in Wilkes County, an area now covering ten counties.

1795 to 1798 Tennessee, probably Blount County or vicinity.

1800 to 1801 Tennessee, in Blount County.

1799 to 1805 Georgia, in Oglethorpe County and probably elsewhere.

1807 on Tennessee, in the area of Warren and Overton Counties and in between.

Many unnamed relatives of these Middle Tennessee Ledbetters are believed to have moved from North Carolina to Georgia by 1790 and remained there.[2] One of Arthur's Tennessee grandsons was visiting relatives in Georgia in 1833 when the "stars fell".

The earliest land grant to a Ledbetter in the State of Tennessee was 140 acres in Warren County[3] to James on 11 Sep 1809. This property, when granted, was adjacent to that of George Ledbetter, a son of Buckner. These lands of James and George were located in the vicinity of Laurel Cove, which is now in Van Buren County. The North Carolina land grants in Tennessee included no Ledbetter as grantee. The earliest recorded land transaction by a Ledbetter in Overton County, Tennessee, was a purchase by Buckner in November 1811 on Nettle Carrier Creek. This creek, which cradled the settlements of early Ledbetters, was named for the Cherokee Indian Chief, Nettle Carrier, who ruled the area until he departed in the summer of 1799. The first settlers had arrived in the spring of that year.

Arthur moved to some place in the "west," where he died by drowning in 1814. His widow returned to Overton County to live with her son Washington. His sons John C. and Washington served together in the War of 1812, John C. later moving to Illinois and Washington to Arkansas. Son Buckner lived and died in Overton County. Buckner and John C. were children of his first marriage, and Washington of his second. It is believed he had a son named James, but no record has been found to prove it.

In 1832 a few of Arthur's descendants left Overton County and went by ox-drawn wagon train across Kentucky to a "cow and hog heaven" in southern Illinois. They probably settled near the Ohio River in the vicinity of Elizabethtown and Cave-in-Rock. This area is now in Gallatin and Hardin Counties. The move was headed and financed by Isaac Robins, one of the early settlers of the Overton County area, whose daughters married Ledbetters.

Their stay in Illinois was short-lived. Due to the "shaking ague" (malaria), they returned to Overton County in less than a year, flat broke. Arthur's son John C. had taken his family to this area about 1826 and James, the oldest son of Washington, soon followed his Uncle Johnny. These two did not return with the Robins group.

This small section of Illinois had been populated by Ledbetters before John C. arrived. These included family heads named Henry b 1808 and Asa b 1812.[4] John C. and the others evidently alternated their residences between the two southern counties of Gallatin and Hardin and the counties of Bond, Fayette, Shelby and Effingham, which are located about 100 miles to the north.

As early as 1831, a descendant of Arthur migrated from Overton County to northwest Arkansas. Others are known to have moved in the 1840's to Texas and Missouri. A few made the trek to the California gold fields in 1858-62.

Tradition tells us the first three Ledbetters listed below were sons of Arthur, although it is reasonable to believe that he had four or five times that many children:[5]

2. Buckner, b about 1760 possibly in North Carolina, d 1840-54 in Overton County, Tennessee.[6]

3. John C., b 16 Jan 1785 in Virginia, d about 1870 probably in Effingham County, Illinois.

4. Washington, b 1789 in Virginia, d 1860 in Madison County, Arkansas.

5. James. This individual is assigned as a son to Arthur based only on his apparent age and association with the other older Ledbetters as shown in records pertaining to Warren, White and Overton Counties, Tennessee. He is not listed in the various appropriate census schedules. Evidently he did not marry before 1840 and either left Overton County or died before 1850.

Third Generation—Grandchildren of Arthur Ledbetter

(2) Buckner, son of (1) Arthur, was probably married more than once. He m last Tabitha ———, b 1771 in NC, d after 1850 in Overton Co, Tenn. She was probably a Jones. He probably moved about 1785 from NC to Ga. Buckner was in Wilkes Co, Ga in 1791, and in 1792 he apparently moved to Franklin Co, Ga where his lands were located. He resided 1794, part of 1795 and from 1799 to at least 1803 in Oglethorpe Co, Ga. This county's 1803 tax returns show Buckner owned lands in adjoining Jackson Co. (probably in current Oconne Co) on Apalachee River. Births of his children would indicate he was in Tenn 1795-98, in Ga again 1800-05, and back to Tenn by 1808 when he was in his late 40s. He was the first Ledbetter to be recorded in the land transactions of Overton Co. This was a purchase of 100 ac on the south side of the upper reaches of Nettle Carrier Creek in November 1811. He and Tabitha remained and died there. His children numbered at least 9 sons and 6 daughters, as follows:

6—George, b 1783 in NC, d 1863 on War Eagle Creek in Madison Co, Ark.

7—A son, b 1775-94. No further record; listed only in the 1820 census.

8—Frances "Fannie", b about 1792. m about 1817 to Wilson Conner, b 1780-90. They removed from Overton Co to Hamilton Co, Tenn 1830-36 and both died there 1844-50.

9—Elizabeth, b 22 Nov 1795 in Tenn, probably Blount Co or vicinity, d 1850-60 in Madison Co, Ark. m about 1820 in either White or Overton Co, Tenn to William McElhaney, b 3 Jun 1791 in Tenn, d 1850-60 in Madison Co, Ark, son of John, b 1760-70 in Va and Hannah (nee Bowen) McIlhaney. She removed 1831 from White Co, Tenn to Madison Co, Ark. Their dau Sarah H. m (45) Harvey Carrol Ledbetter, a first Cousin.

10—Reverend Arthur, b 3 Jun 1798 in Tenn, probably Blount Co or vicinity, Tenn, d 7 Nov 1859 in Dallas Co, Tex.

11—Jones, b 10 Nov 1799 in Ga, probably Oglethorpe Co, d about 1870 in Overton Co, Tenn.

12—Aram (Aaron), b 1801 in Ga, probably Oglethorpe Co, d after 1856.

13—Beverly (son), b 1802 in Ga, probably Oglethorpe Co, d at age 68 in Fentress Co, Tenn.

14—James, b 1804 in Ga, probably Oglethorpe Co, d after 1850 possibly in west-central Indiana.

15—Winifred "Winnie", b 1805 in Ga, probably Oglethorpe Co, d after 1880 probably in Overton Co. m William Lynn, d about 1848. Residence included Overton Co from 1820 thru 1880.

16—Tabitha "Tabby", b 1808 in Tenn. m before 1840 Richard Lea, b 1808 in Ga, probably son of James Lee. Resided in Overton Co until at least 1860.

17—Buckner H., b 1811 in Overton Co, d after 1850 probably in Overton Co.

18—A son, b 1810-15. Listed in 1820 and 1830 census. Probably d young.

19—Louisa, b 1814 in Tenn, d after 1856. m about 1840 Vincent Coleman, b 1823 in Tenn. Resided in Overton Co from 1820 through 1850.

20—Hettie, b 1817 in Tenn, d after 1860. Her residence included Overton Co from 1820 thru 1850 with her family and finally with her widowed mother, in Fentress Co, Tenn in 1860. William Ledbetter, b 1844 resided with her in 1850 and 1860, and Mary Ledbetter, b 1840 with her in 1850.

(3) John C., son of (1) Arthur. Served in the War of 1812. He volunteered on 4 Oct 1813 in Overton Co, Tenn and served with Canady's Co of Bradley's regiment until he was discharged on 28 Dec 1813 at Monroe, Overton Co, Tenn. He was then drafted on 20 Jun 1814 in Overton Co and served in Kilpatrick's Co, 1st Regt West Tenn Militia. He and his brother Washington "deserted" on 20 Sep 1814 and "returned" 12 Oct 1814. They were both discharged at Fort Charlotte, Mobile on 8 Mar 1815. He resided in White Co, Tenn on 1 Jan 1812 and 30 Jul 1815, and in Overton Co in 1820. He and his family removed in 1826, when he was age 41, to probably what is now Hardin Co, Ill.

Resided alternately in Hardin and Effingham Co, Ill in 1851 and in Hardin Co in May 1855 and May 1856. Possibly m about 1806 Rachel S. —————, b 1779 in Tenn, d about 1870 probably in Effingham Co, Ill. His children included:

21—John, b 1807 in Tenn, probably Overton Co, d after 1880, probably Hardin Co, Ill.

22—A son, b 1810-20.

23—A son, b 1810-20.

24—A daughter, b 1810-20.

25—Job, b 1826-29 in Overton Co, Tenn, d of war wounds 22 Jun 1864 at Resaca, Ga.

(4) Washington, son of (1) Arthur. Served in the War of 1812 in Kilpatrick's Co, 1st Regt West Tenn Militia; joining at Fayetteville, Tenn 20 Jun 1814 and, with his brother John, "deserted" on 20 Sep 1814 and "returned" 12 Oct 1814. Service included 14 days in the Creek Indian War in 1815. Was discharged 8 Mar 1815 at Fort Charlotte, Mobile. Resided in Franklin Co, Tenn in 1816, and in Overton Co in 1820-50. He spent some of his early days in Warren and White Co, Tenn. In 1828 he purchased a $400 tract of land on Nettle Carrier Creek adjoining the south and east lines of his brother Buckner. He took his family on the round trip to Gallatin Co area of southern Illinois in 1832 with the Isaac Robins train. In the Fall of 1850 he migrated at age 61 to Madison Co, Ark where he remained. m, probably in the Warren-Overton Co area, to Martha "Patsy" Chesser, b 1793 in Va, d after 1860 in Madison Co, Ark, dau of James Chesser, b 1756 in Md, d after or late in 1850 probably in Cannon Co, Tenn. Their children included 9 sons and 7 daughters:

26—James "Jim", b 1804-10, d about 1835 in Ill, probably Gallatin (now Hardin) Co.

27—William, b 23 Jul 1811 in Overton Co, Tenn, d 4 May 1891 near Alpine, Overton Co. A twin to Ben.

28—Benjamin "Ben", b 23 Jul 1811 in Overton Co, Tenn, d 27 Dec 1891 at same place. A twin to William.

29—Winnie, b 1812 in Tenn, d after 1870 probably in Madison Co, Ark. m Hickman Officer, d before 1860.

30—Washington, b 1813 in Tenn, d 1870-80 in Overton
Co, Tenn.

31—Mary "Polly", b 26 Sep 1816 in Tenn, d after 1906. Buried Aurora, Lawrence Co, Mo. m Martin Qualls 27 Sep
1838 in Overton Co, Tenn.

32—Merrill, b 1817 in Tenn, drowned after 1860 in either
Cumberland or Obey Rivers.

33—Martha, b 1820-25 (?). m William McClain.

34—Beverly J., b 1822 in Overton Co, Tenn, d after Jul 1883
probably in either Lawrence or Stone Co, Mo.

35—Wiley, b 10 Jun 1824 near Livingston, Overton Co,
Tenn, d 13 Feb 1915 near Crane, Stone Co, Mo.

36—Elizabeth "Betsy", b 1830 in Tenn. Lived and died in
the southern edge of Ky, in Monroe Co. m ——— King.

37—Sarah, b 4 Feb 1826. Buried Aurora, Lawrence Co, Mo.
Resided before 1860 near Berryville, Carroll Co, Ark. m
Francis Sanders. Removed to Granby, Newton Co, Mo.

38—Arthur, b 1825-30 (?), d young, probably in Ark, leaving a widow and one child, believed to be a son.

39—Samantha, b 1832 in Tenn.

40—Lewis Chesser Jordan, b 1835 in Overton Co, Tenn, d
1900 in Boone Co, Ark.

41—Amanda, b 1838 in Tenn.

Fourth Generation—Greatgrandchildren of Arthur Ledbetter

(6) George, son of (2) Buckner. m in Overton-Warren Co
area Tenn, Susannah Chesser, b 1788 in Va, d 1881 in Madison
Co, Ark at War Eagle on War Eagle Creek, dau of James Chesser,
b 1756 in Md, d after or late in 1850 probably in Cannon Co,
Tenn. He bought land and settled before July 1809 in Warren
Co, Tenn. This land was located on Laurel Creek between Laurel
Cove and Rocky River in what is now Van Buren Co. Evidently
when all his children except Elizabeth and Alfred had left home
for the "west", he removed in 1849 to War Eagle, Madison Co,
Ark at age about 66 to join his son Harvey and others. Their
children included 7 sons and 3 daughters; probably all born in
Warren Co, Tenn:

42—Nancy, b 1808 and m about 1828 both probably in
Warren Co, Tenn to Thomas Elsey, b 1805 in Tenn.

They removed 1830-40 to Madison Co, Ark from Warren Co.

43—Jefferson Brooks "Jeff", b 15 Jan 1810 in Tenn, d 17
May 1896 in Madison Co.

44—Hugh M., b 1811 in Tenn, d during Civil War at Aurora,
Madison Co.

45—Harvey Carrol "Harve", b 18 Apr 1816 in Warren (now
Van Buren) Co, Tenn, d 5 Sep 1902 at War Eagle,
Madison Co.

46—Eli "Eel", b 1818 in Tenn, d 1900 at Poteau (now Le
Flore Co), Okla Territory.

47—Winnie, b 1815-20 in Tenn, m Ab (?) Clark and removed from Tenn to Miss probably after 1840.

48—Elizabeth "Betts", b 1823 in Tenn, believed to have d
1 Dec 1909 near Stidham, McIntosh Co, Okla. Further
information herein.

49—William M. "Bill", b 12 Jun 1824 in Tenn, d 9 Jul 1909
near Bells, Grayson Co, Tex.

50—James, b 1827 in Tenn, d 1862 at Drakes Creek, Madison
Co, of typhoid fever.

51—Alfred, b 1832 in Tenn, d probably 1850-60 in Madison
Co.

(10) Reverend Arthur, son of (2) Buckner. Became a Missionary Baptist preacher about 1828 and preached in Overton Co,
Tenn. He lived and farmed at the head of Nettle Carrier Creek
and did church work until 1832 when he and his family emigrated
to Southern Illinois. In less than a year, because of sickness, they
returned to Overton Co. On 1 Apr 1841 Arthur with Evan Jones
gave a deed of trust for 300 ac on the Middle Fork of Nettle Carrier
Creek to his first cousin (27) William. This property adjoined his
father's south property line as well as the mouth of his brother
Beverly's spring. Arthur witnessed a deed in Overton Co on 19 Jan
1844. On being "induced" to settle on a portion of Texas public
domain, he "broke up" his home and left Overton Co again with
his family on 7 Mar 1848. Just a few miles before reaching the
area to be settled, his family contracted smallpox and he lost his
wife and a child. He failed to meet an agreed deadline for arriving

into the public domain area due to this sickness but later moved in and settled on the East Fork of the Trinity River in present Dallas Co. They relocated in 1850 nine miles west of Dallas. He organized five churches in Dallas and had pastoral charge of four of them. m 1st Elizabeth Robins, b 18 Mar 1802 in Jackson (now Overton) Co, Tenn, d of smallpox 18 Aug 1848 at Garland, Dallas Co, Tex. She was dau of Isaac Robins, a native of Scotland and one of the early settlers of the Overton Co area. To them in Overton Co were born 6 sons and 3 daughters:

> 52—Isaac Anderson, b 1823, d before 1900 at Fort Belknap, Young Co, Texas.
> 53—Martha J., b 1825. m Wesley Ware, son of H. H. Ware, a Baptist preacher. They both died in middle age.
> 54—Oliver Vincent, b 30 May 1827, d 6 Sep 1902 in Dallas Co, Texas.
> 55—Lewis B., b 1830, d at Hazeldelle, Comanche Co, Texas.
> 56—Mary L., b 1833, m ————— Neely.
> 57—Thomas Logan, b 1836, d 1876 in Dallas Co, Texas.
> 58—Cynthia, b 1842, d 1848 of smallpox in Dallas Co, Texas.
> 59—Arthur Brooks, b 19 Oct 1845, d 31 Jul 1917 at Marshall, Searcy Co, Ark.

(10) Reverend Arthur m 2nd 13 Aug 1849 in Dallas Co, Texas to Mrs. Elizabeth (nee Ogle) Pearson, b 7 Jun 1825 in Ky, d 15 May 1901 at Dallas, dau of David Ogle and widow of William H. Pearson. To them in Dallas Co, Texas were born 4 sons and 2 daughters:

> 60—Frances Tennessee, b 1850, d at Tulia, Texas in late 1930's, m George W. Baker.
> 61—James Ogle, b 25 Jan 1853, d 10 Apr 1880 in Dallas Co, Texas. Did not marry. Buried beside his twin brother.
> 62—A twin brother of James Ogle d at age 2 weeks.
> 63—Mary Elizabeth, b 1855, d 1939 in Dallas. m 17 Dec 1876 in Dallas to Alfred Bradley Qualls, b 22 Nov 1851, d 15 May 1929 in Dallas, son of Martin and (31) Polly Qualls.
> 64—William Hughes, b 12 Dec 1856, d in Fall of 1936 in Dallas Co, Texas.

James Franklin "Bud" Ledbetter
(1852-1937)

William Russell Ledbetter (1850-1942)

65—George Washington, b 9 Sep 1859 near Cockrell Hill, d 30 Dec 1938 in Dallas Co, Texas.

(11) Jones, son of (2) Buckner, m 1st by 1820 to Ann Jones, b 1801 in Tenn, d 1850-53 in Overton Co, Tenn, sister of Evan "Ive" Jones, one of the early settlers in the Overton Co area. Purchased land in Overton Co before 1832 and was relatively active in land transactions there; receiving two state grants. He purchased a part of his father's 65 ac place from his brothers and sisters. Jones and Ann are buried on his old farm on the north side of the upper reach of Nettle Carrier Creek. Their children included 6 sons and 6 daughters; all born in Overton Co, Tenn:

66—Isaac Jones "Ike", b 1824, murdered 1861 in Berryville, Carroll Co, Ark.

67—Tabitha, b 1826. Did not marry before she left Overton Co.

68—Buckner Harris T., b 1827, d 1863-75 in Kaufman Co, Texas.

69—Elizabeth "Betsy", b 1830, m Allen Bowman.

70—Evan J. "Ive", b 1832, d after 1880, probably in Benton Co, Ark.

71—Robert, b 1834, d Overton Co and buried beside his father.

72—Winnie, b 1836, d before 1931 probably in Overton Co, m Isaac Stout.

73—Benjamin Laken C. "Lake", b 1838, d 10 Jan 1863.

74—Martha Ann "Patsy", b 1841, d before 1931. Had a son Robert Laken "Lake" Ledbetter, b 1866 in Tenn.

75—Charity, b 1842, d after 1931. m Camel Craig.

76—James K. Polk, b 1845, d 15 Jan 1926 in Overton Co, Tenn.

77—Rachel, d before 1931. Married Mr. Hyter.

(11) Jones m 2nd Elizabeth Craig, b 1835, possibly dau of John, b 1806 in NC and Marguerite Craig, b 1813 in Tenn. Their children were 4 sons only:

78—Will K. P., b 1855 in Tenn.

79—Andrew J. "Drew", b 29 May 1857, d 4 Feb 1951 in Overton Co, Tenn.

80—Jesse, b 4 Dec 1859 in Tenn, d 20 Feb 1931, buried in Overton Co, Tenn.

81—John C., d 1916.

(12) Aram (Aaron), son of (2) Buckner, m about 1817 to Elizabeth Davis, b 1795 in NC, dau of Levi Davis. Aram was a miller. Resided at least from 1820 through 1856 in Overton Co, Tenn on Eagle Creek. He acquired land there in Aug 1838 which he sold in Mar 1850. The 1850 census shows Levi Ledbetter, aged 7 months, residing with the family. The children marked ** below are listed as sons only because they lived in among the other Ledbetters in 1850 and more closely fit into the family's age brackets according to the 1830 and 1840 census schedules than any of the other families which had unaccounted-for children. Aram's children by 1840 included 5 sons and 2 daughters. Based on the foregoing considerations, the following listing of his children is made:

82—Levi, b 1820 in Tenn, d after 1860.

83—Sarah, b 1821 in Tenn, d after 1850.

84—A son, b 1820-25.

85—William B. **, b 1824 in Tenn, d after 1860 probably in southern Mo.

86—A daughter, b 1825-30.

87—Henry **, b 1832 in Tenn, d after 1850.

88—George, b 1836 in Tenn, d after 1850.

(13) Beverly, son of (2) Buckner Sr. m 1st Nancy Robins, dau of Isaac Robins, one of the early settlers in Middle Tennessee and a native of Scotland. See (10) Reverend Arthur and (27) William for sisters of Nancy. Their children included the following; all born in Tenn:

89—Isaac, b 1820-25, d after 1840.

90—Jones, b 1825, d 1 Nov 1862 in Rolla, Phelps Co, Mo.

91—Julia, b 1825-30.

92—Fannie, b 1825-30.

93—Louisa, b probably 1830-35.

94—James W. "Jimmy", b 1835, d after 1880.

(13) Beverly m 2nd Susannah Cravens, b 1809 in Tenn. They moved 1840-50 from Overton Co to Fentress Co, Tenn and she was there late as 1880. Their children, all born in Tenn, were:

95—Margaret, b 1837, d after 1850.

96—Martha "Patsy", b 1839, d after 1860.

97—Winnie, b 1841, d after 1860. m about 1859 to John E. Conatser, b 1839 in Tenn.

98—Armazinda (or Arminta), b 1843.

99—Vina, b 1846.

100—Ewing Mc. "Mack", b 1847, d after 1860.

101—Tabitha Ellen, b 1850, d after 1880. Further information herein.

102—Artilla (or Arminta), b 1853, d after 1870.

(14) James, son of (2) Buckner: He evidently m twice in Overton Co, Tenn. m 1st probably about 1825 to ————, b 1800-10 and 2nd about 1830 to Elizabeth ————, b 1814 in Tenn. James owned three tracts of land on Nettle Carrier Creek adjacent to his father and his Uncle Wash and also land in Fentress Co on the Obey River. The entire family left Overton Co after 1856 and went west; possibly removed to west-central Indiana. The children of James numbered at least 7 sons and 4 daughters, including:

103—A daughter, b 1825-30.

104—A son, b 1830-35.

105—Tennessee, b 1829 in Tenn, d after 1850.

106—Overton, b 1832 in Overton Co, Tenn, d between Jun 1894 and Jul 1897 near Plainville, Daviess Co, Ind. Enlisted 8 Jan 1864 at Columbus, Ind in Co "B", 10 Union Ind Cav. Blue eyes, light hair, light complexion, 5 ft.-10-in. Resided near Steen, Knox Co, Ind during the Civil War. Discharged 31 Jul 1864 at Indianapolis. Resided near Plainville in 1891-93 and removed 1893 to near Wheatland, Knox Co. From official War Dept records: "Party in question has not a reputation to be envied". Overton Co records indicate he was indicted by the State of Tenn for grand larceny in 1854. m before 1854 to Sarilda ————. He had a dau Ella who m ———— Montgomery and resided 1899 in Montgomery, Ala.

107—James, b 1834 in Tenn. Killed during the Civil War.

108—Priscy A., b 1836 in Tenn, d after 1850.

109—Alfred K., b 1839 in Overton Co, d after Jun 1865. Enlisted 26 Oct 1861 in Pikeville, Bledsoe Co, Tenn in Co "C", 43 Conf Tenn Inf and was captured by Federal

forces at Vicksburg on 4 July 1863. He was then recruited
from prisoner status at Camp Morton, Indianapolis, Ind
on 18 Aug 1863 into Co "D", 6 Union Ind Cav. Blue
eyes, sandy hair, fair complexion, 5 ft.-9½ in., a farmer.
Discharged 17 Jun 1865 at Pulaski, Tenn.

110—Hamilton, b 1841 in Overton Co, d after 1880.

111—William, b 1843 in Tenn, d after 1850.

112—Frances, b 1849 in Tenn.

(17) Buckner H., son of (2) Buckner. m about 1828 Virginia Jane Lions, b about 1812 in Va, d after 1860 probably in
Overton Co, Tenn. They probably resided in Overton Co all their
lives. He was visiting relatives in Georgia on 13 Nov 1833 when
the "stars fell". Their children by 1842, all born in Overton Co,
were:

113—A daughter, b 1825-30.

114—A daughter, b 1830-35.

115—Elizabeth, b 1833. m James Ledbetter, a first cousin who
was son of Beverly.

116—A daughter, b 1835-40.

117—Louisa, b 1836. m John Rains.

118—Elijah W., b 1838, d after 1880, probably in Overton Co.

119—Nancy, b 1840, d after 1880, probably in Overton Co.
Further information herein.

120—Rebecca "Beck", b 1842, d after 1860. Had a child named
Margaret.

(21) John, son of (3) John C. Came from Overton Co, Tenn
when a young man of about 19 with his father and settled in
southern Illinois, probably near Elizabethtown. m 5 April 1828 in
Gallatin Co, Ill to Elizabeth Wright, b 1812 in Ky, d after 1880
probably in Hardin Co, Ill. They evidently resided in that part of
Gallatin which became Hardin in 1839. Their children, all born
in Ill, included:

121—James Alexander, b 1829, d after 1880, probably in
Hardin Co. m by 1860 to Selistina T. ———, b 1832 in
Ky, probably dau of James S. Lowry, b 1800 in NC. Resided 1850 through 1880 in Hardin Co. Their children
included Elizabeth, b Jan 1870, d after 1880.

122—Sina, b 1833.

123—Robert H., b 1836 in Hardin Co, d 23 May 1910 in Pope Co, Ill.

124—Mary E., b 1837.

125—Tabitha A. (or Ama J.), b 1840, d after 1860.

126—Nancy J., b 1844, d after 1870. m Allen Hobbs, b 1843 in Ill.

127—Matthew, b 1846, d after 1880.

128—Arthur, b 1848, resided 1870 in Hardin Co. m Maria
————, b 1852 in Ill. Their children included Mary, b Dec 1870 in Hardin Co.

129—Ruth, b 1855.

(25) Job, son of (3) John C. Probably the last child of the family born in Overton Co, Tenn before they went to southern Illinois. m 25 Oct 1855 in Decatur, Macon Co, Ill to Sarah S. Thesser, d 11 Nov 1865, dau of Mary Adams. Served in the Mexican War by joining 21 Jun 1846 at Greenville, Bond Co, Ill, Seller's Co, 3rd Ill Volunteers. Discharged 21 May 1847 at New Orleans, La. Was issued a land warrant for 160 acres for his service. Resided 1847 in Bond Co. In the War Between the States he joined Co "C" Union 70th Indiana Inf and was wounded on 15 May 1864. Died from these wounds on 22 Jun 1864 at Resaca, Ga. Blue eyes, light hair, light complexion, 5 ft., 5 in. Their orphaned children were as follows and all resided near Pittsboro Co, Ind in July 1866:

130—Sidney Jason, b 10 Nov 1857, d after 1932 in Martinsville, Morgan Co, Ind. m 3 times.

131—James William, b 8 Apr 1859, near Decatur, Macon Co, Ill, d 20 Aug 1950 in Indianapolis, Ind.

132—Mary Margaret, b 20 Jun 1861, d 3 Sep 1903 in Indianapolis, Ind. m Reuben Willis Adams, b 2 Dec 1855 in Ky, d 19 Oct 1941 in Indianapolis, a first cousin to her mother. They moved to Nebraska after m. She was taken when a child and raised in Illinois by a Thompson family.

133—Willis Jobe, b 16 Oct 1862, d May 1932 in Indianapolis, Ind of burns. m twice.

(26) James, oldest son of (4) Washington. At about age 20 he married, and removed from Overton Co, Tenn in 1828-30

to where he died about 1835 probably in Gallatin or Pope Co
(an area now Hardin Co), Illinois. He made a crop with his brother
William on the fateful Robins venture of 1832. At his death he
left a wife and one child. This child probably was Francina Jane,
b Gallatin Co, Ill, d 9 May 1859 in Shelby Co, Ill, m 1 Jun 1853
to Evan Baker, b 15 May 1830 in Shelby Co.

(27) William, son of (4) Washington. He went in 1832
with the Isaac Robins ox-wagon train to southern Illinois but was
driven back with the others in about a year's time because of sickness. William with his twin brother Ben bought their father's farm
which was adjacent to their first cousin Jones' property 5 miles
east of Livingston and spent their lives there. m 1st about 1829
Fannie Robins, d 1849 in Overton Co, dau of Isaac Robins above.
Their children, all born in Overton Co, were:

134—Nancy, b 1831, d 1902. m William Jones.

135—Lavina "Vinie", b 1830-35, d at Campbellsville, Taylor
Co, Ky. m Quentin D. Elder who was teacher and
preacher with the Cumberland Presbyterian church before
they left Overton Co and went to Ky.

136—Andrew Jackson, b 1835, d 1860 at Berryville, Carroll
Co, Ark. He had moved there that same year from Overton Co. Did not marry.

137—James Mitchell, b 9 Feb 1836, d 19 Jun 1916 at Campbellsville, Taylor Co, Ky.

138—Martin Van Buren, b 1838, murdered Aug 1861 at
Berryville, Carroll Co, Ark.

139—Adela "Della", b 1849, d before 1932 in northern Mo.
m John Nelson. After her mother died, she was taken
care of as a baby by her first cousin Winnie Lynn.

(27) William m 2nd in 1850 to Jane Delaney Cox, b 1827
in Overton Co, d 4 Jul 1876 at Alpine, Overton Co, dau of Gerarel
T., b 1790 in Md, d 24 Sept 1874 in Overton Co and Mary N.
(nee Berry) Cox. Their children were all born in Overton Co and
were all married there except William Lafayette:

140—MacMiller C. "Mack", b 1 Nov 1850, d 9 Aug 1946 at
Clarkrange, Fentress Co, Tenn.

141—John Dillard, b 30 Sep 1852, d 18 Jun 1933 at Alpine, Overton Co at the old homeplace on Nettle Carrier Creek where he was born.

142—Marinda Ellen "Rinda", b 1855, d after 1932. m 15 Jan 1871 in Overton Co to Soloman W. Winningham, a Union Army soldier. They resided in Overton Co.

143—Amanda B. "Mandy", b 1857, d before 1932 at Nashville, Tenn. m John Eldridge.

144—Martha Isabelle, b Jan 1860. m James Valentine Shepherd, brother of (76) Polk Ledbetter's wife. They removed to Ky.

145—William Lafayette "Fate", b 22 Oct 1862, d 30 Nov 1946 at Elk Grove, Sacramento Co, Calif.

146—Mary Leona m Emmett G. Copeland. Resided 1932 in Overton Co.

147—Benjamin Berry, b 8 Dec 1868, d 19 Jun 1952 at Livingston, Overton Co.

(27) William m 3rd 4 Mar 1880 in Overton Co to Amanda Dillon, b 1829 in Tenn. No issue.

(28) Benjamin "Ben", son of (4) Washington. m 1835 to Elizabeth "Betsy" Medlock, b 1819 in Tenn, d 1877 in Overton Co, Tenn. With his brother William bought his father's farm where they both lived. This was at West Fork in Overton Co. Their 13 children were probably all born in Overton Co:

148—A daughter, b 1835-37, d young.

149—Nancy Jane, b 1837. m after 1870 to Martin Van Richardson. See sister Margaret below.

150—Pleasant Hillary, b 1839, d 1904 in Overton Co.

151—Leann, b 1841, d before 1932. m 3 Jan 1870 in Overton Co to Jasper H. France.

152—Martela or Martha E., b 1843, d young.

153—James Calvin, b Aug 1847, d 8 Jul 1896 in Overton Co.

154—Lavina, b 1849, d before 1860.

155—Margaret S., b 1850, d before 1932. m 20 Sep 1868 in Overton Co to Martin Van Richardson. After she died, he m 2nd Jane above.

156—John Cambell, b 5 Mar 1851, d after 1931 in Overton Co.

157—Winnie Emma, b 1854, d before 1932. m 29 Jan 1868 in Overton Co to Samuel Boswell.

158—William Porter, b Dec 1857 in Overton Co. Resided 1933 in Greencastle, Putnam Co, Ind. He left Overton Co about 1879 when he was 21. m 19 Nov 1885 probably at Fillmore, Putnam Co, Ind to Fannie Newman, b 17 Sep 1862 at Fillmore, dau of William and Rachel Newman.

159—Mary Alice, b about Mar 1860, d before 1933. m after 1880 Marion Richardson.

160—Harriet, b 1863, d before 1870.

(30) Washington, son of (4) Washington. m Mary K. "Polly" Ferrel, b 1813 in Ky, d after 1880. Probably resided in Overton Co, Tenn all their lives. One of their dau m Green Huddleston, a minister. The children, all born in Tenn, were:

161—William Hamilton, b 1838 in Overton Co. Never married. "A doctor with a good practice."

162—Charlotte "Lottie", b 1840. Resided 1860 and 1880 in Overton Co. m before 1860 Phillip Sells who was killed in the Civil War.

163—Tabitha Emeline, b 1844.

164—Julie, b 1847.

165—George W., b 1849.

166—Mary C., b 1852. m Jacob Shote, b 1851 in Tenn.

167—Louisa Jane, b 1858. Resided 1880 with her sister Lottie in Overton Co. Never married.

(32) Merrill (Merrel), son of (4) Washington. Resided in Overton Co until at least 1860. m Margaret ————, b 1830 in Tenn. He was a mail carrier and drowned while driving his team in the swollen Obey or Cumberland River. Their children included:

168—Thomas B., b 1849 in Tenn.

169—Louis J., b 1850 in Tenn.

(34) Beverly J., son of (4) Washington. Resided 1850 with his father's family in White Co, Tenn; 1860 in Johnson Co, Ark; 1870 in Madison Co, Ark; and 1880 in Stone Co, Mo. Enlisted in Co "C", 21 Confederate Ark Inf at Clarksville, Ark on 18 Nov 1861. Accidentally wounded in the hand on 10 Apr 1862 by pistol

shot. He probably went along as a 27 year old bachelor with his father to northwest Ark in the fall if 1850. m Ellen C. ————, b 1835 in Ky. Their children were:

170—Minerva, b 1854 in Ark.

171—Martha E., b 1860 in Ark.

172—Artimissa, b 1862 in Ark.

173—William M., b 1864 in Ark.

174—Charity A., b 1866 in Mo.

175—Beverly W., (son), b 1869 in Ark.

176—Washington, b 1871 in Ark.

177—Mary, b 1872 in Ark.

178—Ophelia, b 1873 in Ark.

179—Camelia, b 1878 in Mo.

(35) Wiley, son of (4) Washington. m 1st 16 Mar 1846 in Overton Co, Tenn to Zidia Ann Crabtree, b 10 Feb 1831, d 11 Mar 1901 in Stone Co, Mo. Removed in the Fall of 1850 from Overton Co to Madison Co, Ark with his father; later, after two years in Carroll Co, Ark removed to Dallas Co, Texas and stayed for 18 months in 1859-60; then returned to Madison Co, Ark. Enlisted 9 Feb 1863 at Fayetteville, Ark in Co "D", 1st Union Ark Inf with his brother Lewis Chesser Jordan Ledbetter. Blue eyes, fair complexion, light hair, 5 ft., 5 in., a farmer. Discharged for disability at Fort Smith, Ark on 1 Mar 1865. Later removed to Stone Co, Mo where he was in 1870. Resided 1890-91 in Lawrence Co, Mo. Wiley m 2nd 19 Aug 1902 at Lick Branch, Boone Co, Ark to Lydia Whitfield (nee Brown; Inman), b 22 Mar 1847 in Hamilton Co, Mo, dau of Jackson and Elizabeth Inman, widow of R. A. Brown, d 5 Feb 1884, and divorcee of J. M. Whitfield who deserted her on 4 Jul 1887; both husbands of Carrollton, Ark. She resided 1916 in Ada Co, Idaho. Wiley and Lydia had no children. The children of Wiley and Zidia Ann included:

180—Sarah E., b 19 Aug 1847 in Tenn.

181—William Seyburn, b 15 Dec 1852 in Ark. Resided 1931 near Green Forest, Carroll Co, Ark.

182—Lewis Dillard, b 13 Dec 1855 in Mo. m Saphronia Grisham, sister of his brother Seyburn's wife Susan.

183—Christopher Columbus, b 21 Sep 1857 in Ark. m Elizabeth "Bettie" Bell.

184—Martha J., b 25 Apr 1860 in Dallas Co, Texas.

185—Mary T., b 17 Apr 1866 in Mo, probably Stone Co.

186—Surle Hershel, b 27 Aug 1870.

(40) Lewis Chesser Jordan, youngest son of (4) Washington. He with his brother Wiley enlisted in Co "D", 1st Union Ark Inf at Fayetteville, Ark on 9 Feb 1863. Black eyes, dark hair, dark complexion, 5 ft., 5 in. Mustered out at Fort Smith, Ark on 10 Aug 1865. Probably removed from Tenn to Madison Co, Ark as a 15 year old youth with his father in the Fall of 1850. Resided 1860 near his brother Wiley in Dallas Co, Texas. Removed from Stone Co, Mo to Boone Co, Ark in 1872. m before Aug 1860 in Dallas Co, Texas to Emily Amanda Mandeville Brown, b 1840 in Ill. Their children included:

187—Mary D. or Martha, b 1869 in Mo.

188—Safrona C., b Jan 1870 in Mo.

189—James Hilary, b 1872 in Mo. Resided 1931 at Harrison, Boone Co; Ark. m 1st Susan Mabel Miller; m 2nd Lilly Presley; m 3rd Mrs Mattie (nee Daniel) Curry.

Fifth Generation—Arthur Ledbetter Line

(43) Jefferson Brooks "Jeff", son of (6) George. m 3 Jan 1830 probably in Warren Co, Tenn to Elizabeth Herriman, b 3 Sep 1812 in Tenn, d 4 Jan 1875 in Madison Co, Ark. Removed in the early 1830s, probably with his brother Hugh, from his father's home on Rocky River in eastern Warren Co (now Van Buren Co) to Wilmouth Creek in western Warren Co (now Cannon Co); then in 1851 from Cannon Co, Tenn to Madison Co, Ark. He owned land and farmed at the head of Jackson Creek in Madison Co. He was also a tanner and shoemaker. They were Primitive Baptists. The first 9 of their 12 children were born in Tenn and the others in Madison Co, Ark:

190—Nancy Elizabeth, b 11 Nov 1830, d 7 Feb 1916 in Madison Co. m 18 Jan 1847 in Cannon Co, Tenn to Alexander McDougal, b 1825 in Tenn.

191—Burwell, b 14 Apr 1833 in Warren Co (now Cannon Co), d 12 Oct 1908 near Washburn, Sebastian Co, Ark.

192—James Harvey, b 24 Mar 1835, d 16 Apr 1858. He and his brother George Washington went to the California gold fields in wagon trains. One of them died a few days before reaching his destination and the other a few days after arrival. Married but no issue.

193—George Washington, b 3 Jun 1837, d 14 Nov 1862. See above. Never married.

194—Thomas Eli "Tom", b 4 May 1839, d 13 Apr 1899 in Indian Territory (Okla). m Jane McElhaney, b 1847, dau of Arthur "Arts" McIlhaney, b 4 Dec 1817, son of William and (9) Elizabeth (nee Ledbetter) McIlhaney. No issue. Tom enlisted in the 1st Confederate Ark Field Battery. Captured at Vicksburg, Miss on 4 Jul 1863 and paroled three days later on his oath that he would not further assist the Confederate cause. Removed after 1870 from Madison Co to Okla Territory.

195—Minerva Jane, b 23 Jun 1841, d 29 Feb 1853.

196—Suzanna, b 7 May 1844, d 18 Nov 1860 in Madison Co. m Tucker Upton.

197—John Allen, b 13 Dec 1846, d 24 Apr 1859 in Madison Co.

198—Lewis Cass, b 6 Mar 1849 in Cannon Co, Tenn, d 6 Jan 1942 at Asher, Madison Co, Ark.

199—Starling Monroe "Bud", b 7 Apr 1852, d 1 Mar 1918, m 20 Nov 1881 at Fayetteville, Washington Co, Ark to S. J. "Dolly" Winkler, b 1860.

200—Winnie Parline, b 4 Dec 1854, d 21 Jun 1955 at Japton, Madison Co at age 100. m 1875 William Enoch "Willie" Spurlock, b 1855 in Tenn.

201—Isaiah, b 25 Jan 1859, d 29 Nov 1947 at Elkins, Washington Co, Ark.

(44) Hugh M., son of (6) George. Removed in the early 1830s, probably with his brother Jeff, from near Rocky River in eastern Warren (now Van Buren) Co, Tenn to Wilmouth Creek in western Warren (now Cannon) Co, then, at some time between June 1849 and the 1850 census-taking, removed from Cannon Co to Madison Co, Ark. m Mary "Polly" Herriman, b 1810 in Tenn, d about 1880 at the home of dau Nancy at Aurora in Madison Co. In addition to 3 daughters who died young and whose names are not known, their children were:

202—Eliza, b 17 Jul 1826 in Tenn, d 21 Jan 1913 in Madison
Co. m Claiborne Thomas, b 1824, murdered 1863-65 in
Madison Co after he returned home from the Civil War
for a visit.

203—Nancy, b 1835 in Tenn, d after Nov 1914 at which time
she resided in Madison Co. m John Guinn, b 1835 in
Tenn, d after Nov 1914.

204—Charlotte "Lottie", b 29 Aug 1837 in Tenn, d 3 Jan
1925 in Madison Co. m Thomas Carrol Jackson, b 1842
in Tenn.

205—James M., b 1840 in Cannon Co, Tenn, d 10 Jan 1885
in Sebastian Co, Ark.

206—Sarah, b 14 May 1843 in Tenn, d 4 Feb 1925 near St
Paul, Madison Co. m 11 Jan 1866 near Aurora, Madison
Co to John C. Teague, b 7 Aug 1841 near Woodbury,
Cannon Co, Tenn, d 4 Nov 1914 near St Paul, son of
John and Mary Teague. He was a "Musician" in Co "B",
1st Union Ark Inf during Civil War.

207—Zady Ann, b 1846 in Tenn.

208—William, b 1848 in Tenn.

209—John Dillard, b 20 Jun 1854 in Ark, d 28 May 1927 on
War Eagle Creek, in Madison Co.

(45) Harvey Carrol "Harve", son of (6) George. Removed
from his father's home of Rocky River in eastern Warren (now
Van Buren) Co, Tenn to near War Eagle Community in Madison
Co, Ark in 1836 when he was 20 years old. A farmer. m 1st 30
Apr 1837 in Madison Co to Sarah H. McElhaney, a first cousin, b
28 Jul 1821 in Tenn, d 11 Aug 1844 in Madison Co, dau of William and (9) Elizabeth (nee Ledbetter) McIlhaney. The children
of this marriage, all born in Madison Co, were:

210—Nancy Emeline, b 30 Apr 1840, d age 16 years in
Madison Co.

211—Laura Ann, b 24 Dec 1841, d 11 Aug 1926 at Springtown, Parker Co, Texas. m 19 Jul 1861 in Madison Co
to Harlan Keeling, b 5 May 1834 in Tenn, d 7 Nov 1911
in Parker Co, Texas, son of Thomas and Mary "Polly"
(nee Irick) Keeling.

212—George Washington, b 24 Nov 1843, d 17 Jan 1927 in Madison Co.

(45) Harve m 2nd 8 Jan 1846 in Madison Co, Ark to Mary Ann Bowen, b 29 Dec 1827 in Grainger Co, Tenn, d 31 Mar 1907 in Madison Co, dau of John and Jane (nee Bridgeman) Bowen; John b 1799, d 1844 in Madison Co, was first judge of Madison Co. The children of Harve and Mary Ann, all born in Madison Co, were:

213—Charles M., b 25 Dec 1847, d age 6 months in Madison Co.

214—Sarah Harris, b 25 Dec 1848, d 10 Feb 1925 in Madison Co. m 1865 James Washington Officer, b 1847 in Tenn.

215—William Russell "Bill", b 5 Aug 1850, d 14 Apr 1942 at Speegleville, McLennan Co, Texas.

216—Julia A., b 2 Jun 1852, d age 9 years in Madison Co.

217—Alfred M., b 18 Apr 1854, d age 3 years in Madison Co.

218—Mary Jane, b 23 Mar 1856, d 11 Nov 1930 in Madison Co. m 1st 10 Apr 1918 in Madison Co to Carl Emil Reehling, b 27 Mar 1860, d 24 Dec 1919 in Madison Co. m 2nd H. B. Walters.

219—James Alfred, b 31 May 1858, d at age 15 years in Madison Co as result of a kick by a work steer.

220—John Henry, b 23 Jun 1861, d 23 Nov 1882 in Madison Co. Did not marry.

221—Tennessee Elnor "Tennie", b 1 Apr 1863, d Aug 1890. m William "Bill" Cox, b 28 Mar 1857, d 28 Mar 1934, son of Stephen and Elizabeth (nee Bowen) Cox.

222—Mildred Armanda "Mindie", b 12 Jan 1867, d 19 Feb 1946 in Waurika, Jefferson Co, Okla. m 24 Sep 1891 in Okla Terr (now Muskogee Co) to Rufus M. Mock, b 1857 in Randolph Co, Ark, son of Griffith C. and Margaret J. Mock.

223—Martha Elizabeth "Mat", b 23 Feb 1869, d 1938 in Parker Co, Texas. m 22 Dec 1889 in Aurora, Madison Co to James Upton, b 1870 in Ark, d 1950 in Parker Co, Texas, son of Josephus S. "Seephie" and Mary Jane (nee Robinson) Upton.

224—Marion Willard "Bud", b 23 Dec 1870, d 9 Aug 1937 in Bristow, Creek Co, Okla.

225—Caroline Melvina, b 24 July 1873, d 1 Jun 1957 at Poolville, Parker Co, Tex. m 11 Jan 1890 in Aurora, Madison Co to Josephus R. "Joe" Upton, b 10 Aug 1866 in Ark, d 14 Dec 1951 in Parker Co, son of John and Lucinda (nee Robinson) Upton. Joe was a first double cousin to Jim Upton, above.

(46) Eli "Eel", son of (6) George. It is likely he left his father's home on Rocky River in Eastern Warren (now Van Buren) Co, Tenn to live with or near his brothers Jeff and Hugh in Western Warren (now Cannon) Co where he married at about age 20. Removed 1850 to Madison Co, Ark where he resided until at least 1880. Later removed to Poteau (now in Le Flore Co), Okla Territory. m 1st 25 Apr 1838 in Cannon Co to Mary "Polly" Ashford, b 1820 in Tenn, d 1860-63 in Ark. Their children were:

  226—Lucinda, b 1841 in Tenn, d Dec 1869 in Madison Co. m 22 Feb 1865 at Fort Smith, Ark to Joseph Thomas of Co "B", 1st Union Ark Inf, b 1 Jan 1840 in Madison Co, d 4 Nov 1919 in Ore. He m 2nd 7 May 1871 Livona Drake.

227—James, b 1843 in Tenn, probably d young. Note 2nd son James.

228—Eliza Jane, b 1844 in Tenn. m Ashley Wages, b 1848 in Ark. Resided at Ryker, Newton Co, Ark.

229—Josiah, b 9 Jan 1846 in "Middle Tennessee", d 30 Nov 1911 at North Powder, Union Co, Ore.

230—Harvey Carrol "Heavy Harve", b 6 Aug 1848 in Tenn, d at Westville, Adair Co, Okla.

231—Nancy Ann, b 1852 in Ark. m ————— Thomas.

232—Elizabeth "Lizzie", b 1854 in Ark. m 1st after 1880. m 2nd ————— Burchett.

233—Mary P., b 1857 in Ark, d at Coal Dale near Bates, Scott Co, Ark. m Dan H. Minor, a coal miner, b 1857 in Ark, d at Coal Dale.

(46) Eli m 2nd 1862-63 in Ark to Mrs Jane Robinson, b 1830 in Ala who had dau Rhoda Robinson, b 1861 in Ark. Their children were:

234—Alice "Allie", b 1865 in Ark. m Charlie Lyons. Resided Fort Smith, Ark.

235—Josephine "Josie", b 1868 in Ark. m Jimmy Reeves. Resided 1942 Cisco, Texas.

236—James (2nd), b 1873 in Ark.

237—Ellen, b 1875 in Ark, d when a child.

238—Washington. Accidentally shot and killed by an older brother when a little boy.

(48) Elizabeth "Betts", daughter of (6) George. Removed 1848-49, most likely with her father and mother, from Tenn to Madison Co, Ark and resided there as late as 1880. m after 1850 to ——— Alexander without issue. Lived most of her life with her children in various parts of Arkansas, Texas and Oklahoma. She gave birth to 2 sons and 2 daughters:

239—Nancy Arminda "Mindie", b 7 Oct 1839 in Tenn, d 12 Nov 1919 at Nimrod, Eastland Co, Texas. m 8 Apr 1856 to Isaiah T. Hock, b 4 Aug 1829 in Tenn, d 27 Jan 1921 in Eastland Co, Texas, son of George Washington and Mary (nee Thomas) Hock.

240—Mahetabel "Hetty", b 1844 in Tenn, d in Johnson Co, Texas. m 1860 to George Washington Hock Jr, b 28 Jul 1837 in Tenn, d 23 Jan 1918 at Joshua, Johnson Co, Texas, brother of above Isaiah T. Hock. Resided in McLennan Co, Texas in 1880.

241—James Harvey "Jim", b 1 Mar 1848 in Tenn, d 15 Feb 1925 in Madison Co, Ark.

242—Monroe N. "Bud", b Feb 1850 in Ark, d after 1921 in Porter, Wagoner Co, Okla. m Nanny Harrison.

(49) William M. "Bill", son of (6) George. Removals: 1849 Cannon Co, Tenn to Madison Co, Ark; back to Cannon Co by Jan 1852; 1877 to Taney Co, Mo; 1878-80 to Madison Co; again to Cannon Co in 1889; 1894 to Bell Co, Texas; and finally in 1903 to near Bells, Grayson Co, Texas. m 1st 17 Apr 1842 in Cannon Co to Susannah Sullens, b 17 Mar 1823 in Tenn, d 1870-74 in Cannon Co. Their children, all born near Gassaway, Cannon Co, Tenn, were:

243—John, b 4 Dec 1844, d 15 Nov 1866 near Gassaway. Did not marry.

244—Thomas, b 15 Sep 1846, d 12 Nov 1891 near Gassaway.

245—Alfred "Little Alf", b 15 Nov 1848, d 11 Feb 1940 in Fullerton, Orange Co, Calif.

246—Elizabeth, b 31 Jan 1852, d 31 May 1854.

247—Caroline, b 15 Aug 1854, d 1915-20 at Princeton, Collin Co, Texas. m 13 Feb 1876 in Cannon Co to William "Billy" Smith.

248—Tilford "Tilf", b 9 Jun 1858, d 8 Jun 1924 near Gassaway.

249—George Washington, b 16 Jun 1861, d 3 Mar 1939 at Bixby, Tulsa Co, Okla.

250—James, b 11 Aug 1863, d young; before 1870.

(49) William M. "Bill" m 2nd 15 Mar 1874 in Cannon Co, Tenn to Martha A. Murphy, b 10 Sep 1852 in Ala, d 12 July 1926 in Grayson Co, Texas, dau of D. F. and Eliza (nee Dennis) Murphy. Their children were 6 sons and 5 daughters:

251—Elijah Franklin, b 20 Jan 1875 in Cannon Co. d 4 Nov 1905 at Denton, Denton Co, Texas of typhoid fever.

252—Eliza, b 30 Oct 1876 in Cannon Co. d 6 May 1877 in Mo.

253—Sarah Paralee, b 7 Feb 1878 in Taney Co, Mo. Resided 1956 at Nashville, Tenn. m 25 Jan 1894 in DeKalb Co, Tenn to John W Beaty, b 17 Dec 1877 in DeKalb Co, Tenn, d 12 Dec 1928 in Warren Co, Tenn.

254—Mary F., b 15 Apr 1880 in Madison Co, Ark. Resided 1956 at Menard, Menard Co, Texas. m 1900 in Bell Co, Texas to J. E. Kinney.

255—William Hiatt "Bill", b 20 May 1882 in Madison Co, Ark, d 5 Sep 1953 in Grayson Co, Texas. m 1st 1902 in Bell Co, Texas to Bessie Willis. m 2nd 15 Dec 1907 in Grayson Co to Maude Carver.

256—Birttie, b 11 Feb 1884 in Madison Co, Ark. Resided 1956 in Houston, Texas. m 1st 1902 in Collin Co, Texas to Will Cupp. m 2nd 1916 in Grayson Co, Texas to Lawrence Hicks.

257—Monroe M., b 9 Feb 1886 in Madison Co, Ark. Resided 1961 near Denison, Grayson Co, Texas.

258—Helen (Heelen), b 27 Apr 1888 in Madison Co, Ark.

Resided 1956 in Honeygrove, Fannin Co, Texas. m 1903 in Fannin Co to M. F. Clark.

259—Cleveland, b 14 Jul 1892 in Warren Co, Tenn, d 13 Apr 1906 in Grayson Co, Texas.

260—Dock H., b 16 Apr 1895 in Bell Co, Texas. Resided 1962 near Viola, but in Grundy Co, Tenn.

261—Early, b 29 Sep 1897 in Bell Co, Texas. Killed in a railway accident 10 Aug 1914 at Van Ormy, Bexar Co, Texas.

(50) James, son of (6) George. Farmed on War Eagle Creek eight miles south of Huntsville, Madison Co, Ark after leaving Cannon Co, Tenn in 1849 at age about 22. m 11 May 1849 in Cannon Co, Tenn to Sabrina "Tennessee" Reeves, b 1832 in Tenn, d 1870 in Ark. Their children included 4 sons and 4 daughters, all born in Madison Co, Ark. After James' death, Sabrina m 2nd James Clark. To the latter was born only one son in 1868 named Jason A. Lincoln Clark who resided 1937 in El Reno, Okla. James Ledbetter's children were:

262—George Washington "Big George", b 27 Jun 1850 near Aurora, d 21 Jun 1921 at Drakes Creek, Madison Co, Ark.

263—James Franklin "Bud", b 15 Dec 1852, d 8 Jul 1937 in Muskogee, Muskogee Co, Okla. This was the Oklahoma Marshal.

264—Alfred Payne, b 14 May 1855, d 14 May 1940 in Fullerton, Orange Co, Calif.

265—Elizabeth "Lizzie", b 1856, d near Vinita, Craig Co, Okla. m Brink Dennis.

266—Susan Jane "Susie", b 1858, d near Mulberry Creek, Crawford Co, Ark. m 1st ——— Dare, m 2nd Albert Bass.

267—Samantha E., b 1859. m Ben Vick.

268—Jerry Turner, b 8 Aug 1861 near Drakes Creek, d 10 Aug 1933 at Vinita, Craig Co, Okla.

269—Luvena T. "Venia", b 1863, d in Okla, probably near Shamrock in Creek Co. m Plumber Dwyer.

(52) Isaac Anderson, oldest son of (10) Reverend Arthur.
m Cynthia Jones, b 1824 in Tenn, dau of Evan Jones, one of the
early settlers of Overton Co, Tenn. They resided in Overton Co
until at least 1850 at which time he cleared up a number of
debts. He is the only brother who did not go to Dallas Co, Texas
in 1848 with his father, however he settled near Graham, Young
Co, Texas before 1860. Enlisted 17 Mar 1862 at Houston, Texas
in Co "A", Griffin's Bn, 21st Confederate Texas Inf. Served as
musician and in the Quartermaster Dept, and quite a bit of time
in pursuit of escaped prisoners and deserters. They had a grandson
named Joseph A. Ledbetter, b 1877 in Texas, and their children
included:

270—Armilda, b 1846 in Tenn.

271—Alexander T., b 1848 in Tenn.

272—Calvin, b winter of 1849-50 in Tenn.

273—Porter E., b 1853 in Texas.

274—Martha J., b 1855 in Texas. m ——— Weatherford.

275—Lucy B., b 1865 in Texas.

(54) Oliver Vincent, son of (10) Reverend Arthur. Left
Overton Co, Tenn with his father's family on 7 Mar 1848 and
settled in Dallas Co, Texas where he remained. m 4 Mar 1848 in
Overton Co to Margaret Fox, b 24 Jul 1828 in Ala, d 2 Feb 1899
in Dallas Co, Texas, dau of Joseph and Lucy (nee Evans) Fox.
Joined 31 Aug 1862 at Dallas, Co "A", Griffin's Bn, 21st Confederate Texas Inf. Served in the Quartermaster Dept at Beaumont,
Texas with specific duties as mechanic, carpenter, wagon-maker
and wheelwright. Their children included the following; all born
in Texas, probably Dallas Co:

276—Thomas J. (1st), b 10 Feb 1850, d 20 Mar 1851 in
Dallas Co.

277—Nathaniel B., b 1852, d at age 24 while surveying in
Brown Co, Texas. Drowned in Pecan Bayou near Brown-
wood. Body never recovered.

278—Wesley C. "Lum", b 1854. m Rebecca ———, b 1854
in Ala. They resided with his father's family in Dallas
Co in 1880. His sons Ed and William b 1876 in Tex,
lived in Marlo, Okla. Lum lived longer than the other
children.

279—Minerva Jane "Sissy", b 1856. m ———— Denson.
280—William Oliver "Ollie", b 21 Aug 1856, d 30 Jun 1917
    in Dallas Co.
281—Melvina M. "Linnie", b about Jun 1860. m ————
    Spillers of Garland, Texas.
282—James J. "Bud", b 1862, d in Dallas, Texas.
283—Arthur Lee, b 1863, d 1912 in Dallas, Texas.
284—Thomas John, b 1865. Resided in Mineral Wells, Texas.
285—Carrol E., b 1868, d 1929 in Dallas Co. m Etta ————,
    b 1869, d 1945 in Dallas Co.

(55) Lewis B., son of (10) Reverend Arthur. Evidently left Overton Co, Tenn with his father's family on 7 Mar 1848; settling in Dallas Co, Texas only a short time before moving on and finally settling in McCulloch Co, Texas. Joined Co "K", 5th Confederate Texas Cav on 20 Jun 1862 at Weatherford, Parker Co, Texas. Appointed 4th Sergeant on 20 Oct 1862. m Jane Blackwell. They resided in or near Brady, McCulloch Co, Texas. They had 12 children including:

286—Claude
287—Bob
288—Mollie
289—Ellen m ———— Moore.
290—Ora

(57) Thomas Logan, son of (10) Reverend Arthur. m Lois Almeda Hughes, a widow with children, b 1834 in Tenn, d 23 Aug 1861 at age "29 yr, 6 mo, 12 da" in Dallas Co, Texas "about 3 years after marriage". Joined 10 Apr 1862 at Breckenridge, Stephens Co, Texas, Co "K" 19th Confederate Texas Cav. Was shot in the right arm "about two inches below the shoulder" and on 11 Jan 1864 was determined not fit for duty. Blue eyes, light hair, 5 ft., 10 in. Resided Dallas Co, Texas in Mar 1864. Almeda's children of former marriage were probably Sarah E., b 1855, and William T., b 1856 as shown in 1860 Census of Dallas Co, Texas. The only children of Logan and Almeda were the two sons listed below who each had large families living in Dallas Co in 1957:

291—Arthur Lonnie "Lon", b 9 Nov 1859 in Texas, d 14 Jan
    1922, m Perdita ————, b 1 Mar 1873, d 14 Feb 1939

in Dallas Co, Texas. Their children included two infant sons both b and d in Dallas Co 1908 and 1914 respectively.

292—Lois Davis, b 21 Aug 1861, d 17 Sep 1938. His children included Elmer B., b 23 Feb 1895, d 22 Apr 1959, who served in Co "E", 111th Engrs, 36 Div in World War I.

(59) Arthur Brooks, son of (10) Reverend Arthur. His mother died when he was almost three years old and he was taken to the home of his elder brother, Oliver Vincent, where he lived for a short time before returning to live with his father and stepmother by Nov 1850. Volunteered on 28 Apr 1862 at Houston, Texas in Co "A", Griffin's Bn, 21st Confederate Texas Inf. He returned home after the war and m 6 Sep 1866 to Mrs Mary Pell (nee Wright) Jones, b 12 Dec 1848 in Giles Co, Va, dau of Tyrie and Mary Wright. Removed 1882 from Young Co, Texas to Searcy Co, Ark. To this union were born 10 sons and 2 daughters:

293—James Oliver, b 17 Nov 1867 in Dallas Co, Texas, d 10 Sep 1940 at Broken Arrow, Tulsa Co, Okla.

294—Thomas Lewis, b 29 Oct 1869 in Hood Co, Texas, d 29 Apr 1852 at Pryor, Mayes Co, Okla.

295—William Columbus, b 23 Dec 1871 in Dallas Co, Texas, d 24 Nov ———— at South Canadian (now Pittsburg Co), Okla Terr. m 9 Feb 1898 in Okla Terr (now Pittsburg Co) to Pearl Jones, b 1880.

296—Horace Alfred, b 31 Dec 1873 in Dallas Co, Texas. Resided 1956 at Wier, Kansas.

297—Anderson, b 20 Jan 1876 in Comanche Co, Texas, d there 11 Jul 1876.

298—Arthur, b 15 Sep 1877 in Young Co, Texas, d 29 Apr 1899 in New Okmulgee (now Okmulgee Co), Okla Terr.

299—Lacy Edwin, b 2 Dec 1879 in Young Co, Texas, d there 7 Apr 1880.

300—Floyd, b 11 Mar 1881, in Young Co, Texas, d 13 Mar 1949 in Blythe, Riverside Co, Calif. m Maude Brown.

301—Mary Elizabeth, b 27 Jul 1883 in Searcy Co, Ark, d 13 Dec 1951 at Hayward, Alameda Co, Calif. m in Searcy

Co, Ark to John T. Plant. Removed after 1931 from Tulsa Co, Okla to Calif.

302—Early Lee, b 13 Dec 1886 in Searcy Co, Ark, d 15 Apr 1949 at Broken Arrow, Tulsa Co, Okla.

303—Medora Belle, b 1 Feb 1888 in Searcy Co, Ark, d 21 Oct 1926 at Pryor, Mayes Co, Okla. m Ben F. Mayes, son of Jasper M. and Eliza (nee De Priest) Mayes.

304—Orchard Brooks, b 21 Aug 1891 in Searcy Co, Ark, d 1 Apr 1915 at Drumright, Creek Co, Okla of flu. Never married.

(64) William Hughes, son of (10) Reverend Arthur. m 27 May 1890 at Ferris, Ellis Co, Texas to Mattie S. Malone, b 1 Apr 1867, d 1938 in Dallas Co, dau of George L. and Emma D. Malone. He was an inventor of farm machinery, including the Ledbetter One-Seed Cotton Planter. Their children were 2 sons and one daughter; all born in Dallas, Dallas Co, Texas:

305—James Camrod, m a Dallas girl. No issue. Patent attorney in New York City in 1960.

306—William Broadus. Resided 1932 at Merced, Calif.

307—Elizabeth Emily, m F. W. Fields of Milwaukee, Wisc.

(65) George Washington, youngest son of (10) Reverend Arthur. m 23 Nov 1881 Sarah Elizabeth Smith, b 19 Apr 1859 at Smyrna, Rutherford Co, Tenn, d 22 Nov 1930 in Dallas, Texas, dau of Robert N. and Elizabeth (nee Creel) Smith. She removed 1869 from Tenn to Dallas Co, Texas. He was a Commissioner of Dallas Co for 8 terms; 1916-1933. "Ledbetter Drive" in Dallas is named for him. Their children were all born in Dallas Co. Lena, Ruth and Irene lived unmarried together in 1962 at the old home place which had been in the family since 1846. The children were:

308—Nellie, d 1917. m Thomas B. Goode.

309—Jesse, d 1915.

310—Ella Maude, m J. R. Brandenburg. Resided 1960 in Dallas.

311—Annie Elizabeth "Bessie", m W. C. Overton. Resided 1960 in Dallas.

312—James Garfield, d 1957 in La. m Odessa Savone in La. Served in the Army Aviation Corps in World War I. No issue. Resided 1934 at Port Barre, La.

313—Lena.

314—Robert M., m early in 1919 Sallie Smith. Resided 1960 in Dallas. Their children were Marie, Jean, Margie and George Robbins.

315—Lucy L., b 7 Jun 1894, d 13 Apr 1942 in Dallas Co. m M. G. Campbell.

316—Frankie L., m 24 Dec 1919 Morgan Millican of El Paso, Texas. Resided 1960 in El Paso.

317—Ruth.

318—Billie Margaret, m 1925 E. F. Hale. Resided 1960 in Dallas.

319—Irene.

(66) Isaac Jones "Ike", son of (11) Jones. m in Overton Co, Tenn to Minerva Jane Raines, b 1829 in Tenn, d 1890 at Berryville, Carroll Co, Ark, dau of William Raines. They removed 1856 to Carroll Co, Ark. Enlisted in the Union Army and was shot and killed by bushwhackers in Berryville early in the war. They had 4 sons and 4 daughters:

320—Sarah J. "Sallie", b 22 Oct 1847. Resided 1930 in Muskogee, Okla. m Lem G. Wright of Muskogee.

321—William Jones, b 27 Apr 1848, d 11 Aug 1917 at Berryville, Ark.

322—Andrew J. "Drew", b 1850, d Feb 1906 in Stone Co, Mo.

323—Mahala Ann, b 1853. Resided 1880 in Carroll Co, Ark. m Charles Davis, b 1848 in Ark.

324—Charity J., b 1855. m William Standlee.

325—Albert P., b 1857, d young; thrown from a horse.

326—Rachel Mallie, b 1859. Resided 1931 in Eureka Springs, Carroll Co, Ark. m 1st Ardell Davis. m 2nd Charles Cunningham.

327—Bud, b 1863, d at age 2 years.

(68) Buckner Harris T., son of (11) Jones. m Susannah C. Jackson, b 1823 in Tenn, d after 1883 in Kaufman Co, Texas, dau of Jane Jackson, b 1801 in NC, d about 1860 in Overton Co. Purchased land northwest of Locust Springs schoolhouse and resided as late as Dec 1851 on Nettle Carrier Creek in Overton Co, Tenn.

Removed to Texas by 1857. Military record: "Traveled from Little Rock, Ark to Douglas, Nacogdoches Co, Texas where he enlisted 10 Mar 1862 in Co "H", 17th Confederate Texas Cav. Black eyes, black hair, dark complexion, 5 ft., 9 in., a blacksmith by trade. Furnished his own horse. Promoted to Corporal 1 July 1862. Discharged 17 Jun 1863 at Little Rock, Ark." Their children included:

328—Richardson, b Sep 1849 in Overton Co, d young.

329—Nancy Jane, b 25 Mar 1851 in Overton Co, d 6 May 1937 on a visit in Corpus Christi, Texas but buried near Kemp, Kaufman Co, Texas. m J. T. Barnes, b 27 Jul 1848, d 4 Mar 1915 in Kaufman Co.

330—Dillard, b 22 Sep 1852 in Overton Co, d about age 9.

331—Robert Parris, b 5 Feb 1854 in Overton Co, d 10 May 1934 in Lynn Co, Texas.

332—Sarah Elizabeth, b 2 Oct 1855 in Overton Co, d 1952 in Kaufman Co, Texas. m 1st 3 Jan 1877 to Allen Willis, b 8 Aug 1854 in Hardin Co, Tenn, d 30 Dec 1884 in Praireville, Kaufman Co. m 2nd William H. McDougald who was husband of her sister Winnie. Both marriages in Kaufman Co. Issue both m.

333—Winnie Ann, b 10 May 1857 at Nacogdoches, Nacogdoches Co, Texas. d 1951 at Sweetwater, Texas. m 5 Nov 18— to William H. McDougald, b 1855, d 1950 in Kaufman Co. m 2nd ———— Richberg. Issue both m.

334—Mary Susan "Susie", d Muskogee, Okla. m Sam Hall.

335—John Thomas, d about age 16 in Kaufman Co, Texas.

336—Martelia E. "Teelia", d Kaufman Co. m after 1882 ———— Guthrie.

(70) Evan J. "Ive", son of (11) Jones. Removed 1850-60 from Overton Co, Tenn to Benton Co, Ark where he resided in 1870 and 1880. m Martha ————, b 1835 in Tenn. Enlisted 15 Aug 1862 at Bentonville, Benton Co, Ark in Co "H", 2nd Confederate (Gordon's) Ark Cav. Their children included 5 sons and 2 dau, all born in Ark:

337—James, b 1859, d 1870-80.

338—Robert, b 1861.

339—Charity Jane, b 1863.

340—William, b 1866.

341—Mary Bell (Mollie), b 1868.

342—David, b Feb 1870.

343—Allison, b 1873.

(73) Benjamin Laken C. "Lake", son of (11) Jones. m Marinda "Rinda" Bilbrey, b 1838 in Tenn. Joined 5 August 1861 at Livingston, Tenn, Co "H", 25 Conf Tenn Inf and attained rank of 2nd Corporal. A gunshot severely wounded his arm at the Battle of Murphreesboro on 31 Dec 1862. He was captured and then died from the wound on 10 Jan 1863 within Federal lines. Their two children, both born in Tenn, were:

344—Nancy, b 1858.

345—George Dallas, b 1860. Removed "west".

(76) James K. Polk "Poke", son of (11) Jones. m Armilda Shepherd, b 1843 in Tenn, d 7 Mar 1905 in Overton Co, Tenn, sister of James V. Shepherd who m (144) Martha Isabelle. Their children, all born in Overton Co, Tenn, were:

346—Isaac Granville, b 1865. m 21 Jun 1895 in Overton Co to Mrs. N. J. Rich.

347—Albert M., b 1867.

348—Mary Ann, b May 1870.

349—Burr E., b 1872.

350—Andrew V., b 1874.

351—William L., b 1877.

352—Robert Winston, b 24 May 1879 in Overton Co. Resided 1931 at Livingston, Overton Co. m 21 May 1901 in Overton Co.

353—Birdie

354—Rachel

(78) Will K. P., son of (11) Jones. m 2 May 1872 in Overton Co, Tenn to Mary Stout, b 1854 in Tenn, dau of Sam Stout. Their children, the first 4 born in Tenn, were:

355—James Daily, b 1873, m Lou Ellen Hammonds. Had sons Bob and Luther.

356—J. Porter, b 1875.

357—Alta J., (dau) b 1877, m 1st Logan Carr, m 2nd —— Neal.

358—N. A. (dau), b 1879. Probably died young.
359—Elizabeth "Lizzie", m Sherly Webb.
360—Perlie, m —————— Crawford.
361—Willie.
362—Jones. Killed himself.
363—Quillen.

(79) Andrew J. "Drew", son of (11) Jones. m 1st Nancy
Vaughn, dau of Vince Vaughn. His children were:
364—Sally, d before 1962. m Emmett Keisling.
365—Liza, d before 1962. m J. W. Hill.
366—Horace, b about 1882. m Fannie Margaret Hill, b 1884,
  d 1959, sister of J. W. Hill above. Had a son, Carl.
367—Vincent.
368—Granville, m May Norris. Resided 1961 east of Alpine,
  Tenn.
369—Rillie, m Wiley Little.
370—Dillard, twin to Rillie. m away from Overton Co, Tenn.
371—Fannie, m John Henry Smith.

(80) Jesse, son of (11) Jones, m Mary Lucy Cantrell, dau
of Reverend W. C. Cantrell, b 1836, d 1911. Their children were:
372—Hiram, m Effie Allred.
373—Lizzie, m————Oakley.
374—Lee (dau), m————Oakley.
375—Cora, m Grover Gill.

(81) John C., son of (11) Jones. m 1st Louisa Cantrell,
sister of Mary Lucy Cantrell who m his brother Jesse. Their children were:
376—William Jones, m Ora Smith.
377—Mae, m Dan Harris.
378—Nola, m Jones Hancock.
379—Ed, m Nora Smith. Had one son, Paul.
380—Pearl, m Foster Ledford.

(81) John C. m 2nd 10 Mar 1897 in Overton Co, Tenn to
Vestina Presley. Their children were:
381—Walter, d young.
382—Bertha, m Everett Copeland.

(82) Levi, son of (12) Aram (Aaron). Resided in Overton Co, Tenn from birth thru 1860 with adult life in the Roaring River area. No trace thereafter. m Nancy ————, b 1870. Their children, all born in Tenn, were:

383—Martha J., b 1839, d after 1860.
384—Mary E., b 1842, d after 1860.
385—Sarah C., b 1844, d after 1860.
386—Nancy E., b 1846, d after 1860.
387—Tabitha, b 1847, d 1850-60.
388—Adelia M. or Delila, b 1848.
389—James C., b 1851.
390—William, b 1854.
391—Lucinda, b 1856.

(85) William B., son of (12) Aram (Aaron) (?). Removed from Roaring River area in Overton Co, Tenn to Texas Co, Mo in 1850-55. m Mary ————, b 1825 in Tenn. Their children included:

392—Alvin C., b 1846 in Overton Co, d 5 Apr 1883 at Licking, Texas Co, Mo.
393—William, b 1849 in Tenn, d probably 1850-60.
394—Levi M., b 1855 in Mo.
395—John S., b 1857 in Mo, d after 1880.
396—James G. H., b 1858 in Mo, d after 1917. Resided 1894 in Texas Co, Mo.

(87) Henry, son of (12) Aram (Aaron) (?). m Ladz ————, b 1832 in Tenn. The family is not accounted for after 1850 at which time they resided in Overton Co, Tenn. Their children included Sarah, b 1850, probably in January in Tenn.

(90) Jones, son of (13) Beverly. m in Tenn to Catherine Nation, b 1824 in Tenn, removed from Mo to Ark possibly 1888, d 1912 at Peel, Marion Co, Ark while living with her dau Fannie. After death of Jones, she m 2nd ———— Tabor and had sons Henry and Jake. Jones enlisted 4 Aug 1862 in Co "I", 32nd Union Mo Infantry and died in the Post Hospital at Rolla, Mo on 1 Nov 1862. Their residence was near Clear Springs, Texas Co, Mo and their children included:

397—Isaac Tillman, b 1845 in Tenn, d before 1933.

398—Margaret Jane, b 1847 in Tenn. m 30 Jul 1864 at Rolla, Phelps Co, Mo to David M. Johnson, b 31 July 1840, son of John Price and Rachel R. Johnson.

399—James Beverly, b 1849 in Tenn, d before 1933.

400—George Washington, b 18 Jul 1850 in Tenn, d Mar 1888 at Clear Springs, Texas Co, Mo.

401—Lucinda, b 1855 in Tenn.

402—Nancy E., b 1858 in Mo.

403—Fannie, b 1861 in Mo, d after 1912. m ———— Risley and they resided at Peel, Marion Co, Ark.

(94) James W., son of (13) Beverly. m (115) Elizabeth Ledbetter, b 1833 in Tenn, his first cousin. They resided 1860 in Fentress Co, Tenn, and 1870 and 1880 in Overton Co. Their 14 children, all born in Tenn, were:

404—Buckner H., b 1854. m Emyline A. ————, b 1848 in Tenn. Listed in the 1880 census of Overton Co. Their children included James W., b 1875 in Tenn who m 6 Jul 1895 in Overton Co to Mahala Anne Sells; and Alfred W., b 1878 in Tenn.

405—Nancy Jane, b 1856.

406—George Beverly, b 1857.

407—Jones W. "Jonah", b 1859. m, probably in Fentress Co, Tenn to Tennessee J. Upchurch, b 1863 in Tenn, dau of Joseph Upchurch of Fentress Co. Their children included a dau, Rebecca J., b Nov 1879 in Tenn.

408—Arthur A., b about Dec 1859.

409—James Mathias, d in infancy.

410—Winefred "Winnie", b 1862.

411—Elijah "Tice", b 1863.

412—Delila Adela, b 1865.

413—Phillip, b 1867, d before 1870 according to census.

414—John Mc., b Jan 1870. Is possibly the John Mc who m 24 Dec 1890 in Overton Co to Martha Hensley.

415—William "Will", b 1870.

416—Lafayette, b 1872. m 28 Nov 1893 in Overton Co to (506) Angy Ledbetter.

417—Henrietta, b 1874.

(100) Ewing Mc "Mack", son of (13) Beverly. m probably in Fentress Co, Tenn to Sibbia A. Rooker, b 1843 in Tenn, d after 1909. They spent their lives in Fentress-Overton Co, Tenn. Their children, all born in Tenn, were:

    418—James Marion, b 14 Jul 1866, d before 1962. Possibly is the James M. who m 10 Oct 1897 in Overton Co to Etta Sells.

    419—Campbell, b Mar 1870, d before 1962. m 7 Oct 1897 in Overton Co to Lou Jones.

    420—John A., b 1875, d before 1962. m 14 May 1893 in Overton Co to Lee Tayse.

    421—Alexander "Alex", b 1876. Resided 1962 near Livingston, Overton Co with his youngest daughter.

    422—Lou Dora, b 1878, d summer of 1961.

(101) Bitha Ellen, daughter of (13) Beverly. Born and lived with parents in Fentress Co, Tenn until at least 1880. The 1880 census indicates she had the following children named Ledbetter, all born in Tenn:

    423—Lareen F., b 1868.

    424—James McJ., b May 1870.

    425—Sousy C., b 1873.

    426—Mary E., b 1878.

    427—Rhoda A., b Jun 1880.

(110) Hamilton, son of (14) James. m Harriet ———, b 1835 in Ga. Spent their lives on Obeds River in Overton Co, Tenn. Joined 2 Aug 1863 at Camp Nelson, Ky, Co "A", 11th Union Tenn Cav. Captured 22 Feb 1864 at Wineman's Mill, Lee Co, Va and paroled 21 Mar 1864 at Richmond. Blue eyes, light hair, fair complexion, a farmer. Their children included the following; all born in Tenn:

    428—Martha A. E., b 1859.

    429—William H., b 1863.

    430—James J. H. H., b 1865.

    431—E. Stokely, b 1869.

    432—L. F. (dau), b 1875.

(118)   Elijah W., only son of (17) Buckner H. m Ann Eliza Garrett, b 1845 in Tenn. They resided in Overton Co, Tenn prob-

ably all their lives. Their children included 3 sons and 6 dau; all born in Tenn, probably Overton Co:

    433—Maria J., b 1860.
    434—George J., b 1863.
    435—Laken, b 1865.
    436—Evalina, b 1866.
    437—Lou Dora, b 1868.
    438—Katie, b 1871.
    439—Nancy, b 1874.
    440—Mary Lou, b 1876.
    441—Ras Turner, b 1878.

(119) Nancy, daughter of (17) Buckner H. m a man named Robbins. In the 1870 census of Overton Co, Tenn she used the name Robbins and had no husband listed. The census listed the names of the oldest three children below as Robbins. However in 1880, she and these three youngest children resided in that same county near her brother Elijah W. and she used the name Ledbetter for her family. Her children evidently were as follows; all born in Tenn:

    442—Mary J., b 1862.
    443—Nancy Elizabeth, b 1864.
    444—Charles C., b Nov 1869. m possibly 23 May 1890
        in Overton Co to Nancy Gunnels.
    445—James M. "Jim Matt", b 1876.

(123) Robert H. son of (21) John. Enlisted 29 Jul 1861 at Elizabethtown, Hardin Co, Ill in Co "A", 29th Union Ill Inf. Blue eyes, light hair, fair complexion, 6 ft., 0 in., a farmer. Served extra details as waterhauler and in hospital in St Louis as a cook and nurse. Transfered 2 Sep 1863 to Co "A", 1st Battalion of Cav, Mississippi Marine Brigade. Discharged 6 Mar 1865. m 1st Minerva ——————, d 1861 at Cave-in-Rock, Hardin Co, Ill. m 2nd Becca Tucker, d 1885. m 3rd Nancy L. Oxford on 14 Dec 1889 in Hardin Co, Ill. m 4th Mary M. —————— on 2 Jul 1908 probably in Pope Co, Ill. Resided variously in Pope and Hardin Co, Ill from 1890 to 1910 and in Spring of 1888 at Hurricane, Crittenden Co, Ky. His children included:

    446—Mary J., b 26 Jan 1866.

447—Ollie, b 27 Jul 1871. Resided 1917 at West Point, Ky.
448—Robert L., b 6 Feb 1872.
449—Alex, b 16 Aug 1874.
450—Allen, b 28 Aug 1877.
451—Florence, b 23 Feb 1881.

(127) Matthew, son of (21) John. m Charlotte ————, b 1844 in Ill. Resided 1850, 1860 and 1880 in Hardin Co, Ill. Their children included the following; all born in Ill:
452—John, b 1870.
453—Eliza, b 1872.
454—Oscar, b 1876.
455—Dora, b 1878.
456—Rosetta, b winter of 1879-80.
457—Pronetta, b same as Rosetta above. Probably twins.

(131) James William, son of (25) Job. Orphaned at the age of 6 and went to live with people named Davidson or Holtzclaw in Hendricks Co, Ind. m 23 Feb 1885 at Boody, Macon Co, Ill to Anna Mariah Muirheid, b 28 Apr 1856 in Mo, d May 1935 at Indianapolis, Ind, dau of William and ———— (nee Hill) Muirheid. They had 8 children, 4 of whom died in early childhood. The 4 listed below were born in Greencastle, Putnam Co, Ind:
458—Harrison, b 26 Jun 1888, d Sep 1957 at Indianapolis, Ind. m 1916 at Indianapolis to Myrtle Engle and resided 1957 in Speedway City, Ind. He was a soldier in World War I. Their children were Harrison, David, and Robert.
459—Hazel, b 14 Mar 1892. Resided 1960 in Indianapolis. m 1911 George R. Anderson, d 1947.
460—Mearl, b 19 Jun 1897. Resided 1957 in Indianapolis. m 14 Oct 1914 in Indianapolis to Wilbur H. Meele. No issue.
461—Marion Carl, b 22 Aug 1899, d 4 Nov 1945 at Indianapolis. m about 1920 in Indianapolis to Helen Smalley. Their children were Duane Marion who resided 1957 in Lake Worth, Fla; Comrade Marguerite m Malcolm Gordon; and Anne Laurel.

(136) James Mitchell, son of (27) William. m 22 Jan 1861 at Livingston, Overton Co, Tenn to Margaret Ann France, b 31 May

1839, d 25 Apr 1922 in Taylor Co, Ky. Served in "Morgan's Cavalry" during the Civil War; Co "D", 10th Confederate Ky Mounted Rifles. Removed to Taylor Co, Ky after the war, where they bought land by his sister, Vinie Elder; lived and died there. They had the following children; all born in Taylor Co, Ky except as noted:

462—Vina Adeline, b 12 Nov 1861 in Cumberland Co, Ky, d 14 Feb 1930. m Robert Henry Miller on 15 Feb 1883 in Taylor Co, Ky.

463—Fannie Elizabeth, b 6 Aug 1863, d 11 Dec 1911. m R. L. Logan of Cumberland Co, Ky.

464—Nannie Officer, b 2 May 1868, d 29 Mar 1950 at Santa Anna, Calif. m in Cumberland Co, Ky to Emmett Brans-ford Huddleston of Narrowbone, Ky.

465—Mattie Clementine, b 8 Mar 1866, d 27 Jul 1882 in Taylor Co, Ky.

466—Lois Elmer, b 18 Jul 1870, d 23 Aug 1871 in Taylor Co, Ky.

467—William Alonzo, b 10 Sep 1873, d 7 Dec 1953 at Glascow, Montana.

468—Maggie Jane, b 5 May 1875. m at Burkesville, Cumberland Co, Ky to ——— Owens.

469—Andrew Jackson, b 12 Sep 1877. Resided 1961 in Louisville, Ky.

(138) Martin Van Buren, son of (27) William. m 25 May 1861 near Berryville, Carroll Co, Ark to Mary Jane Roper. When he first arrived in northwest Ark he lived with his Aunt (37) Sarah Sanders near Berryville. When the Sanders removed to Granby, Mo, he went along but later returned to Berryville. In Aug 1861 he was murdered by a man named Bullington. His only child was the posthumus son listed below. After Van's death, Mary Jane m 2nd in 1871 in Ark to ——— Tschudi who was 3 years older than she, a native of Switzerland, and a Confederate soldier. They lived in Aberdeen (1871-91) and Tupelo (1891) to at least 1894), Miss.

470—Martin Van Buren II, b 11 Apr 1862 in Mo, d 6 Jan 1896 at Corinth, Alcorn Co, Miss.

(140) MacMiller C. "Mack", son of (27) William. m 11
Jan 1871 at West Fork, Overton Co, Tenn to Margaret J. Sells, b
1854 in Tenn, dau of Tice and July Sells. The 1880 census lists
his occupation as "huckster". Their children, all born in Overton
Co, Tenn, were:

471—Christina, b 11 Aug 1872, d 20 Sep 1893 in Overton
   Co. m Westley Beats. Her father so strongly objected to
   the marriage that he placed her maiden name on her
   gravestone.

472—Julie Canzanda, b 1874, d 1900. m James Teeple.

473—Alonzo D., b 1876, killed by a train in 1927. m Sallie
   Walker whose parents were from Florida. Their children
   were Jim, Henry, Magenta, Roy, William, and Sara
   Catherine.

474—Loranzo Don, b 1 Oct 1878, d 29 Nov 1890 in Overton Co.

475—Fanny L., b 1879.

476—Dora, b 1880. m Henry Peters and resided 1931 in
   Clarkerange, Tenn.

477—Gilbert, b 1882. Resided 1931 near Monterey, Putnam
   Co, Tenn. m Annie Whitaker. Their children were Frank
   Walter, Mabel, Mitchell, Reagon, Ruby, Marie, Robert
   Grover, and Talmadge.

478—Forster, b 1884, killed by a train in 1900. m Ellen
   Anderson. Their one child was named Olen, who resided
   1931 in Nashville, Tenn.

479—Mitchell Elder, b 24 Nov 1886. Resided 1931 in Mon-
   terey, Putnam Co, Tenn. m Dec 1904 to Jemima A.
   Bagwell, b 24 Jan 1884. Their children were Louise,
   Roy, Blanche, Ruth, Willie Pauline, Woodrow, Margaret
   Frances, Paul, and Betty Ann.

(141) John Dillard, son of (27) William. m 22 Jun 1876
at Livingston, Overton Co, Tenn to Eliza Frances Neely, b 8 Mar
1853 in Va, d 27 Apr 1941. Their children were all born on the
old farm which originally belonged to William's grandfather,
Washington. One daughter died in infancy; the other children
being:

480—Landon "Lannie" Joe, b 12 Mar 1877, d 1 Mar 1956 at Nettle Carrier, Overton Co, Tenn. m Delia Carmack; divorced; no issue.

481—Charlie Virgil, b 28 Dec 1870. d 1962 near Monroe (Nettle Carrier), Overton Co.

482—William Chester, b 15 Sep 1883. Resided 1962 near Livingston, Overton Co. m Verna Allred, b 8 Sep 1895. Their children were Ray, Ralph m Lucille Brown, Oren m Mary Jo Poindexter and 2nd Pauline McDonald, Casto, Glen m Claudine Stover, Ella V., and Gentry m Elise Smith.

483—Samantha Lovenia "Beanie", b 8 Oct 1887. Resided 1962 at Decherd, Franklin Co, Tenn. m J. F. "Bill" Deck.

484—Allie Beulah, b 10 Jun 1893. Resided 1962 in Nashville, Tenn. m Maurice McDonald.

(145) William Lafayette "Fate", son of (27) William. m 1 Dec 1890 at Burkeville, Cumberland Co, Ky to Mary Agnes Paull, b 1868, dau of Martin and Adda (nee Phillips) Paull. They removed in Mar 1904 from Oak Grove, Overton Co, Tenn to Sacramento Co, California. In 1930-31, Fate furnished to Justus R. Moll most of the information used in determining the older family connections in this Arthur Ledbetter line. Their children were all born near Livingston, Overton Co, Tenn except the last two who were born at Elk Grove, Sacramento, Calif:

485—Perlie May, b 25 Aug 1891. m Van Huffman, brother to Franklin D. Huffman below. Resided 1957 at Gridley, Butte Co, Calif.

486—Leland, b 13 Jan 1893. m Newton Booth. Resided 1957 Elk Grove, Calif.

487—Read, b 5 Oct 1894. m Sam P. Biggs. Resided 1957 Sacramento, Calif.

488—Lucy, b 27 May 1896. m Franklin D. Huffman. Resided 1957 Sacramento, Calif.

489—Paull b 1 Apr 1900. m Lillian Sehlmeyer. Resided 1957 Sacramento, Calif.

490—Lester, b 15 Nov 1901. Resided 1957 near Elk Grove, Calif.

491—Victor, b 11 Nov 1906. m Norma Stanley. Resided 1957 Lakeport, Lake Co, Calif.

492—Clifford, b 9 Dec 1909. m Naomi Brown. Resided 1957 Elk Grove, Calif.

(147) Benjamin Berry, youngest son of (27) William. m 23 Sep 1897 at Nettle Carrier, Overton Co, Tenn to Eula Belle Keisling, b 27 Mar 1882 at Nettle Carrier, dau of A. G. and Eliza (nee Farley) Keisling. Removed 1898 from Nettle Carrier to Livingston where his wife resided in 1962. Their children were all born in Overton Co, Tenn and are as follows:

493—Conway Bernice, b 15 Apr 1901. Resided 1962 at Livingston, Overton Co, Tenn. Did not marry.

494—Roxie Anne, b 30 Nov 1902. Resided 1962 at Livingston also. Did not marry.

495—Ruby May, b 26 Jun 1904. d 21 Mar 1906 at Livingston.

496—Sallie Esther, b 25 Feb 1907. Resided 1958 at Hilham, Overton Co, Tenn. m J. B. Pigg.

497—Ethel Turner, b 6 Jun 1911. Resided 1958 at Royal Oak, Mich. m Homer Carr.

498—Auda Magdaline, b 9 Jan 1915. Resided 1958 at Colorado Springs, Colo. m Larry Spence.

499—Roy Berry, b 31 Dec 1916. Resided 1958 at Harlem, Ga. m Viola Nelson.

(150) Pleasant Hillary, son of (28) Benjamin. m in Overton Co, Tenn to Icy Ann Collins, b 1843 in Tenn, d 1921 in Overton Co, Tenn. They resided through 1880 in Overton Co, Tenn. Their children were all born in Overton Co:

500—Evert E. Lexes, b 29 Sep 1865, d 25 Jun 1940 at Caddo Gap, Montgomery Co, Ark.

501—Alvin, b 1868, d about 1928 in Overton Co, Tenn. m Dell Eads.

502—William "Billie", b May 1870, d about 1951. m 4 Apr 1890 in Overton Co to Emily Lou Eads.

503—Mary E., b 1872, d probably young in Overton Co, Tenn.

504—Francis E., b 1873. Resided 1957 in Overton Co, Tenn. m 2 Apr 1896 in Overton Co to Laura Crabtree.

505—Sidley, b 1878. Resided 1932 in Livingston, Overton
Co, Tenn. d before 1957. m R. H. Carr.

506—Angie, b 1878. Resided 1957 in Overton Co, Tenn. m
1st (416) Lafayette Ledbetter on 28 Nov 1893 in Overton Co. m later Charlie Maddox.

507—Lona, died Feb 1951 or 1954 at Glennwood, Ark. m
James Smith.

(153) James Calvin, son of (28) Benjamin. m 1874 at
Livingston, Overton Co, Tenn to Aquilla Collins, b 13 Jul 1854 in
Tenn, d 15 Mar 1917 in Overton Co. They had 4 sons and 4 daugh-
ters, all born in Overton Co, Tenn:

508—Andrew Virgil, b 12 Jun 1875, d after 1931.

509—Margaret, b 1878. Resided 1931 in Livingston, Overton
Co, Tenn. m Elbert McCormick.

510—William Porter, b Feb 1880. Resided 1931 in Livingston, Overton Co, Tenn. m Ethel Moore.

511—Ida, m Alex Collins. Resided 1931 in Livingston, Tenn.

512—Leona, m Floyd Ledford of Alpine, Overton Co, Tenn.
Resided 1931 in Alpine.

513—James Overton, b 9 Mar 1886, d Aug 1952 at Black
Springs, Montgomery Co, Ark. m (765) Martha Ledbetter.

514—Martley Alice, m Martin Smith. Resided 1931 in Norman, Montgomery Co, Ark.

515—Oliver, b 1891, d 1919 in Overton Co. m Madie Eldridge, b 1888, d 1913 in Overton Co.

(156) John Cambell, son of (28) Benjamin. m 1st 21 Mar
1870 to Sarah Jane Swallows, b 1849 in Tenn, dau of Joe Bealk
Swallows. m 2nd 11 Apr 1880 in Overton Co, Tenn to Jane P.
"Necy" Hammock, b 1863 in Tenn. They resided in Overton Co in
1880. Children of the first marriage, all born in Overton Co, were:

516—Isaac Egwart, b 20 Oct 1871.

517—Rasmus Haywood, b 19 Oct 1873.

518—Joseph Ben, b 18 Jan 1876.

(181) William Seyburn, son of (35) Wiley. m 1st Susan
Grisham, sister of his brother's wife Saphronia. m 2nd Yreka Lee.

The following, and two who died as infants, were his children (which wife is not recorded):

519—Alfred, b 24 Jun 1880. Resided 1931 in Lambert, Okla.

520—Lewis, d unmarried at age 44 years.

521—Robert, d at age 2 years.

Sixth Generation—Arthur Ledbetter Line

(191) Burwell (Burrel), son of (43) Jefferson Brooks. Removed to Sebastian Co, Ark from Madison Co, Ark on 25 Oct 1879; to Parker Co, Texas in 1883; and back to Sebastian Co in 1887 where he remained. Enlisted on 2 Feb 1863 at Fayetteville, Ark in Co "B", 1st Union Ark Inf. Blue eyes, light hair, fair complexion, 5 ft., 10 in. Promoted to corporal in Feb 1865. Mustered out 10 Aug 1865 at Fort Smith, Ark. m 20 Apr 1854 Jane H. Cox, b 10 May 1835 in Mo, dau of Jacob Cox. Their children, all born in Ark, were:

522—Sarah Catherine, d during the Civil War.

523—Mary Tennessee, b 1858, d during Civil War of burns from boiling wash water.

524—John William, b 2 May 1860 in Madison Co, d 12 May 1930 near Oden, Montgomery Co, Ark. m after 1880 Margaret Jackson, b 1859, dau of (204) Lottie.

525—Louisa Jane "Liza", b 23 Mar 1863, d 1947 near Loveland, Tillman Co, Okla. m 13 Apr 1878 near Aurora, Madison Co, Ark to John Calvin Lee, b 1860, d 1948.

526—Ulysses Grant, b 2 Aug 1866 near Aurora, Madison Co, d 12 Aug 1957 at Clovis, New Mexico.

527—Elizabeth Josephine (listed as Julia in 1880 census), b 22 Sep 1868 near Aurora, Madison Co, d 25 Sep 1955 near Washburn, Sebastian Co, Ark. m in Sebastian Co to George Washington Howard. d 1953. She had red hair.

528—Ida Emeline, b 22 June 1872 near Aurora, Madison Co, d 8 Feb 1957 in Chickasaw, Okla. m Zanie Spoon on 20 Jan 1890 near Washburn, Sebastian Co, Ark.

529—Lewis Monroe, b 12 Feb 1875 near Aurora, Madison Co, resided 1957 in Chickasaw, Okla. m 1st 29 Jul 1893 at Washburn, Ark to Mamie Campbell, d 1905 in

Sebastian Co. m 2nd 15 Mar 1908 at Washburn to
Minnie Rogers.

530—Burl Calvin, b 16 Oct 1878 near Aurora, Ark. Resided
1957 at El Reno, Okla. m in Madison Co to Esther Spurlock, niece of William E. Spurlock, b 1855 in Tenn who
m (200) Winnie.

(198) Lewis Cass, son of (43) Jefferson Brooks. m 12 Dec
1879 in Madison Co, Ark to Fairy Elizabeth Watson, b 13 May
1859 in Ky, d 5 Apr 1952 in Madison Co. Their children were
one son and eight daughters:

531—Tera Vivia, b 20 Nov 1880 in Madison Co, Ark, d 17
Feb 1905 at same place. Did not marry.

532—Mahala Elizabeth "Betty", b 10 Apr 1882. Resided 1956
at Haskell, Okla. m 3 Nov 1901 in Madison Co to H.
Doyle Sisemore, b 1881.

533—Mary Ellen "Ella", b 26 Feb 1884. Resided 1956 in
Asher, Madison Co. m 25 Aug 1901 in Madison Co to
Frank Atha, b 1876, d 21 Oct 1956.

534—Ida May, b 15 Nov 1885, d 1 Feb 1886.

535—Eliza Jane "Lizie", b 25 July 1888, d 20 Jan 1941. m 2
Jun 1907 in Madison Co to Fred Brooks, b 1883.

536—Lula Frances, b 24 Jun 1890, d 4 Jul 1890.

537—William Isaiah "Willie", b 4 Apr 1893 on Jackson Creek,
near Aurora, Madison Co. Resided 1956 in Corcoran,
Calif.

538—Winnie Maranda, b 23 Dec 1895, d 28 Sep 1927. m 11
Aug 1913 in Madison Co to John Sisemore, b 1893.

539—Telitha Melvina, b 8 Nov 1898. Resided 1956 in Fayetteville, Washington Co, Ark. m 18 Aug 1922 in Madison
Co to David Doyle Counts, b 1900.

(201) Isaiah, son of (43) Jefferson Brooks. Removed Dec-
ember 1907 from Madison Co, Ark to White River near Elkins,
Washington Co, Ark. Was a farmer and harvester. m 1st 1 Jan
1879 to Mahala Jane Neal, b 13 Aug 1858 near Ball Creek in
Madison Co, d 7 Mar 1910 at Elkins, dau of James and Rutha (nee
Drake) Neal. The couple were Primitive Baptists and devout

Christians. Their children were 1 son and 5 daughters; all born in
Madison Co, Ark:

> 540—Florence Effie, b 28 Sep 1879 near Aurora. m 22 Dec
> 1899 to William Henry Muncy, b 16 Jul 1878, d 27 Apr
> 1907, son of William and Polly Muncy. She resided 1957
> at Fayetteville, Washington Co, Ark.
>
> 541—Bertha Ethel, b 18 Jan 1883 near Drakes Creek. m 31
> Jan 1904 in Madison Co, Ark to Samuel Neal, b 19 Jul
> 1884, d 30 Sep 1952, son of Richmond and Sarah Eliza-
> beth (nee Ham) Neal. She resided 1957 near Huntsville,
> Madison Co, Ark.
>
> 542—Esir Freeman, b 30 Oct 1885 near Japton. d 10 Mar 1951
> in Madison Co, Ark. m 6 Feb 1933 in Fayetteville, Ark
> to Mary Henson. No issue.
>
> 543—Saphronia Estella, b 6 Apr 1889 at Drakes Creek. m
> Otto Bray in Fayetteville, Ark, son of William and Minnie
> Marguerite (nee Failor) Bray. Resided 1957 in Fayette-
> ville, Ark.
>
> 544—Dovie Esther, b 6 Apr 1893. d 3 Mar 1912 at Elkins,
> Washington Co, Ark. Did not marry.
>
> 545—Sina Mae, b 8 Nov 1898 near Drakes Creek. m 19 Jan
> 1921 at Harris, Washington Co, Ark to Ottis Orble
> Stephens, son of Seymour and Effie (nee Fleener)
> Stephens. Resided 1957 at Evansville, Indiana.

(201) Isaiah m 2nd 21 Apr 1913 in Washington Co, Ark to
Martha Ann (nee Ham) Alderson, b 1870 in Mo.

(201) Isaiah m 3rd 20 Aug 1922 in Washington Co, Ark
to Arma Dell "Della" (nee Dunaway) Allison, b 1872 in Ark.

(205) James M. "Jim", son of (44) Hugh. Joined Co "I",
16 Confederate Ark Inf on 16 Nov 1861 at Fayetteville, Ark. "Left
sick on march in Crawford Co, March 28, 1862." Enlisted in Co
"G", 1st Union Ark Inf on 13 Feb 1863 at Fayetteville, Ark. Promoted to Principle Musician (Fife Major) on 1 Jul 1863. Mustered out 10 Aug 1865. Removed from Madison Co, Ark to Indian
Territory (Okla). m 10 Sep 1865 near Huntsville, Madison Co to
Mary E. Robinson, b 8 Aug 1846 in Ark, d 16 Aug 1921 at Cal-
ington, Leflore Co, Okla, dau of Sinclair Robinson. She resided 1891

in Washburn, Sebastian Co, Ark. Their children, all born in Ark, were:

546—Hugh Lafayette, b 17 Nov 1866 in Aurora, Madison Co, d Tulsa, Okla. m Joe Etta Roberts, dau of Joel Roberts.

547—Mary Jane, b 9 Oct 1868, d 13 Mar 1959 at Fort Smith, Ark. m ———— Harrington.

548—Martha Elizabeth, b 6 Jan 1870, d Hanney, Okla. m Dave Kidwell.

549—Margaret C., b 15 Apr 1872, d 18 Oct 1875 in Aurora, Ark.

550—Joseph Howard, b 17 Jun 1875 at Aurora, Madison Co, Ark. Resided Jan 1962 near Muskogee, Okla.

551—John Wilson, b 10 Oct 1877, d Muskogee, Okla. Did not marry.

552—Doctor Franklin, b 6 Mar 1880, d Wewoka, Okla. m Mona Taylor.

553—Rosa Bell, b 13 Dec 1882 at Chisnville, Logan Co, Ark, d Kinta, Okla.

(209) John Dillard, son of (44) Hugh. m Mary Katherine Fields, b 4 Oct 1854 in Ark, d 27 Dec 1906 near Aurora, Madison Co, Ark. Their children were 6 sons and 7 daughters, all born near Aurora, Madison Co, Arkansas:

554—Stillborn baby—sex unknown.

555—Thomas Jerry "Tom", b 1875, d at Marshall (?), Okla.

556—Mahala Jane "Hala", b 1877, d at Arkoma, LeFlore Co, Okla. m Jess Hull.

557—Zadie Ann "Anna", d near Tulsa, Okla. m Noah Lewis.

558—Henrietta "Etta", b Oct 1879, d at Carthage, Jasper Co, Mo. m 11 Jun 1905 in Madison Co, Ark to Joe Hulstine, b 1879.

559—Hugh, b 1881. m 24 Dec 1911 in Madison Co, Ark to May Miller, b 1896. Resided 1956 in Arkoma, Le Flore Co, Okla.

560—Lizie, d at Vian, Sequoyah Co, Okla. m Bill Wells.

561—Johnny, d at age 9 years.

562—Willie, d at age 6 months.

563—Julie, resided 1956 in Kansas. m John Lewis.

564—Mary Hettie, b 23 Nov 1888, d 26 Jul 1961 at Springdale, Washington Co, Ark.

565—Charlottie "Lottie", m Frank Fields.

566—Voal Walker, b 12 Sep 1892. Never married. d 10 Oct
1957 at Springdale, Washington Co, Ark.

567—Samuel "Sam", b 1 Jul 18—. m Maude Robison. Resided
1956 north of Tulsa, Okla.

(212) George Washington, son of (45) Harvey Carrol. Enlisted 12 Jul 1862 in Madison Co, Ark in Co "I", 27th Confederate
Ark Inf. "Deserted and joined the enemy". Enlisted 27 Feb 1863 at
Fayetteville, Ark in Co "D", 1st Union Ark Inf. Served as musician
(drummer) from Feb 1864 to Jul 1865. Blue eyes, fair complexion,
5 ft., 6 in. Mustered out 10 Aug 1865 at Fort Smith, Ark. m 8 Nov
1865 Mahala Jane Baker, b 11 Sep 1844 in Huntsville, Alabama,
d 18 Jan 1927 in Madison Co, Ark within a few hours of her
husband of pneumonia. Their children were 4 sons and 1 daughter;
all born in Madison Co, Ark:

568—William Andrew "Willie", b 12 Jul 1866, d 12 Nov
1924 in Fayetteville, Washington Co, Ark. m 15 Apr
1895 at Fort Smith, Sebastian Co, Ark to Rosa L. Spoon
of Fannin Co, Texas, b 1875.

569—Elizabeth "Lizzie", b 25 Nov 1870, d 8 Mar 1906 in
Madison Co, Ark. Did not marry.

570—Henry Carrol (Listed as Harvey in 1880 Census), b 3
Aug 1872, d 7 Mar 1933 in Madison Co, Ark. m 1st
1 Sep 1895 Maggie Hillis in Huntsville, Madison Co; m
2nd Effie Burnett Cox.

571—John Plummer, b 7 Mar 1875, d 28 Apr 1844 in Springdale, Washington Co, Ark. m 3 Aug 1898 in Aurora,
Madison Co, Ark to Meady Whitely.

572—James Walter, b 21 Sep 1881. Resided 1961 near Mountain Home, Ark. m 1st 2 Aug 1903 in Madison Co, Ark
to Elizabeth Whorton, b 1883; m 2nd 14 Feb 1909 in
Huntsville, Madison Co, Ark to Grady Nell Hawkins.

(215) William Russell, sixth of the eighteen children of
(45) Harvey Carrol, probably was named for a paternal uncle and
for his maternal uncle, Russ Bowen. A stern father caused him to

leave home on War Eagle Creek in Madison Co, Ark in 1868. He joined a wagon train where he drove a buggy and went to Texas to visit Bowen relatives. Bill was an expert horseman and cowhand; making a number of trips up the Chisholm Trail to Kansas from Bastrop, Fort Clark at Bracketville, and other areas in southern Texas. His trail-driving was done for a Mr. Adams, and on making enough money, he bought a farm in 1882 in McLennan Co, Tex. This was his choice along the trail not far from where it crossed the Brazos River. m 18 Jul 1878 in McLennan Co to Eunice Ann Holstead, b 27 Nov 1858 in Davidson Co (now Cheatham Co), Tenn, d 14 Jan 1932 at Speegleville, McLennan Co, Tex, dau of Richard Ezra and Nancy Caroline (nee Haley) Holstead. Their children, all born at Speegleville, McLennan Co, were:

573—Mary Ann, b 25 Aug 1879, d 7 Nov 1879 at Speegleville.

574—Richard Harvey "Dick", b 13 Jan 1881, d 30 Nov 1956 at Speegleville.

575—John Thomas "Tom", b 19 Nov 1885, d 10 Jan 1941 at Waco, Texas.

576—Clay, b 13 Jun 1889, d 24 Dec 1959 at Waco, Texas.

577—Clara Lee, b 29 Oct 1894. Resided 1962 near Crawford, McLennan Co, Tex. m 22 Dec 1920 in Waco, Tex to Judson Frank Burr, b 11 Nov 1887 near Crawford, d 11 Nov 1949 at Waco, son of George Frank and Jennie (nee Boyd) Burr. Son, Julian Frank Burr, b 1922.

578—William Lawrence "Buster", b 12 Sep 1898. Resided 1962 at Speegleville.

(224) Marion Willard "Bud", son of (45) Harvey Carrol. A farmer. Removed about 1935 from Madison Co, Ark to Okla. m 1st 1894 in Huntsville, Madison Co, Ark to Amanda Jane Allen, b 5 Apr 1873, d 9 Aug 1937 (?). m 2nd 22 Nov 1941 to Rosa Mitchel. No issue from latter. Bud's children, both born in Madison Co, were:

579—Lemon Willard, b 1895, d 1 May 1952 at Bristow, Creek Co, Okla. m 11 Jun 1916 in Madison Co, Ark to Oleva Dennis, b 1898.

580—Orange Elbert, b 21 Feb 1899. Resided 1956 near Bristow, Okla. m 25 May 1928 in Madison Co, Ark to Lily Faubus, b 26 Feb 1907 in Franklin Co, Ark. No issue.

(229) Josiah, son of (46) Eli. The Bible containing his birth data washed away in Madison Co, Ark during a "water spout" in 1884. m 5 Sep 1867 at Mount Vernon, Lawrence Co, Mo to Mary J. Irby, b 13 Aug 1843 in Greene Co, Mo. After his death she m 2nd on 2 Nov 1920 to William W. Haskell, d 1 Nov 22 at Orting, Wash. She resided Dec 1922 in Pierce Co, Wash. Josiah joined on 8 Aug 1861 at Fayetteville, Ark, Co "L", 1st Union Ark Cav. Part of service was mail rider "to and from Cassville, Mo". Grey eyes, brown hair, fair complexion, 5 ft., 8 in. Discharged 8 Aug 1865. His Mo residences are recorded as Stone Co in 1866 and 1898; Greene Co in 1891 and 1899; Christian Co in 1896 and 1900; Lawrence Co in 1870. Removed Oct 1900 from Stone Co, Mo to Union Co, Oregon. Their children were:

581—Alfred Porter, b 27 Aug 1868 in Mo.

582—Ida Eveline, b 16 Mar 1871.

583—Melvina Jane, b 19 Aug 1873.

584—Edward Lafayette, b 26 Jan 1879.

585—George Washington Garfield, b 29 Jan 1881.

(230) Harvey Carrol "Heavy Harve", son of (46) Eli. Probably removed from Cannon Co, Tenn to Madison Co, Ark at the age of two years with his parents. m Nancy Catherine Rector, b 18 Feb 1844 in Clay Co, Mo, d 18 Aug 1929 at Westville, Adair Co, Okla. Their children were:

586—Sarah Frances, b 13 Jul 1869 in Ark, d 9 Jan 1958 in Chico, Glen Butte Co, Calif. m Joe Rowland.

587—Robert Eli, b 1871, d at age about 2 years.

588—Allen Lafayette, b 30 Aug 1875 at St Paul, Madison Co, Ark, d 16 Nov 1942 at Rocky, Washita Co, Okla.

589—William Charles "Charlie", b 9 Jan 1878 in Madison Co, Ark, d 8 Jul 1956 in Washington Co, Ark. m Apr 1901 Addie Burk, d 14 Dec 1947 in Madison Co, younger sister of wife of Allen above.

(241) James Harvey "Jim", son of (48) Elizabeth. A farmer. m Sarah Ellen Evans, b 13 Feb 1851 in Madison Co, Ark, d 7 Jun 1921 in Madison Co, dau of Hiram and Charity (nee Lueallen) Evans. Their children were one son and seven daughters:

590—Roba Jaqueline, b 18 Feb 1870 in Ark, d 18 Dec 1954

in Bentonville, Benton Co, Ark. m 17 Sep 1891 John Andrew Ball d 23 Sep 1940.

591—Pheba Cordelia, b 27 Aug 1871 in Ark, d age about 2 years at Drakes Creek, Madison Co.

592—Charity Lenora, b 9 Sep 1874 in Ark, d 20 Jul 1904 at Combs, Madison Co. m Cleve Smith.

593—Nancy Elizabeth, b 2 Apr 1877 in Ark, d 8 Mar 1907 at Park Hill, Cherokee Co, Okla Terr. m Al Smith.

594—Frances McAlester, b 14 Jun 1879 in Ark, d at Combs, Madison Co. m Joel Ball.

595—Millie Myrtle, b 18 Dec 1883, d 7 Jul 1914 at Drakes Creek, Madison Co. m 10 Feb 1907 in Madison Co to John H. Hillis, b 1883.

596—Zanie Ann, b 7 Feb 1886, d 15 Jan 1949 at Hulbert, Cherokee Co, Okla. m 16 Jul 1905 in Madison Co to Charles Reed, b 1886.

597—William Warren "Will", b 26 Jul 1888 at Drakes Creek, Madison Co. Resided 1962 near Huntsville, Madison Co.

(244) Thomas "Tom", son of (49) William M. One of the few descendants of his Grandfather George Ledbetter who remained in Cannon Co, Tenn after the others went "West". Joined 27 Sep 1864 at Liberty, De Kalb Co, Tenn, Co "F", 4th Union Tenn Mounted Inf. Dark eyes, black hair, fair complexion, 5 ft., 8 in. Discharged 25 Aug 1865 at Nashville, Tenn. He resided 1865 in Dallas Co, Mo. m 9 Aug 1868 in Cannon Co, Tenn to Martha Jetton, b 1848 in Ala, d 1 Apr 1925 at Gassaway, Cannon Co. He was killed when returning home on horseback the night of 12 Nov 1891 near Gassaway. Their children included 3 sons and 5 daughters; all born in Cannon Co:

598—Martha "Mattie", b Sep 1869. m 1 Jan 1888 in Cannon Co to Samuel Markum (Markham).

599—Elizabeth "Bettie", b 1871. m 1st 4 Jul 1885 in Cannon Co to Isaac Bogle. m 2nd to Hall Markum (Markham).

600—Susan, b 1874. m Sutten Tossuy.

601—Sarah F., b 1 Oct 1877. m Dillard Northcut.

602—William, b 1879, d when a child.

603—Hattie Ann, b 3 May 1881. m George Vandygrift.

604—George A., b 21 Nov 1883. m Shelah Vandyygrift.

605—Thomas "Tommie", b 4 Apr 1886. m Ila Walker.

(245) Alfred "Little Alf", son of (49) William M. Removed from Cannon Co, Tenn to Madison Co, Ark in about 1883. m 10 May 1873 in Cannon Co to Zana A. "Zanie" Powell, b 1840 in Tenn, d 1889 in Madison Co, dau of Henry and Nancy (nee Driver) Powell. He removed in 1927 along with dau Parallee to Orange Co, Calif. Their children were 2 sons and 2 dau; all born in Tenn:

606—Burley Comer, b 13 Nov 1874, d 20 Sep 1949 at Huntsville, Madison Co, Ark.

607—Rhoda Parallee, b 7 Dec 1877. Resided 1960 in Fullerton, Orange Co, Calif. m 3 Oct 1897 in Madison Co, Ark to Elhannon S. Boyd, b 1878 in Ark, brother of Mary Jane, who was mother-in-law of his brother Burley above and son of John and Paulina Adaline Boyd.

608—William H. "Bill", b Dec 1879, d at age of about 12 years.

609—Sarah, b 1881, d 18 Oct 1921 on Bohannon Mt, Madison Co, Ark. Had a son Luther Ledbetter who resided in California in 1956.

(248) Tilford "Tilf", son of (49) William M. Removed 1877 from Cannon Co, Tenn to Taney Co, Mo with his father. Remained there (thru 1880) and other parts of the "west" including Silver City, N.M., until he returned to Cannon Co, Tenn about 1890 to stay. m 20 Nov 1890 in Cannon Co to Can Delah Bratton, b 2 Feb 1866 in Gassaway, Cannon Co, d 30 Dec 1924 at Gassaway, dau of George and Mary (nee Hale) Bratton. Their first child was stillborn and subsequently were born 3 sons and 2 daughters; all near Gassaway, Cannon Co, Tenn:

610—Bee Alton, b 25 June 1892. Resided 1961 near Gassaway.

611—George, b 18 Oct 1894, d about age 2 years as result of burns.

612—Mary Eller, b 30 Oct 1897, d about age 3 years of diphtheria.

613—Lillian Irene "Lillie", b 17 Dec 1900. Resided 1957 in Nashville, Tenn. m at Woodbury, Cannon Co, Tenn to Roy Stephens.

614—James Robert, b 8 May 1909. Resided 1957 near Cleveland, Ohio. m at Gassaway to Birdie Waldron.

(249) George Washington, son of (49) William M. Removed about 1893 from Madison Co, Ark to Indian Territory (Okla). m 1882 at Harrison, Boone Co, Ark to Sarah Ann Dennis, b near Woodbury, Cannon Co, Tenn, d 29 May 1956 at Tulsa, Okla, dau of James Edward and Nancy (nee Tittle) Dennis. The first 4 of their 6 children were born at Aurora, Madison Co, Ark:

615—Johnson, b 14 Feb 1885, d 10 July 1900 at Chickasha, Indian Terr (now Grady Co, Okla).

616—John Dillard, b 24 June 1888. Resided 1957 near Bixby, Tulsa Co, Okla.

617—Lilly Mae, b 1891, d 16 Sep 1892 at Aurora.

618—Myrtle, b 3 July 1893, d about 1946 at Bixby, Tulsa Co, Okla. m Eddie Seago.

619—Audie, b 7 Apr 1895 at Cartersville, Indian Terr (now Haskell Co, Okla). Resided 1957 in Tulsa, Okla. m 13 July 1922 to Vera Lucille Leland, dau of L. and ——— (nee Herkimer), Leland. They had one son, Eddie Jean, b 16 Aug 1930.

620—Addie, b 24 July 1900 at Stampede, Bell Co, Texas, d Oct 1905 at Haskell, Muskogee Co, Indian Terr.

(251) Elijah Franklin, son of (49) William M. m 1895 at Temple, Bell Co, Texas to Ella McDowell, b 1869, dau of Samuel Smith and Martha Ann (nee Cooper) McDowell. Removed in the summer of 1904 from Hugo, Okla Territory to Denton Co, Texas. After death of Elijah, wife and children moved to Kempner, Texas where they lived with her parents for about 2 years and then moved to McGregor, McLennan Co, Texas where she remained. Their children were:

621—Rosa Ann, b 9 Dec 1896 at Moody, McLennan Co. Resided 1956 in Waco, Texas. m Arthur A. Walker, d.

622—William Charles (Samuel), b 21 Oct 1897 at Moody, McLennan Co. Resided 1956 at Killeen, Bell Co, Texas. m Eunice May.

623—George, b at Kempner, Lampasas Co, Texas, d age 9 days.

624—Mary Frances, b 29 Oct 1901 at Moody, d 17 Sep 1915.

625—Robert Allen, b 4 Feb 1904 at Hugo, Okla Terr. Resided 1960 in McGregor, McLennan Co, Texas. m 1 Sep 1933 in McGregor to Ruby Mae Talley, dau of Arnold Lee and Donnie Mae (nee Denton) Talley. Their children, both born in McGregor, were Leila Don, b 11 Mar 1938; and Linda Claire, b 24 Aug 1944.

(257) Monroe M., son of (49) William. m 1st 13 July 1907 in Grayson Co, Texas to Mrs. Julia (nee Reed) De Board. No issue. m 2nd 30 Sep 1910 in Fannin Co, Texas to Safronie Davis, b 8 Apr 1893 in Fannin Co, dau of T. A. and Adar D. (nee Marcum) Davis. Removed 1930 to Grayson Co, Texas. Their one son and five dau were all born in Fannin Co:

626—Roby Arlis, b 16 June 1911. Resided 1960 near Mule-shoe, Texas. Removed 1938 from Texas to Bakersfield, Calif and returned to Muleshoe in 1959. m 15 June 1948 in Old Mexico to Lena Higgins (?), dau of Henry and Maggie (nee Gresham) Myers. Their one child is Shirley Faye, b 3 Mar 1949 at Bakersfield.

627—Irene, b 31 May 1913, resided 1956 in St. Louis, Mo. m Gene Guidi.

628—Naoma, b 30 Sep 1915, d 10 Nov 1916 in Fannin Co, Texas.

629—Burna, b 30 Aug 1917, d same day.

630—Eudell, b 19 Aug 1918, resided 1956 at Anton, Hockley Co, Texas. m M. B. Cundiff.

631—Oma, b 12 Oct 1922, resided 1956 at White Deer, Carson Co, Texas. m W. C. Williamson.

(260) Dock H, son of (49) William H. m 1912 in Warren Co, Tenn to Rachell Qualls, d 26 July 1952, dau of Robert and Leah Qualls. They removed 1915 from Bells, Grayson Co, Texas to near Morrison, Grundy Co, Tenn. He resided 1960 with daughter Bonnie. Their children were 3 sons and 4 dau, all born in Tenn except the first:

632—Gladys Lorene, b 28 Feb 1914 at Bells, Grayson Co, Texas, d 13 Oct 1914.

633—Mildred Corene, b 23 Feb 1916, d 8 Dec 1916.

634—William Fred, b 25 Dec 1917. m Zelma Fults. Resided 1957 near Morrison, Tenn.

635—Willmer Homer, b 2 Nov 1920. m Georgia Loucinda Daniel. Resided 1957 near Roanoke, La.

636—Dewey Kenneth, b 26 Mar 1923, d 10 Apr 1945 in service of US Army in Germany. m Anna Mae Randolph. No issue.

637—Bonnie Lee, b 16 Apr 1927. m Hervy H. Myers. Resided 1957 at Fults Cove, Grundy Co, near Viola, Tenn.

638—Bobbie Jane, b 18 Mar 1933. m Jesse Fults. Resided 1957 near Morrison, Tenn.

(262) George Washington "Big George", son of (50) James. Farmer and livestock raiser. Enlisted 1 Feb 1865 (at age 14) in Co "B", 1st Union Ark Inf. Blue eyes, light hair, fair complexion, heavy, 5'-5". Discharged 10 Aug 1865 at Fort Smith, Ark. m 20 Jan 1867 at Drakes Creek, Madison Co, Ark, Mary Sisemore, b 8 Jan 1850 in Ark, d 20 Nov 1934 at Japton, Madison Co, dau of James and Mary "Polly" (nee Ball) Sisemore. Their children, all born in Madison Co, were:

639—Sarah E., b 8 Apr 1868, d in Okla, m James Jones.

640—Mary Etta, b 4 Jul 1871, d in Mountainburg, Crawford Co, Ark. m Calvin Creekmore.

641—Alfred P., b 15 Dec 1873 at Aurora, Madison Co, d 23 Nov 1959 near Fullerton, Orange Co, Calif.

642—Willis Turner, b 26 Aug 1876, d 4 Oct 1956 in Springdale, Washington Co, Ark. m 1st Fannie Gage, d 29 June 1938 at Huntsville, Ark. No issue. m 2nd 8 May 1946 Amanda Caroline Lewis Drake. No issue.

643—Marion Gerome "Rome", b 30 Dec 1878, d of measles when his children were small, m Fannie R. West, b 1878. After Rome died she m George Satterfield on 11 Jan 1920 in Madison Co, Ark.

644—Walter Scott, b 26 Nov 1881 near Combs, d 2 Feb 1955 at Little Rock, Ark. Never married.

645—John Floyd, b 13 Apr 1884 near Combs, d 24 Feb 1955 at Little Rock, Ark. Never married.

646—George Washington Jr, b 17 Jun 1888 near Combs, d 27 Oct 1944 in Madison Co. m 22 Jul 1906 in Madison Co to Ella Drake, b 1888.

647—Oscar B., b 16 Nov 1890 near Combs. Resided 1960 near Huntsville, Ark.

648—Ida A., b 7 Jan 1892. Resided 1957 in La Habra, Orange Co, Calif. m 1st 16 Dec 1909 in Madison Co to A. Newton Richardson, b 1887. m 2nd Sterling Hood.

(263) James Franklin "Bud", son of (50) James. Removed from his mother's farm on War Eagle Creek in Madison Co, Ark a few months after her death. Arriving in Johnson Co, Ark in 1872 when he was 19 years old, he started peace officer work along with farming at Coal Hill. His outstanding record obtained him an appointment as Deputy Sheriff of Johnson Co in about 1880 which he held until 1894. Removed in July 1894 to Vinita in the Okla Territory where he took a job as Wells Fargo Express guard on MKT railroad trains between Oswego, Kan and Checotah, Okla Terr. In the Territory he served in many phases of law enforcement: Deputy US Marshall with stations at Vinita, Okmulgee and Muskogee from 16 Oct 1897 to 11 Apr 1899 and from 10 May 1903 until Okla became a state in Nov 1907; Town Marshall of Vinita from Apr 1899 to May 1903; Town Marshall of Haskell and Okmulgee; Chief of Police of Muskogee from 1909 to 1913; Sheriff of Muskogee Co 1913 to 1917 and again on a Ku-Klux-Klan platform from 1922 to 1926; plain clothes policeman at Okmulgee from 1917 to 1922. "Marshal Bud" retired from a long peace officer career to his farm seven miles southeast of Muskogee in 1928. m 28 Jun 1874 in Madison Co, Ark to Mary Josephine Terry, b 27 Mar 1856 in Mo, d 12 May 1930 at Muskogee, dau of William and America Jane (nee Ewing)) Terry. Their children were:

649—George Washington, b 28 Aug 1875 near Huntsville, Ark, d 2 Jul 1943 in Muskogee, Okla.

650—America Jane "Dolly", b 30 Oct 1877 near Huntsville, Madison Co, Ark, d 14 Sept 1961 in Kansas City, Mo. m 23 Apr 1903 at Vinita, Okla Terr to Fred Morton Young, b 11 Dec 1875 at Cissna Park, Ill, d 11 Mar 1926 at Kansas City, Mo, son of William Harrison and Celia Maria (nee Bonebrake) Young.

(264) Alfred Payne, son of (50) James. Was a farmer and member of the Church of Christ where he did some preaching. Removed from Madison Co, Ark to Orange Co, Calif. m 1st Rebecca Herriman who d not long after marriage. No issue. m 2nd 26 Nov 1876 at Drakes Creek, Madison Co, Ark to Lydia McCarver, b 1 June 1859 in Madison Co, d 18 June 1935 in Ark, dau of A. J. and Lucinda McCarver. Their children included 5 sons and 3 daughters, all born in Madison Co:

651—George Augusta "Gus", b 15 Nov 1877, d Dec 1956 at Great Bend, Kan. m Maude Brown near Vinita, Craig Co, Okla.

652—James Franklin, b 4 Sept 1879, d 16 Feb 1900 at Drakes Creek of measles. Did not marry.

653—Helen Ella, b 27 Dec 1880. m 22 Jun 1906 in Madison Co to Calvin Stanfill, b 1881.

654—Robert L., b 9 Nov 1883. Resided 1956 at Muskogee, Okla. m 12 Jul 1908 in Madison Co to Essie Calico, b 1891.

655—Troy Edward, b 13 Dec 1885 at Drakes Creek. Resided 1956 near Wesley, Ark.

656—Ethel S., b 31 Oct 1892. Resided 1956 in Tulsa, Okla. m 1 Mar 1914 in Madison Co to Will J. Ghormley, b 1889.

657—Clarence H., b 14 Aug 1898. d 13 Nov 1962 at Claremore Okla. m 22 Jun 1918 in Madison Co to Myrtle Dorsey, b 1902.

658—Elizabeth S. "Lizzie", b 14 Feb 1900. Resided 1957 at Chino, Calif. m 1st 12 Oct 1918 in Madison Co to Willie C. Neal, b 1894. m 2nd————————Owens.

(268) Jerry Turner, son of (50) James. Was a farmer and Church of Christ Minister; preaching in Madison and Washington Counties, Ark and in eastern Okla. Removed to near El Reno, Okla in 1912. Remained there four years on a farm owned by his half brother, Jason A. L. Clark; then back to Madison Co. Removed further to Wainwright, Muskogee Co, Okla in 1921. m 1st Mary E. "Mollie" Brooks, b 25 Oct 1861 and d 15 Apr 1883 in Madison Co. They had one child, Winnie M., b 10 Feb 1883, d 27 Feb 1883.

Jerry m 2nd 13 Sep 1883 near Drakes Creek, Madison Co to Ida Belle Ramey, b 28 Oct 1865 in Louisville, Ky, d 22 Feb 1949 in Los Angeles, Calif. Their 9 children were all born near Drakes Creek, Madison Co, Ark:

659—Maudie Lee Dellar, b 18 Jul 1884 on Cobb's Creek, d 20 Dec 1886 in Madison Co.

660—Pearla May, b 28 Dec 1885, resided 1956 Los Angeles, Calif. m Allison Cornelius Stone of Georgia.

661—Guy Payne, b 25 Aug 1889, resided 1956 Yorba Linda, Orange Co, Calif.

662—James Arnold, b 2 Nov 1891, d 7 Mar 1959 at Mc-Minnville, Ore. A school teacher, printer and photographer. m 1st 22 May 1914 in Madison Co to Stella Auslam, b 1896. Divorced 1924. They had one child named Clifford, b Huntsville, Madison Co, m Beulah Allen. m 2nd 1926 in Tulsa, Okla to Flora Belle Jones, d 21 Oct 1951 at McMinnville, Ore. They had no children but adopted Ruth Esther Simmons, m Arch Bass.

663—George Ramey, b 29 Aug 1893, resided 1956 in Oildale, Calif. m 10 Jan 1914 in Madison Co to Mae Harrison, b 1896 in Ark.

664—Jerry Isaiah, b 22 Feb 1896, d 3 Jun 1945 at El Reno, Okla. as result of a fall. m 1st 6 Sep 1917 in Madison Co to Eula Auslam, b 1898, d about 1925. To them were born Gale and Ralph. m 2nd Billy Patton and was divorced. m 3rd Lillian————shortly before his death.

665—Benjamin Clyde, b 6 Jan 1898, resided 1956 in Fillmore, Calif.

666—Albert Clarence, b 10 Oct 1900, resided 1956 in Anaheim, Calif.

667—Ira Elton, b 22 Sep 1902, d 1912.

(280) William Oliver, son of (54) Oliver Vincent. m Margaret Ella Smith, b 1858, d before 1929. Lived near his father's family in Dallas Co, Texas in 1880. Their two children were:

668—Lucy, b and d 14 Dec 1892 in Dallas Co.

669—Robert E. Lee, b 1895, d Nov 1959 in Dallas Co.

(283) Arthur Lee, son of (54) Oliver Vincent. Served as Deputy Sheriff (1893-1900), police officer (1900-1904), and Sheriff (1906-1912) of Dallas Co, Texas. m Lula E. Boren of Iowa. He was killed by a falling awning at the Linz Building in Dallas in 1912. Their children, except the first two resided in Dallas in 1944:

670—Bessie M., m V. G. Foster and resided 1944 in Tulsa, Okla.

671—C. Fred, resided 1944 in Tulsa, Okla.

672—Wilbur M. b 1898, d 28 Dec 1944 in Dallas. m———
Wilbur. She later m James Earl Boots Jr. Wilbur served in the Navy in 1917. His children were Gene C., and Lucy Ann m 19 Apr 1947 in Dallas to Claude G. Killingsworth Jr.

673—Mary V., m 1st Stanley Aulsbrook, m 2nd Roy Bickle.

674—Arthur L., b 1905.

675—Margaret, m Frank A. Lumbey.

(293) James Oliver, son of (59) Arthur Brooks. Removed 1882 with his parents to Searcy Co, Ark. Taught in public schools in Searcy, Marion and Boone Co, Ark from 1885 to 1926. Was a member of the 43rd General Assembly of State of Ark in 1921-22. Removed 1926 from Marion Co, Ark to Pryor, Mayes Co, Okla; after a year there, removed 1927 to Broken Arrow, Tulsa Co, Okla where remained. Was a Master Mason and member of the Christian Church. m 4 Oct 1893 to Lillie Bell Wall, b 4 Jan 1875 at Marshall, Searcy Co, Ark, adopted dau of William G. and Emily Catherine (nee Greenshaw) Wall. To them were born 6 sons and 3 daughters; all in Arkansas:

676—Joseph Verazani "Joe", b 7 Aug 1894 at Marshall, Searcy Co. Resided 1956 in St. Louis, Mo.

677—Arthur Cort, b 12 Apr 1897 at Eros, Marion Co. Resided 1962 in Waco, McLennan Co, Texas.

678—Mary Arkie, b 15 Oct 1899 at Eros, Marion Co. Resided 1957 at Altus, Jackson Co, Okla. m 9 Dec 1920 at Pyatt, Ark to Fletcher Poe Graham, b 3 Apr 1896 at Leslie, Ark, son of Lindsey Luster and Martha Arena (nee Griffin) Graham.

679—William Shem, b 21 Mar 1903 at Eros, Marion Co. Resided 1956 at Portsmouth, Va. m 17 Jun 1949 at Portsmouth, Va to Mrs Emma (nee Gannaway) McKay, b 24 April 1905 in Amherst Co, Va, dau of Gideon and Minnie Alice (nee Bowles) Gannaway. No issue.

680—James Oliver, Jr, b 13 Jan 1906 at Eros, Marion Co. d 20 Nov 1955 in Marion Co, Ark.

681—Carl Scotius, b 19 Aug 1910 at Pyatt, Marion Co. Chaplain (Lt Col) in U S Army in 1956.

682—Emily Blanche, b 14 Sept 1912 at Pyatt, Marion Co. Resided 1956 at Gore, Sequoyah Co, Okla. m 26 Dec 1935 at Muskogee, Okla to Kermit Glenn Horn, b 9 Feb 1911 at Clovis, N. M., son of Noah Sr and Lucy Lovada (nee Coone) Horn.

683—Leslie Lowell, b 4 Sep 1916 at Pyatt, Marion Co. Resided 1956 in Los Angeles, Calif.

684—Lois Elizabeth Rose, b 24 Aug 1920 at Pyatt, Marion Co, Ark. Resided in 1956 in Cincinnati, Ohio. m 15 Sep 1941 in Canton, Ohio to Hugh Faris Sensibaugh, b 4 Jul 1915 at Frazeyburg, Ohio, son of Andrew H. and Elva (nee White) Sensibaugh. He is a minister of the Christian Church.

(294) Thomas Lewis, son of (59) Arthur Brooks. Removed 1882 from Dallas Co, Texas via ox-wagon to Searcy Co, Ark where he grew to manhood. About 1894 removed to Okla Territory, settling near Maud (now Seminole Co) where m 5 Mar 1895 Amanda Elizabeth (nee Smyth) Thomas, b 14 May 1870 in Trigg Co, Ky, d 3 May 1936 at Pryor, Mayes Co, Okla, dau of James Clark "Muck" and Amanda Elizabeth (nee Lawrence) Thomas. They lived among the Pottowatomie Indians. Removed Jan 1909 to near Pryor, Mayes Co, Okla. He m 2nd Mrs May Horton of Memphis, Texas with no issue. The children of Thomas Lewis and Amanda were:

685—Ruth, b 17 Jan 1897 at Maud, d 18 Jan 1897.

686—Leslie Orchard, b 5 Jan 1898 at Maud, d 27 Jul 1905.

687—Alpha Pell, b 27 Aug 1900 at Maud, d 16 Feb 1903.

688—Ruby Pearl, b 24 Oct 1902 at Maud. Resided 1956 at 1921 S Ridgeway, Sapulpa, Okla. m Clayton G. Williams, b 5 Nov 1883 at Joplin, Mo, d 3 Jul 1948 at Pryor, Okla, son of Billy and Angelina (nee Brazil) Williams.

689—Arthur Brooks, b 13 Oct 1905 at Maud. Resided 1956 at Pryor, Okla.

690—Mary Esther, b 9 Jan 1908 at Maud, Seminole Co, Okla. Resided 1956 at Pryor, Okla. m 30 Jan 1932 to Howard Vernon Trogdon, b 2 Apr 1911 at Prue, Okla, son of John Monroe and Effie Ann (nee Miller) Trogdon.

691—Thomas Logan, b 26 Nov 1910 at Pryor. Resided 1956 804 8th St, Alamagordo, N. M.

692—James Luther, b 17 May 1913 at Pryor. Resided 1956 at 1114 N. Sandusky St, Tulsa, Okla.

693—Oliver Vincent, b 16 Oct 1914 at Pryor, d 15 Jul 1915 at same place.

(296) Horace Alfred, son of (59) Arthur Brooks. m 18 Oct 1899 to Flora McVay, b 27 May 1877 in Douglas Co, Mo, dau of John T. and Adelia E. (nee Burns) McVay. To them were born 4 sons and 4 daughters:

694—Okla J., m 4 Dec 1900 in Searcy Co, Ark. Resided 1956 in Gardena Calif. m Ignazio Simone, son of Mike and Giovanni Simone.

695—Oliver Clyde, b 10 Jul 1903 in Searcy Co, Ark. Resided 1956 in Canoga Park, Calif.

696—Nellie Ray, b 7 Jun 1906 in Searcy Co, Ark. Resided 1956 in Portland, Ore. m 1st Jack Martin; divorced. m 2nd Vernon Combs, son of William Combs; divorced.

697—Harold Elmo Carroll, b 2 Nov 1908 in Cleburn Co, Ark. Resided 1956 in Stockton, Calif.

698—Mary Adelia, b 29 Oct 1911 at Searcy Co, Ark. Resided 1956 in Buffalo, N. Y. m Jess Dees; divorced.

699—John Clifford, b 6 Dec 1913 in Searcy Co, Ark. Resided 1956 in Torrence, Calif.

700—Alfred Brooks, b 26 Jun 1918 in Searcy Co, Ark. Killed 25 Feb 1951 in Korea.

701—Marjorie Ray, b 22 Jun 1821 in Wagner Co, Okla. Resided 1956 in Portland, Ore. m 1st Clifford Dees, d 8 Dec 1941 in Alaska. m 2nd Lee Pope, son of Harry and Gladys Pope.

(300) Floyd, son of (59) Arthur Brooks. m 1st Apr 1900 at Marshall, Ark to Maude Ann Brown, dau of Joe E. and Molly (nee Cargill) Brown. Maude lived 1958 in California with their children who were:

702—Beulah, b 2 Feb 1902 in Searcy Co, Ark, d 1956. m Guy Henry Griffin, son of William A. and Emma Griffin. She resided 1958 at Artesia, Calif.

703—Gladys B., b 1904 in Okla Terr, d in infancy.

704—Berl D., b 26 Jan 1905 in Okla Terr. Resided 1958 at Long Beach, Calif.

705—Ora Lee, b 8 Feb 1907; d 9 Mar 1930. m Lloyd Willmore.

706—Edith, b 14 Apr 1910. m Prestor De Graffenreid. Resided 1958 at Oklahoma City, Okla.

707—Jack Paul, b 3 Jun 1912 in Okla. m Buena Hudson. Resided 1958 at Midwest City, Okla.

708—Lucille, b 14 Jun 1914 in Okla. m Marshall U. DeGraffenreid. Resided 1958 at Oklahoma City, Okla.

709—Samuel L., b 2 Sep 1916 in Okla. Resided 1958 in Sterling, Colo.

710—Floyd Jr., b 17 May 1920 in Okla. Resided 1958 in Sterling, Colo.

711—Joe E., b 7 Jan 1923 in Okla.

(302) Early Lee, son of (59) Arthur Brooks. m 30 Jul 1904 in Ark to Nettie Doshier, dau of Wiley and Atsay Elizabeth (nee Humphrey) Doshier. Their children were one son and 5 daughters:

712—Mabel Etta, b 29 May 1905 at Marshall, Searcy Co, Ark. Resided 1956 in Broken Arrow, Okla. m Richard Owen, son of Milt and Donnie (nee Boswell) Owen.

713—Murrel Leon, b 17 Oct 1906 at Marshall, Searcy Co, Ark. Resided 1956 at Broken Arrow, Okla. m Ben Harlan, son of Wedsell Maywood and Elizabeth (nee Hlae) Harlan.

714—Willie Bethel, b 27 Nov 1908 at Marshall, Searcy Co, Ark. Resided 1956 at Broken Arrow, Okla. m Lester Cobb, son of Jim and Anna (nee Dill) Cobb.

715—Eula Louise, b 14 Jan 1911, d 15 an 1914.

716—Rose, b 15 Feb 1914, d 19 Feb 1914.

717—Orchard Early, b 27 Jan 1916, d 11 Jan 1954 in Tulsa, Tulsa, Co, Okla.

(309) Jesse, oldest son of (65) George Washington. m Eva Bohny. The following son and dau who grew up at Comfort, Kendall Co, Texas:

718—Gertrude, b 6 Jul 1910, m————Bohnert. Resided 1960 Comfort, Texas.

719—J. L., b 1 Jan 1912. Resided 1960 possibly at Laredo, Webb Co, Texas.

(321) William Jones, son of (66) Isaac Jones. m 1st 22 Oct 1868 at Berryville, Carroll Co, Ark, Sarah Jane Wyrick, b 9 Dec 1845 in Tenn, d 16 Apr 1882 at Berryville, dau of Alexander and Vina (nee Rogers) Wyrick. He was a large property holder in Carroll Co. The children of this marriage were 2 sons and 3 dau; all born at Berryville:

720—Edna Jane, b 6 Aug 1869. m Tom J Edmondson and they resided 1831 at Columbus, Kan.

721—Mary Alice, b 7 Jun 1872, d 15 Apr 1953 at Springfield, Mo, m William Hoeting Atkinson of Phillipsburg, Mo, b 1867, d 1948. Further information herein.

722—William Robert A., b 25 Jan 1875. Resided 1950 at Alice L., Ore. m 24 Dec 1896 at Berryville, Carroll Co, Ark to Elsie E. McCammon, b 1877.

723—Binyard Aby, b 18 Jan 1879, d Feb 1905. m Will Walker who resided 1931 at Berryville.

724—Thomas Charles, b 19 Jan 1882. Resided at Glen Springs, Idaho. m in Berryville to Jewell Standlee.

(321) William Jones m 2nd 9 Nov 1882 at Berryville to Margaret Eugenia "Sis" Marshall, b 31 Jul 1851, d 31 Jul 1953 in Carroll Co, Ark, dau of John and Cynthia Ann (nee Rule) Marshall. The children of this marriage were 3 sons and 2 dau; all born at Berryville, Carroll Co, Ark:

725—Gertie Alta, b 6 Sep 1883. m before 1930 to Finn Freeman of St Joseph, Mo.

726—Edgar Rudolph, b 5 Mar 1886. World War I service. Resided 1932 at La Grande, Ore and not married.

727—John Isaac, b 24 Dec 1888. Resided 1930 at Berryville. m 1st at Berryville to Queenie M. Fancher, b 6 Oct 1892, d 19 Feb 1913. They had one son Leslie E, b 27 Jun 1912 and d 13 June 1913 in Carroll Co, Ark. m 2nd Grace Burks and they had 2 children.

728—Earl Jones, b 5 Apr 1891, d at age 11 months.

729—Eartle Ruth, b 12 Mar 1895. Resided 1932 at Arkansas City, Kan. m Frank Rutledge.

(322) Andrew J. "Drew", son of (66) Isaac Jones. m 7 Nov 1872 at Berryville, Carroll Co, Ark to Elizabeth "Betty" Standlee, b 1856 in Ark, d after 1931. They resided in Stone Co, Mo in 1880. Their children included:

730—Isaac Jones, b 17 Jul 1874 at Berryville, Carroll Co, Ark. Resided 1931 at Springfield, Mo. m 25 Dec 1899 in Crane Co, Mo to Amelia Long, b 10 Jun 1880, dau of Isaac and Rosa Long. Their children were Andra b 10 Feb 1901, and Jerold b 21 Aug 1908; both b in Crane Co.

731—Melvin, b 1877 in Ark.

(331) Robert Parris, son of (68) Buckner Harris T. m 1st 29 Mar 1879 in Kaufman Co, Tex to S. E. Carpenter, m 2nd 8 Dec 1886 same place to Emma Ware, d 18 Sep 1946 in Lynn Co, Tex. Left Kaufman Co in 1906 and settled 1916 at O'Donnell, Lynn Co, Tex. He was a farmer and his children were:

732—Walter Roy, b 13 Oct 1887 near Kemp, Kaufman Co, Texas. Resided 1961 near O'Donnell, Lynn Co. Did not marry.

733—Jesse Floyd, b 11 Feb 1889, d 31 Dec 1957.

734—Robert Garland, b 17 Feb 1891, d 23 Jan 1959.

735—William Audy, b 30 Nov 1892. Resided 1961 at Tahoka, Lynn Co.

736—Mary Ethel, b 14 Feb 1895. Resided 1961 Crowell, Texas. m F. A. Traweek.

737—Myrtie May, b 28 Sep 1896 near Kemp. Resided 1961
near O'Donnell, Texas. Not married.

738—Franklin Michael, b 16 Apr 1899, d 8 Sep 1900.

739—Ina Vesta, b 29 Jan 1901 near Kemp. Resided 1961 near
O'Donnell, Texas. Not married.

740—Della Lennie, b 5 Aug 1904, d 1 Aug 1907.

(392) Alvin C., son of (85) William B. m 11 Aug 1867 at
Licking, Texas Co, Mo to Lydia Ann Young, b 22 Apr 1847, d
after 1919. Resided 1860, 1870 and 1880 at Licking, Mo. Joined
25 Feb 1865, Co "I", 13th Union Mo Cav. Hazel eyes, brown hair,
fair complexion, 5'-6", a farmer. Discharged 3 Jul 1866 at Ft
Leavenworth, Kan. Lydia Ann m 2nd 16 Dec 1889 to Cornelius W.
Payne, d 11 Jun 1941 in Phelps Co, Mo. She resided 1919 in Seaton,
Phelps Co, Mo. The children of Alvin C and Lydia Ann included
two who died before 1883 and:

741—John William, b 28 Feb 1871.

742—Mary Elizabeth, b 14 Aug 1875.

(400) George Washington, son of (90) Jones. m 1881 at
Clear Springs, Texas Co, Mo to Hariett Morris, d 30 Nov 1888 at
Clear Springs, dau of John and Hariett Morris. Their children were
all born at Clear Springs and when the parents both died in 1888,
they all went to live with their grandmother Morris. The children
were:

743—Jones Walter "J W.", b 22 Aug 1882. Resided 1958 at
Jonesboro, Craighead Co, Ark.

744—John Ledher, b 30 Sep 1884, d 31 Dec 1945 at Hot
Springs, Garland Co, Ark. m Myrtle Wills.

745—Stella, b 23 Mar 1886, d Mar 1926 at Summerville,
Texas Co, Mo. m Frank Wuertley.

746—Lottie, b 20 Apr 1888, d 20 Aug 1956 at Twin Falls,
Twin Falls Co, Idaho. m J. C. Vest.

(467) William Alonzo, son of (136) James Mitchell. m 3
Nov 1905 in Fesenden, Wells Co, N. D. to Frances Falness. To
them was born 1 son and 3 dau:

747—Zalda, b 14 Sep 1908 in Ruso, McLain Co, N. D. Resided 1956 in Sebastopol, Calif. m Robert Thomas.

218   LEDBETTERS FROM VIRGINIA

748—Iown, b 22 Jul 1911 in Ruso, McLain Co, N. D. Resided 1956 in Vallejo, Calif. m George Iverson.

749—Yvonne, b 22 Jun 1913 in Plaza, Montrail Co, N. D. Resided 1956 in Havre, Mont. m Glenn Crosby.

750—Budd A., b 9 Feb 1916 in Minot, Ward Co, N. D. Resided 1956 in Arnold, Md.

(469) Andrew Jackson, son of (136) James Mitchell. m 26 Jun 1916 to Lucy Gertrude Allen, b 22 Mar 1886 in Cumberland Co, Ky, dau of Robert G. and Mary Hellie Allen. They had one child only:

751—Ira Louise, b 10 Jan 1918 at West Point, Clay Co, Miss. m 26 Jun 1942 at Louisville, Jefferson Co, Ky to Lonnie Lee Carter, b 17 Oct 1914 near Chattanooga, Tenn.

(470) Martin Van Buren, son of (138) Martin Van Buren. m 11 Nov 1882 at Aberdeen, Monroe Co, Miss, niece of his stepfather, Maggie Catherine Tschudi, d 13 May 1926 at Denver, Colo, dau of a native of Switzerland. He operated a livery stable at Aberdeen prior to 1894. Their children were 1 son and 4 dau; 1 dau died before 1894:

752—Mary Elizabeth, b 24 Aug 1883 at Aberdeen, resided 1932 at Amory, Monroe Co, Miss. m 24 Dec 1911 at Corinth, Alcorn Co, Miss to G. C. McClamroch, b 28 Aug 1875, son of G. W. and Mary Boone McClamroch.

753—Lillie Adele, resided 1932 at Albuquerque, N. M. m 1st J. G. Moore, m 2nd Dr. W. T. Jones.

754—Martin Van Buren III, b 20 Nov 1891 at Aberdeen, d 1 Nov 1934 at Denver, Colo. m Hazel Hay. Their children were Martin Van Buren IV, b 31 May 1934; Leslie Hay; John Frederick; and Richard.

755—Margaret L., resided 1957 at Booneville, Prentiss Co, Miss. m 1st C. R. Grisham of Booneville; m 2nd——— Walker.

(481) Charlie Virgil, son of (141) John Dillard. m 1902 Etta Lee Sells, b 1 Sep 1880, dau of William and Elizabeth Sells. To them were born 3 sons and 4 dau; all on Nettle Carrier Creek near Alpine, Overton Co, Tenn:

756—Della Ruth, b 6 Jan 1903. M 1925 Waitson N. Mc-
Donald, d 31 Dec 1957. Resided 1962 on Nettle Carrier
in her Great Grandfather William's original house and
home.

757—Fannie Violet, b 5 Feb 1905, d 24 Dec 1960. Never
married.

758—Lawrence Dewey, b 2 Feb 1907. m Ruby Anderson. One
son Billy Carl. Resided 1962 in Nashville, Tenn.

759—Leila Blanche, b 21 Oct 1909. Not married. Resided
1962 with her parents on Nettle Carrier.

760—Ruby Gwendolyn, b 27 Feb 1912. m Cortes Allred. Resided 1962 at Alpine.

761—Clarence Chester, b 18 Oct 1914, m Wilma Ringley, divorced. Resided 1962 in New Brunswick, N. J.

762—Charles Jr, b 21 Apr 1923. m Mamie Jackson. No issue.
Resided 1962 near Anderson, Ind.

(490) Lester, son of (145) William Lafayette "Fate". m
Fay Barton. He is a farmer and owns land in the Cosumne River
District in Eastern Sacramento Co, California. Their two children,
both graduates of Sacramento College, are:

763—Melba Ouida, b 1 Jun 1927. m William Grant Mosher.
Resided 1957 at Elk Grove, Sacramento Co, Calif.

764—William Barton, b 15 May 1930. m Beverlee Ann Gross.
Resided 1957 at Stateline, El Dorado Co, Calif.

(500) Evert E. Lexes, son of (150) Pleasant Hillary. m 12
Jan———inMonroe Co, Ky to Nancy Adeline Smith, b Jackson
Co, Tenn, d 27 Jul 1953 in Caddo Gap, Montgomery Co, Ark, dau
of Enoch Chapman and Martha (nee Hull) Smith. They removed
1905 from Overton Co, Tenn to Ark. Their children were:

765—Martha Ray, b 1890 in Overton Co, Tenn, d 27 Oct
1931 at Pearcy, Garland Co, Ark. m (513) James
Overton Ledbetter.

766—Mary, b 1892 in Overton Co, Tenn. 1957 at Norman,
Ark. m Clay Garrett.

767—Francis Harrison, b 1894 in Monroe Co, Ky. Resided
1960 at Caddo Gap, Ark.

768—Ora (twin), b 1896 in Overton Co, Tenn. Resided 1957 at Caddo Gap, Ark. m Harrison Cogburn.

769—Nora (twin), b 1896 in Overton Co, Tenn. Resided 1957 at Norman, Ark. m Cleave Rowton.

770—Hessie May, b 1900 in Overton Co, Tenn. Resided 1957 at Bakersfield, Calif. m Millard Caughran.

771—Alice, b 1907 at Norman, Montgomery Co, Ark. Resided 1957 at Mount Pine, Ark. m Ember Golden.

(508) Andrew Virgil, son of (153) James Calvin. m 9 Aug 1896 in Overton Co, Tenn to Minnie Grey West, b 17 Nov 1878 in Overton Co, dau of Granville and Emiline West of Livingston, Overton Co, Tenn. Their children were:

772—Sophia Pearl, b 7 Aug 1897.

773—Daisy Emma, b 3 Nov 1899.

774—William Vanis, b 4 Oct 1904.

775—Anna Lee, b 6 Mar 1907.

776—Ernal Mai, b 31 Mar 1909.

777—Wilmuth Luke, b 26 Mar 1911.

778—Andrew Simon, b 29 Jan 1914, d before 1932.

779—Dewey McCoy, b 4 Oct 1916, d before 1932.

780—Heny Juanita, b 3 Aug 1921.

(513) James Overton, son of (153) James Calvin. m (765) Martha Ray Ledbetter, b 1890 in Overton Co, Tenn, d 27 Oct 1931 at Pearcy, Garland Co, Ark, dau of (500) Evert and Nancy Adeline (nee Smith) Ledbetter. Their children were:

781—Clarence, b 25 May 1906.

782—Oscar, b 12 Jul 1908, d 28 Mar 1947.

783—Bloice, b 22 Oct 1917.

Seventh Generation—Arthur Ledbetter Line

(526) Ulysses Grant, son of (191) Burwell. Resided in Parker Co, Texas from Dec 1885 until removed to Washita Co, Okla Terr where he homesteaded on 5 Sep 1892. m 1st 30 Jan 1890 at Springtown, Parker Co, Texas to Laura Viola Lynn, b 2 Sep 1870 in Mo, d 12 Feb 1896 in childbirth near Cordell, Washita Co, Okla Terr. Their children were:

Lewis Calvin, b 14 Jan 1891 near Springtown, Parker Co,

Texas. m Rena Green. Resided 1957 at PO Box 643, McAlester, Okla.

Thomas Jefferson "Tom", b 18 Feb 1893 near Cordell, Okla Terr. m 1st Bertha Atkinson, d 4 years after marriage; m 2nd Oma Beulah Barbee; m 3rd Myrtle Hutcherson. Resided 1957 in Forrest, N. M.

(A son), b and d 12 Feb 1896 near Cordell, Okla Terr. Buried with its mother.

(526) Ulysses Grant m 2nd 9 Apr 1901 near Cordell, Washita Co, Okla Terr to Winifred Jane Benton, b 28 Apr 1872 near Medina City, Medina Co, Texas, d 24 Aug 1935 at Clovis, NM. Removed to Plain, NM in 1921 and to Clovis in Sep 1926. Their children were:

John Burl, b 2 May 1906 near Cordell, Washita Co, Okla Terr. m 1st 1936 in Clovis, NM to Velma Ruth Harrell. m 2nd after 1945 to Grace Darris.

Harold, b 25 Dec 1913 at Cordell, Washita Co, Okla and d there 28 Dec 1913.

(537) William Isaiah, the only son of the 9 children of (198) Lewis Cass. m 2 Sep 1915 in Madison Co, Ark to Elvie Sisemore, b 1898 on Drakes Creek of same county, dau of George and Fannie (nee Drake) Sisemore. All their children were also born on Drakes Creek:

Mildred, b 9 Mar 1917. m Earl Duncan, b Madison Co, Ark, son of Comodore and Mary (nee Drake) Duncan. Resided 1958 at Wesley, Ark.

Lether, b 9 Jul 1919. m Wylmia Thompson, dau of D. L. Thompson. Resided 1957 at Wesley, Madison Co, Ark.

Imogene, b 25 Aug 1921. m Loy Counts, b Madison Co, Ark, son of Norman Leslie and Temperence Tabitha (nee Drake) Counts. Resided 1958 near Huntsville, Ark.

George, b 6 May 1923. m 14 Aug 1948 to Dorothy Napier, b 1932, dau of Verlon and Mary (nee Drake) Napier.

Wanda Lee, b 25 Jul 1924. m Roy Boyd, son of Robert and Flora (nee Counts) Boyd.

Genevie, b 12 Aug 1925. m Reno Guinn on 13 Mar 1948, son of Bill Guinn. Resided 1958 near Huntsville, Ark.

Junior, b 17 Nov 1926. m Norma June Sisemore, dau of
Montgomery and Nettie (nee Drake) Sisemore. Resided
1958 at Wesley, Ark.

Afton, b 12 Oct 1928. m Bettie Thompson, dau of D. L.
Thompson. Resided 1958 at Wesley, Ark.

Kenneth, b 6 Feb 1929. m 9 Oct 1952 at Vada Joyce Logue,
dau of Wayne Logue. Resided 1958 at Buckeye, Ark.

Virginia May, b 17 Mar 1931. m Junior Kisor, son of David
and Ellar (nee Counts) Kisor.

John Carl, b 11 Nov 1932. m Barbara Boyd on 6 Sep 1957,
dau of Gilbert and Maggie (nee Pennington) Boyd.
Resided 1957 in Fayetteville, Ark.

(550) Joseph Howard, son of (205) James M. m 6 Jan 1898
in Aurora, Madison Co, Ark to Ida Hull. They removed 1908 from
Ark to Oklahoma. Their children were:

Mart Edmond, b 5 Nov 1901. Resided 1962 in Muskogee,
Okla. m Gracie May ————.

Clellan, b 26 Mar 1905. Resided 1962 Muskogee, Oklahoma.
m D. C. Hobbs.

Oakley Leonard, b 13 Dec 1911. Resided 1962 Walla Walla,
Wash. m Betty Anna ————.

(574) Richard Harvey Sr "Dick", oldest son of (215) William Russell, was named for both his grandfathers. Farmer, stock
raiser and merchant. m 1st 26 Feb 1908 at Speegleville, McLennan
Co, Tex to Mae Lou Lillard, b 1886 in Dallas Co, Tex, d 18 Aug
1938 at Speegleville, dau of Franklin Lafayette "Fate" and Margaret
America "Pinkie" (nee Burton) Lillard. Their children were all
born at Speegleville; 1956 residences being shown:

Bonnie Lee, b 21 Jan 1909, m 11 Sep 1926 at Waco, Texas
to Charlie Ewing. Resided Speegleville.

Joe Dean, b 19 Sep 1910, m 1st 28 Oct 1939 at Waco, Texas
to Mrs. Geraldine (nee Dunn) Reynolds, d 10 Jan 1954.
m 2nd 9 Sep 1955 at Irving, Texas, Mrs. Hester Good.
Resided Irving, Texas.

Eunice Margaret, b 2 Nov 1912, m 1st 21 Apr 1933 at
Atlanta, Ga to Carl Hampton Buice, accidentally killed
23 Apr 1934 in McLennan Co, Tex. m 2nd 11 Nov

1937 in McLennan Co to Jefferson V. "Jay" Davis. Resided Speegleville.

Lina Mae, b 4 Dec 1915, m 30 Aug 1939 at Speegleville to Telford G. Ferguson. Resided Austin, Tex.

Richard Harvey Jr "Dick", b 17 Feb 1918, m Jul 1947 at Waco, Tex to Louise Bernard Oliver. Resided 1962 near Speegleville.

Tom Connally, b 21 Aug 1920, m 21 Aug 1952 at Speegleville to Mrs. Ruby Ray Hawkins. Resided 1962 at Waco, Tex.

Glenn Franklin, b 17 Aug 1924, m 31 May 1947 at Speegleville to Jackie Elizabeth Golson. Resided at Speegleville.

John Ray, b 11 Dec 1926, m 8 Nov 1946 at Speegleville to Frances Marie Thompson. Resided near Speegleville.

(574) Richard Harvey Sr m 2nd 24 Sep 1940 in McLennan Co, Tex to Mrs. B. L. "Nan" Hunt. No issue.

(575) John Thomas "Tom", son of (215) William Russell. m 24 Nov 1909 at Speegleville, McLennan Co, Tex to Vera Weaver, b 11 Mar 1889 at Gainesville, Ga, d 1960 at Waco, Tex, dau of Floyd Daniel and Minnie Narcissus (nee Boggs) Weaver. Their children were three daughters:

Mildred Pauline, b 15 Aug 1911 at Speegleville, d there 9 Oct 1920.

Nell Marie, b 12 Sep 1920 at Speegleville. m 1 Jan 1941 at Waco, McLennan Co, Tex to Herman Lee Wilson. Resided 1962 in Waco.

Elizabeth Ann, b 7 Oct 1922 at Waco, d there 11 Oct 1922.

(576) Clay, son of (215) William Russell. m 4 May 1914 in Waco, McLennan Co, Tex to Fleta Cecilia Gambrell, b 15 Jan 1892 near Gatesville, Coryell Co, Tex, dau of Duffy Watson and Molla (nee Key) Gambrell. Their children were two sons:

William Russell "Bill", b 23 Jan 1918 in Waco and resided there in 1962.

James Patrick "Pat", b 28 Aug 1919 in Waco and resided there in 1962.

(578) William Lawrence "Buster", son of (215) William Russell. Farmer and civil service employee. m 6 Oct 1920 near

Speegleville, McLennan Co, Texas to Harriet Dent Moore, b 29 Sep 1899 near Robinson, McLennan Co, Texas, d 11 Dec 1960 at Waco, Texas, dau of William Walter and Ella Lucinda (nee Moore/no relation) Moore. Their children, all born in McLennan Co, were:

> Robert Wayne, b 26 Sep 1921 at Speegleville and resided 1959 in Waco, Texas. m Dorothy Irene Travis, b 28 Jul 1926 at Crawford, McLennan Co, Texas, dau of Henry Barrett and Lydia Irene (nee Brown) Travis. They had a son, Stephen Wayne, b 11 Aug 1949.

> David Lawrence, b 6 Oct 1926 at Waco, d 20 Dec 1932 at Speegleville, Texas.

> Suzanne, b 24 Feb 1933 at Speegleville and resided 1960 at Waco. m James Wiley Eagan, b 30 Mar 1932 at Waxahachie, Ellis Co, Texas, son of Earl and Frances (nee Roberts) Eagan.

(588) Allen Lafayette, son of (230) Harvey Carrol "Heavy Harve". m 7 Oct 1900 near Boston, Madison Co, Ark to Joe Anna Burk, b 8 May 1880 in Kingston, Madison Co, Ark, dau of James Henry and Elizabeth Ann (nee Williams) Burk. She resided 1962 in Rocky, Washita Co, Okla. Their children, all born in Madison Co and whose 1956 residences are shown, were:

> Ethel, b 23 Jul 1905 at Boston, m Lonzo Inman. Resided Huntsville, Ark,

> Lena Violet, b 1 Dec 1905 at Boston, m Archie Haggard. Resided near Gotebo, Okla.

> William Thomas, b 8 Mar 1908 at Boston. Resided Rocky, Okla.

> Ted, b 14 Oct 1910 at Boston. Resided Edmond, Okla.

> Arlie, b 2 Jan 1913 at Wharton, m June McSpaddon. Resided Ponca City, Okla.

> Cletus Virgil, b 28 Jun 1917 at Wharton, m Dorothy Klimer. Resided Ponca City, Okla.

> Ruth, b 1 Jul 1921 at Wharton, m Glen Southall. Resided Tulare, Calif.

> Christine, b 23 Nov 1926 at Kingston, m Loran Deming. Resided Wichita, Kan.

(597) William Warren "Will", son of (241) James. m 13 Jul 1910 in Madison Co, Ark to Effie Glenn, b 13 May 1894 in Madison Co, dau of Clarence Jackson and Eva (nee Stringfield) Glenn. Their children were: Cleo, b 21 May 1911; Richard, b 9 Mar 1913; Hiram, b 4 Oct 1916; Pheba, b 19 Feb 1920; Virgie, b 24 Feb 1922; Conard, b 12 Nov 1932; Lishie, b 15 Jun 1934; and Alice, b 5 Oct 1935.

(606) Burley Comer, son of (245) Alfred. m 11 Aug 1905 at Huntsville, Madison Co, Ark to Minnie Mertle Parker, b 22 Jan 1884 in Madison Co, Ark, dau of John and Mary Jane (nee Boyd) Parker. Their children were 6 sons and 3 dau, all born in Madison Co, Ark:

Ada, b 6 Nov 1906. m John Baggatt. Resided 1957 Anaheim, California.

Arthur, d 11 Apr 1911 at Madison Co, Ark.

Alice, b 26 Oct 1910. m Ed Baughman. Resided 1957 in Fullerton, Calif.

Omer, b 1 May 1913. m Callie Stanfield. Resided 1957 at Fullerton, Calif.

Lester (twin) b 7 Oct 1915. m Mozel Bookout. Resided 1957 at Huntsville, Ark.

Vester (twin) b 7 Oct 1915. m Mary Cox. Resided 1957 at Fayetteville, Ark.

Bill, b 25 Apr 1919. m Lavon————. Resided 1957 at Fullerton, Calif.

Cuba, b 10 Feb 1922. m John Dubois. Resided 1957 at Middleville, Michigan.

Lee, b 1 Sep 1922. m Eula Neal. Resided 1957 at Springdale, Ark.

(610) Bee Alton, son of (248) Tilford. m 5 Oct 1912 to Vassie Hobbs at Gassaway, Cannon Co, Tenn. They are the only known descendants of this line still remaining in the Gassaway area where Alton's grandfather William and William's brothers and sisters resided before they went "west". Their 12 children were all born near Gassaway, and in 1956 all lived near Woodbury, Cannon Co, Tenn unless noted otherwise:

Willie Opal, b 27 Jun 1913. m Fred Stone.

Pauline, b 11 Jul 1915. m John D. Bogle.

Eulah May, b 21 Nov 1916. m John Y. Preston.

Claire Bee, b 3 Apr 1918, d age 3 mo and 8 days.

Anah Bell, b 2 Apr 1919. Resided 1956 near Daylight, Warren Co, Tenn. m Bill T. Preston, brother of above John
Y. Preston.

Benn Edmond, b 17 Mar 1921. Resided 1956 in Nashville,
Tenn. m Christine McIlhaney.

Myrtle Irene, b 2 Jul 1923. m Alf Gannon.

Margaret, b 12 Oct 1925. Resided 1956 near Smithville, Tenn.
m Garland Davenport.

Clyde Bratton, b 30 Aug 1927. Resided 1956 near Reliance,
Ohio. m 1st Jo Ann Parker, no issue. m 2nd Anna Bell
Relyah.

Alice Dean, b 20 Oct 1929. Resided 1956 near Daylight, Warren Co, Tenn. m Arthur Gannon, first cousin of above
Alf Gannon.

James Hubert, b 14 Apr 1932. m Martha Thomas.

Emma Warden, b 11 Aug 1936. Resided unmarried in Nashville, Tenn in 1956.

(616) John Dillard, son of (249) George Washington. m
13 Feb 1913 at Washburn, Barry Co, Mo to Zylfa Hall, b 16 Sep
1892 at Washburn, Mo, d 1953 at Bixby Okla, dau of John Patton
and Ida M (nee Ethridge) Hall. Their children were 3 sons and
1 daughter:

John DeMoss, b 27 Nov 1916 at Mounds, Creek Co, Okla, d
14 Dec 1946 in the Alps Mountains of Europe as result
of plane crash.

Orlee Hall, b 24 Aug 1919 at Bixby, Tulsa Co, Okla. m Phyllis
Brown.

Elmo Ward, b 7 Apr 1924 at Bixby, Tulsa Co, Okla. m
Imagine Pullam.

Maxine, b 28 Oct 1922 at Bixby, Tulsa Co, Okla. m————
Beeson.

(641) Alfred P., son of (262) "Big George" m 1 Jan 1893
at Aurora, Madison Co, Ark to Isabelle Scott, b 8 Jul 1873 at Drakes
Creek, Madison Co, Ark, d Aug 1953 at Fullerton, Orange Co, Calif.

Their children included the following, all born in Madison Co, Ark:

W. P. "Pat", b 19 Mar 1895 at Drakes Creek. m Nettie Counts on May 6 1920, b 6 May 1897 at Drakes Creek. They had one child, Donna b 18 May 1922.

Annie, b 30 Jun 1897 at Japton. m 28 Dec 1913 at Drakes Creek to Berry Frank Duncan, b 6 Jun 1893 at Drakes Creek.

Walter Marvin, b 25 Mar 1903. m Alma Counts, b 30 May 1902. Their 6 children were Gerald b 1928, Colleen, Hoye, Van, Larry b 1937, and Garry b 1957.

Lucy, b 26 May 1910 at Drakes Creek. m at Drakes Creek to Noval Hill.

Euna Mary, b 23 May 1913. m 15 Jul 1930 at Drakes Creek to Alva Platz, b 10 May 1902.

(647) Oscar B, son of (262) "Big George" m 12 Jul 1908 in Madison Co, Ark to Mary Tenpenny, b 23 Dec 1890, dau of David and Tersie (nee Brown) Tenpenny. Their children were 4 sons and 3 daughters, all born at Hindsville, Madison Co, Ark and resided 1957 in Madison Co, Ark except Elmer:

Lloyd, b 1909. m Clea Ledbetter. Resided 1960 near Wesley, Ark.

Wayne, b 1913. m Floy Fritts. Resided 1957 at Hindsville,

Mildred, b 1915. m Orval Taylor. Resided 1957 at Huntsville.

Marie, b 1917. m Victor Burnett. Resided 1957 at Huntsville.

Fern, b 1919. m Raymond Cline. Resided 1957 at Hindsville.

Jerry, b 1921. m Leona Vaughn. Resided 1957 at Marble.

Elmer, b 1922. m Iva Evans. Resided 1957 at Best, Benton Co, Arkansas.

(649) George Washington, son of (263) James Franklin "Bud", the Oklahoma Marshal. m 8 Nov 1893 in East Liverpool, Ohio to Annie Elizabeth Proctor, b 18 Mar 1878 in Prairie Grove, Washington Co, Ark and resided 1956 in Muskogee, Okla, dau of John and Harriett Minetta (nee Green) Proctor. Their children were:

George Lanslot Ladled "Lance", b 16 Sep 1895 in Johnson Co, Ark. Accidentally shot and killed while hunting on 26 Dec 1909 in El Paso, Texas.

Dolly Mae, b 16 Aug 1903 near Vinita (now Craig Co) Okla Terr. Resided 1956 in Hayward, Calif. m 29 Sep 1922 to Harold Freudenthaler, b 1901.

Mary Josephine, b 22 Aug 1905 near Muskogee, Okla Terr. Resided 1956 in Barkersfield, Calif. m 6 Mar 1923 in Muskogee Co, Okla to Harold Simpson, b 1901.

Nettie Estelle, b 15 May 1906 near Muskogee. Resided 1956 in Muskogee. m 11 Jun 1924 in Muskogee Co to Earl D. Corliss, b 1906.

James William, b 16 Jun 1908 at El Paso Co, Texas. d 18 Jul 1943 in Muskogee Co, Okla. m Judie Miller. El Paso records list the name James Franklin at birth.

John Franklin, b 14 Feb 1911 at El Paso, Texas. Resided 1956 at Costa Mesa, Calif. m 1st Harris————; m 2nd Zona Hassen.

Marc Leroy (twin), b 14 Apr 1917 at Muskogee. Resided 1956 at Vinita, Craig Co, Okla. Never married.

Annie Marthelle (twin), b 14 Apr 1917 at Muskogee. Resided 1956 inBaltimore, Md. m Percy E. Faust.

(655) Troy Edward, son of (264) Alfred Payne. m 17 Dec 1911 in Madison Co, Ark to Lydia Neal, b 28 Jul 1892, dau of Sam and Rhoda (nee Thomas) Neal. Their children both born at Drakes Creek, Madison Co, Ark:

Mildred, b 24 Jun 1913. m J. V. Wilson and resided 1957 in Fayetteville, Washington Co, Ark.

Irene, b 31 Jan 1915. m Max Counts and resided 1957 in Wesley, Madison Co, Ark.

(661)Guy Payne, son of (268) Jerry Turner. m 8 Jun 1905 in Madison Co, Ark to Livonia Drake, b 1890. Their children were 8 sons:

Otho, m Mary Margaret Cramer.

Theo, m Ethel Olson.

Tolbert, m Mattie Lohrli.

Leo, m Marie Lashley.

Charles, m Rema Neal.

Paul, m Peggy Milroy.

Roy, m Betty Slabaugh.

Rodney, m Carol Strickland.

(665) Benjamin Clyde, son of (268) Jerry Turner. m 31 Jul 1917 at Fayetteville, Washington Co, Ark to Bertha Jackson, b 21 Jun 1894, dau of John D. and Delia (nee Spurlock) Jackson. Their children were:

> Delia Imogene, b 17 Sep 1918 near Japton, Madison Co, Ark. m 1 Sep 1937 Charles Bowker.
>
> Girvis Erwin, b 2 Oct 1920 in Ark. m 22 Jun 1942 Dorothy Singer.
>
> Naomi Clydine, b 4 Jun 1924 in Alhambra, Calif. m 1 Jan 1944 Charles Chapman.
>
> Wanda Lee, b 26 Oct 1930 in Venus, Calif. m 13 May 1951 Robert McMullen.

(666) Albert Clarence, son of (268) Jerry Turner. m Dwina White. Their two children were:

> Leta Mae, m Ralph Michael.
>
> Stanley, m Hazel Piantoni.

(676) Joseph Verazani "Joe", son of (293) James Oliver. m 19 Nov 1916 at Marshall, Searcy Co, Ark to Lillian Ray Reece, b 30 Jun 1894, dau of Brice Smart and Amanda Caroline (nee Baker) Reece. Their children, listed below, resided 1956 in St. Louis, Mo:

> Maizie June, b 20 May 1918 in Miami, Ottawa Co, Okla. m 1942 John Settles. Divorced.
>
> Joe Ray, b 8 Sep 1925 in St. Louis, Mo. m 24 Sep 1955 in St. Louis to Stella Caroline Stroh, b 24 Jan 1924, dau of Dr. Christopher Paul and Stella Elizabeth (nee Logan) Stroh.

(677) Arthur Cort, son of (293) James Oliver. m 18 May 1918 at Glendale, Ariz to Arkie Mary Whitlock, b 14 Feb 1897 at Lead Hill, Boone Co, Ark, dau of James Lindsey and Elizabeth (nee Derryberry) Whitlock. Their children are:

> Willie Evalou, b 9 Mar 1919 at Pyatt, Marion Co, Ark. Resided 1957 in Waco, Texas. m 25 Jan 1942 at Waco, McLennan Co, Texas to William Bruce Hiatt Jr, b 9 June 1920, son of William Bruce and Corrie Jeanette (nee Southard) Hiatt.

Betty Belle, b 3 Aug 1924 at Pyatt, Marion Co, Ark. m 14 Oct 1950 at Waco, McLennan Co, Texas to Marshall Smith, b 2 Oct 1923 at Imboden Ark, son of Henry and Nema (nee McLaughlin) Smith.

(680) James Oliver Jr, son of (293) James Oliver. m 9 Jul 1928 at Harrison, Boone Co, Ark to Eula Cynthia Pierce, b 17 May 1906 at Yellville, Ark, dau of Augustus Garland and Rachel Arminta (nee Tuttle) Pierce. Resided in Pyatt, Ark when he died on 20 Nov 1955 of a heart attack while duck hunting. Their only child was Peggy Jean, 13 Jan 1931 at Cotton Plant, Woodruff Co, Ark. m 20 Dec 1952 at St. Louis, Mo to Dr William J Blake (DDS), b 22 Jun 1929 at Crystal City Mo, son of Emery Ellis and Florence (nee Stovesand) Blake. She is a registered nurse and they resided 1956 at Cape Girardeau, Mo.

(681) Carl Scotius, son of (293) James Oliver. m 1st 16 Jan 1920 at Pyatt, Ark to Zoe Tilley; divorced and no issue. m 2nd at Enid, Okla to Mildred Koons; divorced and no issue. m 3rd 2 Jul 1935 at Grayson, Ky to Ethel Dotson, b 28 Jul 1914. m 4th 20 Jun 1948 in Yokohama, Japan to 1st Lt Ruth Slocum Weymouth, ANC, b 15 Dec 1920 at Rockland, Maine, dau of Milton Wedgewood and Iris Ruth (nee Emery) Weymouth. His children were:

Twin sons, b 1939 in Ind, d both on same day as birth.
Carla Sue, b 7 Jul 1940 in Indianapolis, Ind.
Carl Scotius Jr, b 28 May 1949 at Fort Riley, Kan.
Charles Stephen, b 8 Nov 1950 at Augsburg, Germany.
Craig Slocum, b 7 Jan 1952 at Augsburg, Germany.
Candace Sybil, b 27 Nov 1953 at Ozark, Alabama.

(683) Leslie Lowell, son of (293) James Oliver. m 14 Oct 1939 at Fort Worth, Tarrant Co, Texas to Inez Curtis, b 12 May 1920 at Eldorado, Jackson Co, Okla, dau of Raleigh F. and Flavel M. (nee Knight) Curtis. Their children are:

Janice Kay, b 9 May 1941 at Tulsa, Okla.
Cheryl Anne, b 6 Dec 1946 at Los Angeles, Calif.

(689) Arthur Brooks, son of (294) Thomas Lewis. m 12 Jan 1931 at Claremore, Rogers Co, Okla to Effie Taylor, b 30 Jul 1907 in Ark, dau of Robert and Eller Taylor. Their children, all born at Pryor, Mayes Co, Okla, were:

Mary Elizabeth, b 2 Sep 1932. Resided 1956 in Tulsa, Okla.
m Jan 1954 to Lloyd Higgs, son of Jim Higgs.
Amanda Jean, b 30 Sep 1937.
Arthur Brooks Jr, b 12 Sep 1940.
Margaret Faye, b 29 Aug 1943.

(691) Thomas Logan, son of (294) Thomas Lewis. Removed 1933 from Pryor, Okla to Clovis, N.M. then to Artesia, N.M. where he m 25 Nov 1939 to Elsie Ivans. Their children were:
Alpha Nell, b 5 Mar 1941.
Dixie Mell, b 13 Sep 1942.
Thomas Leon, b 12 Dec 1944.
Andrea Lorraine, b Jan 1946.

(692) James Luther, son of (294) Thomas Lewis. Was granted an MA degree from Okla A & M College. Taught at Univ of Minn and in various schools and colleges in Okla and Texas. m 9 Jul 1944 at Memphis, Tenn to Mildred Morgan, b 3 Oct 1918, dau of Clyde Morgan. They had no issue but adopted the following children:
Allen Thomas, b 5 Oct 1949 in New Orleans, La.
Marlis Ann, b 2 Jan 1954 in Tulsa, Okla.

(695) Oliver Clyde, son of (296) Horace Alfred. m 1st Lillian Dotson, dau of John Dotson. Divorced. m 2nd after 1928 to Jerren Jones, dau of Jessey Wright Jones, Their children were:
Wanda Lee, b 28 Jun 1927 in Tulsa, Tulsa Co, Okla. Resided 1956 at Broken Bow, Okla. m Herman Bowline, son of Clem and Babe Bowline.
Dorothy Jean, b 17 Jun 1928 in Tulsa, Tulsa Co, Okla. Resided 1956 in Wichita Kan. m H. Hackenberger.
Barbara Ray, b 31 Jul 1937 in Claremore, Rogers Co, Okla. Resided 1956 in Hollywood, Calif.

(697) Harold Elmo Carroll, son of (296) Horace Alfred. m Theresa Niedermeyer, b 1906 in Elek, Hungary, dau of John Niedermeyer. Their children were:
Norma Louise, b 7 Apr 1934 in Claremore, Rogers Co, Okla. m Melvin Trotter.
Carol Sue, b 30 Jan 1939 in Claremore, Rogers Co. Okla.

(699) John Clifford, son of. (296) Horace Alfred. m at Tulsa, Okla to Harriette Ursula Looper, b near Tulsa, dau of Clifford D. and Dola M. (nee House) Looper. Their children both born in Tulsa, were Sandra Sue, b 11 Feb 1940 and Linda Kay, b 3 Nov 1943.

(700) Alfred Brooks, son of (296) Horace Alfred. m Aldena Watts, b Jun 1922 in Prescott, Ariz, dau of Eugene Alden and Ruth Elizabeth Watts. Alfred died as a War casualty in Korea on 25 Feb 1951 at which time his wife resided in Hollywood, Calif. Their children were Richard Brooks, b 15 Nov 1943 in San Benardino, Calif and Ronald Eugene, b 9 Nov 1946 in Stockton, Calif.

(704) Berl D., son of (300) Floyd. m James Victoria Palmer, dau of S. S. and Ida Rebecca Palmer. They have one son, Berl D. Jr, b 22 Sep 1929 in Kansas. m Henna Jean Bell, dau of John Morris and Lola Bell.

(709) Samuel L, son of (300) Floyd. m Lavelle Bridges, dau of Oliver and Opal (nee Bell) Bridges. Their children are:
Wanda Lee, b 19 Dec 1939 at New Hall, Calif.
Billie Jean, b 19 Jan 1943 at Lindsay, Okla.
Josephine, b 19 Jan 1943 at Lindsay, Okla.
Patricia Ann, b 17 Apr 1946 at Los Angeles, Calif.
Carol, b 1 Oct 1948 at Escondido, Calif.

(711) Joe E., son of (300) Floyd. m Doris Smith, dau of Fred and Ruby Smith. They have one son, Larry Lee, b 29 Sep 1947 in Calif.

(717) Orchard Early, son of (302) Early Lee. m Mamie Self, dau of William Self. She resided 1956 at Jennings, La. with her children. The children all born in Tulsa, Okla, except Frankie, b 12 Jun 1934 at Broken Bow, Wagoner Co, Okla: Wayne, b 26 Feb 1936; Barbara, b 28 Aug 1939; and Beverly, b 22 Apr 1947.

(721) Mary Alice, dau of (321) William Jones. m William Hoeting Atkinson. Among their ten children was Cleadie Edith Atkinson, b 6 May 1894 at Phillipsburg, Mo, m 10 Jan 1917 at Lebanon, Mo to Justus R. Moll, b 16 Apr 1893 at Mason City Iowa, son of Alexander Henry and Viola Belle (nee Reiniger) Moll. Justus R. Moll is an attorney who ended a long career in Washington, D.C. and returned home to Springfield, Mo in 1962. Beginning

in 1930 he collected information which forms the source for most of the kinship of the earlier Arthur Ledbetter descendants. Justus had one son, William Alexander Moll, b 13 Jan 1918 at Springfield, Mo, m Mary Helen Holmes. Their children were Carol Sue, b 6 Jul 1953 and William Justus, b 14 Oct 1955.

(743) Jones Walter, son of (400) George Washington. m 17 Apr 1907 at Malone, Texas Co, Mo to Maude Evans, d after 1958, dau of Thomas Rhys and Betsy Ann (nee Robinson) Evans. His parents died when he was 6 years old and he with his brother and sisters went to live with their grandmother Morris. He moved to Jonesboro, Ark in 1928 and in 1958 retired there after serving 52 years with the Frisco Railroad. Children were:

> Joseph Walter "Joe", b 1 Jul 1915 at Hoxie, Lawrence Co, Ark. m at Jonesboro, Craighead Co, Ark to Joy Gregory. MD at Jonesboro in 1960.
>
> Betsy Ann, b 15 Aug 1917 at Hoxie, Lawrence Co, Ark. MD and resided at 5718 River Road, Shreveport, La in 1960. Not married.
>
> John Paul, b 2 Aug 1922 at West Plains, Howell Co, Mo. m at Dallas, Texas to Joyce Mayo. MD at Jonesboro, Ark in 1960.

(767) Francis Harrison, son of (500) Evert E. Lexes. m 1918 at Caddo Gap, Montgomery Co, Ark to Ava Duke, b 1903 at Caddo Gap, dau of Sidney and Fannie (nee Hilton) Duke. Their children all born at Caddo Gap, Montgomery Co, Ark except Loyd Hugh. They are as follows:

> Vela Frances, b 1918. Resided 1957 at Glenwood, Ark. m Audry Pounds.
>
> Lela Vernice, b 1920. Resided 1957 at Glenwood, Ark. m Dale Digas.
>
> Loyd Hugh, b 1921 at Glenwood, Pike Co, Ark. Resided 1957 at Delphos, Ohio. m Melba Turner.
>
> Velma Marie, b 1923. Resided 1957 at Portland, Ore. m H. J. Laasch.
>
> Clifton Charlie, b 1927.
>
> Jessie James, b 1929. Resided 1957 at Prescott, Ark. m Marjorie Beckner.

J. T. Gerald, b 1931. Resided 1957 at Payette, Idaho.

Tressia Lonetta, b 1934. Resided 1957 at Glenwood, Ark. m
Jim Lock.

Dayce Ralph, b 1937.

Mary Christine, b 1939. Resided 1957 at Curtis, Ark. m
Glenn Stewart.

Eighth Generation—Arthur Ledbetter Line

(William Russell "Bill"), son of (576) Clay, was named for
his grandfather. He was raised in Waco, Tex and received a degree
in Engineering from Texas A&M College in 1940. m 27 Sep 1940
in Burbank, Los Angeles Co, Calif to Frances Marie Hooper DAR
No. 478473: Charles Ward b 18 June 1920 at Eddy, McLennan Co,
Tex, dau of Murray Robertson and Ersey (nee Cawthon) Hooper,
descendant of Obadiah Hooper of Franklin Co, Ga. He served in the
Antiaircraft Artillery during World War II, then later with the
Army Corps of Engineers. Their children:

William Russell Jr, b 5 Apr 1943 in El Paso, El Paso Co, Tex.

Joan Elaine, b 5 May 1947 in Waco, McLennan Co, Tex.

Janis Lynn, b 6 Apr 1955 at Selfridge AF Base, McComb Co,
Mich.

(James Patrick "Pat"), son of (576) Clay. Raised in Waco,
Tex and chose it for home after World War II. He received a degree
in Civil Engineering from Texas A&M College in 1941. Served in
the 26th Field Artillery of the 9th Division during the war; making
the initial landings in North Africa, Sicily and Normandy. Attained
the rank of major and was awarded Bronze Star, French Croix de
Guerre, French Service Cross and eight battle stars (Algeria-French
Morocco, Tunisia, Sicily, Normandy, Northern France, Ardennes,
Rhineland, and Central Europe). m 1 Jun 1946 in Waco to Helen
Louise Hooper, sister of Pat's brother's wife, Frances. Helen b 24
Apr 1924 at Bryan, Brazos Co, Tex. He is an engineer for the
Texas Highway Dept. Their children, all born in Waco, McLennan
Co, Tex, are:

Kathryn Jane, b 12 Aug 1947.

Susan Louise, b 22 Sep 1949.

James Douglas, b 12 Oct 1952.

NOTES

1. Blood and marital relationships, dates, places and activities in this presentation were obtained from many and varied sources. They spread from wills and marriage records with their definitive specifications on the one extreme, through the 1850 US Census and its probabilities, on to family tradition on the other. Some families have been assembled using several definitive references whereas others are organized solely on the indication provided by one census schedule; each subject to expansion and many subject to revision. Footnote references to documents in this chapter are limited to those of an unusual nature.

2. Ephraim with family came to the Province of Georgia in 1770. William with family petitioned for 400 ac in St Phillips Parish (now Chatham and Bryan Counties) on 7 May 1771. Thomas and Jain witnessed a will in Chatham County in 1777. Records of the 1780s show John and Frederick to be in Washington and Wilkes Counties; Henry, Isaac and Matthew in Wilkes County; and Drury and Lewis in Liberty County. Ephraim was there in an unknown county in 1782.

3. The earliest Ledbetter grantees in the State of Tennessee were (first name, grant number, acres, date, county): James 1619 140, 11 Sep 1809 Warren; James 16870 36, 9 Apr 1822 Lincoln; Henry 1745 50, 14 Jul 1825 Lincoln; Rowland 1744 50, 14 Jul 1825 Lincoln; George 2497 90, 31 Aug 1825 White; William 4372 50, 8 Nov 1826 Rutherford; Jesse 4461 50, 15 Nov 1826 Lincoln.

4. HENRY b 1760-70 in Md, m Charity Edwards b Ga, dau of Edmond Edwards d Robertson Co, Tenn. Children were Hardamon; Van H. b 1805 in Ga; William B.; George Washington b 1808 in Ill; Burling Lee b 1809 in Ill; Doctor Jackson b 10 Nov 1815 in Gallatin (now Hardin) Co, Ill; and Rebecca W., m Samuel Taylor. ASA was appointed Lieutenant in the 4th Regiment of Illinois Territorial Militia 13 Feb 1812 and Captain in the same unit 18 Aug 1817. Was commissioned Justice of the Peace on 27 Feb 1819 in Gallatin County, and the same in 1826 and 1827 in Shelby County after arriving there about 1822. He died 13 Mar 1828 while serving the latter term leaving a widow, Margaret, b 1791 in NC, d after 1860, and children. ASA, being a poor swimmer, drowned while trying to save his mill from flood waters.

5. Ledbetters of early southeastern Tennessee who might have been descendants of Arthur were: (a) LEWIS of Blount Co, who d before Sep 1815 and left an estate to Catherine "Catty" Leadbatter. Catty m 3 Sep 1819 in Blount Co to John Keeble; (b) GEORGE Jr, who obtained two tracts of land as a general enterer in the Hawasee District of Monroe Co in Mar 1827; (c) JAMES Sr of the 1840 census of McMinn Co, b 1770-80.

6. The only child of Buckner to be found in the 1880 US Census was Winnie Lynn at age 81. This schedule shows her birthplace as Georgia but birthstates of her parents were not entered by the census taker.

7. Overton Co deeds N/396 and N/413 dated 1856, and O/397 dated 1857 altogether name Buckner's heirs as Fannie, Aram, Beverly, James, Winnie, Tabitha, B. H. Louisa, and Hettie. Deed N/396 indicates Buckner's wife was named Tabitha.

8. File 59, Texas Memorial Records contains a petition by Reverend Arthur and Lewis. It is dated 23 Oct 1851 and presents the plight of Arthur's family on arrival in Texas.

9. Overton Co deed M/541 dated 21 Oct 1854 provides the descending relationship, Buckner-James-Overton, and indictment data.

10. During the Civil War in the border states there were many instances of soldiers, both Confederate and Union, being captured and forced into service on the other side. We may not rely upon military Service Record entries of "desertion" as an indication of voluntary desertion.

CHAPTER 7

OTHER FAMILIES WHICH HAVE BEEN TRACED TO VIRGINIA

By Roy C. Ledbetter

In the three preceding chapters a connected line of Ledbetters has been traced from Prince George or Brunswick County, Virginia, to the present with all known descendants of the ancestor. There are several other Ledbetters from Virginia whose descendants have been traced in successive generations to the present. In each instance the research of an individual descendant has been responsible for discovering the connected family line to the first known Ledbetter ancestor. In the present chapter the successive generations are set out in general outline. Wherever possible the name and address of the descendant who did the work is given.

From Richard, Senior (1690-1767) and wife Hanna several lines have been traced.

In the chapter on Ledbetters of Early Virginia and Their Probable Family Relation, information has been given on (9) Richard and Hanna and succeeding generations, (20) Drury (24 Nov 1734-1789) and wife Rebekah and their only son (46) Nathan (1755-1802) and wife Susanna Mayes and their ten children, including (68) Gardner (1786-1864).

Gardner m Nancy Jones, dau of John Jones and Angelina Vaughn Jones and they had three sons and four daughters, including Martha Claiborne Jarrett Ledbetter (1820-1909) who m John Jefferson Slaughter and had eleven children, including the youngest Jennie Botterill Slaughter (13 June 1870-22 May 1944) who m Charles Henry Marshall and had five children, including the first child Florence Louise Marshall (5 Oct 1886). She m Charles Henry Heinemann and they had one son Charles Henry Heinenmann II b 22 Jan 1919. Mrs. Heinemann was born in Petersburg, Virginia, and began research in Virginia records about 1912. In 1939 the family moved to Albany, Ga.

Richard and Hanna had as their youngest child (22) William (1740-1812) who had (47) Coleman (1762-1826) who had (77) William, who in turn had a son William (1806-1855). The last named William m Unice Siler and they had five daughters and five sons, including the first Wesley Ledbetter (1829-1911) who m Margaret Kime, and were the parents of Christian Albert Ledbetter (1864-1938), who did the extensive research in the records of North Carolina. A son Charles A. Ledbetter, 1016 Portland St, Greensboro, N.C., has the records in his posession.

Richard and Hanna had as their oldest child Richard, who in turn had as his oldest child Richard, the famous Revolutionary soldier who lived to be 103 years old. Edward B. Stephenson of Corinth, Miss, in his letter 8 Nov 1954 says the soldier and his wife Nancy Johnson had a son Isaac who m Sally Bradley of Rutherford Co, N. C. and had dau Elizabeth. She m Ambrose Sitton of Bumcombe Co, now Henderson Co, N. C. and they had dau Winifred Matilda Sitton, who m Joseph Johnson Stephenson of Bedford Co. Tenn, and they became the parents of Edward B. Stephenson. Mr. Roy W. Black, Bolivar, Tenn, aided Mr. Stephenson in tracing his ancestry back to Virginia. Mr. Black traced his own ancestry through Elizabeth Ledbetter, dau of Henry (d 1751) and her husband Isaac Rowe Walton.

Richard and Hanna's son Richard had as his youngest son (42) Isaac, who had son (66) Isaac, listed in the chapter on Ledbetters of Early Virginia and Their Probable Family Relation. The last named Isaac m Nancy King and about 1816 they migrated to Rutherford Co, Tenn, near Murfreesboro. Will Book 5, p 52, Rutherford Co, Tenn, contains the will of Isaac, showing he had three sons:

1. William b 1800 Brunswick Co, Va, d 1862 Rutherford Co, Tenn;

2. Richard b May 1810 in Brunswick Co, Va, d about 1877 in Benton Co, Miss.

3. Isaac, the youngest son of Isaac and Nancy King, was b 1817 in Rutherford Co, Tenn, and migrated after 1850 to Liberty Co, Texas.

William, the oldest son of Isaac and Nancy King, remained in Rutherford Co, Tenn. He m Rebecca Wellborn and had children Anne, Emma, Adaline, Richard, Laura, Kate, Newton, Frank, and a son William b 21 April 1831 d 15 July 1906 at Murfreesboro, Tenn.

The last named William m 1 April 1866 Mary Catherine Lytle and they had only one child:

Doc Lytle Ledbetter b 2 Dec 1872, Murfreesboro, Tenn, m 11 May 1901 Sarah Maud Doughty at Chicago, III, b 9 July 1879 Leavenworth, Kansas, dau Edwin L. and Elizabeth Doughty, and they had two sons born at Murfreesboro, Tenn:

William Chase Ledbetter b 27 March 1902.

Edwin Logan Ledbetter b 23 April April 1904.

Richard, the second son of Isaac and Nancy King, migrated about 1840 to Benton Co, Miss, and there in 1844 m Martha Ann Hendricks. Richard and Martha had children including:

James H. b 1848 d 9 April 1899, Benton Co, Miss, m Mary Ellen Rucker.

Susan m K. W. Exum. They are the grandparents of Kinchen Williams Exum, Chattanooga News Free Press, Chattanooga, Tenn. He has written an account of the descendants of Isaac Ledbetter and wife Nancy King.

Richard, third child of Richard and Martha, m Estelle King and d 1943.

Charles, another son of Richard and Martha, b 20 Sept 1858 d 22 March 1930, m Nora King Nelson.

Ann, the youngest child of Richard and Martha, m Samuel Elam.

In the chapter on Ledbetters of Early Virginia and Their Probable Family Relation are shown (8) William and wife Francis Vandiver, their son (17) James (1730-1821) and wife Mary, who were the parents of (32) Osborne, and wife Polly Delbridge and their children including (52) David Egbert Ledbetter.

Osborne and wife Polly with their seven children in 1835, with about 150 others, including the families named Williams, Delbridge, Tarver, Pearson, and Smith, migrated in covered wagons from Brunswick Co, Va, to Tallapoosa Co, Ala. Five of the children remained in Tallapoosa Co. In 1941 some of the descendants included William Alexander, Warren Crawford Ledbetter, and Benjamin Franklin Ledbetter living at Natasulga, Ala. The two remaining children, David Egbert and John James Ledbetter, moved to Lowndes Co, Ala. David Egbert and wife Polly H. Smith had a dau Saphronia Jane b 1841 who m Madison Shackelford. They had dau Lelia who m Franklin Moseley, who had one son Rev. (Methodist) Franklin Shackelford Moseley, No. 1 Traction St, Montgomery, Ala. Rev. Moseley, beginning about 1930, did immense research in tracing the family.

William, numbered 84 on the list of Ledbetters of Early Virginia and Their Probable Family Relation is likely the father of Edmund, Laban, and Robert Chalmers Ledbetter. At any rate, the ancestor William is claimed by the family to be from Prince George Co and to have m there about 1765. All three of the above supposed sons served in the War of 1812 in the same company from Prince George Co. The most convincing evidence that William was the father is that he appeared on tax list of Prince George County from 1783 to 1810, then from 1809 to 1817 Edmund, Robert C, and Laban appeared on the same list as shown on the tax list of Prince George Co at the State Library at Richmond. Nothing further is known of Edmund and Laban. Robert Chalmers d 1867, Tupelo, Miss. Robert Chalmers m Sarah Elizabeth Cates and they had four sons who lived to manhood:

John W. m 3 Jan 1844 Harriet Suggs and lived at Memphis, Tenn.

Leonadas

Samuel Peterson

Laban, the only one whose descendants are known. Laban, son of Robert Chalmers, b 1826 d 1855 at Birmingham, Ala, m 1850 Mary Henrietta Thomas of Hopkinsville, Ky, and they lived at Tupelo, Miss and had three sons:

Charles L. who lived in Birmingham, Ala.

James Robert b 1853 Tupelo, Miss, d Oct 1927 at Water Valley, Miss.

Dr. Samuel Leonidas b 17 Aug 1855 Lee Co, Miss, lived at Magnolia Springs, Ala. The doctor m Jan 1882 Margaret Antoinette Morrow, dau of John C. and Mary (Walker) Morrow of Birmingham and they had one son who lived to manhood:

Dr. Samuel Laban b 1886 and was a surgeon in Birmingham, Ala.

On 23 Oct 1943 Dr. Samuel Laban Ledbetter filed a sketch of the family with the Department of Archives and History, Montgomery, Ala.

CHAPTER 8

LEDBETTERS IN THE REVOLUTION

By Roy C. Ledbetter

In such an important matter as those who help make their country an independent nation, one might naturally assume that a list had been made of enlistments or otherwise preserved. Nothing could be more removed from the actual facts. Usually the soldier was in the militia of the colony of his residence. In many cases, the soldier was called in or gathered in a more or less irregular way when the British invaded his area. The colonies were joined only by a loose federation. When the constitution was adopted later apparently no one thought to require the making of a list of those who had freed the nation from England. In fact, such a list would not be complete because of the almost accidental participation in most instances.

Accordingly, at the present time, the highest record proof of service in the Revolution is the finding of a record of application for a pension for such service. The National Genealogical Society, 3123 Adams Mill Rd., N.W., Washington, D.C., undertook the tracing out of all names of Revolutionary War soldiers found in the General Administration National Archives and Records Service, Washington 25, D. C. At the conclusion of such search, only three Ledbetters (Coleman, Richard, Rowland) were included in their list in Vol. XL, December 1952, Page 633 and one Leadbetter.

The Daughters of the American Revolution and other patriotic organizations accept record proof that the ancestor aided the Revolution by money or otherwise.

Georgia is perhaps the easiest State in which to trace soldiers of the Revolutionary War. The other states, for the most part, had already granted their public lands. The legislature of the State of Georgia, on 17 February 1783, passed the Lottery Certificate Act. There were later acts also. The soldier's commanding officer made a certificate as to his service in aid of the Revolution. A private soldier was entitled free to 250 acres of land and 37½ additional, making a total of 287½ acres if the soldier began paying taxes

240

after the grant was made. This caused a great number of soldiers from other states to procure free land and many of them to remove to Georgia, at least for a short period. The original records are in the Georgia State Archives on Peachtree Street in Atlanta.

The chief auhority for tracing the soldiers in Georgia is Georgia's Roster of the Revolution whether enlisted from Georgia or settled in Georgia after the close of Hostilities compiled under authority of the Legislature from all State and Federal documents by Lucian Lamar Knight, Atlanta, Georgia, Index Printing Company, 1920. In the list below, he is cited as Knight by the page.

In this account, only the war service is cited. Reference to the index will show other information generally found in the chapter of Ledbetters of Early Virginia and Their Probable Relation.

Coleman, N. C., Pension files on application of Elizabeth R 6236, B L Wt 47513-160-55.

Colonel Drury, the son of Henry of Brunswick County, Virginia, was colonel of Militia in Anson County, North Carolina and by 1777 was supposed to be Colonel of Militia of Georgia. The record of John Wilson of Pendleton District South Carolina states in part: "John Wilson of Greenville in the State of South Carolina who was a pri. infty & Cav in the company commanded by Captain Bell of the Regt. commanded by Col. Ledbitter in the North Carolina Line for 17 months." Strangely, Colonel is not set out in Knight directly but on p. 242 a grant of 287½ acres, being survey 13 as bounded on the south by Drury Ledbetter land and on the north by land of his son, Lewis Ledbetter. A second bounty to Joseph Lewis, 24 Februray 1785, was bounded on the west by Drury Ledbetter Survey 15. DAR Lineage Book, No. 11,423 Volume 12, page 162, shows Miss Miriam Ballenger joined as a great great grand-daughter of Colonel Drury and his first wife (so described although Colonel was married only once then to) Winnefred Lanier. DAR Lineage Book, Volume 80, page 352, shows Mrs. Lillie Scales Slaughter, No. 79,958 joined as a descendant of Col. Drury but Julia A. Russell, now deceased, of Anderson, S. C. and Orlando, Florida, said this should be private Drury who was a soldier from Virginia.

Private Drury, son of Richard and Hanna of Brunswick County, Virginia. Drury was a private in Sixth Virginia Regiment in 1771 as shown in Crozier's Records, Vol. 2, p 127. Drury was discharged as private in Captain Nathaniel Fox's Company of Sixth Virginia Regiment commanded by Col. James Hendrecks, as shown by the War Department Records and Crozier's Records.

Frederick served with Georgia troops, Knight—p. 385. On certificate of Col. James McNeil, 287½ acres in Washington County, Georgia, was surveyed for Frederick.

George, brother of Richard and Isaac, also soldiers, was certified in Knight, p. 420. Clarence W. Griffin, in his "History of Old Tyron and Rutherford Counties, North Carolina, 1730-1936," printed by Miller Printing Company, Ashville, N. C., says at page 117, George "was an officer in the Revolution and commanded a company under Col. Andrew Hampton at the Battle of King's Mountain."

Henry, brother of Col. Drury. Henry was commissioned Captain, Militia in Brunswick County, Virginia, in the year 1781, as shown in Vol. 24, pages 107-08 of William & Mary's Quarterly.

Henry is certified in Knight, p. 398. In 1793, he received land for services in Georgia troops which land was located in Liberty County, as shown in Wilson's Annals of Georgia, page 188. There is a possibility that this is the above named Henry who remained a resident of Brunswick County, Virginia where he died in 1793.

Rev. Henry (Calvinist). North Carolina Department of Archives and History, Revolutionary Army Accounts, Vol. X, p. 7, folio 4, "a List of Warrants and other Vouchers Paid into the Treasury in 1776 & 77" states H. Ledbetter (number 99), contributed 25 pounds. H. G. Jones, State Archivist in certifying says, "His name headed a list of other people (I thought they were members of his church.)" On the basis of this record, Mrs. Claude A. Brewer, 5606 Merrimac, Dallas 6, Texas, was accepted as a member of the DAR.

Increase Leadbetter of Massachusetts was in the Navy Pension File S.37164.

Isaac of Brunswick County, Virginia, a younger brother of Revolutionary soldiers Richard and George, gave aid to the Revolution as shown by the approval of the claims dated April, 1782, of Henry (same as above brother of Col. Drury), Isaac and Richard in Brunswick County, Virginia Order Book No. 13, pages 417-425 to 527 and is also shown in Tyler's Quarterly, pages 110-113. I am sure that Richard, George and Isaac were sons of Richard, Jr., who died 1751 in Bruswick County, Virginia. The three are grandsons of Richard, Senior, and wife, Hanna.

John Senior-John Junior, each of Georgia, but not yet traced as to parents or descendants. Knight, page 398 shows that for bounty in Washington County, Warrant 1281. Knight, page 267 shows certificate of James McNeil, 5 February 1784, Washington County and a second certificate by James McNeil, 21 July 1784, on which Richard Wilkes petitioned as lawful heir of John Ledbetter for 287½ acres in Washington County. Johns are also mentioned in Knight, pages 288 and 385. Deeds in Washington County, each for 287½ acres to a John Ledbetter are shown at Vol. GGG, page 15 in year 1785; and Vol. 111, page 860 in year 1786.

Lewis, oldest son of Col. Drury is not certified by Knight, but at page 242 is shown a grant of Survey 13, East of Altamaha River, Liberty County, Georgia. A. S. Sally, Jr., Secretary of The Historical Commission of South Carolina, Book X, Part 1, page 213, under "Stub Entries to Indents issued in Payment of Claims against South Carolina Growing out of Revolutions" shows: "No. 1817, Issued 4th March, 1786, to Lewis Ledbetter, L-43-6-3/4, Military Duty as Private and Lieutenant of Horse."

Richard, born 1738 in Brunswick County, Virginia, died 22 January, 1841, on Hightower River, Lumpkin County, Georgia. Knight, pages 420, 452; Mrs. Howard H. McCall, Roster of Revolutionary Soldiers in Georgia by Georgia Society, DAR, John T. Hancock, Publishers, Atlanta, Georgia (1941) page 199, also at page 457, reference is made to "Historical Collection of Joseph Habersham," DAR Vol. 2, pages 610-613 as consisting of a biography of Richard Ledbetter. Details of service are shown by pension applications W 26202; BLWt 29049-160-55 made by Richard in Rutherford County, North Carolina on 10 December 1832, when he was aged 94; and by his widow Elizabeth, made in McDowell County, North Carolina, 30th November 1854.

As taken down in open court and written in long hand, Richard described his service as follows:

"To the best of my recollection I Settled myself and family

in the year 1775 in Mumford Cove, Tyron County, now Rutherford County, North Carolina; about that time we was entirely on
the frontiers and very thinly settled, we all had to take sides. I
became a volunteer to guard the frontiers. I served under Captain
Potts, Capt. McDowell and Capt. McDaniel. The length of Time
I was out on these Different Routes I am not able to say, but my
first Tour was in persuit of the Indians, Capt. McDowell Com-
mander.

"My next Service was a Volunteer for the Seige Ninety under
Coln. Hampton but he turned his course down Broad River in
persuit of the British and Tories. We came in Sight of them at
Shiers Ferry. About or before we Reached that place we joined the
main Armey under Gen'l Sumpter we fired a few Rifles across the
River, I think I saw several fall. We shortly after had the Battle
at Black Stock where our General was wounded. From that place
we Returned to the Mountains. Soon after our Return we was
Ordered and again we was under Coln. Hampton but before the
Company had Collected the Indians Broke into the Settlement and
Killed Two of my little Daughters and Scalped them and a Negroe
girl about 10 years of age. My Wife with a Child at her Breast made
her escape, they was Immediately persued.

"Shortly after, I think in year 1780, I took the ballance of
my family and moved back to Virginia. I was Immediately Numbered and placed on thhe Muster Roll under Capt. Vaugn of Brunswick County, State of Virginia; we was Marched on in persute
of the British, to the point of the fork of James River where we
came up with them and had an engagement. We was there under
the command of Coln. or Gen'l. Lawson. We had to Retreat but
when we was Reinforced we followed after them to Little York.

"I left that place a few days before the Capture of Cornwallis
and his Army and returned home. . . . "

Robert. Knight, page 420, shows Robert included in Miss
Margaret B. Harvey's list of Georgia Revolutionary soldiers, published as Appendix F in Third Annual Report of National Society
DAR to the Smithsonian Institution Senate Document, Vol. 16,
Number 219. Fifty-Sixth Congress, Second Session, 1900-1, Pages
369 to 393. Robert is not shown in any other record that has come
to my attention.

Rowland, N.C., pension application R. 6237 also is Executive Document No. 37 of 32nd Congress, Report of Secretary of the Interior, 16 February 1852, bound Vol. VII, page 383. Application was made by Rowland, 2 September 1839 at a time when he had lived on the waters of Bradshaw Creek in Marshall County, Tennessee, showed he was born in Brunswick County, Virginia in 1764; was drafted about May 1, 1780, when he was 16 and served three months under Gen. Butler, Col. Lane, Capt. James Hillsman and Lt. John Walls; was discharged by Major Hardin Griffin in Wayne County, N.C. Again, about March 1, 1781, Rowland volunteered to protect the General Assembly meeting of Wake County from the Tories mobilized under Col. Fanning at Hillsborough, N.C. The pension was rejected because he had not served six months.

William and William, Jr. were in Virginia Militia in 1758 and Edward Goodrich was their captain and their lieutenant was Maclin in B Company as shown in Crozier's Records, Vol. 2. In September 1758, William and William, Jr. were paid for services or supplies for Militia of Brunswick County as shown in Henning's Virginia Statutes, Vol. 7, page 211. In February 1760, William Ledbetter took oath as Lieutenant in Militia of Brunswick County before Lemuel Lanier. In 1765, William took oath as Captain, First Company Foot Militia, Brunswick County. as shown in Book 9-B, Brunswick County Records. In 177— William was a member of 6th Virginia Regiment during the Revolution according to Crozier's Records, Vol. 1, page 136.

I cannot positively identify the two Williams or know whether three Williams are named in the above records. At the dates Junior did not necessarily mean a son, but at least a younger William in the same community. The oldest and perhaps the most prominent landowner in Brunswick County named William was one who moved there about 1726 from Prince George County. I place him as a son of the original Francis Ledbetter and as having been born about 1696 and married Frances Vandiver about 1712 and as having two identifiable sons, John born about 1714 and James born about 1730. There was plenty of room for a son named William, but I have never found any indication of such a son. William, as a fact, died in Brunswick County in 1775. His age counts against his being one of the soldiers, but he might be the senior. There was a William born 22 March 1740, youngest son of original Richard and Hanna. He sold land in Brunswick County in 1767 and is said to have moved to Chatham County, N.C. in 1771. Accordingly, it is unlikely that this was the last William named as being in the 6th Regiment in Brunswick County. There was a William born 19 February 1720 in Prince George County, Virginia, the son of John and wife Francis. I have been unable to trace this last William.

An unknown Ledbetter died before 1782 while a citizen of Georgia serving in the Revolution leaving a widow Neomia Ledbetter and five children. Neither the name of the father or the five children is given in the record. The Colonial Records of Georgia by Allen D. Candler by order of the Legislature, printed 1907 by Franklin-Turner Co., Atlanta, Georgia. Vol. III, page 43, Jan. 4, 1782, "A Petition from Neomia Ledbetter was read and referred to this committee on Petitions." The Journal of the House of Assembly, Tuesday, Jan 8, 1782, "Mr. Coleman from the committee of Petition Reports in part, viz: "No. 4, That the Petition of Neomia Leadbetter be referred to the Law now before the House" Revolutionary Records of Georgia, Vol. III, page 54.

Minutes of the Executive Council, Friday, Jan. 25, 1782, the Board met. "Whereas the House of Assembly has granted certain sums to the widows and children of those brave citizens of this State who have fell in cause of America, Therefore,

"Ordered, that Milly Horn, Neomia Ledbetter, Sarah Glover and Ann Boyles be allowed to draw thirty-seven bushels of corn from the commissary, in such proportion as their necessities require same to be deducted out of the sums granted them by the House of Assembly, viz:

Milly Horn—4 children, 10 bushels.
Neomia Ledbetter—5 children, 11 bushels
Sarah Glover—2 children, 5 bushels   } 37 bushels."
Ann Boyles—5 children, 11 bushels

Vol. III, pages 310-11, The Revolutionary Records of Georgia by Allen D. Candler.

The above may truly stand as the unknown soldier of the Revolution.

CHAPTER 9

LEDBETTERS IN THE WARS AFTER THE REVOLUTION

By Lt. Col. Wm. R. Ledbetter

Ledbetter Soldiers—1784-1865

The arrival of Ledbetters in the New World prior to the establishment of our nation resulted in their being among the arms bearers in all wars our country has been engaged in. The information in this chapter, except for that pertaining to the War Between the States, has been compiled exclusively from indices, military service records, and claims applications for bounty lands and pensions deposited with the National Archives at Washington, D. C. (There are no cross-references between service record and claim files at the National Archives.) Information relative to the War Between the States has been compiled from the various National Archives indices only, except for county locations, which have been determined after study of data in the various State archives as well.

Claim files in the National Archives for Civil War Federal veterans are a rich source of genealogical information, including birth and marriage data, lists of children with birth dates, and, in some cases, pages torn from the old family Bible. Such information is not included in this chapter. Confederate claim files are maintained by the State concerned.

The historical records include over thirty different ways of spelling the name, but most are cross-referenced to either "Leadbetter" or "Ledbetter." If copies of records are requested from the National Archives, the name should be spelled as shown herein.

Duplicate listings of individuals, due to various spellings of a name, separate periods of service, etc., have been eliminated as far as can be determined. Names listed are those to which all other spellings have been cross-referenced in the National Archives. Since a number of our soldiers in the War Between the States fought on both sides of the cause, some intentional duplication exists between U.S.A. and C.S.A. names.

247

The following listings except for the War Between the States contain all information that could be found concerning the individual in indices, service records, and the various claims applications. All soldiers were volunteers or conscriptees except for the four listed as Regular Army. The wars follow in chronological order with names of Ledbetter soldiers listed alphabetically by state.

REGULAR ARMY 1798-1902

John Ledbetter: Pvt, Company G, 13th United States Infantry Regiment. (See: Mexican War—Georgia)

John Ledbitter: Pvt, Battery C, 5th United States Artillery. Enlisted 19 May 1889 at Fort Columbus, New York City for 5 Years. Born at Rugby, England. Age 22 at Enlistment.

John W. Ledbetter: Sgt, Preston's Company, 35th United States Infantry Regiment. (See: War of 1812—Virginia)

Robert W. Ledbetter: Pvt, 9th United States Calvary Regiment. Enlisted 23 Mar 1872 at Paducah, Kentucky for 5 Years. Born in Hickman County, Tennessee. Age 24 years and 11 months at enlistment.

POST REVOLUTIONARY WAR PERIOD 1784-1811

Herbert Ledbetter: Pvt. Turner's Company, Benn's Battalion, Campbell's Regiment of Virginia Militia. Served from 1 Sep 1794 to 4 Dec 1794 in "an expidition against insurgents in Pennsylvania". (No claim record found)

WAR OF 1812 1812-1815
Names: 47

Official records show this war began 18 June 1812 in Canada, ended 8 January 1815 in New Orleans, and included 6 campaigns. Of the 527,000 United States troops utilized at one time or another during the war, not one entered the service through conscription.

GEORGIA

James W. Ledbetter: Pvt, Turner's Co, 1 Regt Ga Militia; jnd 2 Oct 1812 at Sparta, Hancock Co, Ga; dschg 2 Apr 1813 at Camp

Pinckney Point (as a substitute for William Lockhart). Also Pvt, Shriven's Co, 3 Regt Ga Militia; jnd 25 Sep 1814 at Camp Jackson, Hancock Co, Ga; dschg 2 Mar 1815 at Waynesboro. Age 72 and resided Hancock Co, Ga 21 Jan 1851. Letter 5 Mar 1873 from son T C Ledbetter at Iuka, Tishomingo Co, Miss re land bounty claim of James W near Peoria, Illinois.

Richard Ledbetter: Pvt, Huckaby's Co, 3 Regt Ga Militia; jnd 1 Dec 1814 at Camp Hope; dschg 8 Mar 1815 at Darien, McIntosh Co, Ga. Resided at Clinton, Jones Co, Ga. (No claim data found)

Silas Ledbetter: Pvt, Harvey's Co, 3 Regt Ga Militia; jnd 14 Dec 1814 at Camp Hope; dschg 8 Mar 1815 at Darien, McIntosh Co, Ga. Resided Milledgeville, Baldwin Co, Ga. (No Claim data found)

Timothy Ledbetter: Pvt, Brodnax's Co, 1 Regt Ga Militia; jnd 23 Aug 1813 at Eatonton, Putnam Co, Ga; dschg 6 Mar 1814 at Milledgeville, Baldwin Co, Ga. Out of service 12 Oct to 17 Oct 1813 by furnishing substitute. In Alexander's Separate Bn 18 Oct 1813 to Mar 6 1814 which was asgd to 1 Regt Ga Militia. Age 60 and resided Heard Co, Ga 29 Jan 1851 and age 63 and resided same place 30 Jul 1855. Letter 6 Oct 1908 from J. W. Ledbetter at Rockford, Ala re pension claim.

Williamson Leadbetter: Pvt, Cocke's Co, 3 Regt Ga Militia; jnd 16 Oct 1814 at Athens, Clark Co, Ga; dschg 28 Feb 1815 at Waynesboro (Camp Covington), Ga. Resided in Clarke Co, Ga on dschg. Age about 82 and resided Jackson Co, Ga on 18 Apr 1855.

INDIANA (ILLINOIS)

Merrel Ledbetter: Pvt, Whitside's Co, US Mounted Rangers; jnd 3 Jun 1812 at Vincennes; dschg 3 Jun 1813 at Fort Russell, Illinois Territory. (No claim data)

Murrell Ledbetter: Pvt, Short's Co, US Mounted Rangers; jnd 27 May 1813 at Huggin's Station; dschg 25 Aug 1813. Absent without leave after 20 Jul 1813. (No claim data found)

MASSACHUSETTS (MAINE)

Daniel Lebeter: Pvt, Blood's Co, 1 Regt Mass Militia; served 4-5 Jul 181?. Total pay for 1 day $0.36.6 (wages 26½c; clothes 8.4c; firearms 1.7c) (No claim)

Gurdon A. Leadbetter: Pvt, Fairbanks' Co, 3 Regt Mass Militia; served 9 days and dischg 10 Oct 1814. Total pay $3.30. (No claim data found)

James Leadbetter: Pvt, Wallace's Co, 4 Regt Mass Militia; jnd 3 Sep 1814 at Montville, Berkshire Co, Mass; dschg 20 Sep 1814 at Sheepscut Bridge, New Castle, Lincoln Co, Maine. Resided Montville, Mass. Duty at Belfast and on sea-coast between Belfast and Sheepscut Bridge. (No claim data found)

John Leadbetter: (Data identical to James Leadbetter just preceeding)

Luther Leadbetter: Pvt, Foss' Co, 2 Regt Mass Militia; 13 Sep 1814 at Leeds, Androscoggin Co, Maine; dschg 24 Sep 1814 at Gardiner, Kennebec Co, Maine. Marched 28 miles from Leeds to Pittston, Kennebec Co, Maine. Resided Leeds at dschg. Age 68 and resided at Leeds on 13 Sep 1858. Attest Orson Leadbetter.

Samuel Leadbetter: Pvt, Wallace's Co, 4 Regt Mass Militia; jnd 3 Sep 1814 at Montville, Berkshire Co, Mass; dschg 20 Sep 1814 at Belfast, Waldo Co, Maine. Duty at Belfast and on sea-coast between Belfast and Sheepscut Bridge. Resided Glenburn, Penobscot Co, Maine in 1858. Attest Samuel Leadbetter Jr in 1858. (Evidently Jacob Wortham performed this military service for Samuel as the "substitute" was paid for it. Claim for bounty land was rejected) Resided at dschg Palermo.

Thomas Leadbetter: Pvt, Morrison's Co, 2 Regt Mass Militia; jnd 14 Sep 1814; dschg 24 Sep 1814. Also Pvt, same Co, Ryerson's Regt Mass Militia jnd 25 Sep 1814; dschg 5 Nov 1814. Resided Livermore, Maine at dschg. b 3 Apr 1776. d 20 May 1848 Somerset Co, Maine. m Eunice Clark 8 Dec 1799 at Leeds, Kennebec Co (now Androscoggin Co), Maine; b 14 Jan 1775; age 80 and resided Bingham, Somerset Co, Maine on 31 Mar 1855. Removed from Leeds to Livermore soon after marriage, then later to Bingham. "Reared a family of children".

MISSISSIPPI (ALABAMA)

Daniel Ledbetter: Pvt, Hamilton's Co, 7 Regt Miss Territory Militia to repel an invasion by the Creek Indians; jnd 27 Sep 1813 at Huntsville, Miss Terr (now Madison Co, Ala) dischg 13 Nov

1813 same place, age 54 and resided Madison Co, Ala 2 Dec 1850; age 65 and resided same place 7 Apr 1855. d 15 Mar 1856 in Madison Co, Ala m 18 May 181X (written over but apparently 7, 8 or 9; 7 is most recognizable) in Madison Co, Ala, Harriett B. Buford; age 55 and resided in Madison Co 23 Apr 1856; attest E C and P E Ledbetter 1856. Gardner C Ledbetter was Justice of Peace in Madison Co 2 Mar 1852.

Ephraim Ledbetter: Pvt, Hamilton's Co, 7 Regt Miss Territory Militia to repel invasion by the Creek Indians; jnd 22 Sep 1813; dschg 13 Nov 1813. d 4 Jul 1841 in Pope Co, Ark. M 24 Jan 1808 in Elbert Co, Ga, Hester T Smith, age 61 and resided Madison Co, Ala on 4 Mar 1852. Marriage, death and burial of Ephraim witnessed by David Ledbetter. G C Ledbetter was Justice of Peace in Madison Co, Ala on 4 Mar 1852.

Joel Ledbetter: Pvt, Neely's Co, 7th Regt Miss Territory Militia to repel an invasion by the Creek Indians; 7 Oct 1813; dschg 5 Nov 1813. This company was organized in Madison Co, Miss Territory (now Alabama). (No claim data)

NORTH CAROLINA

Henry Ledbëtter: Pvt, Irvine's Co, North Carolina Detached Militia from Rutherford Co, NC; jnd 20 Feb 1815 at Wadesboro, Anson Co, NC, dschg 6 Mar 1815 at Rutherfordton, NC. Age 58 and resided Cleveland Co, NC on 10 Apr 1855. Resided same county 4 Dec 1855. Age 82 in Mar 1878. d 8 Jan 1885. m 11 Aug 1881 in Cleveland Co, NC, Mrs. Nancy Gladden age 60 and resided Cleveland Co in Jul 1889.

SOUTH CAROLINA

Edward Ledbetter: Pvt, Goss Co, Austin's Regt South Carolina Militia; present for duty 1-25 Feb 1815. (No claim data found)

TENNESSEE

Ephraim Ledbetter: Pvt, Sitton's Co, 1 Regt West Tenn Militia; jnd 13 Nov 1814 at Camp Hynes; dschg 13 May 1815 at Nashville, Tenn. Resided Lincoln Co, Tenn on 23 Jun 1815. Age 72 and resided Tuscaloosa Co, Ala on 11 Jan 1851. d 22 Sep 1851 in Mississippi. m 13 Feb 1808 in Christian Co, Ky, Margaret Morgan; age about 80 and resided Talladega Co, Ala in 1855. Attest sons Isaac and Ephraim 1852 in Talladega Co, Ala.

George Leadbetter: Pvt, Lewen's Co, 2 Regt Mounted Gunmen, East Tenn Volunteers; jnd 10 Jan 1814 at "Coke" Co, Tenn; dschg 25 May 1814 at Kingston, Tenn. d 4 Jul 1846 in Bradley Co, Tenn. m "1801 or 1802" in Pendleton Co, SC, Sarah Harmon; age 74 and resided Bradley Co, Tenn on 4 Jun 1851; age 76 and same residence on 26 Mar 1855. Witness William Ledbetter 1855. (Claim filed Ledbetter)

George W. Ledbetter: Pvt, Anderson's Co, 2 Regt West Tenn Volunteers, jnd 4 Oct 1813; dschg 10 Dec 1813 at Fort Strother. Resided on dschg Sparta, White Co, Tenn. (No claim data found)

James Ledbetter: Pvt, Delany's Co, 2 Regt West Tenn Volunteers; jnd 20 Sep 1814 at Fayetteville, Lincoln Co, Tenn; dschg 10 Apr 1815 at Nashville (or Fayetteville), Tenn. Resided Madison Co, Tenn 5 May 1851. Age about 70 and resided at Eagle Creek, Bradley Co, Ark on 12 May 1855; alive there 15 Sep 1856.

John Ledbetter: Pvt, Robertson's Co, 1 Regt Tenn Militia; jnd 29 Jul 1814 at Fayetteville, Lincoln Co, Tenn; present for duty 3 Oct 1814. (No claim data found)

John Ledbetter: Pvt, Kennedy's Co, 1 Regt Tenn Militia; jnd 4 Oct 1813 in Overton Co, Tenn; dschg 28 Dec 1813 at Monroe, Overton Co, Tenn. Also Pvt, Kilpatrick's Co, 1 Regt West Tenn Militia; jnd 20 Jun 1814 in Overton Co, Tenn; dschg 8 Mar 1815 at Fort Charlotte, Mobile, Ala. Deserted 20 Sep 1814 and returned 12 Oct 1814. Resided White Co. Tenn 30 Jul 1815. Age 64 on 31 Jan 1851 with address c/o Eli Philbrook, Ewington, Effingham Co, Illinois. Age 69 and resided in Hardin Co. Illinois on 28 May 1855. Resided Hardin Co, Illinois on 6 May 1856. Witness 1855 Doctor J Ledbetter.

Merrell Ledbetter: Blacksmith, Russell's Co, Tenn Volunteer Mounted Gunmen; jnd 28 Sep 1814 Fayetteville, Lincoln Co, Tenn; dschg 27 Mar 1815. Resided at Winchester, Franklin Co, Tenn when jnd. (No claim data found)

Millenton Ledbetter: Pvt, Russell's Co, Tenn Volunteer Mounted Gunmen; jnd 28 Sep 1814 at Fayetteville, Lincoln Co,

Tenn; dschg 27 Mar 1815. Resided at Winchester, Franklin Co, Tenn when jnd. Resided in Franklin Co, 12 Jun 1815. (No claim data found)

Washington Ledbetter: Pvt, Kilpatrick's Co, 1 Regt West Tenn Militia; jnd 20 Jan 1814 at Fayetteville, Lincoln Co, Tenn; dschg 8 Mar 1815 at Fort Charlotte, Mobile, Ala. Deserted 20 Sep 1814 and returned 12 Oct 1814. Resided Franklin Co, Tenn on 20 Jul 1816 and Madison Co, Ark on 30 Nov 1850. Age 65 and resided in Madison Co, Ark on 4 Jul 1855. "In the Creek War of 1815 for 14 days."

Wesson Ledbetter: Pvt, Porter's Co, 1 Regt West Tenn Militia; jnd 4 Oct 1813 at Fayetteville, Lincoln Co, Tenn; dschg 11 Jan 1814 at Nashville (Fort Strother), Tenn. Resided on dischg at Fayetteville, Tenn and on 6 Apr 1816 at Lincoln Co, Tenn. Witness 1816 Jess Ledbetter. Age 61 or 64 and resided near Linden, Perry Co, Tenn on 19 Aug 1851. Resided Perry Co on 26 Mar 1855. Age 84, not married and resided in Perry Co on 2 Oct 1871. (Service record indexed Western Ledbether and claim file indexed Wesson Ledbetter)

VIRGINIA

Edmond Ledbetter: Pvt, Raine's Co, detached from 62 Regt Va Militia of Prince George Co; present for duty 28 Jun 1813 to 10 Jul 1813. (No claim data found)

Edmund Ledbetter: Pvt, Raine's Co, 6 Regt Va Militia; jnd 24 May 1814 at Norfolk, Va; dschg 25 Nov 1814 at Norfolk, Va, 100 miles from his place of residence. (No claim data found)

Gardner Ledbetter: Pvt, Fraser's Co, 83 Regt Va Militia of Dinwiddie Co, Va, present for duty 1-6 Jul 1813 at Petersburg, Dinwiddie Co, Va. (No claim data found)

Hamlin Ledbetter: Pvt, Fisher's Co, Perkins' Va Artillery; present for duty 30 Jul 1814 to Aug 1814 at Fort Powhatan, Prince George, Prince George Co, Va. (No claim data found)

Henry Ledbetter: Pvt, Richardson's Co, 1st-Corps d'Elite, Va Militia from the City of Richmond; present for duty 26 Aug 1814 to 5 Oct 1814 and at Richmond 5-7 Dec 1814. d 26 Aug 1846. m 10 Nov 1819 in Hanover Co, Va, Mary T Harris; age 55 and resided in Hanover Co on 23 Aug 1852; age 58 and resided same county on 11 Jul 1855. Attest 1855 Joseph E Ledbetter.

Hubbard Ledbetter: Pvt, Palmer's, Co, 5 Regt Va Militia; jnd 30 May 1814 in Brunswick Co, Va; dschg 30 Sep 1814 at Norfolk, Va. Age 65 and resided in Brunswick Co, Va on 23 May 1851; age 71 and resided same county on 4 May 1855, attest Wiley G Coleman and Edward Dromgoole.

Isaac Ledbetter: Pvt Jones' Co, 19 Regt Va Militia; jnd 18 Mar 1813 at Richmond, Va and dschg 9 days later on 27 Mar 1813. (No claim data found)

Isaac Ledbetter: Pvt, Turner's Co, 19 Regt Va Militia from City of Richmond atchd to 6 Regt Va Militia; jnd 25 Jan 1814 at age 18 and a store clerk; dschg 12 Apr 1814 Norfolk, Va. Was a Quaker and refused to accept his military pay for religious reasons. b Charles City Co, Va. d 7 Mar 1853 at Westerville, Hanover Co, Va. Blue eyes, dark hair, fair complexion. m 8 Dec 1820 in Hanover Co, Jane W Harris; age 78 and resided in Hanover Co on 5 Oct 1878. Witness 26 Feb 1879 in Hanover Co, Edward Leadbetter. "Family record of Jane Leadbetter": (all Leadbetter) Joseph E b 9 Sep 1823. Eliza Matilda b 19 Dec 1825 d 31 Dec 1827, unnamed son b 19 Dec 1827 d 25 Dec 1827, Joseph E b 14 May 1829, Mary Matilda b 12 Nov 1834, Isaac Abner b 25 Feb 1836, Victoria b 15 Feb 1839, Adelaid b 3 Oct 1842, Ella b 4 May 1845, Henry d 31 Dec 1827, Isaac d 7 Mar 1853. Letter 23 Mar 1914 from Gonzales, Gonzales Co, Tex by (Miss) Virginia Leadbetter re bounty claim. (Claim filed Leadbetter)

Jeremiah "Jerry" Ledbetter: 2nd Cpl, Lamkin's Co, 121 Regt Va Militia; jnd 9 Jul 1813 in Botetourt Co, Va; dschg 28 Sep 1813. 3rd Sgt, same organization; jnd 29 Sep 1813 at Norfolk, Va; dschg 10 Jan 1814 at camp near Lambert Point, Norfolk Co, Va. Atchd to 4 Regt Va Militia 29 Sep 1813 to 21 Oct 1813 as 4th Sgt and atchd to 6 Regt Va Militia 22 Oct 1813 to 10 Jan 1814 as 3rd Sgt. d 7 Jul 1829 in Botetourt Co, Va. m 16 Jul 1817 in Botetourt Co, Jane Crawford; age 58 and resided Roanoke Co (from Botetourt Co in 1838) on 21 Apr 1855; had not remarried.

John W. Ledbetter: Pvt, Lamkin's Co, 121 Regt Va Militia; jnd 9 Jul 1813 in Botetourt Co, Va; dschg 28 Sep 1813. Also Pvt,

same organization atchd to 4 Regt Va Militia; jnd 29 Sep 1813 at
Norfolk, Va; dschg 21 Oct 1813 at same place. Also Pvt, same
organization atchd to 6 Regt Va Militia; jnd 22 Oct 1813; dschg
10 Jan 1814 at camp near Lambert Point, Norfolk Co, Va. Stationed
18 Dec 1813 at camp outside Lynnhaven Inlet, Princess Anne Co,
Va (No claim data found)

John W Ledbetter: Sgt, Preston's Co, 35 Regt U. S. Infantry;
dschg 27 Mar 1815 at Norfolk, Norfolk Co, Va. Age 20 and resided in Botetourt Co, Va on dschg. b Botetourt Co, Va. Blue eyes,
light hair, fair complexion, 5'-8", a farmer. Single and residing
near Breckenridge, Botetourt Co on 17 Apr 1816. (Data from claim
file only)

Laban Ledbetter: 3rd Cpl, Baugh's Co, detached from 62
Regt Va Militia of Prince George Co, Va. Present for duty 28 Jun
1813 to 10 Jul 1813 at Fort Powhatan, Pince George Co, Va. (No
claim data found)

Leban Ledbetter: Pvt, Conway's Co, 1 Regt Va Militia. Present
for duty 28 Aug 1814 to 30 Nov 1814; latter date went on fur-
lough to Prince George Co. Dschg at Camp Powell's Creek. (No
claim data found)

Osborn Ledbetter: Pvt, Dancy's Co, 1 Regt Va Militia. Present
for duty 28 Aug 1814 to 30 Nov 1814, dschg on latter date at
Camp Powell's Creek. (No claim data found)

Peter M. Ledbetter: Cpl, Fraser's Co, 83 Regt Va Militia of
Dinwiddie Co, Va. Present for duty 1-6 Jul 1813 and 28 Aug 1814
to 13 Sep 1814; dschg latter date at Petersburg, Dinwiddie Co, Va.
Resided in Dinwiddie Co. (No claim data found)

Robert Ledbetter: Cpl, Comer's Co, 62 Regt Va Militia of
Prince George Co, Va. Present for duty 1-10 Jul 1813 at Fort
Powhatan, Prince George, Prince George Co, Va. (No claim data
found)

Robert C Ledbetter: Quartermaster Sgt, Conway's Co, 1 Regt
Va Militia. Present for duty 28 Aug 1814 to Dec 1814. Promoted
27 Sep 1814 from Pvt to Sgt of QM. Dschg at Camp Powell's
Creek. Resided in Prince George Co, Va. (No claim data found)

William Ledbetter: Pvt, Fraser's Co, 83 Regt Va Militia of
Dinwiddie Co, Va. Present for duty 1-6 Jul 1813 at Petersburg,
Dinwiddie Co, Va. (No claim data found)

INDIAN WARS 1817-1839

Names: 17

The official Indian Wars covered far-scattered places for 101 years from January 1790 to January 1891. However, soldiers named Ledbetter are recorded as serving only in campaigns of the southeast United States. These consisted of the Seminole Wars of 1817-1818 and 1836-1839, the Creek War of 1836-1838, and operations against the Cherokees in 1836-1838.

ALABAMA

Berry Ledbetter: "Cherokee Removal 1838" Pvt, Wann's Co, Norwood's Bn, Ala Militia; jnd 13 Jun at Bellefonte, Jackson Co, Ala; dschg 17 Jul 1838 at Gunter's Landing, Marshall Co, Ala. Made claim 9 Jan 1852 in Jackson Co, Ala and gave age 36 and residence Wayne Co, Mo. Age 40 and resided same place on 2 Jun 1855.

Francis Ledbetter: "Creek War, 1837" Pvt, Pouncey's Co, Wellborn's Regt Ala Mounted Volunteers; jnd 4 Jul 1837 in Dale Co, Ala; dschg 10 Sep 1837 at Fort Breach, Ala. A wagoner. (No claim data found)

Gardner C Ledbetter: "Cherokee Removal, 1838" Pvt, Otey's Co, Norwood's Bn, Ala Militia; enl Huntsville, Madison Co, Ala; jnd 26 May 1838 at Bellefonte, Ala; dschg 16 Jul 1838 at Gunter's Landing, Marshall Co, Ala. Age 43 and resided Madison Co, Ala on 14 Aug 1852; age 47 and resided same place on 11 Jan 1856. "Collected Cherokee Indians".

Jarrett Ledbetter: "Cherokee Removal, 1838" 2nd Cpl, Wann's Co, Norwood's Bn, Ala Militia; jnd 13 Jun 1838 at Bellefonte, Jackson Co, Ala; dschg 17 Jul 1838 at Gunter's Landing, Marshall Co, Ala. Claim made 5 Aug 1851 in Jackson Co, Ala and gave age 42 and residence Union Co, Ill. Age 42 and resided Union Co, Ill on 7 Nov 1855.

John S Ledbetter: "Creek War" Pvt, Ledbetter's Co, Wellborn's Regt, Ala Mounted Volunteers; jnd 3 Apr 1837 in Dale Co, Ala; dschg 4 Jul 1837 at Fort Breach, Dale Co, Ala. (2 service records: John and John S) b 29 Sep 1809 (in Jones Co, Ga), d

15 Sep 1854 in Henderson Co, Texas. m 18 Jun 1846 in Nacogdoches Co, Texas to Mary Ann Elizabeth Webb, b 13 Mar 1828, d Nov 1855 in Henderson Co, Texas. Children were: John R, b 27 Nov 1847, d 26 Nov 1848; Aaron, b 14 Jan 1849, d 22 Jan 1851; Mary Ann, b 22 Sep 1851; Sarah Lydia, b 7 Dec 1852; John S b 21 Jan 1855. (Pages from large family Bible in claim file)

Seaborn Ledbetter: "Creek War, 1837" Capt, Ledbetter's (his own) Co, Wellborn's Regt, Ala Mounted Volunteers; jnd 3 Apr 1837 in Dale Co, Ala; dschg 4 Jul 1837 at Fort Breach, Dale Co, Ala. Commanded the company. Letter envelope marked "River Ridge, Ala, 1st October 1837". d Feb 1851 near Crockett, Houston Co, Texas. m 2 Jul 1835 at Claiborne, Monroe Co, Ala to Mary Ann Bradley. She resided near Larissa, Cherokee Co, Texas on 16 Apr 1857. (Seaborn b 1802 in Ga per US Census)

Shellman P. Ledbetter: "Cherokee Removal, 1838" Pvt, Otey's Co, Norwood's Bn, Ala Militia; jnd 26 May 1838 at Bellefonte, Ala; dschg 16 Jul 1838 at Gunter's Landing, Marshall Co, Ala. Enl in Madison Co, Ala. Age 33 on 19 Feb 1851, age 36 on 28 Oct 1854; age 37 on 7 Apr 1855. Resided in Franklin Co, Ala on each of the three dates.

Martin S. Ledbitter: "Creek War" Pvt, Seal's Co, Webb's Bn, Ala Mounted Militia; jnd 2 Jun 1836 at White Plains, Calhoun Co, Ala, dschg 1 Sep 1836 at La Fayette, Chambers Co, Ala. (No claim data found)

GEORGIA

Isaac Ledbetter: "Seminole War, 1817-1818" Pvt, Irvin's Co, Ga Militia; jnd 8 Dec 1817; dschg 9 Jun 1818. Listed at Fort Gaines, Ga on an undated muster roll. (No claim data found)

John Ledbetter: "War of 1837-1838" Pvt, Saur's Co, 2nd Ga Mounted Volunteers; jnd 5 Oct 1837 in Hall Co, Ga; dschg 11 May 1838 at Forsythe Co, Ga. Resided 1850 Gwinnett Co, Ga. Age 51 and resided Gordon Co, Ga on 23 Mar 1855. Resided Gordon Co, Ga on 17 May 1869. "Action against the Seminole Indians".

Martin G Ledbetter: "Creek War" Two service records: (1) Pvt, Horton's Co, Stokes' 1st Ga Militia; jnd 14 May 1838 at New Echota, Gordon Co, Ga; dschg 26 Jun 1838 at same place. (2)

Pvt, Ligon's Co, Porter's 1st Ga Infantry; jnd 4 Jun 1836 at Columbus, Muscogee Co, Ga, dschg 12 Jul 1836 at same place. Evidently resided at Jefferson, Jackson Co, Ga in 1836 and Watkinsville, Clarke (now Oconee) Co, Ga in 1838. Age 41 and resided Cobb Co, Ga on 25 Nov 1850; age 46 and resided same place on 22 Mar 1855.

Moses Leadbetter: Two service records: (1) "Florida War, 1836-1837" Pvt, Barker's Co, Nelson's Bn, Ga Mounted Militia; jnd 20 Nov 1836 at Kellog's Store, Forsythe Co, Ga; dschg 23 Sep 1837 in Hall Co, Ga. (2) "Florida War" 2nd Lieut, Barker's Co, Nelson's Bn, Ga Mounted Militia; jnd 28 Mar 1839 at Fort Henderson, Ga; dschg 4 Jul 1839 in Forsythe Co, Ga. Age 39 and resided Cherokee Co, Ga on 10 Feb 1852. "War with the Seminole Indians".

NORTH CAROLINA

Wiley Ledbetter: "Cherokee War" Pvt, Angel's Co, 3rd North Carolina Militia; jnd 1 May 1838 at Franklin, Macon Co, NC; dschg 6 Jul 1838 at same place (No claim data found)

TENNESSEE

John Ledbetter: "Cherokee War" Pvt, Dodson's Co, Tennessee Mounted Volunteers; jnd 2 Mar 1838 at Calhoun, McMinn Co, Tenn; dschg 8 Jul 1838 at Fort Cass, Cherokee Nation, Tenn. Age 40 and resided at McMinn Co, Tenn on 3 Aug 1852, age 42 and resided Bradley Co, Tenn on 28 Apr 1855. Letter from "hier" J E Ledbetter at Carterville, Williamson Co, Ill on 8 Sep 1890 states John "was engaged with the Indians during their removal from the Hywassee Purchase". (Claim data filed Leadbetter)

John W. Ledbetter: "War of 1818" Pvt, Andrew's Co, 2nd West Tenn Volunteer Mounted Gunmen; jnd 31 Jan 1818 at Camp Blount, Tenn; dschg in absentia 30 Jun 1818 at Columbia, Maury Co, Tenn. Deserted 15 Feb 1818. (No claim data found)

William Ledbetter: "Cherokee War" Pvt, Caldwell's Co, 1st Tenn Mounted Infantry; jnd 30 Jun 1836 at Madisonville, Monroe Co, Tenn; dschg 31 Jul 1836 at same place. Age 38 and resided Bradley Co, Tenn on 5 Jul 1851; age 41 and resided same place on 19 Mar 1855. Resided same place on 5 Feb 1857. Claim rejected because he served less than 30 days.

William H. Ledbetter: "Cherokee War" Pvt, Cooke's Co, 3rd Bn, Tenn Infantry; jnd 29 May 1838 at Fort Cass, Cherokee Nation, Tenn; dschg 24 Jun 1838. Mustered-in 1 Jun 1838 at Calhoun, McMinn Co, Tenn. (No claim data found)

MEXICAN WAR 1846-1848

Names: 16

This war was the first in which the United States deployed troops great distances beyond its frontier. Other firsts for its 117,000 troops were use of troop ships, house-to-house fighting, and the establishment and administration of a military government over a defeated nation. Service by Ledbetter troops was from widely separated areas.

GEORGIA

John Ledbetter: Pvt, Co G, 13 United States Inf Regt; enl 22 May 1847 at Atlanta, Ga; dschg 15 Jul 1848 at Mobile, Ala. b DeKalb Co, Ga. Age 26 on enl. Blue eyes, light hair, light complexion, 5'-10", a mason by trade. Removed 1870 from Newman, Ga to Winchester, Tenn and d there 31 May 1871 at age 62 m 17 Jan 1850 at Center, Cherokee Co, Ala, Catherine W. ——————, b 8 Jul 1821; removed 1876 to Pulaski, Tenn and 1879 to Louisville, Ky. Sons Burt A and probably HH. From family Bible pages in claims file: Cornelia J. Ledbetter m 2 Jul 1873 W E Turner; Charlcie E. Ledbetter m 12 Jan 1876 W. E. Pierce; John Ledbetter b 10 Apr 1826 d 31 May 1871; Catherine W. Ledbetter b 8 Jul 1827; Cornelia J Ledbetter d 21 Oct 1878.

Wiley W. Ledbetter: Pvt, Loyall's Independent Co, Ga Mounted Volunteers; jnd 27 Mar 1848 at Dalton, Whitfield Co, Ga; dschg 11 Aug 1848 at same place. Age 23 on dschg.

ILLINOIS

Henderson Ledbetter: Pvt, Co C, 2 Ill Inf; jnd 2 May 1847 at Vandalia, Fayette Co, Ill; lost his canteen, 1 pair bootees and 2 pair sox; dschg 20 Jul 1848 at Alton, Ill. b Gallatin Co, Ill. Age

23 on dschg. Served again during Civil War in Co E, 32 Union Ill inf. Blue eyes, light hair, fair complexion, 5'-7", a farmer. d 3 Jan 1862 at Camp Butler, Ill. No issue by first marriage; m 2nd Hester E. ———— 18 May 1855; d 1 Jul 1922; two children only—Willard Maxey b 12 May 1858 & Miranda Isabel b 28 Dec 1860. (Civil War claim data incl)

James C Ledbetter: Pvt, Co C, 4 Ill Inf; jnd 13 June 1846 at Springfield (Ill?); dschg 6 Oct 1846 at Matamoros, Mexico on surgeon's certificate of disability. Claim made 15 Jul 1847 in Macon Co, Ill. Widow, Lydia resided at Aurora, Mo in May 1892. Son, James Y resided Springfield, Mo in 1901. Served again during Civil War in Co I, 7 Union Ill Inf. Age 38 on 3 Sep 1861. Grey eyes, dark hair, dark complexion, 5'-10", a farmer. b Tenn. (Civil War Service Record data incl).

James L. Ledbetter: Cpl, Co C, 2 Ill Inf; jnd 2 May 1847 at Vandalia, Fayette Co, Ill; dschg 20 Jul 1848 at Alton, Ill. Promoted to Cpl 16 Feb 1848 at Jalapa, Mexico. b Fayette Co, Ill. Age 19 on dschg. Black eyes, black hair, dark complexion, 5'-10", a farmer. d 29 Jul 1848 in Bond Co, Ill leaving neither wife nor children. Mother was Elizabeth Ledbetter.

Job Ledbetter: Pvt, Sellers' Co (Co E), 3 Ill Volunteers; jnd 21 Jun 1846 at Greenville, Bond Co, Ill; dschg 21 May 1847 at New Orleans, La. Age 19 on dschg. Claim made 12 Aug 1847 in Bond Co, Ill. Served again during Civil War in Co C, Union 70 Ind Inf. b Overton Co, Tenn, d of wounds 22 Jun 1864 at Resaca, Ga. m Sarah S. Thesser. (Civil War claim file contains additional data).

Joseph Ledbetter: Pvt, Co A, 3 Ill Inf; jnd 21 Jun 1846 at Vandalia, Fayette Co, Ill; dschg 23 May 1847 at New Orleans, La. b Shelby Co, Ill. Age 19 on dschg. Blue eyes, fair complexion, 5'-5", a farmer. Claim made 17 Aug 1847 in Fayette Co, Ill.

LOUISIANA

William B Ledbetter: Pvt, Co H, 3 La Militia Inf; jnd 12 May 1846 at New Orleans, La; dschg 8 Aug 1846 same place. (No Claim data found)

NEW JERSEY

George R Leadbetter: Pvt, Co D, New Jersey Inf; jnd 10 Aug 1847 in New York; dschg 25 Feb 1848 at Vera Cruz, Mexico on surgeon's certificate of disability. b Birmingham, England. Age 19 on dschg. Grey eyes, brown hair, 5'-3", brass founder by trade. (No claim data found)

TENNESSEE

Isaac N Leadbetter: Pvt, Co A, 1 Tenn Inf; jnd 29 May 1846 at Centerville, Hickman Co, Tenn; dschg 12 Sep 1846 at Comargo, Mexico on Surgeon's certificate of disability due to "severe relapse" of fever attended with the diarrhea". b Lincoln Co, Tenn. Age 22 on dschg. Blue eyes, dark hair, fair complexion, 5'-9", a farmer. Claim made 26 Jul 1847 in Hickman Co, Tenn (Claim filed Ledbetter)

James H Leadbetter: Pvt, Co K, 3 Tenn Inf; jnd 17 Sep 1847 at Centerville, Hickman Co, Tenn; "left sick at Molino del Rey 23 Feb 1848"; dschg 24 Jul 1848 at Memphis, Tenn. Age 19 on dschg. Father, Stephen Ledbetter made claim 2 Sep 1848 at Centerville, Tenn. James H d "on his return—having been discharged" and left neither wife nor children. Stephen signed letter 22 Nov 1851 in Perry Co, Tenn. (Claim filed Ledbetter)

John Leadbetter: Pvt, (musician-drummer), Co H, 5 Tenn Inf; jnd 6 Nov 1847 at Athens, McMinn Co, Tenn. promoted to Company Drummer 4 Dec 1847; dschg 20 Jul 1848 at Memphis, Tenn. Age 21 on dschg. Land warrant sent to Calhoun, McMinn Co, Tenn. (Claim filed Ledbetter)

John C. Leadbetter: Pvt, Co K, 3 Tenn Inf; jnd 17 Sep 1847 at Centerville, Hickman Co, Tenn; "left sick at Molino del Rey 23 Feb 1848;" dschg 24 Jul 1848 at Memphis Tenn. b Lincoln Co. Tenn. Age 22 on dschg. Blue eyes, light hair, fair complexion, 6'-1", a farmer. Claim made 14 Sep 1848 at Hickman Co, Tenn. (Claim filed Ledbetter)

Samuel W. Ledbetter: Pvt, Co G, 1 Tenn Mounted Inf; jnd 29 May 1846 at Memphis, Tenn; dschg 13 Oct 1846 at Port La Vaca, Texas on surgeon's certificate of disability. b Roanoke Co,

Va. Age 36 on dschg. Bluish grey eyes, dark hair, light complexion, 6'-0", a tailor by trade.

William A Leadbetter: Pvt, Co K, 3 Tenn Inf; jnd 17 Sep 1847 at Centerville, Hickman Co, Tenn; "left sick at Molino del Rey 23 Feb 1848"; dschg 24 Jul 1848 at Memphis, Tenn. Age 25 on dschg. Claim made 29 Aug 1848 at Centerville, Tenn. (Claim filed Ledbetter)

TEXAS

James Ledbetter: Pvt, Co G, 3 Texas Mounted Volunteers; jnd 2 Jun 1846 in Fannin Co, Texas; dschg 5 Sep 1846 probably at San Antonio, Texas. (No claim data found)

CIVIL WAR 1861-1865

Names: USA 123; CSA 374

The Civil War began 12 April 1861 and ended 9 April 1865. It included 25 official campaigns for which the Union enlisted 2,865,028 troops. Estimates of Confederate enlistments vary from 600,0000 to 1,500,000 but the more recent authorities place them between 800,000 and 1,000,000. According to the U. S. Census, the population of the United States in 1860 numbered 31,443,321 persons; 26,922,537 being white. Approximately 23,000,000 of the overall total were in the 22 Northern states and 9,000,000 in the 11 Southern states. Of the latter 3,500,000 were slaves. The following lists of Ledbetter soldiers include 496 white and 1 negro. Legend for their location is:

    b County of soldier's birth

    r County of soldier's residence

    e County of soldier's enlistment or enrollment

    f County from which soldier's company was formed

Information for each entry is: Name, Rank, Company, Regiment, Location:

ALABAMA—CSA

LEADBETTER

A Montgomery Pvt B 5 Ala Cav e Montgomery
Burton Pvt C 49 Ala Inf r Jackson
G A Sgt H 31 Ala Inf f Talladega
H Pvt F Mead's Conf Cav e Madison
Henry Pvt H Moreland's Ala Cav e Franklin
Jacob M Cpl D 1 Ala Inf f Talladega
James B Pvt A&B 47 Ala Inf f Tallapoosa
James W Pvt B 47 Ala Inf f Tallapoosa
J W O Pvt B 27 Ala Inf f Franklin
J H Sgt E Mead's Conf Cav e Madison
Martin Van B Pvt C 49 Ala Inf e Jackson
P H—F 16 Ala Inf f Lawrence
R A Pvt D 29 Ala Inf f Talladega
W Pvt C 55 Ala Vols f Madison

LEDBELLER

James Pvt D 1 Ala Inf f Talladega
John Pvt Henderson's Res f Talladega

LEDBETTER

A B Pvt G 3 Ala Inf f Loundes
A J Pvt H 3 Bn Ala Res e Pike
A P—E 8 Ala Cav f Marengo
Allison W Capt K 9 Ala Inf f Marshall
Asbury Pvt D 41 Ala Inf f Pickens
Augustus B Pvt G 3 Ala Cav f Calhoun
Benjamin Pvt Hurt's Btry Lt Arty e Chatahoochee Ga
Charles H Pvt B 5 Ala Inf e Tallapoosa
Charles M Pvt A 39 Ala Inf f Pike
D V Pvt A 17 Bn Ala Sh Sh f Pickens
Daniel Pvt D 41 Ala Inf f Pickens
Daniel L Pvt H Ala Inf r Madison
David S Pvt A 2 Ala Inf f Calhoun
David S Pvt A 51 Part Rngrs e Montgomery
David V Pvt A 19 Ala Inf r Pickens
E Pvt G 1 Ala Inf f Talladega
Ephraim B Pvt G 62 Ala Inf f Talladega
F M Pvt H 4 Ala Cav e Lauderdale
G W Pvt E 5 Bn Ala Cav f Sumter
Gardner C Capt H 49 Ala Inf r Madison
George J Pvt K 13 Inf f Randolph
George W Pvt E&K 18 Ala Inf e Talladega
H T Pvt A 17 Bn Ala Sh SH f Pickens
Henry Pvt K 4 Ala Inf r Blount

Henry T Pvt A 19 Ala Inf f Pickens
Humprhey P Pvt—4 Ala Cav e Lauderdale
J Pvt K 23 Ala Inf f Clarke
J Pvt H 31 Ala Inf f Talladega
J B Pvt B 5 Ala Inf f Talladega
J D Pvt F 17 Ala Inf f Montgomery
J D Pvt F 18 Ala Inf f Butler
J D—"CP of INSTR" f Talladega
J J Pvt—McDonald's Cav
J J Pvt—McQueen's Cav
JMG Pvt G 31 Ala Cav f Montgomery
J N Pvt D 31 Ala Inf r Calhoun
J R Pvt D 31 Ala Inf f Calhoun
J W Pvt G 31 Ala Inf f Montgomery
Jacob M Pvt G 31 Ala Inf f Montgomery
James A Pvt G 3 Ala Cav f Calhoun
James M—D 17 Ala Inf f Coosa
James P Pvt E 8 Ala Cav f Marengo
James M S Pvt G 31 Ala Inf f Montgomery
Jarred Pvt A 18 Bn Ala Vols f Jackson
Joel C Pvt K 4 Ala Cav e Jackson
John Pvt Stone's Res f Talladega
John J Pvt Brook's Ala Cav Res r Loundes
John Malone 1Lt C 26 Ala Cav Bn r Calhoun
Joseph W Pvt G 31 Ala Inf f Mongtomery
M J Pvt G 23 Ala Inf f Choctaw
M J—C 31 Ala Inf f Shelby
M T Sgt C 27 Ala Inf f Lauderdale
M T Pvt G 55 Ala Vols f Madison
M W R Pvt C 62 Ala Inf e Shelby
Martin Tyler Pvt C 5 Bn Ala Inf r Calhoun
Montgomery Pvt B 51 Part Rngrs e Montgomery
Osborne Pvt B 5 Ala Inf f Talladega
Paschal E Pvt H 49 Ala Inf e Madison
R B Pvt H 19 Ala Inf f Cherokee
R J Pvt F&K 7 Ala Cav f Montgomery
Reuben B Pvt H 49 Ala Inf e Madison
Richard B Pvt B 40 Ala Inf f Pickens
Robert Pvt B 5 Ala Inf f Talladega
Robert Pvt B 55 Ala Vols e Tallapoosa
S M Pvt H 49 Ala Inf f Madison
W L 2Lt A 19 Ala Inf f Pickens
W R 2Lt—Forrest's Ala Cav
William H Pvt B 5 Ala Inf e Tallapoosa
William H Pvt K 39 Ala Inf f Barbour
Wiliam H 1Sgt B 17 Bn Ala Sh Shooters

ARKANSAS—CSA

LEADBEATER

J M Pvt H 51 Ark Militia

LEADBETTER

A J Sgt H 24 Ark Inf e Dallas
J M Pvt D 34 Ark Inf e Sabastian
J R Pvt D 2 Ark Cav e Montgomery
James M Pvt I 16 Ark Inf r Madison
R S Pvt H 19 Ark Inf e Garland
W E Pvt D 2 Ark Cav e Montgomery

LEDBETTER

A J Pvt E Hardy's Ark Inf e Dallas
Alexander P Pvt H 19 Ark Inf e Garland
Beverly J Pvt C 17 Ark Inf e Johnson
Evan Pvt H 2 Ark Cav e Benton
G W Pvt I 27 Ark Inf e Madison
George Pvt D 9 Ark Inf e Jefferson
James Pvt A Hardy's Ark Inf e Dallas
John A—K 19 Ark Inf e Sevier
Johnson Sgt H 5 Ark Inf e Randolph
Thomas E Pvt 1 Fld Btry Ark Arty r
 Madison

ARKANSAS—USA

LEADBETTER

Josiah Pvt L 1 Ark Cav r Madison

LEDBETTER

Burrell Cpl B 1 Ark Inf r Madison
C S Pvt (filed with Senah S)
George W Pvt B 1 Ark Inf r Madison

James M Pvt G 1 Ark Inf r Madison
Senah S Pvt L 3 Ark Cav b Pulaski

LEODBETER

George W Pvt D 1 Ark Inf r Madison
Lewis CJ Pvt D 1 Ark Inf r Madison
Wiley Pvt D 1 Ark Inf r Madison

CALIFORNIA—USA

LEADBETTER

Robert Pvt H 2 Calif Cav b England (Great Britain)

COLORADO—USA

LEADBETTER

Alfred H Pvt 1 Colo Cav e Denver

GEORGIA—CSA

LEADBETTER

George A Pvt D Cherokee Legion f
 Cherokee
George E Pvt I 1 Ga Loc Def Trps f
 Richmond
J Pvt A 16 Ga Inf f Madison
James W Pvt Carlton's Arty e Clarke
J H Sgt A 27 Bn Ga Inf f Richmond
L J Sgt F 44 Ga Inf f Putnam
Leroy Pvt G 2 Ga Res e Fulton
R L Pvt I 8 Ga Inf f Greene

LEDBETTER

Algian S Pvt D 36 Ga Inf e Fulton
Alonzo C Pvt C 27 Bn Ga Inf r
 Washington
B—K 18 Ga Inf f Bartow
Benjamin E Pvt C 17 Ga Inf f
 Muscogee

Charles Pvt A 3 Bn Ga Sh Sh f Bartow
Charles Prt F 1 Ga Cav f Gordon
D Pvt A 3 Bn Ga Sh Shooters
D H W Pvt D Phillip's Legion e Coweta
Daniel Pvt K 18 Ga Inf f Bartow
G A—I 11 Ga Cav f Clarke
G M Pvt D&G 11 Ga Cav e White
G Perry Pvt D 36 Ga Inf e Fulton
H S Pvt A 1 City Bn Ga Inf e Muscogee
Humphrey Pvt F 1 Ga Cav f Gordon
J Pvt C 1 Ga Regulars
J H Pvt A 25 Bn Ga Inf f Fulton
J H Pvt Hamlet's Ga Inf f Bibb
J P 2 Lt A 39 Ga Inf f Murray
J S Pvt B 2 Ga Inf e Merriwether
J S Pvt D 6 Ga Inf St Gds f Upson
J T Pvt G 3 Ga Inf f Richmond
John Pvt H 1 Ga Reserves f Coweta
John Pvt Taylor's Ga Inf f Clarke

John F Pvt G 28 Ga Inf e Gordon
John P Sgt G 34 Ga Inf e Franklin
Joseph Pvt C 11 Bn Ga Inf f Dawson
Joseph S Pvt C 1 Bn Ga Res Cav e
    Spaulding
Lewis J Sgt E 21 Ga Inf e Pike
Ozias D Pvt I 52 Ga Inf f Dawson
R Pvt A 3 Bn Ga Sh Shooters
Richard Pvt K 18 Ga Inf f Bartow
R N Pvt A 39 Ga Inf e Franklin
Thomas Pvt K 25 Bn Ga Inf f Fulton

Thomas J Pvt K 3 Ga Inf f Clarke
William Pvt A 3 Bn Ga Sh Shooters
William Cpl G 8 Bn Ga Inf e Gordon
William Pvt K 18 Ga Inf e Catoosa
William A Pvt K 9 Ga Inf e Sumter
William A Pvt K 51 Ga Inf f Daugherty
William H Pvt K 55 Ga Inf f Coweta
William H H—K 3 Ga Inf f Clarke
William H H Cpl D&E Cobb's Leg f
    Daugherty

ILLINOIS—USA

LEADBETER

John T Pvt F&C Ill Inf r Hardin

LEADBETTER

Jesse Pvt F 48 Ill Inf b Massac
John Pvt A 45 Ill Inf r Livingston
Joseph Pvt D 45 Ill Inf e Sangamon
William H Sgt G 7 Ill Cav e Hardin

LEDBETTER

Berry Cpl F 60 Ill Inf e Union
David Pvt E 101 Ill Inf r Morgan
David W Pvt A 29 Ill Inf r Hardin
George Pvt K 76 Ill Inf r Ford b England
George M Pvt E 32 Ill Inf e Fayette
George W Pvt A 29 Ill Inf r Hardin
George W Sgt B 131 Ill Inf e Hardin
Henderson Cpl E 32 Ill Inf r Fayette
Henry M Pvt E 32 Ill Inf e Fayette
Isaac H Pvt A 29 Ill Inf r Hardin
Isaac D or S Pvt E 101 Ill Inf r Morgan
Jabez E Pvt E 149 Ill Inf r Vermillion
Jacob Pvt E 32 Ill Inf e Fayette
James B Pvt D 59 Ill Inf b Fayette
James C Pvt I 7 Ill Cav e Macon

James T Pvt D 17 Ill Cav f DeWitt
Jesse H Pvt A 60 Ill Inf b Union
Jesse H Musc D 131 Ill Inf b Massac
Job F Pvt D 17 Ill Cav r DeWitt
John Pvt D 33 Ill Inf r Fayette
John A Cpl H&C 131 Ill Inf b Massac
John F Pvt F&C 29&131 Ill Inf r Hardin
John H Pvt A 29 Ill Inf r Hardin
John T Pvt A 29 Ill Inf r Hardin
John T Pvt F&C 131 Ill Inf r Hardin
John W Pvt A 60 Ill Inf r Union
John W Pvt H 131 Ill Inf r Massac
Joseph Sgt B 7 Ill Inf e Sangamon
Joseph Pvt D 41 Ill Inf b Shelby
Joseph 1Lt C 54 Ill Inf b Shelby
Joseph T Pvt D 17 Ill Cav f DeWitt
Millington Pvt A 29 Ill Inf r Hardin
Robert H Pvt A 29 Ill Inf r Hardin
Washington W Sgt G 7 Ill Cav e Hardin
William Sgt F 62 Ill Inf e Richmond
William B Pvt D 30 Ill Inf e Morgan
William B Pvt Unasgd Ill Vols e Morgan
William F Pvt F 129 Ill Inf b Effingham
William J Pvt A 29 Ill Inf r Hardin
William W Sgt G 7 Ill Cav e Hardin

INDIANA—USA

LEADBETTER

Alfred K Pvt D 6 Ind Cav e Bledsoe,
    Tenn

LEDBETTER

Elijah Pvt B 147 Ind Inf r Wayne
Overton Pvt B 10 Ind Cav r Knox
Job Pvt C 70 Ind Inf r Hendricks

KANSAS—USA

LEDBETTER

Isaac S Pvt B 7 Kan Cav e Franklin Mo

KENTUCKY—CSA

LEADBETTER

J M Pvt D 10 Ky Mtd Rifles r
    Cumberland

LEDBETTER

George Pvt D 5 Ky Cav f Fayette
J G W Pvt D 6 Ky Cav f Marion

KENTUCKY—USA

LEDBETTER
Edwin M Pvt C 49 Ky Inf f Fayette
James M or W Pvt F 12 Ky Inf e Casey
James T Pvt K 12 Ky Cav r Bedford
   Tenn

James T Pvt B 16 Ky Cav e McCracken
John Pvt C&L 12 Ky Cav f Jefferson
John H Pvt C 49 Ky Inf f Fayette
Matthew Pvt E 26 Ky Inf f McLean
Matthew Pvt D 48 Ky Inf e Caldwell

LOUISIANA—CSA

LEDBETTER
J P Pvt G 19 La Inf f Caddo
J P Pvt D 7 La Pelican Inf f Orleans

J T Pvt E 3 La Inf f Morehouse
T G Sgt A Red River Sh Sh r Leflore
   Miss

MAINE—CSA

LEADBETTER
Danville BrGen Engrs CSA b Androscoggin bur Mobile Ala

MAINE—USA

LEDBETTER
Charles H Sgt I 23 Me Inf r
   Androscoggin

Herbert Pvt B 1 Me Hvy Arty r
   Penobscot
Lorenzo Pvt I 23 Me Inf f Androscoggin

MARYLAND—USA

LEADBETHLE
John Pvt G 1 Md Inf f Baltimore City

MASSACHUSETTS—USA

LEADBETTER
Samuel Pvt A 6 Mass Mil Inf f
   Middlesex

LEBEDER
Jules Pvt B&K 2 Mass Cav f Middlesex

MICHIGAN—USA

LEADBEATER
Edward S Lt Col F&St 27 Mich Inf r
   Wayne

Joseph Pvt B 3 Mich Inf r Wayne

MISSISSIPPI—CSA

LEADBETTER
A Pvt Swett's Miss Lt Arty f Warren
William Pvt B 18 Miss Cav r Coahoma

LEDBETTER
Absalom Pvt I 41 Miss Inf f Itawamba
Alex Pvt B 44 Miss Inf f Coahoma
Alex H 1Lt F 35 Miss Inf f Lowndes
Alexander H 2Lt E 11 Miss Inf e
   Lowndes

Benjamin F 1Lt G 28 Miss Cav r Scott
F M Pvt H 3 Bn Miss Inf b Lincoln
   Tenn
George F Pvt B 15 Miss Inf e Alcorn
H H Pvt I 2 Bn Miss Inf e Claiborne
   Tenn
Harrison H Pvt I 48 Miss Inf e Knox
   Tenn
J H Pvt Swett's Miss Lt Arty f Warren
J M Pvt B 12 Miss Cav r Lowndes

J M Pvt F 18 Miss Cav f DeSoto
J W O Pvt I 3 Bn Miss Inf e
  Lauderdale Ala
James I Pvt I 2 Miss Cav f Monroe
James W Pvt Duncan's Rangers r
  Tishomingo
James W Pvt I 48 Miss Inf e Knox Tenn
John M Pvt F 35 Miss Inf f Lowndes
Martin Pvt D 18 Miss Cav r Tippah
P Pvt I 41 Miss Inf f Alcorn
Richard R Sgt K 18 Miss Inf e Hinds
S P Pvt H 10 Miss Cav f Lowndes
S W Sgt E 2 Miss Inf e Lee

Samuel B Pvt B 25 Miss Inf e Jackson
  Ala
T G Pvt Armistead's Partisan Rangers
W H Pvt G 28 Miss Cav r Scott
William Pvt C 1 Bn Miss Inf
William Pvt I 48 Miss Inf e Knox Tenn
William B Pvt E 1 Miss Lt Arty
William C Pvt D 25 Miss Inf r Coahoma
William C Pvt H 33 Miss Inf e Coahoma
William J Pvt I 2 Bn Miss Inf e
  Claiborne Tenn
William S Sgt G 28 Miss Cav r Scott
William S Pvt F 20 Miss Inf e Scott

MISSOURI—CSA

LEADBEATER
John C Pvt F 1 Mo St Gd Cav r Dunklin
LEDBETTER
J F H 2Lt I 12 Mo Cav r Jackson Ark

James McC H Pvt F 6 Mo Inf r St. Clair
James McH Pvt K 10 Mo Inf r St. Clair
James McHenry Pvt D 3 Bn Mo Inf
Wm Hamilton Pvt C 8 Mo Inf r Texas

MISSOURI—USA

LEADBETTER
Alvin C Pvt I 13 Mo Cav r Texas

LEDBETTER
Alpheus C Pvt E 35 Mo Inf f Buchanan
Adolphus F Cpl E&B 4 Mo Cav f Holt

Asa P Pvt EH&K 9 Mo Cav e Boone
Henry J Pvt EH&K 9 Mo Cav e Boone
James or Jones Pvt I 32 Mo Inf e Texas
Joseph C Cpl A 15 Mo Cav r Cedar
Myranda H Pvt D 4 Mo Cav f Buchanan
Oliver V Pvt EH&K 9 Mo Cav r Chariton

NEW JERSEY—USA

LEADBEATER
John F Pvt B 11 NJ Inf e Mercer

NEW YORK—USA

LEDBETER
Thomas D Cpl D 53 NY Inf e New York

LEDBETTER
Samuel M Cpl C 161 NY Inf r Chemung

NORTH CAROLINA—CSA

LEADBETTER
J C Pvt G 6 NC Inf e Wake
James C Pvt C 42 NC Inf e Rowan
Sian B Pvt I 60 NC Inf b Transylvania
Wade Cook F 28 NC Inf

LEDBERRY
John A Pvt E 28 NC Inf e Montgomery

LEDBETTER
A B CPL K 50 NC Inf b McDowell
A L Pvt C 3 NC Inf e Lee
Abner Pvt B 2 Bn NC Defense
Alfred W Pvt G 56 NC Inf e Henderson

Allen A Pvt H 43 NC Inf e Wake
Anonamous Pvt H 28 NC Inf e Cleveland
Andy—K 50 NC Inf b McDowell
A M—E Mallett's Bn
Calvin Sgt E 6 NC Senior Res e
  Chatham
Charles W Pvt H 25 NC Inf e Buncombe
Chet E Pvt G 38 NC Inf f Guilford
Coleman Pvt C 25 NC Inf e Haywood
Elijah Pvt C 15 NC Inf e Rowan
Ephraim Pvt E 6 NC Cav e Transylvania
Ephraim Pvt E 7 BN NC Cav e
  Henderson
G W—E 64 NC Inf

George W Pvt F 3 NC Cav b&e Burke
James Pvt K 60 NC Inf e Buncombe
J F Pvt—38 NC Inf
J G Pvt K 60 NC Inf e Buncombe
John A Pvt E 28 NC Inf e Montgomery
John H Pvt A 28 NC Inf
John W Pvt C 34 NC Inf b&e Rutherford
John W Sgt D 60 NC Inf b&e Henderson
Jonathan Pvt K 50 NC Inf e Guilford
Lewis Johnson Sgt D 2 Bn NC Inf
Samuel H Pvt G 16 NC Inf e Rutherford
Shadrach L Sgt D&G 60 NC Inf e Polk
T B Pvt H 18 NC Inf e Columbus

T E Pvt K 60 NC Inf e Buncombe
Thomas Pvt G 60 NC Inf e Polk
Thomas B Cpl D 23 NC Inf e
   Rockingham
Thomas P Pvt H 42 NC Inf e Rowan
U Pvt D 55 NC Inf f Cleveland
William Pvt D 55 NC Inf b&f Cleveland
William O Pvt C 34 NC Inf b&e
   Rutherford
William T Pvt I 51 NC Inf e Cumberland
William K Pvt B 64 NC Inf e Henderson
Z J Pvt D 38 NC Inf e Guilford

NORTH CAROLINA—USA

LEDBETTER

Philo Pvt D 3 NC Mtd Inf r Transylvania

OHIO—USA

LEADBETTER

Alexander B Cpl A 175 Ohio Inf e
   Tuscarawas
David Pvt K 12 Ohio Cav e Cayahoga

LEDBETER

Henry (negro) Cook H 3 Ohio Cav

LEDBETTER

Charles Pvt D 154 Ohio Inf f Greene
Frederick B Pvt E 94 Ohio Inf e Miami
Joseph Pvt 17 Btry Ohio Lt Arty b
   Greene

PENNSYLVANIA—USA

LEADBEATER

George Pvt E 214 Pa Inf e Philadelphia
Henry Pvt G Pa Hvy Arty f Allegheny
Henry Pvt I 8 Pa Cav f Montgomery
Henry Pvt I 27 Pa Inf f Montgomery
James Pvt K 7 Pa Res Inf f Luzerne
James Pvt K 213 Pa Inf f Berks

LEADBETER

Leonard Pvt E 54 Pa Inf f Cambria

LEADBETTER

John Pvt D 2 Pa Hvy Arty r Philadelphia
John Pvt G 147 Pa Inf f Snyder

SOUTH CAROLINA—CSA

LEADBETTER

Daniel Sgt C 11 SC Inf f Charleston
Thomas D Capt C 11 SC Inf f Charleston

LEDBETTER

Daniel A Col F&St 1 SC Rifles r Union

TENNESSEE—CSA

LEADBETTER

John Musc D 8 Tenn Cav f White
John Pvt H 43 Tenn Inf e McMinn
Newton C Pvt H 15 Tenn Cav e
   Rutherford
W 1Lt—1 Tenn Cav f Maury
William Pvt D 8 Tenn Cav f White

LEDBEDDER

A J Pvt E 18 Tenn Cav e McNairy

LEDBETER

D T Pvt I 18 Tenn Inf e Warren

LEDBETTER

A Pvt Scott's Lt Arty f Shelby
A Pvt Cattle's Bn Inf f Davidson
A J Pvt E 19&20 Tenn Cav r Hardin
A M Pvt C 51 Tenn Inf e Chester
Alfred Cpl E 1 Conf Cav f Lauderdale
Alfred K Pvt C 43 Tenn Inf e Bledsoe

Alsey R—A 4 Tenn Cav r Marshall
Andrew Pvt E 47 Tenn Inf r Dyer
Andrew J Pvt A 40 Tenn Inf e
    Limestone Ala
Benjamin L C Cpl H 25 Tenn Inf r
    Overton
Buck Pvt E 13 Tenn Cav e White
Buckner Pvt A 13 Tenn Cav e Overton
E W Pvt B 23 Bn Tenn Inf
G C 2Lt H 42 Tenn Inf r Madison Ala
G P Pvt C 1 Conf Inf f Franklin
G W Pvt K 38 Tenn Inf e Shelby
Green Pvt I 18 Tenn Inf e Warren
H H Pvt E 34 Tenn Inf e Claiborne
H S Pvt C 24 Bn Tenn Sh Sh e
    Humphreys
Hamilton Pvt A 13 Tenn Cav r Overton
Henry C Pvt I 48 Tenn Inf r Wayne
Isaac 2 Lt G 3 Tenn Inf e McMinn
Isaac Pvt K 25 Tenn Inf e Franklin
J Pvt G 4 Tenn Inf e Lauderdale
J A Pvt A 27 Tenn Inf e Gibson
J J Pvt F 15 Tenn Cav e Weakley
J W Pvt F 17 Tenn Inf e Franklin
J W Pvt K 38 Tenn Inf e Shelby
Jackson Pvt G 3 Tenn Inf r McMinn
James Pvt K 38 Tenn Inf e Shelby
James A Pvt I 17 Tenn Inf e Sullivan
James E Pvt G 3 Tenn Mtd Inf r
    McMinn
James W Pvt B&E 34 Tenn Inf e Knox
Jesse M Pvt E 1 Conf Cav f Lauderdale
John Pvt G 3 Tenn Inf r McMinn
John W Pvt E 1 Conf Cav f Lauderdale
Jonathan Pvt K 28 Tenn Inf r Putnam
L Pvt Cattle's Bn Inf f Davidson
Lewis Pvt L 1 Tenn Inf r Davidson
Lewis Pvt G 3 Tenn Inf r McMinn

Louis L Pvt G 3 Tenn Inf r McMinn
Magness T Pvt H 42 Tenn Inf r Madison
    Ala
Marshall M Pvt F 17 Tenn Inf r
    Williamson
Martin V Pvt G 3 Tenn Inf e McMinn
Matthew Pvt G 59 Tenn Inf e Monroe
Merrial Pvt B 28 Tenn Inf f Overton
Newton C Pvt I 1 Tenn Inf r Rutherford
Noah Pvt C 13 Tenn Cav e Putnam
Noah Pvt K 25 Tenn Inf e Putnam
P H Cpl F 16 Tenn Inf e Sumner
R—F 18 Tenn Cav f McNairy
R W 3Lt D 19&20 Tenn Cav r McNairy
R W Pvt A 24 Tenn Sh Sh e Humphreys
Rufus Sgt E 1 Conf Cav r Lauderdale
Rufus A Pvt A 4 Tenn Cav r Marshall
Rufus W Pvt E 34 Tenn Inf r
    Humphreys
S B Pvt B 2 Conf Inf f Maury
Samuel J Pfc D 3 Conf Engr Trps e
    Knox
Sol S 1Lt G 3 Tenn Cav r Marshall Ala
W Pvt Phillip's Lt Arty e Hardin
W R Pvt G 1 Conf Cav f Hardin
W R 2Lt F 18 Tenn Cav f McNairy
Wesson Pvt B 2 Bn Tenn Cav f Maury
Wesson Pvt G 6 Tenn Cav r Wayne
William Jr Capt I 1 Tenn Inf r
    Rutherford
William Capt A 1&27 Tenn Inf f Benton
William A Pvt G 4 Tenn Inf e Tipton
William H Pvt E 1 Conf Cav f
    Lauderdale
William M Pvt—27 Tenn Inf r Madison
    Ala
William M Pvt E 37 Tenn Inf r Marshall
    Ala

TENNESSEE—USA

LEADBETTER
Andrew Pvt I 11 Tenn Cav e Loudon
Andrew J Pvt I 9 Tenn Cav e Loudon
George W Pvt I&C 9&11 Tenn Cav e
    Loudon
Hamilton Pvt G 9 Tenn Cav b Overton
James Pvt B 6 Tenn Inf e Nelson Ky

LEDBETTER
Alfred Pvt H 10 Tenn Cav r Wilkes NC
Fountain C Pvt F 2 Tenn Mtd Inf r
    Perry

Hamilton Pvt A 11 Tenn Cav b Overton
Isaac J Pvt A 14 Tenn Cav e Lauderdale
Isaac J Pvt I 9 Tenn Cav b Lauderdale
James Pvt H 3 Tenn Inf e Knox Ky
James E Cpl A 8 Tenn Cav b McMinn
John Pvt A 8 Tenn Cav b McMinn
Martin V Pvt A 8 Tenn Cav r McMinn
Robert W Pvt E&G 6 Tenn Cav b
    Hickman
Thomas Pvt F 4 Tenn Mtd Inf r Cannon

TEXAS—CSA

LEADBETTER
James R Cpl E 7 Tex Inf e Cherokee

LEDBETTER
A B Pvt D 17 Consol Tex Cav e Brazos

A G Sgt F 8 Tex Cav r Fayette
Albert Pvt F 9 Tex Inf r Fayette
Alex Sgt F 9 Tex Inf r Fayette
Andrew J Pvt I 10 Tex Inf e Bosque
Archibald B Cpl I 10 Tex Inf e Bosque

Arthur B Pvt A 21 Tex Inf r Parker
Buckner H T Pvt H 17 Tex Cav e
   Nacogdoches
Henry Pvt F 12 Tex Inf e Milam
Isaac A Pvt A 21 Tex Inf r Young
J Pvt F 2 Tex Inf
J Alexander Capt Waul's Legion r
   Fayette
James M Pvt F 22 Tex Cav r Lamar
James R Cpl E 7 Tex Inf e Cherokee
Jeff Pvt F 17 Tex Cav e Henderson

Jefferson R Pvt I 18 Tex Inf e Henderson
John B Pvt D 17 Tex Cav e Cherokee
John D Pvt H 14 Tex Cav e Denton
John W Pvt C 31 Tex Cav e Fannin
Lewis B Sgt K 5 Tex Cav e Parker
Oliver V Pvt A 21 Tex Inf r Dallas
S E Pvt F 30 Tex Cav e McLennan
Thomas L Pvt K 19 Tex Cav r Dallas
W H 2Lt K 9 Tex Inf r Lamar
William H 2Lt I 16 Tex Inf r Fayette

VIRGINIA—CSA

LEADBEATER
J Pvt F 2 Va Cav Res

LEADBETTER
Edward Cpl C 15 Va Inf f Hanover
H L Pvt B 40 Bn Va Cav e Richmond
J S Pvt C 15 Va Inf f Hanover
Joseph E Sgt G 4 Va Cav f Hanover
Peter Pvt G 4 Va Cav f Hanover

LEDBETTER
Charles Pvt A 3 Bn Va Res f Petersburg
George W Pvt E 13 Va Cav f Petersburg
George W Pvt Epp's Va Hvy Arty f
   Dinwiddie
J W Pvt H 18 Va Inf f Appomattox

J W Pvt K 18 Va Inf f Charlotte
Joel F Pvt C 9 Va Inf f Chesterfield
Marquis D Pvt E 37 Va Inf f Lee
R F Pvt Pegram's Va Lt Arty f
   Petersburg
R H Art D 1 Conf Engr Trps r
   Dinwiddie
R T Pvt I 56 Va Inf f Charlotte
Robert F Pvt Conscript Cp Lee e Pr
   George
Robert H Sgt C 18 Bn Va Hvy Arty e
   Petersburg
Rufus H J Sgt E 3 Va Inf f Dinwiddie
Stephen G Pvt C 12 Va Inf f Petersburg
W L Phys Gen&St Hq—Richmond
W N Pvt Mtd Gd 4 Cong Dist e
   Dinwiddie

WEST VIRGINIA—USA

LEADBETER
Abraham Cpl I 5 W Va Cav e Ohio

WISCONSIN—USA

LEDBETTER
Lloyd Pvt H 7 Wisc Inf r Adams Ill

CHAPTER 10

LEDBETTERS IN APPELLATE CASES

By Roy C. Ledbetter

The purpose of the search in appellate cases is to discover the name, state, county, date of residence and relationship of Ledbetters. Such information may confirm other records. But more important, a lead is given for further investigation. The county records of marriages, wills, deeds, taxes are the primary and more complete source of research. Most court cases never reach an appellant court. Only the appellate cases which have a Ledbetter in the style, as plaintiff or defendant, are digested here. In the original files of cases, Ledbetters may be discussed as heirs, parties, or witnesses. There is no index to locate such material.

With state, county, name and date, further research can be made in the U. S. Census.

Cases give further proof that Ledbetters arose in Virginia and spread principally to the other southern states. They arrived in the other states generally in order of time as follows: North Carolina, Georgia, South Carolina, Tennessee, Alabama, Mississippi, Arkansas, Louisiana, Illinois, Indiana, Kentucky, Missouri, Texas, California and Oklahoma. This was in the order of the date of settlement of those states or of their nearness to Virginia considering the Appalachian mountain barrier.

There were Leadbetters in Massachusetts as early as 1659. The Leadbetters spread from Massachusetts and Maine principally to the other northern states. J. E. Ames.

There are appellate court cases bearing the name Leadbetter in the states of California, Illinois, Maine, New York, Wisconsin and Washington. But there are no appellate cases in those states with the name Ledbetter. Oregon has one case with a Ledbetter and several cases having the style Leadbetter. California, Colorado, Florida, Illinois, Kentucky, New Mexico, New York and South Carolina are known to have residents named Ledbetter. None of those states has an appellate court case with Ledbetter in the style.

271

Generally the number of appellate cases indicates a greater number of Ledbetters in the state. In order of number, the states stand: North Carolina with 21, Texas with 20, Alabama with 19, and Georgia with 18. A notable exception is Virginia, where only one case was found. This indicates an early migration from the original mother state.

From other sources the Ledbetters who have been traced were first in America in the old state of Virginia. None have been shown to have arrived first from England into any other state. Georgia might have some Ledbetters who arrived there first from England. But the fact that the Ledbetters are not first found in the coastal area of Georgia indicates their migration from Virginia. Certainly before the Revolution there were Ledbetters in Virginia, North Carolina, South Carolina, Georgia and Pennslyvania.

ALABAMA:

Barbour

1842, a Ledbetter was county clerk. Ledbetter v. State, 10 Ala. 241.

Calhoun

1888, a Ledbetter and others sued the railroad in the city court of Anniston. No initials in opinion.
Anniston & A. R. Co. v. Ledbetter et al., 92 Ala. 326, 9 So. 73,

1897, W. G. (I suppose William Gordon) Ledbetter and more than forty other landowners petitioned the probate court of Calhoun County, Ala., for adoption of Stock law. Edmondson et al. v. Ledbetter et al., 114 Ala. 477, 21 So. 989.

1890, J. M. Ledbetter of Ledbetter & Co. Land & Loan Association v. Vinton, 18 So. 692.

1901, J. G. Ledbetter v. Thomas, 30 So. 342.

1905, Andy Ledbetter v. State, 38 So. 836, 143 Ala. 52.

1927, E. W. (Emmett Wesley) Ledbetter was sued in circuit court of Calhoun County, also in equity, to redeem two lots on which he held a lien. Pope v. Ledbetter et al., 216 Ala. 303, 113 So. 20.

Dale

1897, James H. Ledbetter obtained receipt from U. S. Land Office at Montgomery for land in Dale County.

Elmore

1897, Joe Ledbetter v. United States, 108 F. 52.

Jackson

1905, James Ledbetter v. State, 39 So. 618.

Marshall

1858, Solomon S. Ledbetter v. Blessingame, 31 Ala. 495 Solomon S. was constable.

1931, Frank Ledbetter v. State, 136 So. 430.

Pickens

1842, Ledbetter v. Castles, 11 Ala. 149.

Shelby   ?

1926, L. E. Ledbetter v. State, 110 So. 478.

Tallapoosa

1853, Alexander H. Ledbetter v. Walker, 31 Ala. 175. Ledbetter won decree for N. E. one quarter Section 18, Township 19, Range 23, Tallapoosa County, Ala. (Compare Lowndes County, Miss., 1873 for Alexander H. Ledbetter.)

Walker

1913, Mart Ledbetter, Administrator, 63 So. 987.

1932, Joe Ledbetter v. State, 139 So. 299.

ARKANSAS TERRITORY:

Pulaski County, Saline Township

1836, Benjamin M. Ledbetter v. Kendall, Fed. Cas. Co. 8157a, 1 Hemp. 302.

1839, Benjamin M. Ledbetter v. Fitzgerald, 1 Ark. (1 Pike) 448. Ledbetter, who must be same as in preceding case, lived on land which he was laying off a race track.

ARKANSAS STATE:

Cleveland

1927, H. L. Ledbetter. St. Louis Southhwestern Ry. Co. v. Ledbetter, 20 S. W. 2d 632.

Poinsett

1882, a Ledbetter was administrator of Frank Jones, deceased. St. L. I. M. & S. Ry. Co. v. Ledbetter, Admn., 45 Ark. 246.

Logan

1913, J. S. Ledbetter recovered damages for cattle shipped from city of Prescott. Chicago R. I. & P. Ry. Co. v. Ledbetter et al. 153 S. W. 801.

GEORGIA:

Chatham

1910, D N. Ledbetter v. Savannah Brewing Co., 68 S. E. 950.

1930, H. P. Ledbetter attempted to visit his brother, a member of the crew of the S. S. TULSA moored on the south bank of Savannah River in the city of Savannah. Central of Georgia Ry. Co. v. Ledbetter, 168 S. E. 81.

Cobb

1893, James E. Ledbetter was put off train when he had a ticket from Atlanta to Marietta and thence to Ball Ground. Western & A. R. Co. v. Ledbetter, 25 S. E. 663.

1895, Tate Ledbetter v. State, 23 S. E. 823, 97 Ga. 190.

Decatur, city of Bainbridge

1946, Monroe Ledbetter was one defendant alleged to own slot machines in the city of Bainbridge. Thompson v. Ledbetter et al., 39 S. E. 2d 720.

Floyd, Rome, Ga.

1881, A. W. (Allison Woodville) Ledbetter was member of firm of Simpson & Ledbetter who bought land from Samuel, the president of Bank of Rome. Colquitt, Governor v. Simpson & Ledbetter, 72 Ga. 501.

1887, A. W. Ledbetter v. McWilliams, 15 S. E. 634, 90 Ga. 43.

1889, City of Rome, Ledbetter & Harris, Partners. Ledbetter v. Dean, 9 S. E. 720, 82 Ga. 790.

Ledbetter v. McGhees, 10 S. E. 727, 84 Ga. 227.

1939, Billiter v. Ledbetter-Johnson, Contractors, Inc. 2 S. E. 2d 677: also Anderson v. Ledbetter-Johnson, Contractors, 9 S. E. 2d 860.

1926, John W. Ledbetter and William Taylor Ledbetter constituted Ledbetter Brothers (partners). John W. (Whatley) died May 23, 1926 leaving as his sole heirs his son, Allison Woodville Ledbetter III, who became administrator of his estate; his wife, Alice C. Ledbetter, who became guardian of their only remaining child Sarah Dorothy. Ledbetter v. Farrar Lumber Co., 171 S. E. 374, 177 Ga. 779. (There are descendants of Ephrame, b 1784.)

Fulton

1932, L. T. Ledbetter had at least two sons, G. H. and L. T. Jr. Ledbetter v. Goodroe, 175 S. E. 250, 179 Ga. 69.

Hall

1790, Col. Drury gave bill of sale in Wilkes County, Ga., where in 1802 he died.

1846, Washington, a son, after death of his mother Winefred (nee Lanier) sued in Hall County her second husband, James McClesky, also a Revolutionary soldier. Another brother Williamson testified by deposition. Administrators of James McClesky v. Washington Ledbetter, 1 Ga. 551.

Lowndes, city of Valdosta

1931, D. H. Ledbetter filed suit for injury received in Florida. Ousley v. Ledbetter, 161 S. E. 634.

Lumpkin

1938, Johnson & Ledbetter Construction Co. Jones v. Johnson & Ledbetter Construction Co., 194 S. E. 902, 185 Ga. 323.

Putnam

1871, John Ledbetter, b. about 1855, had Wiley C. Anderson as his guardian in 1871. Bullard v. John Ledbetter, 59 Ga. 109.

1931, J. Dennis Ledbetter. Eatonton Oil & Auto Co. v. Ledbetter et al., 163 S. E. 891.

Screven, city of Sulvania

1907, Son Ledbetter v. State, 58 S. E. 1106.

INDIANA:

Blackford

1905, Henry B. Ledbetter v. State, 74 N. E. 1128, 35 Ind. App. 707.

Grant

1889, Henry B. Ledbetter v. Davis, 22 N. E. 744, 121 Ind. 119.

1895, Henry B. Ledbetter v. Winchel, 40 N. E. 1064. Land in name of Ledbetter was foreclosed.

1895, Abigail Ledbetter v. Silas Embree, 40 N. E. 928.

1906, Henry B. Ledbetter v. Coggeshall, 76 N. E. 787, 37 Ind. App. 124.

IOWA:

Appanoose

1896, Lewis Ledbetter v. United States, 170 U. S. 606.

1897, a Ledbetter bought cattle. White v. Ledbetter, 73 N. W. 610.

KANSAS:

Barton

1915, J. W. Ledbetter and wife Nellie recovered for wrongful death of their son. Ledbetter v. Sunflower State Oil Co., 152 P. 763.

————County, Missouri and
————County, Kansas

1878,—————Ledbetter and wife owned land in———— County, Missouri, which house was moved to—————County, Kansas where Mrs. Christina Ledbetter, then separated from her husband, recovered the house. Bricker v. Christina Ledbetter, 26 Kan. 269.

Labette, city of Parsons

1891, a Ledbetter recovered for loss of left hand while working as a helper switchman. Rouse v. Ledbetter, 43 P. 249.

Wyandotte, city of Emporia

1881, Isaac J. Ledbetter who had "his old home in the state of Illinois" was switchman for the Atchison, T. & S. F. R. Co. at Emporia. Atchison, T. & S. F. R. Co. v. Ledbetter, 8 P. 411.

LOUISIANA:

Caddo Parrish

1916, Dr. J. M. Ledbetter wrote a will in 1916 while he was a retired physician at Shreveport.

Dr. J. M. Ledbetter was born about 1845 in Mississippi. He died at Shreveport, La., about 1919. By his first marriage he had only two sons:

Dr. Wiltz M. Ledbetter, died 1946 at Atlanta, Cass County, Texas. Had ony three children:

Wiltz M. Ledbetter, Jr., b. about 1905. William V. Ledbetter, Joanna Ledbetter, Succession of, 147 La. 771. 85 So. 908.

Carroll Parish
Ledbetter. J. F. Ledbetter v. Ledbetter, 88 Mo. 60.

1839, a Ledbetter was administrator of unnamed deceased. Richardson v. Ledbetter, 14 La. 156.

1847, a Ledbetter with his wife owned a plantation as community property. He died first. Later, about 1846, she died. The plantation was partitioned between her and her heirs including a son, born 1811, and son James Ledbetter, who became administrator of his mother's estate. Ledbetter v. Ledbetter, 2 La. Ann. 215. There is now no Carroll Parish but there is East Carroll with Lake Providence as parish seat and West Carroll with Oak Grove as parish seat in the northeast corner of the state.

Orleans Parish, New Orleans

1926, Benjamin A. Ledbetter sold property at 5900 Prytania Street, New Orleans, through his son Karl S. Ledbetter. Schmidt v. Ledbetter, 10 La. App. 337, 119 So. 573. (Dr. J. M. Ledbetter of Caddo Parish was an uncle to Benjamin A.)

MINNESOTA:

Blue Earth

1909, Emma Grace Ledbetter was acquitted of murder of Holland J. Ledbetter. State v. Ledbetter, 126 N. W. 477.

MISSISSIPPI:

Jackson

1828, Henry Ledbetter executed a note to Conway Oldham. Oldham v. Ledbetter, 2 Miss. 43.

Lee

1869, S. P. Ledbetter had sold land to F. F. Freeman. Freeman v. Ledbetter, 43 Miss. 165.

Lowndes, town of Crawfordville

1873, a house and lot in Crawfordville was purchased by Theophilus Harvey and Alexander H. Ledbetter and title taken in the name of his wife Lucy A. Ledbetter. Alexander died before 1873. Harvey v. Ledbetter, 48 Miss. 95.

Monroe, town of Aberdeen

1890, a Ledbetter applied for license to sell liquors at retail in Aberdeen. Perkins et al. v. Ledbetter, 8 So. 507.

Scott

1883, Betsy Ledbetter. Ledbetter v. State, 61 Miss. 22.

MISSOURI:

Adair

1910, Jacey E. Ledbetter (a woman), Filmore and Sixth Sts., City of Kirksville. Ledbetter v. City of Kirksville, 151 S. W. 228

Barton

1874, J. C. Ledbetter owned land. He was the father of J. F. Ledbetter. J. F. Ledbetter v. Ledbetter, 88 Mo. 60.

Gentry

1870, Miranda H. Ledbetter was elected to county court. Ledbetter v. Hall, 62 Mo. 422.

Pemiscot, city of Caruthersville

1925, Bill Ledbetter was the proprietor of Glad Hand Cafe in the city of Caruthersville, Missouri. State v. Ledbetter, 285 S. W. 793.

Greene

1928, H. L. Ledbetter and O. R. Ainsworth, a woman, who later married a Ledbetter, were then, and for many years had been non-residents of the state of Missouri, but in 1928 H. L. Ledbetter owned land in Kansas City, Jackson County Mo. Boone v. Ledbetter et al., 200 S. W. 2d 601.

1931, Roy Ledbetter was charged with aiding Harry Dooley in robbing bank at Ash Grove, Missouri. State v. Ledbetter, 58 S. W. 2d 453.

NORTH CAROLINA

Buncombe, Henderson, McDowell and Rutherford are adjoining counties in the southwestern part of the state.

Buncombe

1914, George W. Ledbetter v. English, 81 S. E. 1066.

1872, Richard Ledbetter v. Osborne, 66 N. E. 379.

1897, Richard Ledbetter and others sued J. H. Pinner and others for partition of land jointly owned. Ledbetter v. Pinner, 27 S. E. 123, 120 N. C. 455.

Burke

1840, George Ledbetter was sued to establish that he was the father of the child born to Eliza Justis. State to the Use of Eliza Justis v. George Ledbetter, 26 N. C. 242. Similar proceeding to establish George as father of child of Susannah Justis was quashed because on oath of mother. State to the Use of Susannah Justis v. George Ledbetter, 26 N. C. 245.

Henderson

1836, Isaac Ledbetter died intestate leaving fifteen children, nearly all of them being infants and six still infants in 1848. Richard Ledbetter purchased from those coming of age until he owned one-sixth and Leander S. Gash purchased from others coming of age so he owned one-sixth. Richard and others with ten-fifteenths sued Gash for partition of 1260 acres of land. Leander S. Gash v. Richard Ledbetter et al., 41 N. C. 183.

1848, partition of 300 acres of land on the French Broad River between Richard Ledbetter, L. O. Gash, John Ledbetter, Ann Ledbetter, Joseph Ledbetter, Elizabeth, wife of Ambrose Litton (all of age) and the following Ledbetter minors: Alford, Augustus, Silas, Asais, Ephraim, Scion. Ledbetter v. Gash. 30 N. C. 462.

Mecklenburg

1862, George Ledbetter v. Arledge, 53 N. C. (8 Jones Law) 475.

1939, L. L. Ledbetter was treasurer of the city of Charlotte. Riddle v. Ledbetter, treasurer, 5 S. E. 2d 542.

1946, L. L. Ledbetter still treasurer. Purser v. Ledbetter, 40 S. E. 2d 702.

McDowell

1850, Johnson Ledbetter (son of Richard 1738-1843) v. Torney, 33 N. C. 294.

McDowell or Rutherford

1854, Richard O. Ledbetter v. Morris, 46 N. C. (1 Jones Law) 545; 48 N. C. (3 Jones Law) 543. (Morgan District)

Rutherford

1862, R. O. Ledbetter v. Anderson, 62 N. C. (Phil. Eq.) 323.

1885, R. O. Ledbetter owned a mill on Holland creek which had been owned by Whitesides. Hardin v. Ledbetter, 9 S. E. 641.

1820, Richard Ledbetter's negro was sold on execution for an amount above the debt. John H. Alley et al. v. Richard Ledbetter, 16 N. C. 449.

1834, Richard Ledbetter, Senior. John Goodbread v. Richard Ledbetter, Sr. 18 N. C. 12.

1830, Jonathan Ledbetter sold land in Rutherford County and refused to give deed unless life estate was reserved in favor of his father (not named). Bradley also was a defendant. Ward v. Jonathan Ledbetter et al., 21 N. C. 496.

Morgan District

1797, George Ledbetter, Corse & Skepton v. George Ledbetter, 3 N. C. 15.

Rowan

1808, a Ledbetter was sued for slaves by Lofton, Administrator, in Montgomery County, North Carolina, of estate of Allen Dunn. The defendant, Ledbetter attempted to appeal to Superior Court of Law for Disrict of Salisbury. Ledbetter v. Lofton, 5 N. C. (1 Murph) 184.

Richmond

    1882, H. S. Ledbetter v. Quick, 90 N. C. 276.

Transylvania

    1925, P. B. Ledbetter was sued to remove cloud from title to land. Stone v. Ledbetter, 133 S. E. 162.

OKLAHOMA (Indian Territory)

Carter, town of Ardmore

    1896, Walter A. Ledbetter, attorney. Ledbetter v. Mandell, 126 N. Y. S. 497. (From genealogical index in Archives, Spanish and Texas, University of Texas Library, Austin, Texas, on May 15, 1947, I found: T. A. Ledbetter lived at La Grange, Fayette County, Texas, as an early settler, m. Alimida Robinson, dau. of Joel W. Robinson, who fought at San Jacinto and had a son, Walter A. Ledbetter. b. March 9, 1863 at Warrenton, Fayette County, d. Jan. 25, 1934 at Oklahoma City, Okla., m. Aug. 19, 1897 at Gainesville, Texas to Letitia Parnteau, located Ardmore, Indian Territory in 1890.)

Muskogee

    1909, J. F. Ledbetter received majority votes as Marshal of City of Muskogee. Ledbetter v. Kinsey, 134 P. 868. Also State ex rel West v. Ledbetter, 97 P. 834.

Carter

    1907, H. A. Ledbetter purchased a tract of land from Buckner Brems. Bowel v. Ledbetter, 122 P. 131, 32 Okl. 513.

    1903, W. A. Ledbetter, lawyer, of Oklahoma City.

OKLAHOMA

Carter

    1915, H. A. Ledbetter lawyer at Ardmore. Chowning v. Ledbetter, 208 P. 829, 86 Okl. 269.

    1921, Guy T. Ledbetter was represented in suit by Ledbetter, Stuart, Bell & Ledbetter, lawyers of Oklahoma City. St. L. & S. F. R. Co. v. Ledbetter, 200 P. 701, 83 Okl. 78.

    1927, H. A. Ledbetter, lawyer.

1927, L. A. Ledbetter, lawyer of Idabel.

1927, E. P. Ledbetter, lawyer of Oklahoma City. Ledbetter et al. v. Wesley, 23 F. 2d 81.

1927, Hugh A. Ledbetter, who had practiced law twenty-nine years, was disbarred. W. A. Ledbetter of Oklahoma City testified. State ex rel. Dabney, Atty. Gen. v. Ledbetter, 260 P. 454, 127 Okl. 85.

1932, Hugh A. Ledbetter, disbarred attorney of Ardmore represented by attorney H. E. Ledbetter of Ardmore and W. A. of Oklahoma City. State ex rel. Dabney, Attorney General v. Ledbetter, 9 P. 2d 728, 156 Okl. 23.

1933, Hugh A. Ledbetter practiced with his son, H. E. Ledbetter, at Ardmore. W. A. Ledbetter, attorney of Oklahoma City, was brother to Hugh. State ex rel. Dabney, Attorney General v. Ledbetter, 18 P. 2d 1085, 162 Okl. 20.

1935, Madgelle Ledbetter was administratrix of estate of Wesley Lester, deceased. Bowman v. Ledbetter, 48 P. 2d 334, 173 Okl. 345.

OREGON

Union

1930, City of La Grande, E. L. Ledbetter maintained a garage and sold automobiles. Williams v. Ledbetter, 285 P. 214.

TENNESSEE

Montgomery

1903, R. Ledbetter was Commissioner of Road District No. 12 of Montgomery County. R. Ledbetter v. Clarksville Turnpike Co., 73 S. W. 117, 110 Tenn. 92.

TEXAS

Coleman

1921, J. P. Ledbetter died in Coleman County, while suit for divorce was pending. Lena D. Ledbetter v. J. P. Ledbetter, 229 S. W. 576.

Dallas

1904, Arthur L. Ledbetter, sheriff of Dallas County. Broadnax v. Ledbetter, 99 S. W. 1111.

1908, A. L. Ledbetter, sheriff v. Dallas County, 111 S. W. 193.

1923, Arthur L. Ledbetter, Sr., was killed in 1912 by awning falling from Linz Building on Main Street, City of Dallas. He had wife Lula E. and six children: Bessie M., who married V. G. Foster and lives in Tulsa, Oklahoma; C. Fred Ledbetter, Tulsa, Okla., Mary V. who married (1st) Stanley Aulsbrook, m. (2nd) Ray Bickle, Dallas, Texas; Wilbur M. Ledbetter, d. Dec. 28, 1944 at Dallas; Arthur L. Ledbetter, Jr., a minor in 1923; Margaret Ledbetter, a minor in 1923; m F. A. Lumby, Dallas. Harper v. Ledbetter, 271 S. W. 213.

1913, St. Louis S. W. Ry. Co. v. George Ledbetter (who was commissioner), 153 S. W. 646.

1927, Forrest Ledbetter, b 1918. Scottino v. Ledbetter, 56 S. W. 2d 282.

1929, W. O. Ledbetter died before July, 1917 leaving wife Ella (Mrs. M. M.) Ledbetter, who died before 1929 leaving a son, R. L. Ledbetter v. Wright, 25 S. W. 2d 271.

1929, Dallas Trust and Savings Bank v. Roy C. Ledbetter, trustee, 36 F. 2d 221.

1930, Lyday v. Roy C. Ledbetter, trustee, 24 S. W. 2d 68.

Falls

1886, R. W. Ledbetter while plowing oxen about one and half miles south of Eddy, Falls County, on Aug. 5, 1886, shot and killed D. P. Rice, Constable of Bell County, while he and three others were approaching to take possessing of the oxen which had been mortgaged. Ledbetter v. State, 9 S. W. 60.

Fannin

1924, Monroe Ledbetter v. State, 260 S. W. 579.

Fayette

1873, W. H. Ledbetter purchased lot in city of La Grange. Ledbetter v. Burns, 42 Tex. 509.

Gillespie

1894, Henry Ledbetter v. State, 26 S. W. 725.

Hardeman

1908, J. E. Ledbetter was sued for land. Carver v. Ledbetter, 147 S. W. 348.

1931, W. L. Ledbetter and wife Emma resided in Chillicothe.

Hildago

1923, a Ledbetter sued for water rights and damages to his crops. Edinburg Irrigation Co. v. Ledbetter, 247 S. W. 335.

McCulloch

1893, a Ledbetter and his son Bob. Ledbetter v. State, 29 S. W. 479.

Mason

1893, R. B. Ledbetter purchased land. Ledbetter v. First National Bank, 31 S. W. 840.

Shackelford

1884, Bill Ledbetter v. State, 17 S. W. 427.

Tarrant

1896, Mary C. Ledbetter and others, as heirs of William M. Logan, sued for land partly in Tarrant and partly in Parker County. Ledbetter v. Higbee, 35 S. W. 801.

Williamson

1871, J. W. Ledbetter. Houghton v. Ledbetter, 37 Tex. 161.

CHAPTER 11

LEDBETTERS IN THE CENSUS

By Justus R. Moll and Lt. Col. Wm. R. Ledbetter

This chapter records indexed information from some of the United States Decenial schedules. In searching these schedules for the name "Ledbetter" in all its various spellings, over 700 county schedules were reviewed. These counties were located in Alabama, Arizona, Arkansas, Georgia, Illinois, Indiana, Kentucky, Massachusetts, Mississippi, Missouri, North Carolina, Oklahoma, South Carolina, Tennessee, Texas, Utah and Virginia. Since searching all areas of all states would have been impractical, effort was directed toward a study of those areas where there was some indication that a Ledbetter might have existed or where an index was readily available.

The information is presented in two parts. The first is a list of census schedules reviewed, including those which did not list the name Ledbetter in order to prevent fruitless search here by others. The first part consists of various schedules from 1790 through 1880. All existing schedules of the 1790 Census were reviewed, as well as the 1782-85 tax lists of Virginia.

The second part is primarily a listing of heads of families as recorded in the schedules from 1790 through 1880. It also includes the earlier Ledbetters who were not heads of families. Over 700 names are listed. The 1850 through 1880 listings show the name of the person who appears to be the wife. The 1860 listing can be associated closely with residences and removals indicated in records of war service and claims for bounty lands. Claims resulting from the War of 1812 and the earlier Indian Wars were processed between 1851 and 1856; Mexican War claims were processed in 1847-1848.

To make this information serve as a better reference, it should be used in conjunction with county formation data.

PART I—CENSUS SCHEDULES SEARCHED

Legend: O—Complete county searched but no Ledbetter found.
L—At least one Ledbetter found in the county.

ALABAMA:

All existing 1820 schedules searched but no Ledbetter found.

	1790	00	10	20	30	40	50	60	70	80
Autauga					0					
Baldwin						0				
Barbour							L			
Benton						L	L			
Blount					0	0				
Calhoun								L	L	L
Clarke					0	0	0			
Conecuh					0	0				
Covington					0					
Dale					L	L				
Fayette					0					
Jackson						0	L	L	L	L
Lawrence						0				
Lowndes					0		L	L		
Madison					L	L	L	L	L	L
Marshall						0	L	L	L	L
Mobile					0	0				
Monroe							0			
Perry					0					
Pickens						0				L
Pike					0					
Talladega						L	L		L	
Tallapoosa							L	L		
Tuscaloosa					0					
Washington					0	0				
Wilcox					0					

ARIZONA:

All 1870 schedules were searched and no Ledbetter found.

ARKANSAS:

	1790	00	10	20	30	40	50	60	70	80
Arkansas						0		0		
Benton						0		L	L	L
Boone									0	L
Bradley							0	L		
Carroll						0	0	L	0	L
Chicot						0				
Clark						0				
Conway						0		0		
Craighead								0		
Crawford						0	0	0		
Crittenden						0				
Dallas							0	L		
Desha						0	L	0		
Franklin						0		L		
Fulton								0		
Greene						0		L		
Hempstead						0				
Hot Springs						0		0		
Independence						0		0		
Izard						0		0		
Jackson						0		0		
Jefferson						0		0		
Johnson						0	0	L	0	L
Lawrence								0		
Madison						L	L	L	L	L
Marion								0		
Mississippi								0		
Montgomery								L		
Newton								0		
Perry								0		
Polk								0		
Pope						0	0	0		
Prairie								0		
Pulaski								L	L	
Randolph								0		

	1790	00	10	20	30	40	50	60	70	80
Saline								0		
Searcy								0		0
Sebastian								L		L
Sevier								L		
Scott								0		
St. Francis								0		
Union								0		
Van Buren								0		
Washington						0		0	0	
White								L	0	
Yell								0		

GEORGIA:

	1790	00	10	20	30	40	50	60	70	80
Atlanta City							L			
Baldwin				L	0		0			
Carroll							L			
Chatham				0						
Clarke				L	L		0			
Cobb							L			
Coffee								0		
Coweta					0					
Crawford							0			
Effingham				0						
Elbert				0						
Fayette					0					
Floyd							L			
Forsyth							L			
Franklin							L			
Fulton								L		
Glynn				0						
Gordon							0			
Greene				L	L	L	0			
Gwinnett				0	0		0			
Hall				0	L	0	L			
Hancock				L	L	L	L			
Harris					0		0			
Hart								0		

	1790	00	10	20	30	40	50	60	70	80
Heard							L			
Irwin					0					
Henry					0					
Jackson				0	0					
Jasper				0	L					
Jones				L	L		0			
Lowndes							0			
Lumpkin							L			
Madison					0					
Merriwether							L			
Morgan					0					
Murray							L			
Oglethorpe				0	0					
Paulding							0			
Pike					L					
Putnam					L					
Richmond				0						
Thomas							0			
Troup					L		0			
Union							0			
Upson					L	L	L			
Walton						L				
Warren				0						
Washington				0						
Wilkes				0						

ILLINOIS: All 1820 schedules were searched. Ledbetters were found on only the two counties indicated below.

	1790	00	10	20	30	40	50	60	70	80
Alexander							0	L		
Bond			L	0	0		L	0		
Christian							0			
Clay					0		0			
Clinton					0		0			
Coles						L	0	0		
Effingham						0	0	0	L	
Fayette					L	L	L	L	L	L
Gallatin			L	L	L		0	0	0	

	1790	00	10	20	30	40	50	60	70	80
Greene							0			
Hardin						L	L	L	L	L
Macon							0	L		
Macoupin							L			
Marion							0			
Montgomery							0			
Moultrie							0			
Pope					0		0	0		
Randolph						L	L			
Saline							0			
Shelby					L	L	L	L	L	L
St. Clair							0	L		
Union							L			
White								0		
Williamson								0		

INDIANA:

	1790	00	10	20	30	40	50	60	70	80
Daviess								L		
Hendricks								0		
Knox								0		
Wayne							L			

KENTUCKY: Tax records for the years 1790 and 1800 do not include the name Ledbetter.

	1790	00	10	20	30	40	50	60	70	80
Bourbon					0					
Caldwell			0	L						
Callaway					0	0				
Fayette					0					
Fleming					0					
Graves						L	L			
Hickman					0	0				
Livingston			0	0		0				
Montgomery					0					
Nicholas					0	0	0			

MASSACHUSETTS:

	1790	00	10	20	30	40	50	60	70	80
Middlesex	L									

MISSISSIPPI: A special index of the complete state for 1820 was searched. The name Ledbetter was in only one county as shown.

	1790	00	10	20	30	40	50	60	70	80
Copiah							0			
Covington				0						
Franklin							0			
Hinds							L			
Jefferson			L							
Lawrence				L	0					
Leake						0	0			
Lowndes						L			L	
Madison							0			
Neshoba						0	0			
Oktibbeha						L	L			
Oregon								0		
Ozark								0		
Perry						L				
Rankin							0			
Simpson							0			
Texas								0		0
Yazoo							0			

MISSOURI:

	1790	00	10	20	30	40	50	60	70	80
Barry						0		0		
Boone								0		
Cedar								0		
Chariton								L		
Christian								0		
Crawford						0				
Dallas								0	L	
Greene						0	0			
Howard								0		
Howell								0		
Laclede							L			
Lawrence								L	L	
Marion								0		
Phelps								0		

	1790	00	10	20	30	40	50	60	70	80
Randolph						0				
Scott						0	0			
Stone								0	L	L
Taney						L	0	0	L	L
Texas								L		L
Van Buren						0				
Wayne							L			

NORTH CAROLINA:

	1790	00	10	20	30	40	50	60	70	80
Anson	L	L	L							
Ashe		0								
Beaufort		0								
Bertie		0								
Brunswick		0								
Buncombe		0								
Burke		0								
Caswell	L	0								
Chatham	L	L					L			
Chowan				0						
Edgecombe					0					
Greene					0					
Hertford			0							
Iredell			0							
Lenoir					0					
McDowell							L			
Montgomery		L								
Nash	L									
Perquimans				0						
Richmond		0		L						
Rockingham		0	0							
Rutherford	L	L	L			L	L			
Surry		0								
Wake		0								
Warren		0								
Wayne		0								

OKLAHOMA (Indian Territory):

	1790	00	10	20	30	40	50	60	70	80
Choctaw Nation								0		

SOUTH CAROLINA:

	1790	00	10	20	30	40	50	60	70	80
Abbeville		0								
Anderson			L	L	L					
Barnwell		0								
Chesterfield	0									
Edgefield		0								
Fairfield		0								
Lancaster		0								
Laurens	L									
Lexington	0	0								
Marion		0								
Marlboro	0									
Orangeburg	0		0							
Pendleton	L	L	L	L						
Williamsburg			0							
Union	L									

TENNESSEE:

All existing 1820 schedules checked and no Ledbetter found.

	1790	00	10	20	30	40	50	60	70	80
Bedford			0	L	L	L	L	L	L	
Bledsoe			0	0		0				
Blount					L	L				
Bradley				0	L					
Cannon				L	L	L	L	L		
Cheatham						0	0	0		
Claiborne			0		0					
Cocke			0	0						
Coffee				L	0					
Davidson		0	0	0	L	L		0		
Decatur					0					
De Kalb				0	0		0			
Dyer				0						

	1790	00	10	20	30	40	50	60	70	80
Fentress					0	0	L	L	L	L
Franklin				L	L	0	0			
Giles				0		L				
Grundy							0			
Grainger					0	0				
Hickman				0		L	0			
Jackson				0	0	0	0			
Knox						0				
Lauderdale						0	L	L		
Lawrence				0						
Lincoln				L			L			
Marshall							L			
Maury				0			0			
McMinn					0	L	L	L		
McNairy						L		L		
Montgomery				0						
Monroe					L	0				
Morgan					0		0			
Obion						0				
Overton				L	L	L	L	L	L	L
Perry					L	L	L			
Polk							0			
Putnam								L		L
Roane					0					
Robertson				0						
Rutherford			0	0	L			L		
Shelby				0		L	L			
Smith				L	L	L				
Sumner				0	0					
Tipton						0				
Van Buren							0			
Warren				0	L	L	0	0		L
Wayne							L			
White				0	L	0	L	0		L
Williamson				L			L			
Wilson				0	L	L	L			

TEXAS:

	1790	00	10	20	30	40	50	60	70	80
Anderson								L		O
Austin							O	L		
Bastrop							O		O	
Bell								L	O	O
Bexar							O			O
Blanco										O
Bosque								O		O
Bowie							O			
Brazos							O	O		
Cass							L	L		
Collin							L	L	O	
Comanche										L
Coryell								L		O
Cherokee							L			
Dallas							L	L	L	L
Denton							O	L		
Eastland									O	
Ellis							O			
Fannin							L			O
Fayette							O	L	L	L
Gonzales							O	O		
Grayson							O		O	L
Henderson							O			
Hopkins							L			
Houston							O			O
Hunt										L
Johnson									O	
Lamar							L	L		
McCulloch								O		L
McLennan								O	O	L
Milam							O	L		
Nacogdoches							O			O
Navarro							O			
Parker								L		
Robertson							O			L
Rusk							O	O	O	

	1790	00	10	20	30	40	50	60	70	80
Smith								0		
Titus							0			
Upshur							0	0		
Uvalde							0			
Van Zandt							L			
Victoria							0			
Washington								0		
Williamson										L
Young								0	0	L

UTAH (Deseret):

	1790	00	10	20	30	40	50	60	70	80
Great Salt Lake							L			

VIRGINIA:

	1790	00	10	20	30	40	50	60	70	80
Albemarle				0	0					
Augusta					0					
Botetourt					L					
Brunswick			L	L	L					
Culpeper					0					
Cumberland		0								
Dinwiddie		L								
Essex		0			0					
Fluvanna		0			0					
Franklin					0					
Goochland		0								
Greensville					L					
Hampshire		0			0					
Hanover		0								
James City					0					
Lee					0					
Louisa				0						
Mechlenburg					0					
Nansemond					0		0			
New Kent					0					
Norfolk			0	0	0	0	0			
Orange					0					

	1790	00	10	20	30	40	50	60	70	80
Prince Edward		L			0					
Prince George		L								
Princess Ann					0		0			
Rockingham					0					
Russell					0					
Scott					0					
Shenandoah					0					
Spotsylvania					0					
Surry		0								
Sussex		0								
Tazewell				0	0					
Washington					0					

Part II—Heads of Families and Elderly Ledbetters

Ledbetter's First Name	Birth	Census Schedule Where Found Year-State-County-Page
A. (Elizabeth)	1820 NC	1850 Tenn Davidson 217
A. G.	1837 Tenn	1860 Tex Fayette 282
A. G.	1838 Tenn	1870 Tex Fayette 382
A. H. (Nancy)	1819 Va	1860 Ala Tallapoosa 151
A. J. (Sarah)	1815 —	1850 Ga Upson —
A. J. (N. E.)	1857-Tenn	1880 Tenn Overton 347
A. W. (Josie)	1844 Ala	1870 Ala Calhoun 592
Aaron	1794-02	1820 Tenn Overton 8
Aaron	1800-10	1830 Tenn Overton 184
Aaron	1800-10	1840 Tenn Overton 1
Aaron (Elizabeth)	1811 Ga	1850 Tenn Overton 17
Abarhom	1800-10	1830 Ala Madison 85
Abner	1780-90	1830 SC Anderson 142
Abram H. (Anne)	1825 Tenn	1850 Tenn Perry 151
Absalom (Mariann)	1808 Ga	1850 Tex Hopkins 334
Albert (Almeda)	1832 Tenn	1870 Tex Fayette 382
Albert (Elmeida)	1835 Tenn	1880 Tex Fayette 19
Alex	1819 NC	1860 Tenn Davidson 330
Alex (Lucy)	1841 Tenn	1870 Miss Lowndes 318
Alexander (Nancy)	1820 Va	1850 Ala Tallapoosa 44
Alford (Zany A.)	1849 Tenn	1880 Tenn Cannon 550
Alford (Safrona)	1855 Mo	1880 Mo Stone 12
Alfred (Mahaly)	1798 NC	1860 Tenn Bedford 98
Alfred	1800-10	1840 Tenn Bedford 9
Alfred (Mahala)	1807 NC	1850 Ala Jackson 32

Name	Date	Year / Location
Alfred (Lydia)	1855 Ark	1880 Ark Madison 574
Alvin H. (Lidda)	1846 Tenn	1880 Mo Texas 412
Alvin (Samantha)	1850 Tenn	1880 Tenn Fentress 563
Amanda	1836 Ala	1860 Ark Sevier 59
Anderson (Polly)	1824 Ky	1850 Ill Hardin 31
Anderson (Mary)	1827 Ky	1870 Ill Hardin 13
Andrew	1776 NC	1850 NC McDowell 515
Andrew J.	1810-20	1840 Ga Upson—
Andrew (Elizabeth)	1850 Tenn	1880 Mo Stone 10
Andrew J. (Margaret)	1843 Tenn	1870 Ala Talladega 563
Ann	1780 SC	1850 Tenn Bedford 193
Archibald	1830 Ala	1850 Tex Lamar 549
Archibald (Margaret J)	1838 Ala	1860 Ala Marshall 753
Arthur	1794-02	1820 Tenn Overton 8
Arthur	1790-00	1830 Tenn Overton 185
Arthur	1790-00	1840 Tenn Overton 10
Arthur (Elizabeth)	1799 Tenn	1850 Texas Dallas 81
Arthur B. (Mary P)	1846 Tenn	1880 Texas Young 382
Arthur (Maria)	1849 Ill	1870 Ill Hardin 46
Asa	bfr 1775	1820 Ill Bond 11 (Vol 2)
Asa	1800-10	1830 Ala Madison 133
Asa	1800-10	1840 Ala Madison 184
Asey (Martha)	1828 Ill	1850 Ill Shelby 188
Augustin (E.)	1831 NC	1850 Ga Hall 343
B. J. (Ellen)	1822 Tenn	1860 Ark Johnson 967
B. J. (Ellen)	1822 Tenn	1870 Ark Madison 367
Banks	1800-10	1830 Ga Putman 199
Barzella	1800-10	1830 NC Rutherford 458
Barzilla (Sarah)	1806 NC	1850 NC Rutherford 655
Ben	1818 Tenn	1880 Tenn Overton 299
Benjamin	1775-94	1820 Ga Jones 134
Benjamin	1810-20	1840 Tenn Overton 12
Benjamin (Elizabeth)	1811 Tenn	1850 Tenn Overton 6
Benjamin (Elizabeth)	1810 Tenn	1860 Tenn Overton 210
Benjamin (Elizabeth)	1812 Tenn	1870 Tenn Overton 307
Benjamin (Elizabeth)	1820 Tenn	1850 Ky Graves 401
Berlin (Nancy)	1842 Ill	1880 Ill Hardin 389
Berry	1810-20	1840 Ala Jackson 46
Berry (Mary A.)	1817 NC	1850 Mo Wayne 212
Berry (Margaret)	1833 Tenn	1860 Ill Alexander 70
Beverly (Male)	1800-10	1840 Tenn Overton 30
Beverly (Susannah)	1802 Ga	1860 Tenn Fentress 6
Beverly (Susan)	1810 Ga	1850 Tenn Fentress 388
Beverly J. (Ellen C.)	1822 Tenn	1880 Mo Stone 7
Buck (Emyline)	1854 Tenn	1880 Tenn Overton 299
Buckner	bfr 1775	1820 Tenn Overton 10
Buckner, Sr.	1750-60	1840 Tenn Overton 1
Buckner	1810-15	1830 Tenn Overton 190

Buckner, Jr.	1810-20	1840 Tenn Overton 1
Buckner (Jane)	1812 Tenn	1850 Tenn Overton 20
Buckner H. (Jane)	1810 Tenn	1860 Tenn Overton 274
Buckner H. (Susanah)	1827 Tenn	1850 Tenn Overton 44
Burfet	1798 SC	1850 Ala Madison 417
Burlin	1810-20	1840 Ill Gallatin 36
Burlin (Susan)	1809 Ill	1850 Ill Hardin 31
Burlin L. (Mahala)	1811 Ill	1860 Ill Hardin 1073
Burlin (Mahala)	1811 Ill	1870 Ill Hardin 30
Burlin L. (Nancy)	1841 Ill	1860 Ill Hardin 1074
Burlin (Nancy)	1841 Ill	1870 Ill Hardin 30
Burl (Jane)	1830 Tenn	1870 Ark Madison 372
Burrell (Jane)	1833 Tenn	1860 Ark Madison 435
Burrell (Jane)	1833 Tenn	1880 Ark Sebastian 679
Burton (Margaret)	1838 Ala	1860 Ala Jackson 493
C. A. (Narcis)	1849 Ala	1880 Ala Calhoun 644
Calvin (Nancy)	1824 NC	1850 NC Chatham 892
Carolin	1839—	1850 Ga Merriwether—
Caroline	1778 Ga	1850 Ala Tallapoosa 175
Catherine	1805 Ky	1860 Mo Chariton 306
Charles	1755-74	1800 NC Montgomery 486
Charles	bfr 1775	1820 Tenn Smith 451
Charles	1770-80	1830 Tenn Smith 41
Charles	1816 Me	1850 Ill Randolph 110
Charles (Arminta)	1828 Tenn	1860 Tenn Overton 224
Charles W. (Araminta)	1825 Tenn	1870 Tenn Overton 336
Charles (Catherine)	1849 Ga	1870 Ala Calhoun 533
Charles P. (Dorinda C)	1850 Ga	1880 Ala Calhoun 670
Chesley (Martha)	1800—	1850 NC Chatham 874
Clark A (Mary C)	1855 Ga	1880 Ala Calhoun 668
Colman	bfr 1775	1790 NC Chatham 88
Coleman	1755-74	1800 NC Chatham 202
Coleman	1765-84	1810 Va Pr Edward 575
D. J. (Nelly)	1815 Ill	1860 Ill Hardin 1053
D. J. (Ellen)	1816 Ill	1870 Ill Hardin 42
D. L. (Narcissa)	1817 Ala	1870 Ala Marshall 107
D. T. (E)	1815 Ala	1860 Ark White 937
D. T. (Nancy)	1817 SC	1870 Ala Calhoun 659
Daniel	—	1790 NC Caswell 82
Daniel	bfr 1755	1800 SC Pendleton 882
Daniel	bfr 1765	1810 SC Pendleton 162
Daniel	bfr 1775	1820 SC Pendleton 5
Daniel	1790-00	1840 Ala Madison 173
Daniel (Harriet B)	1792 Ga	1850 Ala Madison 417
Daniel	1800-10	1830 Ga Hall 128
Daniel	1800-10	1830 Ga Hancock—
Daniel I. (Mary)	1814 Ala	1850 Ala Marshall 179
Daniel (Martha A)	1832 Ill	1860 Ill Hardin 1055

Name	Date/Place	Later Record
Daniel (Martha)	1841 Ala	1870 Ala Madison 6
Daniel (Hannah)	1844 Ill	1870 Ill Hardin 29
Dave (Hannah)	1846 Ill	1880 Ill Hardin 396
David H.	1800-10	1830 Ill Fayette—
David (Pallah H.)	1813 Va	1850 Ala Lowndes—
David (P. H.)	1813 Va	1860 Ala Lowndes 512
David	1810-20	1840 Ala Madison 176
David T. (Nancy)	1820 SC	1860 Ala Calhoun 417
Doctor J	1810-20	1840 Ill Hardin 232
Doctor J (Rebecca)	1809 Ill	1850 Ill Hardin 30
E. (R.)	1832 Ala	1860 Texas Cass 66
E. J. (Martha)	1832 Tenn	1880 Ark Benton 479
E. W. (Analiza)	1843 Tenn	1870 Tenn Overton 333
Ed	—	1790 NC Caswell 82
Edmund	1784-94	1810 Va Pr. George 530
Edward	1770-80	1840 Ky Graves 117
Eli	1810-20	1840 Tenn Cannon 141
Eli (Mary)	1817 Tenn	1850 Ark Madison 289
Eli (Mary)	1818 Tenn	1860 Ark Madison 525
Eli (Jane)	1822 Tenn	1870 Ark Madison 374
Eli (Jane)	1820 Tenn	1880 Ark Madison 534
Elijah (Anne)	1838 Tenn	1860 Tenn Overton 304
Elijah (Ann E.)	1836 Tenn	1880 Tenn Overton 304
Elizabeth	1770 NC	1850 NC McDowell 591
Elizabeth	1823 Tenn	1860 Ark Madison 420-21
Elizabeth	1825 Ky	1860 Tex Dallas 320
Elizabeth	1821 Tenn	1850 Tenn Lauderdale 272
Elizt	1822 Tenn	1860 Tenn Lauderdale 363
Ellenor	1780-90	1830 Tenn Rutherford 117
Ephraim	1770-80	1830 Ga Troup 42
Ephraim	1780-90	1840 Ala Madison 173
Ephraim	1778 Ga	1850 Ala Talladega 458
Ephraim (Martha)	1815 Ala	1850 Ala Talladega 457
Ephraim (Sandy)	1820 Ga	1850 Ga Heard 344
Evan (Martha)	1833 Tenn	1860 Ark Benton 264
Evan (Martha)	1835 Tenn	1870 Ark Benton 261
F. (male)	1810-20	1840 Ala Talladega 271
F. D. or T. D. (M. E.)	1828 Tenn	1860 Tenn Bedford 199
Francis W. (Sarah)	1849 Ala	1880 Texas Young 379
Frank (Mary)	1855 Ill	1880 Ill Hardin 380
Frederick (Delia)	1801 Ga	1850 Ala Talladega 372
Frederick (Adelia)	1809 Ga	1870 Ala Talladega 625
G. (Mary)	1831 Ky	1880 Tenn Putman 122
G. C. (E. C.)	1808 NC	1880 Ala Calhoun 539
G. D. (Elizabeth)	1820 Va	1850 Ala Tallapoosa 19
G. W. (Louisiana)	1809 Ill	1880 Ill Fayette 111
G. W.	1827 Miss	1860 Texas Anderson 27
Gardner	1800-10	1840 Ala Madison 173

Gardner C.
  (Elizabeth C)   1809 Ga   1850 Ala Madison 413
Gardner C.
  (Elizabeth C)   1809 SC   1860 Ala Marshall 935
Gardner C.
  (Elizabeth C)   1809 SC   1870 Ala Marshall 141
George (Eliza)   1824 NC   1850 NC McDowell 555
George (Jane)   1825 Tenn   1850 Ill Shelby 186
George   bfr 1775   1790 NC Rutherford 116
George   bfr 1755   1800 NC Rutherford 125
George   1780-90   1830 Tenn Warren 363
George   1780-90   1830 Tenn Monroe 105
George   1780-90   1840 Tenn Warren 338
George (Susan)   1783 NC   1850 Ark Madison 289
George (Susanah)   1783 NC   1860 Ark Madison 431
George W. (Susanna) 1808 Ill   1850 Ill Fayette 403
George   1810-20   1840 Ky Graves 114
George W. (Cyntha) 1820 NC   1850 Mo Laclede 230
George (Sarah J.)   1825 SC   1850 SC Anderson 221
George (Nancy)   1827 NC   1850 NC Chatham 937
George W. (Mary E.) 1840 Ala   1870 Ala Talladega 563
George (Jane)   1845 Ark   1870 Ark Madison 461
George (Jane)   1844 Ark   1880 Ark Madison 536
George   1851 Tenn   1880 Mo Texas 341
George W. (Mary)   1851 Ark   1880 Ark Madison 548
George (Elizabeth)   1859 Ill   1880 Ill Hardin 422
George (Julia)   -   1860 Tenn   1880 Tenn Putman 137
Glover (Rachel)   1830 Ill   1870 Ill Effingham 437
Gray   1755-74   1800 NC Montgomery 496
Gray   1770-80   1840 Miss Lowndes 211
Green (Elizabeth)   1829 NC   1850 Tenn Wilson 545
Guardiner   1784-94   1810 Va Dinwiddie 152
H. (Male)   1790-00   1840 Ill Fayette 143
H. (J. H.)   1807 NC   1870 Texas Fayette 382
H. (M. H.)   1832 Ill   1880 Ill Fayette 191
H. (Harriet)   1834 Tenn   1880 Tenn Overton 325
H. M. (Mary)   1811 Tenn   1860 Ark Madison 431
Ha—   1830 Ill   1870 Ill Fayette 726
Hamilton   1810-15   1830 Tenn Perry 39
Hamilton (Jane A)   1808 NC   1860 Tex Fayette 277
Hamilton (Harriet) 1845 Tenn   1870 Tenn Overton 399
Hansten   1765-84   1810 Va Brunswick—
Hardamon   1800-10   1830 Ill Fayette—
Harriet   1813 Va   1860 Ala Madison 93
Harriet   1823 Ala   1880 Ala Marshall 132
Harry   1790-00   1830 NC Rutherford 496
Harvey   1810-20   1840 Ark Madison 32
Harvey (Mary)   1815 Tenn   1850 Ark Madison 290

Harvey C. (Mary A)	1816 Tenn	1860 Ark Madison 431
Harvey (Mary A)	1818 Tenn	1870 Ark Madison 367
Harvey (Mary)	1817 Tenn	1880 Ark Madison 536
Harvey (Nancy)	1850 Ark	1870 Ark Madison 374
Harvey (Nancy)	1850 Tenn	1880 Ark Madison 534
Harvey (Martha A)	1836 Ill	1860 Mo Chariton 233
Henderson (Mary Ann)	1823 Ill	1850 Ill Fayette 403, 413
Henderson (Hester)	1823 Ill	1860 Ill Fayette 97
Henry	1755-74	1800 NC Montgomery 496
Henry	bfr 1789	1810 Miss Jefferson—
Henry	bfr 1775	1820 NC Richmond 204
Henry	1775-94	1820 Tenn Lincoln 9
Henry	1760-70	1830 Ill Gallatin 28
Henry	1794-02	1820 Ill Bon 11 (Vol 2)
Henry	1790-00	1830 Ill Fayette—
Henry	1790-00	1830 Ga Jasper—
Henry (Ann)	1790 NC	1850 Tenn Perry 165
Henry	1800-10	1830 SC Anderson 22
Henry C.	1800-10	1840 Tenn McNairy 54
Henry (Ann)	1810 Va	1860 Ala Madison 198
Henry (Shriah)	1819 Ill	1850 Ill Shelby 104
Henry (Sarah J)	1819 Ill	1860 Ill Shelby 603
Henry (Ladz)	1832 Tenn	1850 Tenn Overton 19
Henry (Mrs)	1832 Ill	1870 Ill Shelby 47
Henry (Rebecca)	1836 Ill	1870 Ill Hardin 52
Henry (Rebecca)	1836 Ill	1880 Ill Hardin 417
Herbert	1760-70	1830 Va Botetourt 295
Hesther	1790 SC	1850 Ala Marshall 178
Hetty	1817 Tenn	1860 Tenn Fentress 24
Hetty	1820 Tenn	1860 Tenn Overton 255
Hillery (Ann)	1840 Tenn	1880 Tenn Overton 301
Holding	bfr 1775	1790 NC Nash 70
Hubbard	1784-94	1810 Va Brunswick—
Hubbard	1794-02	1820 Va Brunswick 656
Hubbard	1780-90	1830 Va Brunswick 244
Hubbard	1760-70	1840 Tenn Giles 92
Hugh	1810-15	1830 Tenn Warren 369
Hugh	1810-20	1840 Tenn Cannon 145
Hugh (Mary)	1810 Tenn	1850 Ark Madison 289
I. (S.)	1834 Tenn	1860 Tex Parker 435
I. (or J.)	1800-10	1840 Tenn Perry 163
I. J. (Eliza)	1820 Va	1850 Ala Lowndes 164
I. (or J.) B. (Cynthia)	1829 Tenn	1850 Tenn Bedford 208
I. (or J.) S. (Martha)	1827 Tenn	1860 Tenn Lauderdale 366
Increase	bfr 1775	1790 Mass Middlesex—
Ira	1770-80	1840 Tenn Smith 1
Isaac	1755-74	1800 NC Anson 227
Isaac	1760-70	1830 Ala Dale 4

Isaac	1774-84	1800 NC Anson 214
Isaac	bfr 1765	1810 Va Brunswick—
Isaac	1765-84	1810 Va Brunswick—
Isaac	1765-84	1810 NC Rutherford 401
Isaac	1780-90	1830 NC Rutherford 457
Isaac Jr.	1790-00	1830 NC Rutherford 457
Isaac	1790-00	1840 Tenn Perry 163
Isaac (Martha)	1798 NC	1850 Tenn Perry 163
Isaac	1800-10	1830 Ga Troup 43
Isaac	1800-10	1840 Ala Dale 14
Isaac (Lucinda)	1808 Ga	1850 Texas Van Zandt 219
Isaac (Sarah)	1813 Tenn	1850 Ala Talladega 458
Isaac (Lucian)	1817 Tenn	1860 Texas Milam 33
Isaac (Rebecca)	1820 Tenn	1870 Ill Fayette 660
Isaac J. (Minirva)	1822 Tenn	1860 Ark Carroll 797
Isaac C. (Elizer E.)	1823 Tenn	1850 Tenn Perry 165
Isaac (Ibbey Jane)	1823 Ill	1860 Mo Chariton 249
Isaac J. (Manerva)	1823 Tenn	1850 Tenn Overton 23
Isaac (Rebecca)	1823 Tenn	1850 Tenn Overton 22
Isaac (Eliza)	1823 NC	1850 Ga Lumpkin 141
Isaac A. (Cynthia)	1824 Tenn	1850 Tenn Overton 21
Isaac A. (Scyntha)	1824 Tenn	1880 Texas Young 416
Isaac (Martha)	1835 Tenn	1860 Tenn McMinn 274
Isaac (Catherine)	1847 Tenn	1880 Tenn White 492
Isaiah (Mahala Jane)	1858 Ark	1880 Ark Madison 566
J. (male)	1805 Ga	1860 Ga Fulton 873
J. (M.)	1810 Tenn	1880 Ala Calhoun 569
J. (or I.)	1800-10	1840 Tenn Perry 163
J. A.	1824 Ga	1850 Ala Dale—
J. A.	1831 Tenn	1860 Tex Fayette 277
J. Alex (Selistina)	1829 Ill	1880 Ill Hardin 383
J. M. (Elizabeth)	1814 SC	1860 Tenn Bedford 243
J. P. (J. C.)	1820 Ala	1860 Ala Jackson 605
J. (or I.) B. (Cythia)	1829 Tenn	1850 Tenn Bedford 208
J. C. (Rose A.)	1848 NC	1880 Tex Dallas 91
J. H.	1818 Ga	1860 Tex Bell 11
J. L. (E. E.)	1853 Ala	1880 Ala Calhoun 645
J. M. (Eliza)	1802 NC	1870 Miss Lowndes 332
J. M. (Judea)	1832 Ga	1860 Ark Sebastian 1009
J. M.	1837 Tenn	1860 Tenn Overton 291
J. M.	1840 Ga	1860 Tex Lamar 102
J. M. (M. L.)	1846 Ala	1880 Ala Calhoun 541
J. P. (Susannah)	1809 NC	1850 Tenn Wayne 315
J. S. (Elizabeth)	1817 Ga	1860 Ark Montgomery 917
J. (or I.) S. (Martha)	1827 Tenn	1860 Tenn Lauderdale 366
J. W. (Frances)	1810 Va	1850 Tenn Lincoln 117
J. W. (Martha)	1812 Tenn	1860 Ala Madison 104
J. W. (Ellender)	1812 NC	1870 Ala Calhoun 513

Jackson (Margaret)	1835 Ala	1860 Ala Jackson 489	
Jacob (Ruth)	1838 Ind	1860 Ill Fayette 138	
Jacob M. (Ann E.)	1835 Ga	1870 Ala Talladega 583	
James	bfr 1765	1810 Va Brunswick—	
James	bfr 1775	1820 Va Brunswick 656	
James	1775-94	1820 Ga Baldwin 20	
James	1780-90	1830 Ga Pike—	
James	1775-94	1820 Tenn Lincoln 6	
James	1780-90	1830 Ill Shelby 198	
James	1780-90	1840 Ill Coles 158	
James (Mahala)	1782 NC	1850 Ill Shelby—	
James (Mahala)	1783 Tenn	1860 Mo Chariton 250	
James (Nancy)	1784 NC	1860 Ark Bradley 497	
James (Patsy)	1795 NC	1850 Tenn Blount 246	
James (Martha)	1795 NC	1860 Tenn Blount 136	
James	1800-10	1830 Tenn Overton 205	
James (Delilah)	1804 Ga	1850 Ga Carroll 153	
James (Elizabeth)	1804 Ga	1850 Tenn Overton 19	
James (Martha)	1807 SC	1860 Ala Calhoun 569	
James (Elizabeth)	1810 Tenn	1860 Texas Collin 107	
James	1810-20	1840 Tenn Overton 1	
James (Rebecca)	1814 NC	1850 NC McDowell 517	
James (Caroline)	1820 Tenn	1860 Mo Lawrence 835	
James (Jane)	1821 Ill	1850 Ill Shelby 104	
James (Lucinda)	1821 Ill	1860 Ill Shelby 603	
James (Sophronia)	1828 Tenn	1860 Ark Madison 419	
James (Tennessee)	1826 Tenn	1850 Ark Madison 290	
James (Anna)	1823 NC	1850 Ga Lumpkin 141	
James (Palestine)	1829 Ill	1870 Ill Hardin 46	
James (Mary Frances)	1831 Ohio	1880 Ill Fayette 113	
James (Sarah)	1833 Tenn	1860 Tenn Overton 210	
James (Mary)	1833 Ill	1870 Ill Fayette 732	
James (Isabella)	1834 Ala	1870 Ala Madison 209	
James (Larena)	1836 SC	1860 Ala Calhoun 573	
James (Jane)	1838—	1860 Tenn Bedford 177	
James (Mary)	1840 Tenn	1880 Ark Madison 528	
James (Mary)	1843 Tenn	1870 Ark Madison 373	
James (Lanier ?)	1847 Tex	1880 Tex Fayette 9	
James (Sarah)	1848 Tenn	1870 Ark Madison 428	
James (Aquilla)	1848 Tenn	1880 Tenn Overton 299	
James (Emly)	1848 Ala	1880 Ark Sebastian 609	
James (Mary)	1853 Ark	1880 Ark Johnson 337	
James	1857 Tenn	1880 Tex Grayson 406	
James	1857 Tenn	1880 Tex Hunt 480	
James (Dora)	1857 Ill	1880 Ill Hardin 423	
James (Sarah)	1858 Ga	1880 Ark Sebastian 629	
James (Winnie)	1859 Ill	1880 Mo Taney 253	
James A. (Mary)	1827 Ky	1860 Ill Hardin 1302	

Name	Year	Place	Census
James A. (Mary)	1827 Ky		1880 Ill Hardin 422
James A. (Selistina T.)	1829 Ill		1860 Ill Hardin 1049
James C. (Lydia)	1825 Tenn		1860 Ill Macon 1251
James H. (Sarah M.)	1823 Ga		1850 Ga Hancock 15
James H. (Sarah Ellen)	1848 Tenn		1880 Ark Madison 574
James M. (Missouri V.)	1845 Ala		1870 Ala Talladega 618
James P.	1800-10		1840 Tenn McNairy 32
James P. (Mary)	1819 Tenn (?)		1850 Tenn Perry 165
James P.	1847 Tex		1870 Texas Fayette 521
James V.	1800-10		1840 SC Anderson 123
James W.	1770-80		1840 Ga Hancock 217
James W.	1775-94		1820 Ga Hancock 90
James W. (Elizabeth)	1831 Tenn		1880 Tenn Overton 352
James W. (Elizabeth)	1833 Tenn		1870 Tenn Overton 357
James W. (Elizabeth)	1835 Tenn		1860 Tenn Fentress 6
Jane	1790-00		1830 Ga Upson 110
Jane	1794—		1850 Ga Upson—
Jane	1820-25		1840 Ala Talladega 288
Jarrett	1800-10		1840 Ala Jackson 59
Jarrett (Margaret)	1811—		1850 Ill Union 226
Jefferson	1810-15		1830 Tenn Warren 369
Jefferson	1810-20		1840 Tenn Cannon 145
Jefferson (Elizabeth)	1811 Tenn		1850 Tenn Cannon 367
Jeff B. (Elizabeth)	1810 Tenn		1860 Ark Madison 436
Jefferson (Elizabeth)	1810 Tenn		1870 Ark Madison 369
Jeff	1810 Tenn		1880 Ark Madison 528
Jesse	1775-94		1820 Tenn Lincoln 6
Jessee (Elizabeth)	1814 SC		1850 Tenn Bedford 193
Jessie (Mary M.)	1840 Miss		1870 Tenn Bedford 307
Joel			1790 N Caswell 82
Joel	bfr 1755		1800 SC Pendleton 872
Joel	1774-84		1800 NC Montgomery 502
Joel	1810-20		1840 SC Anderson 123
Joel (Mary)	1811 SC		1850 Anderson 221
Joel C.	1826 Ala		1850 Ala Jackson 134
Joel P. (Jane C)	1819 Ala		1850 Ala Marshall 182
John	bfr1775		1790 N.C. Chatham 88
John (2 of these)	bfr 1775		1790 NC Nash 70
John	1765-84		1810 NC Rutherford 401
John	1765-84		1810 SC Pendleton 154
John	1775-94		1820 SC Pendleton 360
John	1770-80		1830 SC Anderson 24
John	1770-80		1840 Ill Gallatin 37
John	1780-90		1840 Ill Coles 158
John (Mary)	1796 Ga		1850 Ala Tallapoosa—
John (Martha)	1801 NC		1850 Ga Gwinnett 192
John (Polly)	1805 Tenn		1860 Tenn McMinn 277
John (Elizabeth)	1806 Tenn		1850 Ill Hardin 11

Name	Born	Census
John (Elizabeth)	1807 Tenn	1860 Ill Hardin 1049
John (Elizabeth)	1807 Tenn	1870 Ill Hardin 46
John (Elizabeth)	1807 Tenn	1880 Ill Hardin 383
John (Elizabeth)	1809 Tenn	1860 Ark Dallas 969
John (Susan)	1809 SC	1850 Ga Franklin 90
John	1800-10	1830 Ga Hall 20
John	1800-10	1830 Ala Madison 162
John	1800-10	1840 Ala Talladega 268
John	1800-10	1830 Ill Gallatin 43
John (Mary)	1811 Tenn	1870 Ala Madison 209
John (Elizabeth)	1812 Tenn	1870 Ala Talladega 562
John	1810-20	1840 Ky Graves 114
John	1810-20	1840 Tenn McMinn 96
John (Mary)	1813 Tenn	1850 Tenn McMinn 229
John (Ellen)	1816 Ill	1880 Ill Hardin 387
John (Arenia)	1822 SC	1850 Ga Lumpkin 140
John (Catherine)	1826 Ga	1850 Ga Atlanta City 19
John (Jane)	1826 Ala	1870 Ala Marshall 82
John (Irvine)	1834 Ala	1880 Ala Calhoun 532
John	1836 Ga	1860 Ark Pulaski 229
John (Mary)	1845 Ill	1870 Ill Hardin 42
John (Mary)	1844 Ill	1880 Ill Hardin 389
John (Emmaline)	1846 Ala	1870 Ala Talladega 498
John (Mary)	1846 Ala	1870 Ala Madison 209
John (Sarah J.)	1852 Tenn	1870 Tenn Overton 361
John (Mary)	1854 Ark	1880 Ark Madison 529
John (Harriet)	1857 Ill	1880 Ill Fayette 104
John (Nancy)	1858 Mo	1880 Mo Texas 397
John C. (Jane P.)	1851 Tenn	1880 Tenn Overton 312
John H.	1826 N. Y.	1850 Utah Great Salt Lake 195
John H. (Jane)	1824 Ala	1880 Ala Marshall 132
John H. (Jane)	1826 Ala	1860 Ala Marshall 737
John J. (E. A.)	1811 Va	1860 Ala Lowndes 512
John Jr.	1800-10	1830 Pa Philadelphia 53
John M.	1800-10	1840 Miss Lowndes 211
John M. (Judah O.)	1832 Ga	1880 Ark Sebastian 627
John N. (Rebecca A.)	1830 Ky	1880 Ill Hardin 423
John Q. A. (Artemissa)	1850 Ark	1880 Ill Hardin 425
John S. (M. E.)	1809 Ga	1850 Texas Van Zandt 219
John S. (Elizabeth)	1817 Ga	1850 Ga Carroll 156
John S. (Martin R.)	1826 Tenn	1850 Tenn Lauderdale 271
John W.	1800-10	1840 Ala Madison 173
John W. (Martly A.)	1811 Ga	1850 Ala Madison 412
John W. (Elender)	1813 NC	1850 Ala Benton 395
John W. (Leander R.)	1813 NC	1860 Ala Calhoun 563
John W. (Fannie E.)	1831 Tenn	1880 Texas Williamson 567
Johnston	1784-94	1810 NC Rutherford 401

Johnston	1780-90	1830 NC Rutherford 458
Johnston (Jane)	1808 NC	1850 Tenn Perry 153
Johnson	—	1840 Ga Lumpkin—
Johnson (Nancy)	1782 Va	1850 Ga Lumpkin 147
Johnson (Georgia A.)	1832 NC	1880 Ark Madison 514
Jonathan	1790-00	1830 NC Rutherford 457
Jones	1794-02	1820 Tenn Overton 7
Jones	1790-00	1830 Tenn Overton 204
Jones	1790-00	1840 Tenn Overton 1
Jones (Ann)	1800 Ga	1850 Tenn Overton 20
Jones (Elizabeth)	1799 —	1860 Tenn Overton 274
Jones (Catherine)	1825 Tenn	1850 Tenn Fentress 388
Jones (Catherine)	1824 Tenn	1860 Mo Texas 1043
Jones (Tennessee J.)	1858 Tenn	1880 Tenn Overton 350
Joseph	bfr 1775	1820 Tenn Williamson 612
Joseph (Susan)	1772 Va	1850 Tenn Lincoln 117
Joseph	1775-94	1820 Ga Jones 133
Joseph	1800-10	1830 Ga Clarke 319
Joseph	1810 Ga	1850 Ala Tallapoosa 175
Joseph (Dellila)	1810 Ga	1860 Ga Fulton 724
Joseph	1800-10	1840 Ga Walton
Joseph (Jane)	1827 NC (?)	1850 Ga Lumpkin 142
Joseph (Eleanora)	1827 Ill	1850 Ill Fayette 403,413
Joseph (Theresia)	1840 Frankstadt	1870 Texas Fayette 435
Joseph (Sallie)	1846 Ga	1870 Ala Talladega 461
Josiah (Mary J.)	1848 Ark	1870 Mo Lawrence 422
L. (male)	1823 Tenn	1880 Texas Robertson 26
L. (M. A.)	1824 Tenn	1860 Texas Anderson 49
L. (male)	1835 Tenn	1860 Texas Parker 435
L. C. J. (Emily A.)	1835 Tenn	1880 Ark Boone 490
L. J. (Martha)	1824 NC	1850 Ga Forsyth 334
Labon or Sabon	1755-74	1800 NC Rutherford 125
Laken or B.L.C. (Marinda)	1837 Tenn	1860 Tenn Overton 264, 274
Leondus (Mary)	1826 Tenn	1850 Miss Oktibbeha 534
Levi	1825-30 (?)	1840 Tenn Overton 1
Levi (Nancy)	1817 Tenn	1850 Tenn Overton 112
Levi (Nancy)	1820 Tenn	1860 Tenn Overton 204
Levin	1800-10	1830 NC Rutherford 483
Lewis	bfr 1775	1790 SC Union 93
Lewis	1800-10	1830 Ill Shelby 200
Lewis	1800-10	1840 Mo Taney 110
Lewis	1810-20	1840 Tenn Wilson 74
Lewis (Nancy)	1820 NC	1850 Tenn Wilson 544
Lewis (Emily A.)	1835 Tenn	1860 Tex Dallas 317
Lewis (Amanda)	1836 Tenn	1870 Mo Stone 135
Lewis (Sarah)	1856 Ill	1880 Mo Taney 253
McC. (Margret J.)	1851 Tenn	1880 Tenn Overton 351

Name	Birth	Census
M. G. (Dicey)	1808 Ga	1870 Ala Calhoun 667
M. L. (Sarah J.)	1832 Ala	1860 Ala Marshall 909
M. M. (R.)	1831 Tenn	1860 Tenn Rutherford 79
Margaret	1776 NJ	1850 Ala Talladega 457
Margaret	1780-90	1830 Ill Shelby 176
Margaret	1790-00	1840 Ill Shelby 193
Margaret	1800 Unk	1850 Ill Shelby 104
Margaret	1791 NC	1860 Ill Shelby 603
Marion (Alice)	1845 Ga	1880 Tex Dallas 232
Marshall (Rebecca)	1831 Ill	1860 Ill Hardin 1060
Marshal (Rebecca)	1830 Ill	1870 Ill Hardin 48
Martha	1800-10	1840 Ill Randolph 229
Martha	1808 Ky	1850 Ill Fayette 402
Martha	1812 Tenn	1850 Ky Graves 389
Martha C.	1819 Ga	1850 Ala Barbour —
Martha E.	1836 Tenn	1880 Tenn Bedford 221
Martha J.	1830 Tenn	1870 Tenn Cannon 156
Martin	1842 Ala	1870 Ala Calhoun 512
Martin G. (Dicy)	1810 Ga	1850 Ga Cobb 237
Martin G. (Dica)	1810 Ga	1860 Ala Calhoun 551
Martin G. (Dice J.)	1808 Ga	1880 Ala Calhoun 669
Mary	1780 SC	1850 Ga Forsyth 334
Mary	1782 NC	1850 Tenn Davidson 114
Mary	1784 SC	1850 SC Anderson 221
Mary	1783 Va	1850 Ala Tallapoosa 49
Mary	1810-15	1830 Ga Hall 20
Mary	1810-20	1840 SC Anderson 123
Mary	1828 Ala	1870 Ala Marshall 82
Matthew	bfr 1755	1800 SC Pendleton 169
Matthew (Rachel)	1817 NC	1850 Tenn Blount 246
Matthew (Charlotte)	1845 Ill	1880 Ill Hardin 386
Merel (Margaret)	1818 Tenn	1850 Tenn Overton 23
Merrel (Margaret)	1817—	1860 Tenn Overton 263
Micajah	1794-02	1820 Ky Caldwell 30
Middleton	bfr 1775	1820 Tenn Franklin 75 (17)
Middleton	1770-80	1840 Tenn Coffee 180
Millenton	1770-80	1830 Tenn Franklin 40
Millington (Mary)	1848 Ill	1880 Ill Hardin 396
Monroe	1853 Ark	1880 Ark Sebastian 679
Nancy	1793 NC	1850 NC Chatham 936
Nancy	1791 SC	1880 Ala Calhoun 644
Nancy K.	1770-80	1830 Tenn Rutherford 201
Nelson (Rebecca)	1831 Ky	1860 Ill Hardin 1403
Nelson (Rebecca)	1830 Ky	1870 Ill Hardin 13
Noah	1800-10	1830 NC Rutherford 457
Noah (Jinnette)	1807 NC	1860 Tenn Putnam 31
O. V. (Margaret)	1826 Tenn	1860 Tex Dallas 320
O. V. (Margaret)	1826 Tenn	1870 Texas Dallas 360

Oliver (Arminda)	1838 Ill	1860 Mo Chariton 233
Oliver P. (Margaret)	1828 Tenn	1880 Tex Dallas 335
Oliver V. (Margaret)	1827 Tenn	1850 Tex Dallas 88
Osbern	1784-94	1810 Va Brunswick—
Osburn	1775-94	1820 Va Brunswick 656
Osborne	1780-90	1830 Va Greenville 47
Overton	1830 Tenn	1860 Ind Daviess 705
Ozias	1831 NC	1850 Ga Murray 544
P. E. (Harriet B.)	1820 Ala	1850 Ala Madison 417
P. E. (Harriet)	1821 Ala	1860 Ala Madison 93
P. H. (Icyann)	1840 Tenn	1870 Tenn Overton 308
Pennine (female)	1780 NC	1850 Tenn Wilson 545
Polk (Armilda)	1846 Tenn	1870 Tenn Overton 360
Pleasant	1800-10	1840 Ala Jackson 46
Pleasant (Elizabeth)	1810 NC	1850 Ala Jackson 3
Pleasant (Elizabeth)	1811 NC	1860 Ala Jackson 493
Pleasant (Elizabeth)	1810 NC	1870 Ala Jackson 50
Pleasant (Cynthia)	1827 Ala	1850 Ala Jackson 32
R. B. (Martha P.)	1837 Ala	1870 Ala Madison 283
R. B. (Martha)	1834 Ala	1880 Ala Madison 222
R. C. (male)	1780-90	1840 Tenn Shelby 208
R. R. (M. A.)	1854 Ala	1880 Ala Calhoun 652-3
Rachel	1801 NC	1850 Ark Desha 71
Ransom (Nancy)	1825 Ala	1850 Ala Jackson 32
Reubin P. (Nancy)	1822 NC	1850 Tenn Perry 153
Rhoda	1790-00	1840 Miss Oktibbeha 122
Rhoda	1782 Va	1850 Miss Oktibbeha 534
Rd or Richard	bfr 1775	1790 NC Rutheerford 116
Richard	1739—	1840 Ga Lumpkin—
Richard	brf 1755	1800 NC Rutherford 125
Richard	1774-84	1800 NC Rutherford 125
Richard	1784-94	1810 Va Dinwiddie 153
Richard (2 of these)	bfr 1765	1810 NC Rutherford 399, 401
Richard	1730-40	1830 NC Rutherford 457
Richard	1775—	1840 NC Rutherford—
Richard	1780 NC	1850 NC Rutherford 515
Richard (Elizabeth)	1812 NC	1850 NC Rutherford 665
Richard (Zilla)	1815 NC	1850 NC McDowell 517
Richard (Mary)	1848 Ill	1870 Ill Hardin 30
Richard (Hannah)	1848 Tenn	1870 Ark Madison 426
Richard (Hannah J.)	1848 Tenn	1880 Ark Madison 586
Richard C. (Sarah)	1789 Va	1850 Tenn Shelby 192
Riley (Parell)	1839 Tenn	1860 Tenn McNairy 405
Robert (Margaret J.)	1843 Ga	1880 Ala Calhoun 668
Robert (Luller)	1855 SC	1880 Ala Madison 119
Robert B.	1859 Tex	1880 Tex McCulloch 10
Roland	bfr 1765	1810 NC Anson 46
Roland (Mariah)	1821 Tenn	1850 Tenn Lauderdale 271

Roland (Mariah)	1821 Tenn	1860 Tenn Lauderdale 366
Rollin	bfr 1775	1820 Tenn Lincoln 6
Rowland	bfr 1775	1790 NC Nash 70
Rufus (Elizabeth)	1800 NC	1850 Tenn Williamson 260
Rufus (Sarah)	1836 Tenn	1860 Tenn Lauderdale 367
S. (Mary Ann)	1802 Ga	1850 Texas Cherokee Co 823
S. (male)	1824 Tenn	1860 Ark Franklin 287
S. or T. M. (Minerva)	1828 Tenn	1860 Tenn Lauderdale 366
Sabon	1755-74	1800 NC Rutherford 242
Samuel	1775-94	1820 Ga Jones 134
Samuel	1790-00	1830 Ala Madison 117
Samuel (J. A.)	1838 Ala	1880 Ala Madison 358
Samuel B.	1790-00	1840 Ala Madison 173
Samuel W.	1810-20	1840 Tenn Shelby 210
Sarah	1775-94	1820 Ill Gallatin 40
Sarah	1780-90	1830 Ga Putnam 200
Sarah	1820 Tenn	1860 Mo Texas 1095
Sayburn	1765-84	1810 NC Rutherford 402
Seburn	1750-60	1830 Ala Dale 1
Seburn	1800-10	1840 Ala Dale 32
Seborn (Susanna)	1836 Ga	1860 Texas Coryell 17
Shelman	1810-20	1840 Ala Madison 174
Silas	1775-94	1800 Ga Jones 134
Silas	1780-90	1830 Ga Jones 454
Silas (Sarah C.)	1843 Ala	1880 Ala Madison 358
Silas (M. S.)	1854 Tenn	1880 Tenn Putnam 117
Simpson (Martha A.)	1843 NC	1880 Ark Madison 520
Sol S. (Elizabeth W.)	1825 Ala	1860 Ala Marshall 937
Solomen S. (Elizabeth)	1825 Ala	1850 Ala Marshall 181
Solomon (Elizabeth)	1824 Ala	1870 Ala Marshall 92
Solomon S. (Betty W.)	1825 Ala	1880 Ala Marshall 211
Stephen	1790-00	1840 Tenn Hickman 190
Stephen (Margaret)	1800 NC	1850 Tenn Perry—
Susa (female)	1820 Tenn	1870 Tenn Fentress 527
Susan	1835 SC	1870 Ark Pulaski 381
T. or S. (Minerva)	1828 Tenn	1860 Tenn Lauderdale 366
T. D. (Elizabeth)	1821 Va	1860 Ala Tallapoosa 151
T. D. or F. D. (M.E.)	1828 Tenn	1860 Tenn Bedford 199
T. H. (male)	1833 Tenn	1860 Texas Austin 210
Tabitha	1771 NC	1850 Tenn Overton 20
Tabitha	1825 Tenn	1860 Tenn Overton 259
Thomas	1774-94	1800 SC Laurens 233
Thomas (Maria)	1813 England	1870 Ill St. Clair 469
Thomas (Malinda)	1814 Tenn	1850 NC McDowell 556
Thomas (Frances)	1814 NC	1850 NC Chatham 937
Thomas (Frances)	1815 NC	1860 Ark Greene 574
Thomas (Kesiah)	1833 Ill	1860 Ill Shelby 505
Thomas (Harriet)	1835 Ill	1870 Mo Dallas 139

Thomas	1840 Tenn	1870 Ark Madison 369
Thomas (Martha)	1847 Tenn	1870 Tenn Overton 214
Thomas (Martha)	1847 Tenn	1880 Tenn Cannon 557
Thomas D. (Martha)	1827 Tenn	1870 Tenn Bedford 233
Thomas L. (Almeda)	1837 Tenn	1860 Tex Dallas 320
Tilford	1858 Tenn	1880 Mo Taney 257
Timothy (Charlotte)	1791 Ga	1850 Ga Heard 344
Tyler (Sarah)	1842 Ala	1880 Ala Calhoun 659
Van (Rachel)	1805 Ga	1850 Ill Fayete 413
W.	1770-80	1840 Ga Greene—
W.	1780-90	1840 Tenn Perry 170
W. H.	1837 Tenn	1860 Mo Texas 259
W. H.	1837 Ala	1880 Tex Grayson 309
W. K. P. (Mary)	1855 Tenn	1880 Tenn Overton 343
W. M.	1857 Ala	1880 Tex Hunt 448
W. O. (Sarah E.)	1814 Va	1850 Ala Tallapoosa 19
W. O. (Sarah)	1814 Va	1860 Ala Tallapoosa 9
W. R. (E.)	1827 Va	1880 Tex Grayson 306
Walton	1765-84	1810 NC Rutherford 401
Wash (Louisiana)	1809 Ill	1870 Ill Fayette 732
Washington	1775-94	1820 Ga Greene 12
Washington	1770-80	1830 Ga Greene 286
Washington	1775-94	1820 Tenn Overton 14
Washington	1780-90	1830 Tenn Overton 214
Washington	1780-90	1830 Tenn White 2
Washington	1780-90	1840 Tenn Overton 1
Washington (Martha)	1789 Va	1860 Ark Madison 488-9
Washington (Rebecca)	1790 Tenn	1850 Tenn White 115
Washington (Louisianna)	1809 Ill	1860 Ill Fayette 139
Washington	1810-20	1840 Tenn Overton 3
Washington (Mary)	1813 Tenn	1850 Tenn Overton 11
Washington (Mary)	1812 Tenn	1860 Tenn Overton 284
Washington (Mary K.)	1812 Tenn	1870 Tenn Overton 371
Washington (Minerva)	1833 Ill	1870 Ill Hardin 46
Washington (Mary)	1840 Ala	1870 Ala Talladega 593
Wesley L. (Phebe)	1798 NC	1850 Ind Wayne 88
Wesson	1775-94	1820 Tenn Lincoln 6
Wesson (Sarah)	1790 NC	1850 Tenn Perry 184
Wiley	1760-70	1840 Miss Perry—
Wiley	bfr 1775	1820 Miss Lawrence—
Wiley	1774-84	1800 SC Pendleton 171
Wiley	1800-10	1830 Tenn Bedford 20
Wiley (Mary)	1824 NC	1850 Ga Murray 252
Wiley (Zida A.)	1826 Tenn	1860 Tex Dallas 320

Name	Birth	Census
Wiley (Zida An)	1827 Tenn	1870 Mo Stone 140
William	bfr 1765	1810 Va Pr. George 530
William	bfr 1775	1790 NC Chatham 88
William (2 of these)	bfr 1755	1800 NC Chatham 176, 205
William	1775-94	1820 SC Pendleton 397
William	1775-94	1820 Ga Baldwin 29
William	1784-94	1810 Va Dinwiddie 152
William	1784-94	1810 SC Pendleton 163
William	1780-90	1830 Tenn Bedford 156
William	1790-00	1830 Tenn Rutherford 201
William	1810-15	1830 Tenn Overton 204
William (Jane)	1810 Tenn	1850 Tenn Overton 20
William	1810-20	1840 Tenn Overton 1
William (Jane)	1810 Tenn	1860 Tenn Overton 274
William (Jane)	1811 Tenn	1870 Tenn Overton 357
William	1810-20	1840 Ala Benton—
William (Casandra)	1811 Ga	1850 Ala Tallapoosa 50
William (Phebe)	1814 Tenn	1870 Ala Talladega 563
William (Mary A.)	1814 NC	1850 NC Chatham 936
William (Mary A.)	1813 NC	1860 Ark Greene 581
William	1817 Tenn	1880 Mo Taney 253
William	1820 Tenn	1870 Mo Taney 323
William (Pheb)	1820 Tenn	1850 Tenn Bradley 268
William (Hulda)	1821 Ill	1850 Ill Macoupin—
William (Rachel)	1824 Ky	1860 Ill Hardin 1302
William (Susan)	1824 Tenn	1850 Ark Madison 291
William (Nancy)	1825 Tenn	1850 Texas Cass 777
William (Mary)	1840 Tenn	1860 Tenn Bedford 91
William (Susan)	1825 Tenn	1860 Tenn Cannon 361
William (Susannah)	1825 Tenn	1870 Tenn Cannon 208
William (Martha A.)	1825 Tenn	1880 Ark Madison 519
William (Susan S.)	1831 Tenn	1860 Ark Dallas 969
William (Tennessee)	1835 Tenn	1880 Tex Fayette 5
William (Mary)	1846 Ga	1870 Ark Pulaski 379
William (Susan)	1847 Tenn	1880 Tenn Bedford 137
William	— NC	1880 Tenn Warren 301
William B.	1790-00	1830 Ill Gallatin 31
William B.	1800-10	1830 Ill Fayette 248
William B. (Mary)	1824 Tenn	1850 Tenn Overton 60
William B. (Mary)	1824 Tenn	1860 Mo Texas 1093
William B. (Julia A.)	1847 Tenn	1870 Tenn Overton 332
William H.	1835 Tenn	1860 Tex Fayette 303
William H.	1840 Tenn	1860 Tex Lamar 158
William J. (Sarah J.)	1848 Tenn	1880 Ark Carroll 208
William K.	1800-10	1830 NC Rutherford 528
William L.	1800-10	1830 Tenn Wilson 114
William M. (Hariett E.)	1834 Ala	1860 Ala Marshall 737

William O. (Margaret)	1857 Tex	1880 Tex Dallas 335
William R. (Eunice)	1850 Ark	1880 Tex McLennan 193
William W.	1850 Tex	1880 Tex Hunt 537
Williamson	bfr 1775	1820 Ga Clarke 1
Williamson	1770-80	1830 Ga Clarke 319
Willard (Mary)	1858 Ill	1880 Ill Shelby 268
Winneford	—	1790 SC Pendleton 84
Zachariah (Rebecca)	1807 NC	1850 Tenn Marshall 49
Zedekiah	bfr 1775	1790 NC Anson—
Zedekiah	1755 74	1800 NC Montgomery 486

INDEX

Clyde Franklin 120
L L 120
William Clyde 120
Dorsey, Myrtle 209
Doshier, Nettie 214
Wiley 214
Doss, Margaret Ellen 118
Samuel Alexander 118
Dotson, Ethel 230
John 231
Lillian 231
Doughty, Edwin L 238
Sarah Maud 238
Dowdle, Margaret 138
Down, Peter Frank 73
Raiford Franklin 73
Downs, Henry 29
De Priest, Eliza 181
Drake, Amanda Caroline Lewis 207
Ella 208
Fannie 221
Livona 174 228
Mary 221
Nettie 222
Rutha 197
Temperance Tabitha 221
Draper, Daniel D 148
Ida 144
Sarah 148
Driver, Nancy 204
Dromgoole, Edward 254
Dubois, John 225
Duke, Ava 233
Sydney 233
Dun, John 27
Dunaway, Arma Dell 198
Duncan, Berry Frank 227
Comodore 221
Earl 221
Dungan, Byron L 132
Byron Lee 132
Carl Ray 132
Dennis Dawyne 132
Dunlay, Mary 57
Dunn 48 51
Allen 280
Elizabeth 51
Geraldine 222
Luella V 77

Thomas 51
Du Pont 3
Dupuy, Jane 68
Durante, Irene 60
Joe 60
Dusak, Joe 131
Marguerite Mary 131
Duwe, Gertrude Johanna 128
Otto Paul 128
Dwyer, Plummer 177
Dykes, Allen Hill 150
Martha Cleo 150

Eads, Dell 194
Emily Lou 194
Eagan, Earl 224
James Wiley 224
Eakes, J Tillman 92
Earington, Dorothy 22
Eason, John 51
Edge, James 134 136
Edgerton, John W 90
Edmondson 272
Edmonson, Tom J 215
Edwards 2
Charity 235
David Emmett 131
Edmond 235
Edward 38
Emmett 131
Francis Rees 108
John 21
Morgan 95
Eisenhower 6
Elam, Samuel 238
Elder, Quentin D 166
Vinie 191
Eldridge, John 167
Madie 195
Elgin, W M 143
Elliot, Nancy 34
Ellis, R N 91
Susie A 92
Elsey, Thomas 158
Embree, Silas 276
Emery, Iris Ruth 230
Engle, Myrtle 190
English 279
Epps, Francis 19

324 INDEX

Gard, Katherine Joy 79
  Lewis E 79
Gardiner, James 89
Garrett 106
  Ann Eliza 188
  Clay 219
Gash, L O 279
  Leander S 279
Gayle, Lila Louise 77
Ghormley, Will J 209
Gibbs 2
  Anne Kathleen 87
  Annie Ledbetter 86
  Cecile 87
  Edith 87
  James Phillip 86 87
  Jasper Kate 88
  Luteola 86 87
  Mary Alla 86
  Pauline 87
  Sanford 86
  Sarah Elizabeth 87
  Sarah Sanford 86
  Thomas Clifton 86 87
  Virginia Sandford 87
  Wilbourn Sanford 87
  Wilbourn Smith 86 87
Gibson 83
Gilbert 2
Giles, Lottie 112
  Samuel 112
Gill, Grover 185
Gilmer, Robert 99
Givens, Daniel 136
  Robt. 134 136 137
Gladden, Nancy 251
Glasspool 109
Glenn, Clarence Jackson 225
  Effie 225
Glover, Elizabeth Chappell 143
  Martha Ann 143
  Mary B 144
  Sarah 246
Golden, Ember 220
Golson, Jackie Elizabeth 223
Good, Hester 222
  James 2
Goodbread, John 280
Goode, Thomas B 181

Goodrich, Edward 245
  Mary 54
Goodroe 275
Goodwin, Emma 108
  James 108
Gordon 183
  Elizabeth 36
  Jacob 100
  James 136 137
Gosney, Mayne 128
Graham, Doris Joan 127
  Fletcher Poe 211
  Helen Anita 127 131
  Henry 127
  James Albert 127
  Letha Bernice 131
  Lindsey Luster 211
  Stephen Henry 127
Grantham, Paul E 77
Grason, William C 145
Graves, Rhoda 64
Gray, James Mattison 70
  Texanna M 52 70
  William 85
Grayson (see Grason) 137
  Nancy G 142
  William 142
Green, Charlie 111
  Elizabeth Josephine 147
  Frieda Joyce 126
  Hannah 137
  Harriett Minetta 227
  Jacob Ross 147
  John Thomas 111
  Rena 221
  Tom 105
  William 136
  William Ellis 126
Greenberg, Lilla 117
Greenshaw, Emily Catherine 211
Gregory, Joy 233
Gresham, Cornelia H 92
  D C 92
  Maggie 206
Griffin 178 180
  Clarence W 31 242
  Guy Henry 214
  Hardin 245

Martha Arena 211
  William A 214
Grisham, C R 218
  Saphronia 169
  Susan 195
Griskie, Josie 111
Gross, Beverlee Ann 219
Groves, David George 132
  J S 132
  John Charles 132
Guidi, Gene 206
Guinn, Bill 221
  John 172
  Reno 221
Gum, Martha 36
Gunnels, Nancy 189
Gunner, Eva Mae 132
Guolden, Daisy 132
Guthrie 183
Gwathmey, William 44

Habersham, Joseph 30 243
Hackenberger, H 231
Hadden, Allen 38
Haden 144
  Robert 151
Haggard, Archie 224
Haislip, Laban 40
Hale, E. F. 182
  Mary 204
  Mary Pedelta 129
Haley, Nancy Caroline 201
Hall 278
  John Patton 226
  Sam 183
  Zylfa 226
Halstead (see Holstead)
Ham, Ledbetter 71
  Marcus 71
  Martha Ann 198
  Sarah Elizabeth 198
Hamilton, Anne Sigisimunda 55
  Bobby Jack 57
  Caroline 57
  Dr. 4
  James David Tillman 56 57
  John Lloyd 57
  John Moore Taylor 55 56
  John Taylor 56

Mary Ann 57
Rachel Elizabeth 57
Rebecca Jane 56
Sarah Ann 56
Susan Elizabeth 57
William Morgan 57
William Thomas 57
Hamlin, John 20
Hammock, Jane P 195
  Necy 195
Hammonds, Lou Ellen 184
Hampton, Colonel Andrew 31
  242 244
Hamrick, George 72
Hancock, Jones 185
  John T 243
Hand 3
  Carl Edward 132
  Celia Elaine 132
  Clarence Crell 132
  Lisa Caroline 132
Hannah, James 135 136
  Jane 146
  John 136
Hardin 280
  Ana Belle 131
  Clara Ann 126 131
  Dorothy Sue 126 131
  Elizabeth Sharon 126
  James Boone 126
  Jimmie Nell 126
  Lillian Inez 126 131
  Tilden Hendrix 126
Hardison, Hilda 72
  Netta 52 71
Hardy, Adline 110
Harlan, Ben 214
  Wedsell Maywood 214
Harlee, Bettie 49
  David Stuart Eugene 65
  Edgar Cooley 65
  Frederick Earle 65
Harless, Henry 151
  Sarah 151
Harllee, David Stuart 65
  Eleanor Marquis 65
  Frederick Earle 65
  Marjorie Ferne 65

Marquis, Mary 65
Marsh 3
Marshall, Charles Henry 236
    Florence Louise 236
    John 215
    Margaret Engenia 215
    Martha Ann 55
    Sis 215
Martin, Ann K 90
    Elizabeth Washington 90
    Grace 114
    Hagood 58
    Harriett 90
    Jack 213
    James 90
    John 102
    Louisa 90
    Mary F 90
    Matthew 102 105
    Sarah Jane 105
    Susan L 90
    Thomas 90
    W L 143
    William Logan 94 138 145
Masemore, Ann Little 71
    Elizabeth Virginia 71
    John Ernest 71
    John William 52 71
Mason, James 30
    Mildred Marie 129
Massie, Addie 126
Masters 83
May, Eunice 205
Mayes, Ben F 181
    Jasper M 181
    Robert 35
    Susanna 35 236
Mayo, Joyce 233
Mc (Listed between L and M)
Meadow 3
Medlock, Elizabeth 167
Meek, Clistie 115
    J M 115
    William H 190
Meesy, Eliza 40
Meeting, Betty Ann 67
    Herbert 67
    Herbert McLaughlin 67
Mendenhall, George 51

Meredith, Susan M 76
Meroworth 149
Metcalf, J L 86
Michael, Ralph 229
Middleton, Margaret 138
Miller 3 90
    Effie Ann 213
    F L 116
    Judie 228
    Mary 107
    May 199
    O C 114
    Robert Henry 191
    Samuel 107
    Susan Mabel 170
Millican, Morgan 182
Millikin, Jennie 37
Milroy, Peggy 228
Minor, Dan H 174
Mirick, Sarah 45 (See Myrick)
Mitchel, Rosa 201
Mitchell 74
    Sarah 36
Mock, Griffith C 173
    Rufus M 173
Moile (slave) 44
Moll, Alexander Henry 232
    Carol Sue 233
    Justus R i xi 39 94 193 232 233 285
    William Alexander 233
    William Justus 233
Montgomery 163
Moody, Ella 118
Moon, Jasper 134
    Mahala 147
Moore 179
    Ella Lucinda 224
    Ethel 195
    Harriet Dent 224
    Herbert 130
    J G 218
    James K 50
    Mary Ann 124
    Tacolla 119
    William Walter 224
Morgan 191
    Clyde 231
    Jonathan Sam 103

Ratliff, Iva 71
  Mattie 71
Ray 106
Reaves, Carter 110
  Louisa 118
  Narcissus 110
Rector, Mary Chisolm 72
  Nancy Catherine 202
  Nelson 72
  Richard Kellam 72
Redditt, Ada Virginia 62
  Charles A 61
  Charles Harison 62
  Helen Boleyn 61 62
  Helen Elizabeth 62
  Stella Amanda 62
Redwine, Barbara 104
Reece, Brice Smart 229
  Lillian Ray 229
Reed, Charles 203
  Evan L 23
  Julia 206
Reehling, Carl Emil 173
Reeves, Addie 121
  Jimmy 175
  Joe 111
  John 111
  Louisa 111
  Mattie 83
  Sabrina 177
  Tennessee 177
Register 61
Reid, Charles Eckford 62
  James William 71
  Susie 37
Relyah, Anna Bell 226
Revill, W T 91
Reynolds, Geraldine 222
  Kenneth 130
Rhea, Farris W 122
  Regis Farris 122
Rhodes, T N 58
Rice, D P 283
  Joel 136
  Roger 18
Rich, J N 184
Richardson 277
  A Newton 208

Marion 168
Martin Van 167
Richberg 183
Reiniger, Viola Belle 232
Riley, Boyce 71
Ringley, Wilma 219
Risley 187
Riddle 280
  Charles 141
Riddles, Thomas 135 137
Roark, John 134
Robbins 189
  Charles C 189
  Mary J 189
  Mary Louise 72
  Nancy Elizabeth 189
Roberts, Frances 224
  Joe Etta 199
  Joel 199
Robertson, Floyd Ray 132
  H B 118
  John B 90
  John Franklin 118
  Kimberley Jean 132
  Terry 118
Robin (slave) 21
Robins, Elizabeth 160
  Fannie 166
  Isaac 154 157 160 162 166
  Nancy 162
Robinson, Alimida 281
  Ann Eliza 51
  Betsy Ann 233
  Betty Sue 123
  Charles 51
  Cora 51
  Curtis 123
  Grace 123
  Hazel 123
  Herndon Yoakum 86
  James 51
  James Harvey 8
  Jane 174
  Joel W 281
  John 112
  Keziah 51
  Lucinda 174
  Marcelous 112
  Mary E 198

Lula 80
Margaret Machan 88
Marshall 230
Martha Cornelia 63 64
Martin 195
Mary A 79 85
Mary Ann 88
Mary Elizabeth 123
Mary Eugenie 85
Mary Frances 63
Mary Ledbetter 73
Mary Walton 88
Maxwell Chandler 88
Nancy Adeline 219 220
Nora 185
Ora 185
Philip 88
Philip Duffield 87
Polly H 34 238
Presley Nelme 73
Robert N 181
Sallie 182
Sallie Eugenia 88
Sallie Shelton 73
Sally Elizabeth 79 86
Sally Fanny 86
Sarah Elizabeth 181
Selwyn 63
Thomas Frank 88
Thomas J 79
Thomas Jefferson 79
Virginia 86
Virginia Katherine 128
William 176
William Blake 86
William C 49
William Calvin 62 63 79
William Charles 79
William Nathan 128
Smyth, Amanda Elizabeth 212
Southall, Glen 224
Southard, Corrie Jeanette 229
Spears, Caroline 59
Claude 59
Eugenia 59
Speed, Lois 65
Spell, Elizabeth 20
George 20
Spence, Larry 194

Spencer, John 71
Spillers 179
Spoon, Rosa L 200
Zanie 196
Spurlock, Delia 229
Esther 197
William E 197
William Enoch 171
Stable, Edward 40
Stanback, Elizabeth 52
Mary 52
Standlee, Elizabeth 216
Jewell 215
William 182
Stanfield, Callie 225
Stanfill, Calvin 209
Stanley, Norma 194
Steedman, James H 85
Steele, Martha Elizabeth 81
Martha J 80
Mary 51
Polly 48
Robert J 80
Robert Leake 81
Steiner, George Paul 79
Stephenson, C B 85
Edward B 237
Joseph Johnson 237
Stephens, Otis Orble 198
Roy 204
Seymour 198
Stevens, John L 122
Josie 122
Stevenson 90
Mary Ida 122
Stewart, Glenn 234
Stinson, J G 114
Stires, Henry 136
Stitt, Arnold Haymie 68
David Leander 68
David Tillman 68
John Dupuy 68
John Monroe 68
John W 68
Ticia Elizabeth 68
William Tillman 68
Stockard, Frank 132
James Lynn 132

CPSIA information can be obtained
at www.ICGtesting.com
Printed in the USA
BVHW061722170419
545808BV00013B/135/P